THE COMPLETE GUIDE TO

MANAGING YOUR PARENTS'

FINANCES

WHEN THEY CANNOT

A Step-By-Step Plan To Protect Their Assets, Limit Taxes, and Ensure Their Wishes Are Fulfilled

By Bill Swan

The Complete Guide To Managing Your Parents' Finances When They Cannot : A Step-By-Step Plan To Protect Their Assets, Limit Taxes, and Ensure Their Wishes are Fulfilled

Copyright © 2010 by Atlantic Publishing Group, Inc.

1405 SW 6th Ave. • Ocala, Florida 34471 • 800-814-1132 • 352-622-1875–Fax

Web site: www.atlantic-pub.com • E-mail: sales@atlantic-pub.com

SAN Number: 268-1250

Library of Congress Cataloging-in-Publication Data

Swan, W. A., 1966-
  The complete guide to managing your parents' finances when they cannot : a step-by-step plan to protect their assets, limit taxes, and ensure their wishes are fulfilled / by W.A. Swan.
     p. cm.
  Includes bibliographical references and index.
  ISBN-13: 978-1-60138-313-6 (alk. paper)
  ISBN-10: 1-60138-313-4 (alk. paper)
  1. Aging parents--Finance, Personal. 2. Retirement income. I. Title.
  HG179.S894 2009
  332.0240085--dc22
                              2009014868

Printed in the United States

PROJECT MANAGER: Amanda Miller • amiller@atlantic-pub.com
ASSISTANT EDITOR: Amy Moczynski • amoczynski@atlantic-pub.com
ASSISTANT EDITOR: Angela Pham • apham@atlantic-pub.com
INTERIOR DESIGN: Tara Price • tlpricefreelance@gmail.com
COVER DESIGN: Meg Buchner• megadesn@mchsi.com
BACK COVER DESIGN: Jackie Miller • sullmill@charter.net

We recently lost our beloved pet "Bear," who was not only our best and dearest friend but also the "Vice President of Sunshine" here at Atlantic Publishing. He did not receive a salary but worked tirelessly 24 hours a day to please his parents. Bear was a rescue dog that turned around and showered myself, my wife, Sherri, his grandparents Jean, Bob, and Nancy, and every person and animal he met (maybe not rabbits) with friendship and love. He made a lot of people smile every day.

We wanted you to know that a portion of the profits of this book will be donated to The Humane Society of the United States. *–Douglas & Sherri Brown*

The human-animal bond is as old as human history. We cherish our animal companions for their unconditional affection and acceptance. We feel a thrill when we glimpse wild creatures in their natural habitat or in our own backyard.

Unfortunately, the human-animal bond has at times been weakened. Humans have exploited some animal species to the point of extinction.

The Humane Society of the United States makes a difference in the lives of animals here at home and worldwide. The HSUS is dedicated to creating a world where our relationship with animals is guided by compassion. We seek a truly humane society in which animals are respected for their intrinsic value, and where the human-animal bond is strong.

Want to help animals? We have plenty of suggestions. Adopt a pet from a local shelter, join The Humane Society and be a part of our work to help companion animals and wildlife. You will be funding our educational, legislative, investigative and outreach projects in the U.S. and across the globe.

Or perhaps you'd like to make a memorial donation in honor of a pet, friend or relative? You can through our Kindred Spirits program. And if you'd like to contribute in a more structured way, our Planned Giving Office has suggestions about estate planning, annuities, and even gifts of stock that avoid capital gains taxes.

Maybe you have land that you would like to preserve as a lasting habitat for wildlife. Our Wildlife Land Trust can help you. Perhaps the land you want to share is a backyard— that's enough. Our Urban Wildlife Sanctuary Program will show you how to create a habitat for your wild neighbors.

So you see, it's easy to help animals. And The HSUS is here to help.

THE HUMANE SOCIETY
OF THE UNITED STATES.

2100 L Street NW • Washington, DC 20037 • 202-452-1100
www.hsus.org

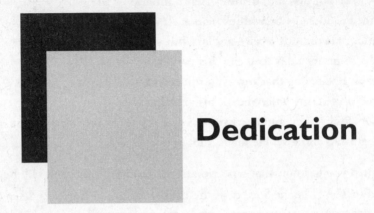

Dedication

To my mother, Elizabeth Swan, who suffered the slow and frustrating decline into dementia over the last few years of her life, which gave me first-hand experience to many lessons of this book.

Table of Contents

CHAPTER 3: THE STRESS OF FINANCIAL CAREGIVING — 47

CHAPTER 4: GETTING AN ACCURATE VIEW OF PARENTAL FINANCES — 59

CHAPTER 5: TAKING OVER — THE FINANCIAL AND LEGAL PROCEDURES — 73

CHAPTER 6: HELPING YOUR
PARENTS LIVE THE WAY THEY WANT   103

CHAPTER 7: THINKING ABOUT
WHERE YOUR PARENTS WILL LIVE   131

CHAPTER 12: WILLS, TRUSTS, EXECUTORS, AND BURIALS   211

APPENDIX A: WORKSHEETS   233

APPENDIX B: CASE STUDIES   261

GLOSSARY OF TERMS   273

RESOURCES   281

BIBLIOGRAPHY   283

INDEX   285

Foreword

Some 60 years ago, a major demographic change began in America as 84 million Americans were born between the years 1946 and 1964. After World War II, the troops returned home and rushed to make up for lost time by getting married and starting families. This birthrate explosion was so dramatic that demographers called the event "The Baby Boom." Longevity is the second cause for demographic change, as many more people are living into their 80s and 90s. Boomers look forward to a long life, but meanwhile, their parents are also living longer.

Demographers and sociologists have published many studies on this population explosion, including its effects on the U.S. economy and the personal finances of that generation. In 2009, there were about 75 million Boomers, ranging in age from 45 to 63 years old. They currently make up about 29 percent of the U.S. population. Many are retired or planning to retire soon, but are caught between their desires and the needs of their aging parents.

Boomers have made many positive contributions to society, but their sheer numbers cause them to be the source of many burdens — to themselves and their children. Most Boomers never considered the fact that they might be "parenting" their parents someday — taking care of the needs of Mom and Dad, who once cared for them. Many Boomers are now looking after an older parent or relative while also raising their own children and working part-time or full-time. They now face a host of complex needs, ranging from managing their retirement accounts to estate planning, tax reporting, aging, and end-of-life issues — for both themselves and their parents.

It is hard for them not to panic when considering what they face, especially when realizing that so few have saved as much as they may want or need for the future. According to the 2007 Retirement Confidence Survey by the Employee Benefits Research Institute, 46 percent of baby boomers have saved less than $50,000 for retirement. With their own financial security in question, the need to take over their parents' financial life, especially if it happens suddenly, can be extremely stressful. However, if approached one step at a time, they can get a handle on what needs to be done.

More than ever, people need help dealing with these major life issues, and educating themselves about their parents' finances is critical. *The Complete Guide to Managing Your Parents' Finances When They Cannot* is a straightforward and well-organized resource that speaks to the diverse demands of family finances in today's economy. It is an indispensable guide that provides a basic primer in personal finance for those who will be involved in their parents' financial lives. It is well organized: You can read it beginning to end, or jump straight to the section you need to consult immediately.

In order to be a financial caregiver, you need to know how to deal with legal and financial paperwork; government agencies and regulations; a host of insurance, investment, and estate-planning issues; and the inevitable emotional and psychological issues that arise whenever money and family mix. *The Complete Guide to Managing Your Parents' Finances When They Cannot* covers all of these topics and more.

This comprehensive guide supplies the knowledge and confidence you need for the many hurdles ahead. It will help you decide who should manage your parents' money; how to communicate with siblings and caregivers; how to manage your parents' stocks, bonds, real estate, and other investments; how to deal with health insurance, Medicaid, and other insurance issues; and how to protect your parents from elder fraud. It covers every eventuality, including insolvency, in capacity and, eventually, death.

Whether you are a Boomer yourself or the child of a Boomer, this book will help guide you through many of the issues you may encounter when thinking about your parents' financial needs. It could mean the difference between boom and bust for you and your parents. I hope you find it as valuable a resource as I did.

Kenneth Ford
President and Founder
Ford Wealth Management

1

Thinking About Your Parents' Finances

There are multiple reasons for wondering if you should think about your parents' finances. Maybe you have not had the conversation with your parents about their finances yet. Maybe they are refusing help, or you are seeing signs that, indeed, there may be trouble coming soon. These reasons are among the few that made you get a copy of this book. Are you worried over nothing? Are you seeing signs that tell you something is wrong? What would you do if there was something wrong? The answers can be obvious and not so obvious, but there will be signs when you have no choice but to get involved.

There may come a time when you may have to deal with the possibility of needing to take over your parents' finances. While this is not an easy topic to handle, using the guidelines provided in this book as a first step when considering this option will help you with gain knowledge and benefits for both the parents and child. This book will examine some basic guidelines to help the person who must manage another person's finances.

As you read through this chapter, you will learn about what lies ahead of you in this situation. You will also learn of the benefits to not only your parents, but to yourself, as well. This chapter will also cover the basics in regard to managing your parents' money.

THE ROAD AHEAD

Have you ever thought of what your parents might be doing in 20 years? This is a question that not many people often think of. Perhaps you never really thought of it, either, or maybe you have the image of your parents living happily into their old age, enjoying their lives and their grandchildren or great-grandchildren.

Maybe there have been thoughts about what would happen if something occurred. The likeliness of one of them dying may have crossed your mind in recent years; or maybe you are wondering how they would cope if they needed to move into a nursing home. Perhaps you never thought about these possibilities until recently.

It is also possible that you have never considered how your parents handle their finances, or if they could afford what they currently have. This is especially true if one parent dies and you realize that you are not sure if the surviving parent can maintain their current lifestyle. While Medicaid will handle many health issues, what happens if a long-term medical crisis strikes? And what happens if the surviving parent is not the one who handled the finances? There is also the possibility that the surviving parent, while able to handle the finances, is not able to handle the daily duties like buying food, handling medication, or knowing how to deal with being alone.

There are many reasons that adult children tend not to worry about any of this until it is forced upon them, such as:

- They are your parents. They dispensed the advice on a range of things, including finances and living better. They have known what to do for years, or at least made it look like they did. They do not need you to help plan their estate, draw up a will, or handle Medicare and their finances.

- It is not any of your business what they do with their money. As you grew up, they learned to let you make your own decisions, so what right would you have to ask them about theirs? And you do not want to imagine the conversation where you ask Mom or Dad where their financial papers are kept. Asking about a will or the estate may give the appearance you are greedy.

- When a parent dies, it hits a nerve. It does not matter if you love them, or even if you get along with them. When a parent dies, time stops, life stops, and it may seem as if there is no tomorrow. But, even if you have seen others go through this, you may have the mentality that your parents will be around for years, and you may feel that you do not need to think about it.

- Having a discussion with your parents about their money and their lives can be an uncomfortable conversation. So why bother?

THE TOTAL CAREGIVER ROLE

While the main focus of this book is about money and financial management, your parents (or surviving parent) will likely need more help from you than helping set up automatic payments or having their home equity provide income in later years. It is quite possible your parents will need more assistance outside of the financial caregiver duties.

- Caregiving for your parents can be a demanding, intensive commitment, and it can be long-term. If you start helping your 70-year-old widowed mother draw up a financial plan for the rest of her life, you may be helping with her finances until she reaches 80, 85, 90, or beyond. The decisions you have to make over the years could change from how to afford to keep your mother in her house to how much money Medicare will pay for long-term care— or how to minimize the tax bite on her estate when she dies.

- Caregiving can become draining and exhausting, particularly if your parents' financial affairs are not in order, and you may find it does not receive all the appreciation it deserves. A parent with dementia may have no idea how much you do for them, and a clear-headed parent may resent being told that he or she does not have the money to keep taking monthly gambling trips to Las Vegas or ordering two dozen pay-per-view films every week.

- Caregiving can also lead to conflict with your siblings, or your surviving parent's partner or second spouse. Even if you have your parents' support and legal authority, the rest of the family may disagree with your decisions or think you are exaggerating the problems — they no more want to think of your parents being old or mentally incompetent than you do. They also may feel you are trying to get special benefits in the will. In worst-case scenarios, you could be accused of spending your parents' money on yourself, or of "undue influence" over their financial decisions.

- Caregiving demands time. The more help your parents' needs, the less time you have for your job, spouse, children, and for whatever you do to relax and de-stress. The impact on your life — financial and emotional — will almost certainly be much bigger than you imagine.

- Caregiving is no picnic for your parents, either. Acknowledging that disability, death, or long-term illness lies somewhere down the road is not a pleasant experience for them, either. Asking you for financial help and guidance — whether they want to give you a power of attorney or have you look for a nursing home — means accepting aging and weakness, and admitting they no longer have full control of their lives. It also means sharing confidential, personal information with you and possibly, at some point, giving up their power to make their own decisions.

POSSIBLE ISSUES

If the day comes when you are needed to help manage your parents' finances, it should go smoothly. Even if your involvement goes smoothly, there will still be stress for both you and your parents — but the stress will be manageable.

If there is a medical crisis and you must intervene immediately without preparation, the stress will be worse. If one parent dies, the stress will increase even more. The surviving parent may be in no condition to handle the finances, the wrapping up of the other parent's affairs, and their daily life. And there will be grief occurring with either cause.

If you have never discussed your parents' finances, multiply the stress factor even more. If something were to happen, would you know such things as:

- Where is the living will?
- Is there a will?
- Who has authority to handle the finances?
- Who has authority to handle the legal issues?
- What is the condition of their finances?
- Where are the financial records?
- Is there a safe deposit box?
- Where is the safe deposit box, if there is one?
- Where are the legal papers?
- Are all the legal papers intact?
- Who are the lawyers, doctors, and bank people you need to find?

It is an honest assumption that you may not want to talk to your parents about their finances or how they manage their lives. It is also a very good assumption that the difficulty you will face having a conversation with them about money is nothing compared to facing a crisis and not being prepared. Having this conversation about financial matters when there is no crisis or imminent need will be less stressful than trying to accomplish all this in the middle of a crisis — whether emotional or financial.

YOUR PARENTS' BENEFITS

One of the biggest benefits for your parents in planning ahead is the saving of their assets and resources to pass along to the younger generations. Most times, this is one of the biggest concerns of aging parents. As of 2006, nearly $95 million per year is lost during the transfer of assets between generations. Most of this is due to improper or complete lack of planning for taxes, medical needs, and missing assets.

Advance planning, no matter what form it takes, offers many other benefits to your parents once the planning is in motion. Here are some of the most important benefits:

- When it comes to investing and retirement, knowing about the 401(k) or the IRA that your parents have can help them use it more effectively. If you parents still work, ask them if they have a retirement account and if their employer contributes to it.

- Knowing the rules of Social Security and Medicaid helps, as both are complex and detailed.

- You should be aware of whether your parents will receive VA benefits. Knowing how to best use the tax codes to keep the most of your parent's income and assets is another key issue. Both the placement and the timing of what assets are tapped — and when they are tapped — can save or cost your parents a lot of money.

- Along a similar path is estate planning. With the proper planning, your parents can minimize the tax payout, keeping more assets in the family where they wanted them to be. Estate planning also ensures your parents will know that their burial wishes are fulfilled when the time arrives. This also includes the area of living wills and final wills, which need to be clear and detailed.

- Should one parent pass away before the other, having the planning in place will help you help them maintain their financial stability and budget. Having a joint checking account, or legal authority to act in emergency situations, will save time and stress for both you and your parents.

- Having your parents go over their retirement plans with you can benefit them by having a second set of eyes to spot potential problems.

Whether your parents are young and in terrific shape, or starting to show the first signs of decline, the more you plan now, the better you can make their lives in the future — and the longer they can stay independent, living the life they choose, instead of a life they have to settle for.

YOUR BENEFITS

When looking at the benefits of advance planning, you should also look at how the issue affects you — and what concerns could potentially arise. There are many benefits to both you and your family, if you make the plans ahead of their need. Let us take a look at your side of the picture.

The Issue

Your parents will likely need you at some point in their lives. While they would not want to feel as if they are a burden — and you would hate feeling like they are — caregiving may seem like a burden to both of you at times. It is also possible that you could spend more time looking after your parents' needs than they did looking after your needs as a child.

Being the caregiver, you will have additional demands on your time, as well as and some of your resources. This adds stress to your life and can be difficult to deal with. There may be times when you want to simply walk out the door and take a week off, but it will not be possible.

Although this book is not about caregiving, it is quite possible that along with watching your parents' money, they will need you to provide other sorts of care, such as performing minor home repairs, doing some shopping, driving them to and from appointments, or making extra visits to spend time with them. Even if money is the only issue, tracking bills, deposits, investments, and figuring out what to do with their house are not responsibilities you can neglect. While this may seem like a lot of additional work to undertake, realize that you are not alone in considering the option of handling tasks within the family.

Potential Concerns

One central concern regarding managing parental finances is the lack of advance planning. If a coma, advanced dementia, or other serious illness leaves your parents unable to sign checks or manage their money, and there is no groundwork laid out for someone to handle the situation, you could be charged with covering the mortgage, insurance, and other monthly bills until they recover. How long can your finances handle the added payments? Would any other family members be able to offer you assistance?

While many parents will not require this much assistance, they may still feel guilty having you reorganize your life to help them manage their financial situation. However, when the time comes, they may not have much choice but to accept your help. Proper planning can help prevent the possibility that this may happen.

Caregiving is always going to be stressful. The more care you have to provide, and the worse your parents' situation, the more stress you will feel. By putting in the work ahead of time while they are in shape to participate in the discussion and the decisions, you can reduce the stress you all may face later. It may be awkward and time-consuming to go over their finances now, but it will benefit everyone in the long run.

With this in mind, here are a few benefits to ensuring your parent's finances are well taken care of:

- You can help your parents become financially secure in their old age.

- If you have their financial information readily accessible, you will be spared the pressure of scrambling through all their papers or trying to piece together information from tax returns.

- If you have already discussed money and their financial resources, you will know what sort of a budget you have to work with and whether your parents need to start liquidating investments.

- If you and your parents have arranged in advance for you to have the authority to help them — whether it is a power of attorney, a joint checking account, or you are the co-trustee on a revocable trust — you can do more for them than if you have to wait for a court to rule on your petition to become your parents' guardian.

- If you have shared your concerns with your siblings and everyone has had a chance to discuss, weigh in, and modify your plans, the result will be less family conflict later. Primary caregivers often feel no one else in the family appreciates their sacrifices; even if they volunteered, they can become resentful that nobody is shouldering the burden. Siblings, meanwhile, may question your financial decisions or even your motives. Involving them in your decisions and asking for help and guidance can not only reduce strife, it will also give you more of a support system to lean on.

- If you know your parents have a will made out and that the will is up-to-date and clear about who gets what, that eliminates another possible source of trouble. There will be a smaller chance of siblings feuding over who inherits what.

- If you have made sure your parents have a living will that spells out what to do if they are in a coma, you will not have to decide yourself whether to turn off life support, and with any luck, you can carry out your parents' wishes without having to fight the rest of your family in court.

- If you can protect your parents from elder abuse and fraud, you can avoid other kinds of tragedies, such as discovering an unscrupulous lover has stolen most of their retirement money.

- When you make the financial picture better for your parents, you make it better for yourself — and that, in turn, will make your parents' life better. Many parents feel guilty for creating a burden on their children by not having their finances adequately prepared. With prior knowledge of your parents' financial picture, and a working knowledge of Medicaid, you can greatly reduce the possibility of lost income or having to pull money from a retirement account early.

- Advance planning will also help reduce the feeling of uncertainty when deciding which task to handle next. Going into your parents' financial future with at least a general direction can help you avoid indecision, lost time, and wrong turns, as well as the feelings of being inadequate and incompetent because you were unable to handle tasks that may be crucial.

Being the caregiver will have an effect on both work and personal life. You will be the one who handles the paperwork, medical forms, household management, and overall budgeting. What does this have to do with parental finances? You will be the one who needs to minimize waste and lost time for both you and your parents. Getting to doctor appointments, making sure the proper forms are filled out correctly the first time, ensuring the bills are paid on time, and watching for signs of elder abuse or neglect are all part of making sure your parents' money goes where and when it is needed to have the best outcome possible for everyone.

Two related issues must also be considered here. If you have children, this will become a family affair. Advance planning will help them adapt as well, so if there are sudden changes in your parents' lives, your children can have a better handle on the situation. The other issue is time. If you start managing your parents' lives when they are 70 and they live to be 92, you will be providing care for most of those 22 years. You, too, will be aging. Your children may need to step in to handle tasks that neither you, nor your parents, can manage anymore. Having plans in place can help them know where — and how — to do what is needed.

MANAGING THEIR MONEY – THE BASICS

- Now that you have decided to take on this task, however small or large, you will need to know some of the basics of what you will be doing as the financial manager of your parents' money:

- Making up a complete picture of your parents' finances. This includes how much money your parents have, such as accounts, stocks, bonds, non-cash assets such as their house, and how many expenses and debts they have. This will give you a look at what you have to work with.

- Figuring out when to take part in, or take over, your parents' finances because it is the only available option.

- Deciding just how much authority you will need to handle your parents' financial affairs and how to best use the authority.

- Learning your parents' bookkeeping methods so they, and everyone else, can follow along with what you are doing with their money.

- Deciding, and recognizing, when or if the situation has gone beyond your abilities, and having to find a professional to handle things further.

Unfortunately, the first issue among many will be to discuss these options with your parents. See the next chapter.

CHAPTER 2

Discussing the Money Issues with Your Parents

When you know there is something wrong with the financial picture in your parents' life, you may find yourself asking two difficult questions. First, do you intervene? And if you choose to intervene, how do you discuss the issue with your parents? This chapter will focus on how to know when to intervene, as well as how to handle this delicate subject. We will also cover the amount of involvement you may need to have in your parents' financial life, as well as the topic of raising this subject with your parents and anyone else closely involved in the situation.

The first issue you will want to face is how to get ahead of the financial problems before they are too difficult to handle. This book provides a set of guidelines to help you know when you need to intervene and how involved you will need to be. This chapter also covers the issue of working with stepparents and partners.

GETTING AHEAD OF
THE MONEY PROBLEMS

There is rarely a good way to bring up problems about finances, especially when it is a grown child talking to their parent about the parent's money. But there is a good time to deal with the issue – before it becomes a problem. Yes, this is easier said than done. But there are sometimes clues that they may be ready to discuss the issue with someone. Some hints might include statements like your mother mentioning how a friend of hers gave her daughter the power of attorney, or your father mentioning how difficult it may be for your mother to handle finances if she became a widow. Even if your parents do not bring it up directly, comments such as this could mean they are willing to talk, and these comments are your way to start the conversation.

What if your parents do not make any comments? Then it is up to you to start a conversation. Some low-key ideas that may help you include telling them you are writing your will; putting together a retirement plan; or creating a power of attorney or a living will and asking them how they wrote their own will or who handled it for them, as if you are asking for advice. Ask them about who to contact about their estates should it be needed.

But what if this fails, too? Find someone else, such as an uncle or aunt, family friend, minister, or rabbi, who can start the conversation for you. You can also enlist the help of family members or your siblings if using a group effort seems easier. You should at least let the rest of the family in on this discussion. They should be aware that you intend to discuss financial issues with your parents. It is possible other family members have either thought of doing this, or have tried and had little luck themselves.

There are two potential issues that may arise if you do not include the family. If your family discovers you have access to your parents' finances or important papers, they may wonder why you did not tell them. And if other members of the family are closer to your parents, either physically or emotionally, they might think you are attempting to trump them into taking over their position in your parents' lives.

How do you include your family? The best way is to hold a group meeting to accomplish three things: It allows everyone in the family to stay informed; it shows that you are not attempting to sidestep any other family members; and it becomes a good brainstorming session in case anyone else has any other ideas. Another issue that rides along with this is when a family member becomes your parents' official caregiver — they will likely need the support of the remaining family members to carry out the duties effectively and with less strain on everyone. Though you could meet with both siblings and the parents at once, it gives more of an advantage to have a "pre-meeting" with just your siblings so that no other issues surface during the handling of this topic. Having a pre-meeting also allows any other issues between family members to be discussed without involving Mom and Dad in other arguments or conversations.

A pre-meeting also allows everyone to know who is capable and willing to take on certain duties of the caregiver role. It also sets aside any unknown preconceived notions that may have gone unnoticed otherwise. If there are siblings who think that they are obligated to carry out certain duties, make sure they are aware that they should not take these duties on if they are not comfortable with them. There may be underlying opinions that need to be addressed as well during this meeting.

There is also the possibility that certain members of the family simply do not want to be involved with their parents' personal lives. This issue also must be considered and accepted.

This pre-meeting is not supposed to be a solution to everyone's problems; it is about planning the best care for your parents when the time comes that they will need that assistance. There will never be complete agreement on every issue. The point of the meeting is to make sure everyone in the family knows what is going on and why; it is the best way to start the conversation and decide who should initiate the discussion. If you and your siblings can decide what advance planning needs to be done, such as power of attorney, trusts, wills, or assisting in balancing the checkbook and making sure the bills are paid each month, this covers half of the work that needs to be completed.

Some tips to helping keep the pre-meeting productive include:

- Setting a time limit and an agenda of topics to be covered beforehand

- Using phrases that express your disagreement with someone in terms of your own thoughts and feelings, rather than accusations

- Keeping the main topic on-track

Other ways to make this meeting more productive include considering the abilities of everyone involved. Is one family member better at confrontational issues, while another is better at the financial front? Is there a family member who is the overall organizer of the group? Showing you are willing and able to share duties will help avoid challenges and confrontations later. It will also allow other siblings to feel that they can be a part of their parents' caregiving if they choose to be.

There is also the possibility you will handle these responsibilities on your own. This may be because there are no family members who are willing or able to be involved, or because there are no other family members. In this situation you may feel as if you are all alone, handling this huge task. While it may seem this way, it is not always true. There are other people who can help you if you need assistance. Beyond the usual answers of the family minister and neighbors, there are community senior centers and associations that have information and support groups available. There are also service agencies such as your local Area Agency on Aging or a local outreach program for seniors offered by your community or local government. These services provide everything from free transportation to doctors' offices and home visits to utility assistance that helps guarantee the lights and heat remain turned-on in your parents' home.

Whatever the situation or the results that come from these brainstorming sessions, make sure the outcome is written down. This is especially true for assignment lists, obligations, lines of communication, and ideas that need further study. Make copies of all these and send them to everyone who will be involved in the family or close to the family.

If you are in a situation where you must make all the decisions yourself, write down in advance the key talking points you want to cover with your parents; have a dry run with your spouse or a friend so that you are aware of any problems that might come up; and try many different approaches to the topic.

If you want to try a slower approach, and your parents use e-mail or text messaging, try raising the subject via those methods first. This gives your parents the chance to digest what you are suggesting while giving everyone time to prepare for the coming discussion. This method helps to keep the conversation calm and possibly at a more civil level if you think an argument may erupt.

One way to ease the possible confrontation you are expecting is to assure your parents that you are not attempting to take over their life, force decisions upon them, or give lectures on how to live. The point you want to make is that you are making sure your parents are ready for any future situations and can live the happy retirement they have been waiting for. It may not happen exactly the way they planned it, but this is the goal that both you and your parents should try to reach together. If both of your parents are still living, this is the time to make sure that when one of them does leave the other behind, the surviving spouse is ready to financially handle the rest of their lives.

Some points to raise, especially if your parents respond with vague answers about doing the estate planning "someday," can include some of the following ideas:

- With good estate planning, they can pass along more of what they have and ensure assets go where they want them to go.

- With living wills, they can avoid possible situations such as the famous Terri Schiavo case (see Ch. 12, p. 217), in which there was no clear idea of what she wanted, eventually devastating the family financially and emotionally.

- With no clear direction, decisions made in later years by you or other family members may not be what your parents would have wanted.

- With written directions on where to find important paperwork and documents, handling a crisis situation will be much easier.

- If something were to happen before the will and planning are completed, you and the remaining family members will need to know what to do.

If your parents resist all efforts to approach this issue, remember that they are adults and cannot be forced into making decisions. Keep the meeting a discussion and do not lower it to the level of a lecture. If you push your parents, they will likely feel resentment, and the whole process and situation will only become more difficult and time-consuming. Make it clear you are not attempting to take over their lives, but ensure that their future is planned out and they are ready for it.

But keep in mind that if there appears to be no immediate agreement, you should drop the subject. If your parents are still

15 years away from retirement or have no real plans to retire, they may not even consider this an important subject. The important considerations are not how they invest, plan, and save now, but how they will spend the last remaining years of their lives and need the best plan in place for them and their family when it is needed.

Coming to an understanding is not the end of the deal, either. Even if your parents are willing to work with you on this issue, gathering and reviewing all the financial details will take time.

What do you do if they do agree to your help?

- If your parents become incapacitated tomorrow, how hard would it be for you to step in immediately?

- Would your parents be willing and able to help you care for their finances? This could be as simple as giving you signature privileges on their bank accounts or allowing you authority to open a safe deposit box in their name for important papers.

- How are your parents planning to pay for insurance and medical needs? Are their medical needs tied to their insurance policies, and if so, what does insurance cover?

- Gather a list of where important documents are located. This includes account numbers for bank accounts, investments, and insurance. This also includes the location of safe deposit boxes, family belongings and records, and important papers such as bank loans, contracts, and contact information for people who hold this information.

- How are the finances handled? How would one parent be able to handle the finances if the other were to die or become unable to help manage finances? This will likely bring up a discussion because this subject is normally not considered.

- What are the plans your parents have for the remainder of their lives? Is there a plan in place to let them live the way they want?

- Is there a will in place for each parent? This involves both a living will and planning on how the estate will be dispersed.

- Are there plans or ideas in place for funerals, the handling of their bodies (burial, cremation, or organ donation), or a burial location? Are these plans written down, or have they been left for later consideration?

All of this becomes a part of parental finances simply because it all must be planned for with the income they have or will have. Budgeting for these events must be considered mandatory by the financial caregiver if your parents are to get what they planned for. Because of this, having this information becomes significantly important in your parents' later years.

WHEN DO YOU NEED TO INTERVENE?

If a parent has had a stroke, or has slipped into a coma, leaving the other parent to manage on their own, you need to intervene. If there has been a major medical crisis and the insurance is used up, or the hospital and medical bills are piling up, you should get involved. If the parent who handled the finances has passed away, you must step in. If an economic crisis strikes, wiping out almost an entire lifetime of financial stability, you may have to take over.

There are other times when the signs will not be as clear and obvious. Examples of the not-so-obvious signs include depression; memory loss; family members and friends passing away, leaving no support system; a new acquaintance gaining more influence over parental opinions and actions — these can all be warning signs that trouble is brewing.

There are times when, even when parents are alert and aware, the simple volume of financial data, bills, medications, special offers, and junk mail can overwhelm anyone. When your eyesight begins to diminish, those once mildly annoying insurance notices, doctor bills, and financial statements can become more complicated, and it can be harder to catch all the details. This is especially true for insurance statements that claim they are not a bill but look just like one. Utility bills are becoming more complex, as taxes and amounts may be handled by other agencies or assistance offices. Seniors are prone to sending money with each mailing simply because they think it is another bill to be paid when, in fact, it is nothing more than a solicitation. The issue may not be one of mental capacity; it may just be that your parents' hands are no longer as steady as they once were. They may not be able to physically handle a stack of bills, or easily write out a legible signature on checks or other paperwork.

How do you know when it is time to intervene? What are the signs to look for?

- Unpaid bills or collection notices for unpaid bills

- Large amounts of money transferred to people unrelated to you

- If your parent is usually a neat and clean person, look for extreme clutter or hoarding

- If your parents show signs of wearing the same clothes for days, or wearing dirty clothes

- If you find rotting food in the refrigerator, especially if it is piled up in back

- Obvious depression

- Unfilled prescriptions, or medicine used haphazardly

- If your parents have had repeated falls or are having difficulty walking

- If your parents are eating less or less frequently

- A loss of interest in activities or people

- Confusion or memory loss

- If there is recurring poor judgment

- If you see sudden mood swings or personality changes

- If you see signs of possibly suicidal thoughts

If you have gained access to your parent's checkbook or credit card bills, look for signs such as these:

- Missing checks

- Inaccurate addition or subtraction (multiple numbers crossed out as mistakes fall into this category, too)

- Repeated overdrafts or larger amounts being withdrawn

- Multiple sequences of checks made out for the same amount to the same business can mean that your parents are paying bills repeatedly or have locked themselves into a payment plan

- If the credit card bill shows items that you know your parents have not purchased, this could be a sign of identity theft

- If your parents are getting medical bills for procedures or prescriptions they never had, this could be a sign of medical identity theft

If you do find signs of a possible problem, you cannot count on your parents to admit there was a mistake or that they need help. Your parents may be facing one of three issues: They may be so afraid of losing their independence that they refuse to admit there is a problem; they may know there is a problem and are too proud to admit the problem, especially to their children; or they may be at a point where they simply do not know there is a problem.

The cause could be the medication they take; it could be grief from the death of their spouse or close family member or friend; it could be a combination of these. The best thing to do is not to read into the situation, do not panic, and look at all options for possible causes. If your gut instinct still tells you there may be a problem, monitor the situation to make sure your conclusions are accurate.

It is possible that you may be too close to the situation— or too far away geographically— to notice any slight changes. If your parents have friends or neighbors whom they see regularly, ask them if they have seen any recent changes in behavior. If you visit your parents often, ask those who only see them occasionally the same question. Having a second or even third opinion can add to your view of the situation. It is possible that the loss of one ability will not affect any other ability. If your parents can no longer drive, it does not necessarily mean that they are now unable to handle medication and financial matters; it is an individual matter for each person.

If the signs of depression, age, or illness have become apparent, bring the subject up with your parents. You need to do this in a way that shows concern and caring for your parents' wishes and their needs. Here are a few suggestions that may help when bringing up this topic:

Action Focused Statement	*"I noticed the electric bill was really late getting paid. Have you received any shut-off notices lately?"*

Concern Focused Statement	*"Mom, when you go to the casino, about how much do you spend each time?"*
Another Useful Statement	*"I notice your checkbook hasn't been balanced in months, and I'm worried about that. Any idea on how that happened?"*

HOW INVOLVED SHOULD YOU GET?

With the ultimate goal being allowing your parents to live the life they wanted to the best of their ability, depending on their ability to handle daily financial duties, they should be allowed to do so until it becomes no longer possible without taking complete control.

The conversation with your parents about their finances will cover almost the exact same issues that the conversation among family members, such as long-term planning and gathering information, for example. Unlike the conversation with your family, this discussion will need definite decisions of how to handle financial issues.

Questions that must be addressed when it comes to handling spending money and paying bills, as well as tracking debit and credit cards, include:

- How much help will your parents need from you? This is a topic you will undoubtedly need to handle on your own.

- Are your parents able to manage the investments and bill payments, but maybe need a little assistance or more time?

- Are your parents able to handle most of the financial management but need someone to help with some items, such as checking the math?

- Are your parents not able to financially manage their lives?

Other questions that will need to be answered at some point include:

- Are your parents overestimating their abilities? Does it look like they already know or sense there is a problem, but do not want to admit to it yet?

- Are your parents showing signs of confusion or memory loss? Is their judgment being affected?

- Are your parents withdrawing from the world around them?

- Is there any one person who appears to be a strong influence on your parents?

- Do your parents need help remembering to pay daily and monthly bills? Is the money there to pay the bills?

The level of involvement could only be as low as showing your parents how to figure out how much their investments are worth, or how to sell off a few items online or at a garage sale. Your involvement could be greater if signs are more serious, such as your parents being unable or unwilling to manage their own finances and still refusing any help. It is at this point where you might be entering the realm of guardianship and conservatorship.

In any case, this is the time to look at the entire situation as honestly and realistically as you can, for both you and your parents' benefit. In most cases, you will likely just need to check on how they are doing to make sure they are still mostly in control; but eventually, it can get to the point where you are doing the financial work for them because it is not possible for them any longer.

CONCERNING STEPPARENTS AND PARTNERS

Assuming that your parent's partner is not engaging in abuse or exploitation, he or she may still complicate things. If your parents are reluctant to let you into their affairs, their partner may take their side against yours. Or, if the partner disagrees with you on solutions, the parent may decide to listen to them.

If you have come to a financial understanding with your parent and the parent then takes a new partner later in life, he or she may decide their new partner should be the one with the power of attorney, or they may replace you as trustee. Nevertheless, do not make the partner an adversary, even if he or she disagrees with you. Treating them as an opponent will not solve anything, and it may even make the situation worse. However, cases of elder abuse and "undue influence" cases are an exception.

If it is a serious relationship, do the best you can to keep the partner in the loop. It is not unreasonable for him or her to know what might happen down the road.

But if your parent remarries, it is time for a new discussion. Does your parent still want whatever plan you may have agreed on before? If the newlyweds plan to sell your parent's house and buy a new one together, how will that change the budget planning? Is there going to be a prenuptial agreement?

Your parent may want to make sure all his or her money goes toward you and your siblings, but the law may prevent cutting his or her spouse completely out of the will. A spouse who receives less than a set percentage — the exact level varies state by state — can challenge the will and ask for more money. In some states, this could be as much as half; in other states, the amount for a short marriage is small but lengthens as time passes.

In the end, how and when you bring the issue of money up with your parents depends on you. What they need from you will depend on them. How to provide them with what they need is the subject of the remaining chapters.

3

The Stress of Financial Caregiving

If you ultimately decide to handle the parental finances, there will inevitably be stress. The stress of handling parental finances will include many issues. Here, we will look at the issues a son or daughter may potentially face when dealing with a parent's finances. We will also discuss how to determine if you are ready for financial caregiving, and what to do if you are not. We will also provide information on where to look for— and how to obtain— financial help.

In this chapter, we will look at the issue of long-distance caregiving, a situation that many families are now facing. There is also the risk of burnout and finding ways to avoid it. Another issue we will handle in this chapter is how to be ready to take control of another person's finances. We will also examine the issues of depression and controlling stress when handling a parent's finances. Lastly, we will offer a guide to help you know when to call a professional, and how to hire one if it is needed.

LONG-DISTANCE CAREGIVING

The definition of "long distance" varies, depending on which source you use when you are talking about caregiving. There are sources who place this as a time of one hour of travel time between points, and others who use a distance measurement of 100 miles one-way. No matter how you measure long distance in your mind, there are numerous Americans who provide this kind of caregiving to a loved one.

While the issues are the same for those living nearby, the problem solving becomes more difficult and more stressful for adult children who must create a travel schedule to care for their parents.

Here are some tips that might help if you are one of these long-distance caregivers:

- Keep in mind that parents may exaggerate a problem, or minimize it; it may be hard for you to know which they are doing

- Communicate regularly, if not daily, with your parents

- Try to check in often with your parents' primary caregiver, neighbors, doctors, and others. If you can, find a trusted person near your parents and give him or her your phone number

- If you can make regular, frequent visits to your parents, do so. This gives you some idea of what their life is like on a daily basis

- If you have Internet access, research resources for seniors or handicapped persons in your parents' area

- If your parents have Internet access, use e-mail and instant messaging to keep in touch more often; if they do not have this option, consider getting them an inexpensive computer with a Web browser

- If paperwork needs to be sent or received by your parents, make use of fax services, or buy an inexpensive fax/scanner/copier

- Make note that your parents may not disclose everything; this may be out of concern for worrying you or embarrassment. Always have someone else around to get a second opinion

- Make the effort to schedule meetings and trips to meet your parents' health care providers. You should establish relationships to get an overview of your parents' health and be able to ask for advice. Check to see if the doctor can receive and will reply to e-mail

- Keeping a copy of the local phone book for your parents' area will help you find local numbers and resources much faster

- Have copies of all key information such as Social Security numbers at your residence, as well as a folder at your parents' house or attorney's office

- Remember to stay organized because this will simplify life for everyone. Schedule appointments, trips, bills, and medication in an appointment book as a way to keep track of everything at a glance

- Signs your parents up for direct deposit or automatic bill payments to simplify long-distance caregiving duties. You can do most of the financial activities over the Internet.

- Soon after you become the financial, or even primary, caregiver, be sure to notify any professionals involved in your parents' care. This includes doctors, attorneys, and professional financial managers. Make sure they know your contact information so they can contact you if there are problems.

Federal law requires many employers to provide up to 12 weeks of unpaid leave for eligible employees during a family crisis. Details of this law can be found at **www.dol.gov/esa/whd/fmla**. If your employer has a human resources department, check with them as well to see if they can help.

THE RISK OF BURNOUT AND HOW TO AVOID IT

One of the main problems you will contend with while being a caregiver to your parents is stress — and your ability to keep it to a manageable limit. Do not make the mistake of thinking you can handle anything that will come along; you are neither a saint nor superhuman. You do have a breaking point. Being a caregiver to your parents may bring you to your breaking point, even though you do not realize it yet.

Being the financial caregiver for your parents will be no different than any other type of caregiver role. What you will need to accomplish is a method or strategy, for either avoiding or limiting the risk of burnout as the caregiver. Let us look at a few ways of doing this:

- For starters, do not be afraid to set boundaries with your parents. If there are things you are not willing to do, say so. If your parents' criticism or complaints become more than you can tolerate, tell them. Do it as calmly and respectfully as possible, but do it; remember, you are not required to be their doormat.

- While it is possible that your parents may have no idea of the strain they are causing, it could also be true that they will refuse to change if they are told about it. If this issue should happen, try bringing someone else with you when you visit them. Most often the tone will be calmer because few want to cause a scene around others outside their family. If the other person knows what you are attempting to do, they could also assist in the conversation, but only do this if he or she is willing, and do not force the other visitor into this position.

- Ask your siblings to trade off some of the caregiver duties if you feel you are nearing a point of boiling over. If you must, limit the time you are around your parents to avoid burnout.

- Even if the relationship between your parents and you is a pleasant one, you should still find time for yourself on a regular basis. This is especially true if you have become more than just the financial caregiver. Make sure you take a day off during the week; consider the role of caregiver like a job where you are allowed time away from the job. Find a back-up caregiver to help you in case of emergencies, illness, or your own burnout.

- Something that you may find invaluable is a quiet place where you can just sit. This is the place where you can scream, cry, talk to someone, or simply take in the silence. It does not matter where this place is, as long as it is safe, comfortable, easily accessible, and it helps release some of the tension. If you find yourself needing therapy, get it; this is not a bad thing if it saves the well-being of both you and your parents.

- Keeping your siblings and your spouse in the information loop is essential when you are a caregiver of any capacity to your parents. You may see yourself as weak or disrespectful because you cannot handle the responsibilities completely alone. On the reverse side, if you do not tell anyone there is a problem, who will know what to look for but you? If you need help, ask.

- If you become both the primary and financial caregiver, you will probably have a different relationship with your parents than the rest of your family does. As the caregiver, your parents are relying on you to handle the problems and emergencies. They will see this as a formal role, whereas, with the rest of the family, there is more of an informal role because there is not the issue of responsibility surrounding the relationship. This is one of many reasons to disperse caregiving responsibilities among family members so no one person is affected.

- If you think it will help — and it may — find a support group in your area. There are a few listed in the resources section at the end of this book. Having a support group of caregivers who know what you are feeling and dealing can help minimize the stress. They may also have tips, tricks, and other resources you did not know about to help you with your own situation.

- If you find yourself losing your temper or belittling yourself for the way you handled something, there is only one thing you must do: Forgive yourself. You cannot make everything perfect. You are human — no more, no less.

Running the risk of burnout as caregiver, in any capacity, is also possible. This is especially true if you are living an already busy life and must add caregiver responsibilities onto the list. You may feel as if you have a handle on everything occurring during the day, but all that is needed to upset the balance is one small accident or misstep. If you have safeguards in place, and you know there is a surefire way to release tension, you can manage your way through the seemingly unending rounds of minor emergencies.

DEPRESSION

Given the intense stress caregiving can put you under, and the pain of seeing your parents weak, incapacitated, or slowly losing their mind, it is not surprising that caregivers are often at risk for depression. This is particularly true if circumstances force you to spend a substantial amount of time taking care of your parents by yourself, causing you to cut back on whatever fun activities you would normally engage in.

While a certain amount of bleak, sad thoughts are normal in caregiving, if you start to find them overwhelming, do not assume that what you are feeling is natural or normal, or that there is nothing you can do about it. Do not make the mistake of thinking "It is all in my head — I should just snap out of it," or that if you cannot conquer your blue feelings, it is a sign of weakness. Depression is not a personal failing or a weakness, and it is treatable.

Clinical depression is characterized by several symptoms: sadness or emptiness; feelings of hopelessness, guilt, worthlessness, or helplessness; loss of interest in activities, including sex; oversleeping or insomnia; overeating or loss of appetite; fatigue and loss of energy; thoughts of suicide; difficulty thinking clearly; and persistent psychosomatic symptoms, such as stomach upsets or chronic pain.

STRESS CONTROL

Even if you are not depressed, stress can take a physical and emotional toll on you. It can spoil sleep, digestion, and weaken your immune system, or can simply make you less able to deal with other stressors — car repair bills, your child's bad report card — when they come.

Do not wait until your stress level reaches a point of breaking. The use of preventive maintenance is more productive and efficient than making major repairs to any type of system, living or mechanical. Here are a few ways to take care of your body to avoid reaching critical limits:

- Exercise can help relieve stress and boost your general health, which will help you withstand stress better. Find something that appeals to you — a walk around the block, push-ups, bicycling, hand weights, or yoga — and start immediately. If that requires someone to watch your parents for 15 minutes, find someone. It will be worth it. Choose a time that works for you and exercise regularly, but check with your doctor first for advice. Pulling a hamstring will not help your situation.

- Try yoga or meditation to relax your body and your mind.

- Find at least a little time to do something you like for a few minutes a day.

- Eat regularly. Even if you are pressured and short on time, eat three meals a day (add snacks according to whatever meal plan or diet theory you follow), eat healthy meals, and do not overeat.

WHEN TO CALL A PROFESSIONAL

One of the first things people do when faced with personal or family crisis is to seek out the self-help books to get advice and information. Being a caregiver is no exception. Walk into any large retail bookstore, or search an online store on the Internet, and you will find evidence that it is possible to handle everything your parents need. There are books and sites full of information about legal issues, selling or buying a house, managing retirement accounts, investing, cutting the tax rate, estate planning, writing any type of will, and yes, there is an *Eldercare for Dummies*.

In practice, though, you may not have the time, knowledge, or confidence to tackle any of these things. Sure, the books and Web sites all say that most anyone can do what they instruct you to do, but what happens if you make a mistake? What happens if one or more things go wrong? This is when it can get terrifying.

While hiring a competent professional for your needs will not guarantee a miracle, it can eliminate the risky elementary errors that you might make without one. Hiring a professional also cuts back on the amount of time and energy needed to handle resource management for your parents' estate. The one major drawback to this is that the more people you hire for different issues, the more income goes out to pay for their services. You will need to consider how much professional help your parents can afford, how much they need, and how much time will be saved.

Some of the professional assistance you might want to look into includes:

- **Financial planners**: Make financial plans for retirement, investments, or your parents' estate. They can have names such as "certified financial planner," which requires several courses in planning and passing a two-day exam; or "personal financial specialist," a title given to Certified Public Accountants who undertake additional studies. Planners may be paid on an hourly fee basis, a commission on the financial services they sell your parents, a percentage of the assets they manage, or some combination of those.

- **Geriatric care managers**: These specialize in planning and overseeing care for seniors. They may be in business for themselves, or work for a government agency or a nonprofit.

- **Elder law attorneys**: They specialize in issues relating to seniors, possibly including wills, estate planning, Medicare (and Medicaid and Medigap), retirement, and guardianship. This kind of attorney may be useful if you are in a dispute with a nursing home over your parents' treatment, if they have been denied government benefits, or if they have been victimized or abused. Not all elder law attorneys have the same strengths, so if you are attorney-shopping for your parent, look for one whose expertise matches the problems you want solved.

- **Financial managers**: They are responsible for handling the checking, billing, and investments.

- **Real-estate agents**: These may be useful if your parents want to sell or buy property.

- **Rental managers**: Their experience in dealing with rental properties may be relevant to your parents' lives.

- **Tax accountants**: They may be of great assistance.

Be honest about what you can and cannot do. You may be confident you can sell your parents' home by yourself or work as their rental manager, but if they have a half-dozen properties in different states, that may be more than you have the time or ability to take care of. Filling out your parents' 1040-EZ tax form should be no problem, but if you have their own business, depreciation of assets, and capital gains taxes, you might want to consider hiring a professional.

There are no set rules for knowing when to hire a professional in any situation. Rely on your judgment regarding what your parents need — and what needs you can handle. If money is tight, aim for using services that are essential, such as appealing a Medicaid rejection, oversight of investment portfolios, or more serious health care issues. As for the books and Web sites, research them as thoroughly as possible and make use of any information you can find. Use the government Web sites frequently, as these can be a more reliable guide for many questions and concerns.

HIRING A PROFESSIONAL

Other online sources can help you screen hires, too. For example, **www.lawyers.com** registers thousands of attorneys with background information about them, their practice, and their specialties. You can also conduct an Internet search to find attorneys or financial planners and see if any newspaper stories or other records associated with their names come up. When typing in keywords for search, combine "professional's name," "profession," and "city of operation" to cut down on the white noise of people with the same name.

By whatever means you search for these professionals, try to gather three to five names, then call and make appointments to interview them in-person. Ask them up-front about their qualifications and experience, and how it relates to your specific problem. Years of expertise as a divorce lawyer will not help if you have a complicated question about estate planning.

But it is not just about qualifications. Try to get a feel for what the professionals are like, their style of doing business, and whether you (and your parents, if they will be dealing directly with them) can work comfortably together. Ask if they can name past clients who would be willing to talk to you about the same.

Of course, it is also about money. Leave your introductory meetings with a clear idea of what their fees are, whether they operate on an hourly or fee-for-service basis, and — if it is hourly — how much the total usually is for the kind of service you require.

Getting an Accurate View of Parental Finances

Now that you are aware of the need to intervene and decided it is time to do so, you need to prepare. You will need to know how to evaluate the situation and how to place it in a comprehensive format.

In this chapter, we will gather the financial information needed, then use a simple guide to calculate both the assets and the liabilities. Finally, we will place all of this information into one comprehensive package that will show everyone an accurate view of your parents' financial situation.

GATHERING THE INFORMATION

There are two methods for gathering all the needed information about your parents' finances. The first, advance planning, is not overwhelmingly difficult, although the list of what you need may make it seem harder than it actually is. The second, gathering information after a crisis has already hit, makes obtaining all the necessary information seem more like detective work.

Let us handle the easier of the two: advance planning. If you are fortunate enough to begin planning in advance of any problems, congratulations, your life will be much easier once all of the planning details are addressed. First, ask your parents to create a file that will give you all the needed information necessary to help them later on.

Here is a list of what you need:

- Personal information, such as addresses, phone numbers, date of birth and birthplace, birth certificates, marriage certificates, any divorce or adoption papers, military records, and passports

- Medicaid and Social Security numbers, photocopies of their cards, and contact information of their caseworker, if they have one

- A list of contact information for their accountant, attorneys, bankers, financial planners, insurance agents, executor of the estate (if not you), employee benefits councilor, minister, and stockbroker

- Access numbers and passwords to online and electronic accounts, such as debit cards and credit cards. You may want to write this data down and keep everything with the other paperwork

- An extensive listing of assets, liabilities, and details of how to find the needed documentation for these

- Legal documentation, such as living wills and anything that gives you authority, such as power of attorney

If your parents are willing to allow it, ask them to let you see their monthly statement from the bank, credit card company, and mortgage company, or at least authorize the businesses to send you duplicate copies. If you review them every month, it might alert you to a problem. Also, have the utilities send you notices of missed payments or copies of bills.

When all of the information is gathered together, the file should be kept at a location where it will be safe from fires or other natural disasters. It also needs to be easily accessible and somewhere where your parents can easily update it when needed. This is especially true if contact information for their professional contacts, or investment and real estate holdings, change.

CASE STUDY: TRACY SHERMAN

My mother became ill and, though her illness was not life-threatening, I realized that my brothers and I had no idea of her financial situation. Should something happen suddenly, we'd have no idea of where her money was or whether she would be able to take care of herself, money-wise. At the time, she was divorced, living with her long-term partner and partner's family, paying minimal rent.

I think, actually, she brought it up with me, letting me know where she kept her financial information and saying I could go through it to see what's what. She was matter-of-fact about bringing it up, and I was glad because I didn't know how to bring it up to her. I'm not sure if she had a will, or at least an updated one, at the time, and I remember saying it would be helpful if things were delineated.

CASE STUDY: TRACY SHERMAN

Fortunately, nothing needed to be done at the time. Since her health has improved and she's back with her partner's family, I admit I've slacked off on the learning curve. In going through my mother's paperwork, I was glad to see she had more financial resources than I thought she did. I felt relief about that. Knowing she wasn't destitute, I then wondered how it works as far as Medicare paying for nursing care or other living arrangements, should they be needed. I added questions to my list. I haven't needed to assume financial responsibility, thank goodness. The difficult part is role-reversal; it was also nerve-wracking to think that when I looked at her finances, I'd find very little money in reserve.

For record-keeping, it was a matter of listing account locations, account numbers, balances, and contact information (names, addresses, phone numbers, Web sites) so that I would have it if necessary. As far as resources, I took the information given to me in the areas of first alert systems and medical transportation, for example, and made a matrix for myself, comparing the different options.

Since then, my mother's health has greatly improved, and she is taking better care of herself. She continues to live with her partner and family. She is more aware of the challenges that were presented to the family as her health declined, and I believe is making a concerted effort to not have those challenges occur again.

As uncomfortable as it may be, it is important to know your parents' financial situation before an emergency arises. Having information ahead of time about assisted living facilities and nursing homes for possible placement (both location and financially) would also be beneficial. Knowing whom and where you can turn to for information is also important.

To avoid getting overwhelmed, make a plan. Decide what information you need to know regarding financial matters — accounts, investments, life insurance, IRAs, mutual funds, any and all.

Now that you have all the information together that you need, where is the best place to put it? Certificates (birth, stock, marriage, etc.), titles, and deeds should be kept in a safe deposit box at a nearby bank. If another bank purchases your bank, your parents will still own the box; if the bank office closes, your parents will be notified and allowed to move their documents to another branch or another bank. For documents that have a more urgent need such as wills, power of attorney, or advanced directives, these should be placed in the care of a lawyer, minister, or other figure who has quick access to a safe place.

So what happens if you are in a crisis mode and need to find the information yourself? One of the best places to start looking is the IRS. Your parents' last tax return will have a lot of information you can use. Schedule B will list dividend and interest income along with the attached institution for each account. Look for bank statements, credit card bills or receipts, or utility bills.

One thing you will want to do in either situation is check the information you receive for accuracy. Trace any paperwork back to its origin, and talk to a person about the information. Make sure there are no other missing pieces of information that go along with it that you might need.

After you have gathered all the needed information, you will be putting it together to create an accurate picture of your parent's assets and their liabilities. You will know what they own — and what they owe.

CALCULATING ASSETS

When figuring out the total assets your parents have, you will have a large amount of information laid out before you. Here is a way to help you organize this information into a more usable format.

Bank Accounts

List the institution, the type of account (savings, checking, money-market, CD, etc.), the account number, and where the monthly statements are located.

Bonds

These are one of three types: Treasury, municipal, or corporate bonds. List the issuer, the due date, the number of bonds, and the location of these documents.

Benefit Plans

This covers both employee benefits and retirement plans. List the type of plan (401k, IRA, pension, profit-sharing, stock plan, etc.), whom it covers, the trustees, the dollar value, and the beneficiaries.

Veterans Benefits and Plans

List the figures, obtain copies of all the paperwork no matter how small, and all contact numbers for the Veterans Administration.

Civil Service Pensions

List the contact information, person, and addresses; the amounts being paid, and when; and the location of any documents that go with this account.

Social Security

List here the amounts your parents receive or will be receiving, the dates, and the method of payment (direct deposit or mail), as well as any other benefits under this category.

Business Records

If one or both parents own a business, list the following information: name and type of business, type of ownership, percent of ownership, and location of all documents for the business.

Insurance Policies

List the type of policy (auto, health, property, life, etc.), what or who is insured, the company or agent, the account number, the location of the paperwork, and the cash value, if it applies.

Mutual Funds

List the account type, number, the company that issued the fund, and the location of any paperwork for the mutual fund.

Stocks and Bonds

List the type of account, the company, the account number, class of stock or bond, the amount of shares, and the location of these stocks.

Other Investments

List in this category any futures or options your parents may hold.

Real Estate

List here the following: the type of property, its location, and the date it was purchased; the cost of the property, the appraised value, any improvements since purchase, and the location of all of this information.

Real Estate Income

List this separately from the real estate. List income such as anything from mortgage payments or rent payments to your parents, the debtor, the contact information, and the amount paid each month.

Other Income or Payments

List here the income or payments from annuities, royalties, alimony, child support payments, or installment payments.

Safe Deposit Boxes

List the bank and the physical location of the branch; create a separate list of the contents and list the location of that information; list the appraised value of items within the safe deposit box if you have one.

Tax Records

List here whose records are kept, the years, and where they are located.

Loans

List the amount total, the amount still due, who made the loan, who it is payable to, and when the loan repayment is due.

Wills and Trusts

List all wills (including living wills and advanced directives), trusts, funeral instructions, the executor, the attorney who drew up the document and their contact information, and the location of everything.

It should be noted that if any of the information listed above is online, you will need the user names and passwords to log in and reference any needed documents. It is also possible, after logging in, to print out this information to obtain a paper copy for yourself.

INVENTORY OF PERSONAL PROPERTY

List here items such as cars, jewelry, furniture, books, electronics, collectibles (stamps, coins, cards, dolls, etc.), antiques, paintings, boats, and other such valuable items.

The Next Step

Now that you have the information for everything listed above, the next step is giving it all a dollar value that tells you your parents' net worth. This will become important when filing for Medicaid or other government programs if they have not already been put into use. It also helps if you must consider turning investments and tangible assets into cash.

Current assets that can be quickly liquidated for cash include bank accounts, money-market funds, T-Bills, savings bonds, and securities. Securities include stocks, bonds, stock options, and futures. The cash value for some of these securities can be found in the latest copy of *The Wall Street Journal*. Securities not listed there can be found with your parents' financial advisor.

Long-term assets that take longer to liquidate include annuities, pensions, retirement plans, insurance policies with a cash value (such as life insurance), interest in a business, real estate, and collectibles. Insurance agents can tell you the cash value of any policies and financial advisors can give a ballpark number for annuities, pensions, and retirement plans. To get the value of the real estate your parents own, look at the most recent tax appraisal, or hire someone to appraise the real estate. When calculating the cash value of real estate, remember that you must subtract closing costs, fees, capital gains, and other taxes from the gross revenue. To evaluate a business, use a certified public accountant or business broker for an estimate. You can also ask a business partner what the fair value would be to buy out your parents' share of the business.

Personal property includes stamp collections, furniture, paintings, jewelry, electronics, DVDs, contents of the wine cellar, or vases. When looking at them as a source of cash, do not guess what they are worth or assume that what your parents paid for them — or what the seller told your parents they were worth — is what they will receive. To get a realistic idea of how much these items could sell for, check out collectible guides, the Kelly Blue Book, or hire an appraiser.

Keep yourself aware of market conditions as they change. The value of real estate and collectibles varies depending on the economy, the market, and the availability of buyers. What price you can get today may be higher or lower than the price you can get when you need to liquidate assets.

CALCULATING THE LIABILITIES

When calculating your parents' liabilities, you will need to know what your parents' monthly and future expenses will be in the following categories:

- Alimony or child-support payments

- Utility bills

- Other monthly bills such as Internet access, credit card payments, and insurance premiums

- Unpaid taxes (from overdue payments, payments due on April 15, or estimated tax from businesses)

You will also need to know the location of all of these bills.

Federal income tax payments will not be the only tax payments; you need to also remember both state and local income tax. There will also be capital gains tax if you sell stocks, real estate, collectibles, or annuities, and there are property taxes, as well. Property taxes are owed on any property they own, not just for the house, and this includes vacation homes, rentals, or unimproved land.

There are also these three categories to take into account:

- Real estate debt
- Loans
- Bills for specific services, such as doctor's payments

As with your property taxes, be sure to include mortgages on any property owned in the list of liabilities; home equity loans are also in this category. Make notes of the terms, the rate of interest, and who holds the loan.

This category includes all borrowed money: the automobile loans, debt-consolidation loans, education loans, furniture and appliance payment plans, loans taken against their insurance policies or retirement plans, and personal loans. Make notes for these loans using the same type of information as you used above: the terms, the interest rates, and who the loan is payable to.

PUTTING IT ALL TOGETHER

Once you have all the information, the next step is simple: Add the total of all the various assets, then subtract the total liabilities. If the net result is positive, be glad: You are starting out with everything at least potentially under control, and you can draw up a budget knowing your parents have money for expenses. If your parents' liabilities total more than the cash coming in, there is no need to panic. While this is not good, there are steps you can take to avoid catastrophe, listed later in this book and in the reference section.

In either case, with this information you will have a much greater view of the complete financial picture. You will be able to better judge situations that will arise, create solutions, and devise plans using knowledge instead of estimating and hoping there is enough.

CASE STUDY: JUSTIN DYCK, CFP

People need to know their parents' cash-flow needs (income and expenses analysis); have an itemized list of assets and liabilities (a net worth statement); and the account numbers, passwords, phone numbers, and e-mails for their assets and liabilities. Parents and children should complete a financial organizer that takes inventory of all financial and health information.

Since change is often sudden and stressful, it's important to be prepared. Having all your financial information in one place can make it easier to deal with the unexpected — both good and bad. A "critical information" document is designed to be an organizational tool that will help you and your family more easily navigate moments of change. Once the document is complete, you should share it with appropriate family members, as well as your financial advisor, tax advisor, and legal counsel.

Signs the children need to intervene are incapacity, missed payments such as late notices or collection-agency calls, and difficulties with activities of daily living.

CASE STUDY: JUSTIN DYCK, CFP

Professionals have experience with the issues you are facing for the first time. They can recommend strategies and advise on how to avoid pitfalls. To find a reliable professionals, use referrals; seek professionals with advanced designations such as CPA, CFP, or CIMA; and interview multiple professionals to gauge expertise and compatibility.

Lack of organization is the primary hurdle for adult children. Problems typically arise suddenly, and it is too late to plan during an emergency. Maintaining an up-to-date critical information log reduces this risk. Children typically have different risk tolerance characteristics than their parents. Therefore, it is important to clarify the purpose of the money and allocate investments accordingly.

Typical surprises are that long-term care facilities are expensive, and that the husband "took care of everything," and the wife is consequently not familiar with the family finances. Many don't seek the advice of professionals until after a death or incapacity, and then it is too late to execute estate planning.

The common regrets are:

- "I wish I (they) would have been more organized."

- "I wish we would have made long-term care preparations."

- "I wish I would have allowed her to be more involved" (Husband). "I wish I would have paid more attention" (Wife).

- "We (they) should have completed estate planning" (wills, trusts, power of attorney, health care surrogates, and so forth).

- Complete the "critical information" document before life happens. Consolidate all assets with one firm to maximize efficiency. Recommended resources include a critical information booklet; online bill paying; the "My Financial Picture" online tool (**https://myfinancialpicture.ml.yodlee.com**); and working with a competent financial advisor.

- Sibling disputes are common and range from "Who gets what?" to "How to manage the assets." One way to reduce this risk is to name co-executors. This allows both brother and sister equal power in the decision-making process. You can also avoid this problem by creating trusts and naming a corporate trustee. Therefore, the surviving beneficiaries don't argue with each other, but rather with the trustee, whose sole job is to interpret the language of the trust and execute its intent.

CASE STUDY: JUSTIN DYCK, CFP

My advice: Delegate or automate as much as possible, and leverage your trust advisors. Meticulous organization reduces stress; ask for help. Start planning with your parents as soon as possible because it is too late once an emergency happens. Take a copy of the critical information booklet with you. This will allow the parents to see the value of such planning. Make certain that you address the legal work necessary to give you authority to make decisions on their behalf if something should happen.

Taking Over — The Financial and Legal Procedures

When you have taken on the responsibility of handling your parents' finances, you will also be taking on the legal issues that come with that responsibility. When you take over another person's finances, there are both financial and legal procedures you must follow. This chapter will discuss those legal issues, and some possible ways to handle them.

We will first look at the legal steps needed in taking over management of another person's finances. There will also be the issue of finding the best way to make everyone happy. You will need to know how to manage expenses, and how to play a significant role even if you simply need to be the helping hand while allowing your parent to maintain most of the control. We will cover financial topics such as joint checking accounts and revocable and irrevocable trust accounts, as well as how to watch out for pure trusts and other scams. Along the way, we will cover power of attorney, guardianships and conservatorships, as well as the issue of privacy protection — and the drawbacks to this protection.

MANAGING YOUR PARENTS' MONEY

One of the most important tasks you will have when managing parental finances is not mixing their finances with yours. Combining finances may seem to be more efficient, less time-consuming, and less paperwork, but it really is not. Keeping everything separated, like you would if you were running a business, is a more reasonable and more accurate accounting and bookkeeping method. The only exception is the joint checking account.

One thing to avoid is spending their money to pay your caregiving expenses, or borrowing their money to pay and putting it back later. If they give you money for assistance, that is one thing, but for you to take their money is a red flag for anyone double-checking your conduct. If your parents can and do choose to provide financial help, make sure the rest of the family knows.

Transparency, or letting everyone see what you do with your parents' money, is essential. The last thing you want your family or your parents to think is that you are hiding something. Your siblings and your parents — assuming they are able — should feel free to check the books at any time.

As a rule, do not do anything your parents have not specifically authorized. This may not be possible, regardless of all your planning. Something may occur that nobody saw coming, but you will be on much safer ground if you can prove your actions are carrying out your parents' wishes.

This is another argument in favor of preplanning: By securing the written authority ahead of time, it keeps your hands clean. This could become doubly important if a financial problem develops that is not your fault. It is not enough to be good; avoid even looking bad.

A final key step is to use the same methods as your parents when you balance their books; whether it is an old ledger, Quicken, or just their checkbook, do the same when working with their money. They know how to read their files, and they will be reassured as long as they can keep reading it the same way.

Even if your personal recordkeeping is sloppy, make sure you do better when working with your parents' money. Keeping receipts, bills, and records is one more defense if anyone questions whether you can be trusted with it.

THE LEGAL STEPS NEEDED

The legal authority to manage your parents' money can come in a variety of forms, depending on how capable of money management they are, how much authority you need, and what everyone is comfortable with.

As a common rule, there is a difference between incapacity and a legal finding of incapacity. Even if you know for a fact that your father cannot manage his money, legally he remains in control until a court hearing decides otherwise. On the other hand, you may believe your father was competent when he gave you power of attorney, but a court might find otherwise or decide he was incapacitated enough to set limits on what you can do with it.

Being unable to do something does not mean your parents are incompetent to do anything. Your parent may no longer be allowed to drive, but that does not mean they cannot manage the money. Your parent may be fully competent in their day-to-day business, but their caregiver could still have convinced them to develop a new will under duress. In many states, having a power of attorney or guardianship over your parents' finances is separate from the power to make health care decisions.

MANAGING EXPENSES

Two questions must be answered before getting too involved with your parents' finances. First, how good are you, realistically, at handling finances? If you are having a hard time budgeting your own family income, you may have a problem that could cross over into the financial management of your parents' affairs. On the other hand, if you have most of your financial world automated, then you have a ready-made template to follow.

The second question is, how much care can you afford to give to your parents? Even if your parents have a good retirement fund, medical treatment options in place, and a good accounting system, it does not mean being the caregiver will not affect your financial matters. There will be indirect costs you will incur as a caregiver, such as travel, meals away from home, attorneys' fees, work days lost, and the odd expenses that you can never see coming. If there are problems with your parents' finances, such as overdue notices piling up or possible insurance coverage lapses because of a premium that soon will be due, then there will be financial issues that will need immediate handling without having time to take proper steps that avoid other problems.

If you have not set up advance provisions such as joint accounts, power of attorney, or another of the steps listed below, you could find yourself having to pay the bills yourself while you straighten out the bigger financial issues. Even if there is a provision that gives you ability to handle finances should your parents become incapacitated, this takes time to come into effect while the incapacitation is confirmed.

While you may tell yourself that you would do anything to keep your parents out of a financial mess, neither your bank nor your credit accounts will share your feeling. With this in mind, here are the few tips regarding establishing financial provisions before they are needed:

- If you are having an advance planning meeting with your parents, do not ignore the question of whether they should repay you, should you need to finance immediate needs. Consider having something in writing stating that they will be responsible for repayment of out-of-pocket expenses to cover their bills. This only works for keeping their bills current, not for your gas or travel time to be there.

- Get any agreements in writing now. Neither your parents nor your family will be under any obligation to repay you for your costs or expenses with a simple verbal agreement.

- If you see the time approaching when you will be assuming the caregiver role, cut down your debts as much as possible ahead of time. Pay off the credit cards, switch to lower cost insurance, and make sure you have your insurance costs calculated automatically into your budget. If you must, set your own bills up with automatic payments.

- Keep your own debt under control. Do not start splurging now — you may not be able to afford it later.

- Even though you are paying down your own debt, do not try to help your parents by adding their debt to yours. Paying for your parents' bills using your credit cards is a mistake. Doing this handicaps the one person your parents need to maintain financial solvency — you.

- Talk to the rest of the family about possibly covering some of the costs involved with travel, lodging, moving, and other costs if these become too much to handle alone. While this may seem cowardly at times, not telling anyone if there is a financial problem on your end will not only cause resentment, but also could tear a family apart.

Make a Caregiver Budget

This is a tool that will come in handy when calculating where the money is and where it is going. How much money will it take to keep your parents out of bankruptcy court? How much can you cover for them? Make a caregiver's budget as soon as you know you will be taking on this role. Figure in expenses such as food, lost work days, travel, and incidental costs that you know you will have.

About Your Family and Your Retirement

Taking care of your parents is a commendable effort, but you must also consider two other important factors with regard to this situation. The first is you. Do not neglect yourself, your health, or your own finances. This includes your retirement. If you have a 401(k), continue contributing to it. This is especially true if you have matching funds from your employer. Do not dip into your retirement to help out your parents. To word it bluntly, you will likely outlive your parents, and without your own retirement taken care of, your children will be placed in a near impossible situation, just as you may be in.

This brings us to the next factor in this equation: your family, your children, and your spouse. If you drive your own family into bankruptcy trying to keep your parents solvent, you are simply trading one problem for a possibly worse one. You must be sure to keep your family fed and clothed while meeting their current and future needs.

A HELPING HAND

This is not a legal step, but in some cases — for instance, a deceased parent handled all the money matters and the survivor is overwhelmed by the task — it might be all that is needed. Visit your parents' house on the weekend and check that the bills are not going out late, and make sure the checkbook stays balanced.

Making Social Security and pension payments direct-deposit, and using automatic withdrawals to pay bills, can eliminate a significant amount of work. Simplifying the amount of paperwork makes it easier on your parents, which eases the demands on you.

JOINT CHECKING ACCOUNTS

One of the simplest steps to helping your parents handle their money is to have a joint checking account, a form of what is called "joint tenancy," on which both you and your parent or parents can write checks. In the event your parents are incapacitated, you will be able to keep paying their bills without any problems. And, if they are withdrawing large sums of money to pay a scam artist, you will find out quickly. In the worst case — death — the money in the account automatically passes to you without going through probate.

Of course, giving you access to their money might make some parents uneasy (and you might feel greedy for asking), but if they are willing and comfortable with the idea, it is a good basic precaution.

An alternative is an agency account, which allows you to withdraw or deposit money on your parents' behalf, without giving you any ownership of the money. It operates less like a shared account and more a limited version of the power of attorney.

One warning: If creditors pursue either you or your parents, there is no way to separate the money they put into a joint account from what you put in. Creditors can take all of it.

Also, because the money passes to you when your parents die, it will become separate from the rest of your parents' estate. Your siblings may see this as cheating them out of their fair share of your parents' wealth.

You should ask your parents about receiving a second key and access privileges to their safe deposit boxes. Some estate planners recommend you open the box with someone who will vouch for a record of the contents so your siblings will know you did not clean out the contents.

POWER OF ATTORNEY

Power of attorney is a legal instrument authorizing one to act as the attorney or agent of the grantor.

In laypersons' terms, this means your parent gives another person the legal authority to make decisions and act on his or her behalf. There are two types of this legal form: limited power of attorney and durable power of attorney. Before we go further, let us take a quick look at each.

Limited Power of Attorney
Limited power of attorney is just that, a limited use of the privilege. This is usually given to someone for the purpose of selling off real estate, paying bills, or for making medical decisions in case your parents cannot do these things. A limited power of attorney has specific authority that cannot be added to unless it is authorized by the person who first gave the authority.

Durable Power of Attorney
This use is most often created to ensure that your parents' wishes are carried out when they are incapacitated and can no longer make their own decisions. Durable power of attorney has a much broader range, and the person granted this authority can make just about all legal decisions needed on behalf of your parents.

Most times, even if a durable power of attorney is filed, it will not go into effect until the grantor has become unable to function without needing great amounts of assistance to live, and this usually requires a doctor to testify to this fact.

The Financial Management Use

A power of attorney in either case does not take away the ability of your parents to manage their own finances; It simply gives you the ability to step in and act as their representative if they need you to. In non-elder care cases, powers of attorney might be used to authorize someone in Wyoming, for instance, to buy or sell real estate for an owner who lives in Virginia. Another example of this is the joint checking account. As your parents' agent, you have use of their checkbook to pay bills, but to do this you must sign your parent's name followed by your name and the words "as POA;" otherwise, you become liable for any documents you sign.

Possible Drawbacks

As a caregiver or potential caregiver, you can see why power of attorney is useful, but it has drawbacks, too. For one thing, your siblings may not be comfortable to see you now that you outweigh them in decisions involving their parents. They may feel they could do the job better, or that this reflects on your relative standing in your parents' affections.

Another problem is that as long as your parents are legally competent, they can revoke the power of attorney just by writing to you to say so. This is especially possible if they are having mental problems or being manipulated by someone else, which could be when they need you most.

A power of attorney becomes void if the principal becomes incapacitated and unable to make decisions. For elder caregivers, the durable power of attorney is more effective because you retain the authority, even if your parents are incapacitated. If your mother is in a coma, a durable power of attorney could give you the authority to sell property to raise money for her care, pay for professional caregivers, or authorize her business to pay its suppliers.

One main drawback to being granted the right to act as agent is the person given this duty cannot pass it off to someone else, unlike being able to hire an accountant or home aide to handle the finances or physical caregiving.

Your parents may also be reluctant to give you what amounts to an open hand with their assets and estate. Plenty of people have abused the power: *The Pittsburgh Gazette* in 2007 reported of a military wife who had her husband's power of attorney while he was overseas, used it to sell his house, then left with the money made from the sale.

Your parents might give you a durable power of attorney with the understanding you will only use it to manage their affairs if they become incompetent, but "understandings" like that are not legally binding. Once you have the title of power of attorney, you could give away their money, "borrow" from them when your own cash runs short, or change the beneficiary of their will or life-insurance policy to benefit yourself or your family. Agents wielding a power of attorney have done all these things.

Abuse of POA

If an agent, or attorney-in-fact, breaches their duties, this is known as fiduciary irresponsibility, and the agent can be taken to court. If convicted, the agent will then be forced to pay restitution, damages, and face jail time. Most times this type of irresponsibility can be discovered years later, but there is no limitation on the time when charges can be brought. Unfortunately, there is no watchdog group that oversees POAs or their agents.

While this may seem irrelevant to you, know that charges can be brought by anyone who may see you as abusing your authority. This can be your parent's partner, their friends, or your own family. This is why having a paper trail of all transactions is necessary to assure no abuse of power has occurred. It is also a good reason to keep all your finances separate from your parents' finances. Even one simple, unexplained error or a missing record can be enough to bring your use of the POA into question. Many adult children have been sued for what looked like breach of fiduciary duty, interference with estate planning, or simple theft.

Restrictions

Because of this legal quagmire, there are attorneys who suggest more emphasis be given to imposing restrictions on the person holding power of attorney in any capacity.

One standard restriction is that the agent cannot give away property. Another is to require the agent make regular accounting statements to your family or your parents' accountant or lawyer. Your parents can set up a supervisor or "protector" who can remove you as agent if it looks like there is a problem, or they can require all your decisions be shared with a co-agent. Of course, the co-agent approach can make it difficult or complicated to carry out necessary decisions, or render decisions impossible if there is a complete disagreement.

The American Bar Association (ABA) recommends that if there is a power your parents do not want you to have, such as giving gifts from their account or changing their will, the power of attorney should spell that out. If there are specific powers they want you to have — to manage your parents' business, to sell the house, to open a safety deposit box, or make loans with your parents' money — the power of attorney should state this. Some attorneys will spell this out in written agreements that are not legally binding upon the agent, but do make clear the parents' intentions in writing the document.

Some actions may be illegal even if the power of attorney authorizes them. In Florida, for example, a person in charge of another's care may not vote in public elections on behalf of the principal, cannot write or revoke a will, and cannot carry out contracts the principal has signed to provide personal services, such as painting a portrait or serving as a home caregiver. A principal who serves as a guardian or conservator for someone else cannot use a power of attorney to authorize you to carry out those duties.

If you have any doubts about whether a particular act is legal, check with the attorney who drew the document up. Check first; act later.

Alternative POAs

Two alternative versions of power of attorney can be as effective but with limits as to when they are activated: Power of attorney subject to disability, and a springing power of attorney.

The first POA mentioned above gives a person the power of attorney but only kicks in when a doctor certifies, under penalty of perjury, that your parent is medically incompetent. The document used can specify what standards should be used and who makes the assessment. For this instrument to be in effect, attach the doctor's written and signed statement to the POA.

The second version is used when certain events trigger them, causing the POA to "spring" into action. Securing authority this way is much quicker than going through a guardianship hearing to establish incompetence, but it is not instantaneous, particularly if your parents are incompetent but not incapacitated. If your parents are unable to make good decisions because they are clinically depressed or slipping into dementia, or a caregiver is exerting undue influence, it will take time before a doctor is ready to attest to incompetence.

An alternative to these forms is to have your parents draw up a durable power of attorney and file it with their financial documents. In this way you can act without having to wait for the doctor if your parents become incapacitated, but authority is not granted until that time.

How to Use a POA

When the time comes to start acting as your parents' agent, your first action should be to read the power of attorney thoroughly until you know exactly what you can and cannot do. Consult a lawyer if anything in it is unclear. Then take the document or a copy to any institutions or people with whom you will have to deal regularly to establish that you are acting as attorney-in-fact. You cannot afford to lose the original document, so you might consider asking if bankers and brokers will accept a "certified true original" copy prepared by a financial professional.

If you have to prove your power of attorney to an out-of-state bank, see if they will accept authentication from your local banker. If you have to mail them the original, send it by overnight mail and insist it be overnighted back.

Dealing With Bank Issues

Some institutions may be wary of accepting the power of attorney at face value. For all they know, the document could be invalid or forged, or it might have been executed improperly. It could have been revoked since you received it, and your parents might have been incompetent when they signed it. They may be particularly wary if the document is an old one.

For this reason, some institutions may ask you to sign an affidavit saying that you are using your authority in a valid fashion. Depending on the law in your state, you may have to sign to get them to honor the power of attorney, but do not hesitate to consult with an attorney first, if you need to.

If you have a springing power of attorney, some institutions may want proof that the triggering event has happened. With an older document, they may not want to honor it at all, or they may want to have you fill out their own power of attorney forms. You may also have to obtain powers of attorneys for multiple states if your parents have extensive investments.

One possible way to simplify this is to establish with the bank ahead of time that you will be acting as your parents' agent under certain circumstances, and find out then what hoops you have to jump through before they will accept you as attorney-in-fact.

A Quick Note About Revocation

If the POA is revoked for any reason, notify everyone you have done business with as your parents' agent. This is to keep you clear of any legal tangles that may result later.

Final Notes

Many states offer simplified power of attorney forms, which allow your parents to list the powers they grant you. Even in these cases, it is better to work with a lawyer to make sure the document will do exactly what you and your parents want.

A health care power of attorney is a separate document, though your parents can make you their agent for health care as well. We will go over this in Chapter 8.

CASE STUDY: LISA K. JONES

In 1995, my mother was diagnosed with a 3-centimeter acoustic neuroma — a non-cancerous brain tumor that grows on the acoustic nerve and frequently attaches to the brain stem and cerebellum. The tumor had already caused the loss of hearing in her right ear before we even knew the tumor existed. The hearing loss was incorrectly explained as nerve damage, and her severe headaches as migraines. The misdiagnosis delayed getting the tumor removed before severe damage was caused. During her brain surgery and twice more after surgery, she suffered strokes that made the promise of full recovery almost impossible.

CASE STUDY: LISA K. JONES

She had to learn to walk and talk again and had some follow-up procedures that, unfortunately, made the matters worse.

Mom not only faced partial paralysis on the left side of her face, reduced use of her tongue and lost the ability to blink her left eye — plus all the damage from the strokes themselves— severe clinical depression resulting from brain damage in the brain stem created numerous ongoing health issues that she continues to battle today. But the effect of severe clinical depression and "mild" personality changes were among the most difficult for the family members to contend with.

Before the event, she was an auditor for a major retail department store. In this position, she was responsible for managing and reconciling the store's daily sales receipts and monies taken in from the cash registers. Managing her own money and personal affairs had been second nature for her.

My sister had always been the secondary owner of Mom's financial matters such as investments and checking accounts, but she lived several hours away, and the arrangement was primarily there for emergency purposes. After her illness, I became responsible for managing all of Mom's insurance and benefits out of necessity. I helped Mom balance her check book and kept an eye on expenses, but never officially took control of the financial matters.

Mom had lost so much of her independence resulting from her illness. She was no longer able to drive or enjoy her social activities, and her relationships had begun to change. She was grateful to have me manage the health insurance, medical bills, and Social Security disability and benefits issues. She forcefully maintained management of her finances for several years.

Mom was always prepared for the what ifs. She had clearly defined her final wishes and division of her property (which was minimal), should the worst happen. She had also obtained a prearranged funeral plan. We made certain that she completed a living will and final medical directives with the hospital prior to surgery, so there would be no doubt on what the family was to have done, should the worst occur.

What we hadn't planned for was long-term disability. When we realized that was what she would be facing — which was within days after surgery — I began investigating her options. Mom did not have any disability insurance and little in the way of savings.

CASE STUDY: LISA K. JONES

With the guidance of friends and research on the Internet, I started the process of applying for Social Security disability for her. Making applications for benefits — Medicaid, Social Security, and having access to medical records — requires having a power of attorney. There are several types of these documents that allow one person to act on behalf of another in legal, medical, and financial matters.

The power of attorney I had been granted allowed me to access my mom's medical records, discuss her condition with doctors, make applications for benefits on her behalf, and so forth.

Navigating the various systems was a complicated and stressful period for me. It took several months to get her approved for the needed benefits despite having signed documentation from all of her doctors stating that she would forever be disabled, unable to work or drive. Perseverance and having the support of friends and family was critical to my being able to come out the other side with some level of sanity.

Any time you take responsibility for another adult's (especially a parent's) personal business interests, be it financial, medical, or property, there are going to be difficulties. As an adult, they are accustomed to managing their own affairs, and all of the sudden, their child is now managing those things for them. It's always difficult for a parent to recognize that their child, regardless of age, may be more capable of managing something. There is a lot of emotion attached to losing what the parent sees as control of their own lives. It's very easy for money or other business and personal affairs to become a source of stress and arguments — even distrust between parent and adult child.

As the caregiver, you always try to remind yourself of this dramatic change and imagine yourself in your parent's shoes. Even when you know you are doing your best, if can still be hurtful if you feel your parent doesn't trust that you are being honest or taking care of their affairs the way they would themselves. It's a very fine and difficult line to walk.

My responsibilities were primarily related to medical issues and disability income. So the goals were maintaining coverage and the federal benefits — which means keeping up with forms and paperwork. Navigating through the federal and state social welfare systems is not for the timid.

Detailed medical and income records, at least five years' worth, is critical. Also, I recommend having a durable power of attorney that allows the caregiver child access to all legal, financial, and medical records.

CASE STUDY: LISA K. JONES

You will need to keep copies of this document with you whenever dealing with issues on behalf of your parent. It's also a good idea to provide copies to primary service providers like doctors, bank, and so on. And keep your money separate.

Educate yourself if you have older parents. Get them (good idea for yourself as well) to put in writing how they would want things handled in the event they would become unable to manage their own affairs. Preparation will make everyone's life easier and could help relationships from being damaged.

If you're going through the same thing, keep thorough records. Seek counsel and help from trusted resources for yourself. Try to remember your parent did not ask for this situation any more than you did — try to be patient with them and with yourself.

REVOCABLE TRUST ACCOUNTS

Creating a revocable trust is a simple, though expensive, legal process by which your parents transfer some or all of their assets to a trust. Then they buy, sell, and spend their money in their authority as trustees. This does not affect their control of their money and assets at all, but it does require them to name a back-up trustee or co-trustee.

If you were named as the back-up trustee, you would assume authority over the trust assets if your parent is incapacitated or resigns as trustee. As co-trustee, you would have to sign off on any expenditure from the trust.

There are both advantages and disadvantages of using a revocable trust. Let us take a look at each side.

Advantages

- A revocable trust gives your parents maximum flexibility in the management of their assets. It also does not require giving over control to any of their money as a power of attorney would.

- Assets that are a part of a trust do not have to proceed through probate to settle the estate. This means that the trustee can distribute the assets immediately.

- Any real estate in another state will also not need to go through probate. This is mentioned here because out-of-state real property is probated in the state where it is located. For families with a lot of property, this is a beneficial tool.

Disadvantages

- Creating a revocable trust is considerably more expensive than setting up a power of attorney.

- As the name implies, a revocable trust can be ended or changed, or the assets can be moved around. It also allows a new backup trustee to be given control at any time.

- A revocable trust and its trustee are not nearly as powerful as an executor of an estate and a written will. While it can complement the will, it cannot replace one.

Issues to be Aware of

- Community property placed in a revocable trust will revert to community status if the trust is ended. This has major legal issues in a community property state.

- Although revocable trusts can avoid probate, this does not mean they avoid estate taxes or creditors.

- Unlike an estate that goes through probate, creditors do not have a limited time to present their right to money owed. Because of this, debts can hang over the estate much longer and can force an estate into bankruptcy.

Using a revocable trust is a good option if your parents wish to keep the assets completely intact and easily accessible once the estate needs to be settled. Remember, though, that there are numerous legal issues that will come into play with the use of this tool.

IRREVOCABLE TRUST ACCOUNTS

This works the same as a revocable trust, but with less power to change or alter the setup. For that reason, it is not as widely used.

One place where an irrevocable trust provides a benefit is if you and your parents think they will have to apply on Medicaid. Assets in a revocable trust are counted as assets when the government calculates Medicaid eligibility; assets in an irrevocable trust are excluded if the trust was set up at least five years before your parents applied for Medicaid. If it was more recent, there will be a waiting period after they apply for Medicaid before they receive any benefits.

This requires some restrictions on your use of the money. To be disqualified as an asset, the money in the trust cannot be transferred back to you. That does not mean you cannot spend it as a trustee, only that the trust rules will prevent you from transferring the money back out of the trust and into your own name.

PURE TRUSTS AND OTHER SCAMS

You can find a variety of Web sites that promise if you put money in their overseas trust or pure trust — for a fee, of course — you can shield your assets from taxation completely. This, though, is a fraud.

GUARDIANSHIPS AND CONSERVATORSHIPS

Guardianships are defined as the overall care and custody of a person in need of protection as well as their personal and real property. A conservatorship is the custody and control of a person's personal finances and property only. Both involve court procedures and are a last alternative to a durable power of attorney. Details vary by state, but usually an office in the local county courthouse handles guardianship. Most often, this is a probate court function.

There are some states where "guardians" are also called "conservators." In still others, the conservator is charged with making the financial decisions, while the guardian is in charge of health care. Both guardianships and conservatorships can be voluntary or involuntary. There are states that allow for these measures only in the areas where the person is proved incompetent. This would be the case for a partial guardianship.

The court requires a hearing by which you must present medical evidence of incapacitation or inability of the person to handle his or her own health and finances. Most often, medical and mental health professionals are involved, and you bear the cost of the entire hearing. There is also a legal defense appointed to the disabled person as well, as well as reporting requirements of the court to which the guardian must conform.

Becoming your parents' guardian is a quantum leap beyond having power of attorney or being a co-trustee. As guardian, you would have full control over your parents' financial and legal affairs; they would no longer have any power. If this sounds like a big step, it is because this is one of the largest steps you can take. This can also be one of the most frightening and most costly steps when taking on legal issues.

As a guardian, you can decide whether to sell your parents' house, how their money is invested, and how much of an allowance they have each month. You have full control of their money, but legally, you have to use it for their needs. You also assume responsibility for their care and upkeep, for their physical health and safety, and that they enjoy all personal, civil, and human rights they are entitled to.

Becoming a guardian has advantages for a caregiver compared to a power of attorney. It is difficult to revoke once established, which puts you in a stronger position if you are trying to protect your parents from anyone trying to milk them as a cash cow. It is the only step you can take if your parents are already incapacitated, and nothing was done ahead of time to delegate financial authority to someone else.

Because guardianship takes away your parents' control over their own life, it will take a lot more work to set up than a revocable trust or a power of attorney, and you will be subject to a much higher level of scrutiny.

The Legal Issues of Guardianship

It is possible your parents at some point might be willing to appoint you as guardian if it becomes obvious to them they can no longer handle their own affairs. If your parents give consent to your becoming guardian, you will file the papers with the court, which will supervise the relationship and make sure you act, as required, in the best interests of your parents.

For your parents to take this step requires their overcoming the natural fear of losing control of their own lives, and also requires a lot of trust in you. What if you exploit your power over their money for your own ends? What if you refuse to let them spend what they want so you will inherit a bigger estate?

It may be that your parents do not think they need a guardian, or that their mental state is so unstable that they cannot give the proper authorization. In these cases, you will have to petition the court for an involuntary guardianship. Even if your parents are incapacitated to the point they cannot make rational financial decisions, it will be hard to secure guardianship if they retain a fair degree of competency. In addition, seeking involuntary guardianship could utterly alienate your parents. The default assumption by the court system is that anyone over the age of 18 is competent to take care of themselves. If you want to impose an involuntary guardianship on your parents, the burden of proof will be on you.

To secure a guardianship against your parents' wishes will require a court hearing to determine competency. This will require you to hire an attorney, and also commonly requires psychiatrists, social workers, or a court-appointed investigator to review the case and evaluate your parents. Guardianship is granted if the court evaluation finds your parents are incapable of making informed decisions for personal and financial matters, and if failure to appoint a guardian would create an unreasonable risk to your parents' health and safety.

The evaluators may also look at whether your parents could recover capacity later, whether medical treatment would help, and if there are less extreme legal alternatives. A supplemental security income representative payee, for example, is someone designated by the Social Security Administration (SSA) to receive and pay out Social Security benefits on behalf of the recipient, reporting annually to the SSA on how the money was spent. A special needs trust can also be created to run your parents' affairs without going to full guardianship.

If the judge decides that your parents are incompetent and that a guardian is the best solution, he or she will appoint one. But another drawback to this process is that there is no guarantee it will be you, even if you petitioned the court. There is no guarantee it will even be a member of your family, if a judge decides none of you satisfy his or her standards; instead, an outside third party could be appointed to have full power over your parents' financial affairs.

If the judge does appoint you as guardian, that authority can only be revoked by another court hearing; for example, if your parents regained competency. As guardian, you will have to make annual reports on the state of your parents' finances, including their income, value, expenses, and liabilities, and post a large bond as insurance against any actions you may take that hurt the value of the estate or are not in the best interest of your parents.

Major transactions will require court approval, which means more legal expenses. It also means the transactions, whether they are land sales or investments, will become part of the public record, exposing your parents' financial affairs for anyone to see.

If you are unsure if this measure can be handled by just you, or just one person, a way around this would be to appoint a co-guardian who is not in line to inherit anything. Given the choices and the legal ramifications of a guardianship or conservatorship, what would the correct legal step be to propose to your parents? This, unfortunately, is not a simple answer and depends greatly on what you and they are most worried about.

If your parents' finances are simple enough, meaning there is not much more than a savings and checking account, joint accounts may be enough to ensure financial safety. If there is a higher level of financial management, consider some form of power of attorney or revocable trust. If there are serious concerns that someone will prey upon or exploit your parents, consider a guardianship. But simply contacting local law enforcement might work just as well.

PRIVACY PROTECTIONS AND THE DRAWBACKS

Several years ago, the federal government passed the Health Insurance Portability and Accountability Act to protect patients' privacy. Under the law, hospitals, doctors, and insurers cannot divulge your medical information to unauthorized people. One of the problems with HIPAA that has cropped up since then is that even if you are your parents' caregiver, you may find yourself on the unauthorized list for receiving their health information.

If that happens, all your careful advance planning could be for naught. If a hospital refuses to confirm that your parents are incapacitated, your springing power of attorney will not activate; if your parents live alone, you may not even be told what has happened.

This may sound ridiculous, but it has happened: Wives have been refused information about their husbands, and children with power of attorney have had to apply as guardians because it was the only way to establish their authority.

This could not only affect a power of attorney, but also your authority with a revocable trust because you cannot step up as successor until your parents' incapacity is on the record.

Some attorneys say hospitals will often accept an adult child who is known to them as the caregiver, as legitimately authorized — even without paperwork. Legal Web sites say that a power of attorney for health care should give you the authority, even without specific authorization, because springing powers only kick in when someone is incapacitated and hospitals realize the necessity of giving that information out.

However, the sites also say that because of the risk of fines up to $50,000 if courts decide the violation was "knowing," hospitals may insist on clearer, specific authorization before telling you anything about your parents' condition. Some attorneys say they have not experienced any problems in their own practice, but believe it is worth considering it as a "what-if" risk.

If you already have a power of attorney from your parents, update it now to include a specific HIPAA authorization that your parents sign. Attorneys will be able to provide one. If your parents have specific health care providers, contact them and ask what documentation they require. Many will have their own forms.

It is possible there could still be trouble. A doctor might refuse to honor an authorization if he or she questions your parent's legal capacity at the time it was signed, or because he or she interprets it narrowly. If a doctor has a "reasonable belief" that you have abused your parent in some fashion, he or she can refuse to divulge information, even if you have authorization.

If your parents only gave you limited authority — to decide whether they should placed on life-support, but nothing more, for instance — you are only entitled to information relevant to that subject. Likewise, if the circumstances under which you assume your authority are not triggered, hospitals may decide there are not grounds for divulging information.

If you cannot obtain the information to go ahead, you may have no choice but to petition the court to become your parents' guardian.

Like everything else, HIPAA forms should be reviewed periodically to make sure the authorized person is not a person no longer in a caregiver role, such as an ex-spouse. The review should also check if there are any changes in the law down the line. Some attorneys say HIPAA is also an argument in favor of durable power of attorney over springing powers because the former does not depend on incapacity to be effective.

CASE STUDY: TINA HARBUCK

My mother who had handled all the bill-paying died, and Dad really had no clue as to what was due when, or even how to deal with it. Before mom passed away, she turned over the checkbook to me and went over all the bills — when what was due and so forth. Dad, however, still had access to the checking account.

Mom had died, and it was just Dad. He had a home, but was too restless to stay home by himself. He spent most of his time on the road and spent most of his money on who knows what. Plus, his health was failing. We eventually had to put him in an assisted living retirement home — which he enjoyed because there were other folks there all the time.

As for the money situation — when his extra money was all gone (money my mother had invested from an inheritance) — all that was left was his monthly retirement check and his Social Security check. Combined, they were not enough for us to pay bills. That's when he went to the retirement home, and his access to the checking account was cut off. He first lied about the inheritance money — then he cried when he realized he did not have enough to make ends meet.

When Mom died, we hadn't really had any talk about money. We should had discussed with her about the inheritance she had invested. But we figured that was between she and Dad. Who knew he would squander it away in a matter of months? When the money was gone we had no choice but to step in.

As for debts and bills that his retirement and Social Security didn't cover — my sister and brother and I split. I paid for his cable bill, my sister paid for his hygiene stuff like razors and shaving cream and so forth, and my brother brought him cigarettes and tobacco. It wasn't that hard, once we got credit cards paid off, and it was just down to paying for the home each month. At the home, he had food and pretty much every thing he needed.

CASE STUDY: TINA HARBUCK

When I'd go visit Dad at the home, he'd often ask if I had a few dollars he could have. I tried not to give him more than about $5. He really didn't need any money because everything was provided at the home. The only thing he had to pay for was for a haircut every month — they had a lady who would come in once or twice a week and cut hair.

We didn't really set any financial goals; we just tried to keep any expenses down. My sister and brother kept up with what they were spending on essentials for Dad and I would reimburse them out of Dad's checking account. We added my name to Dad's checking account so I could sign and write checks to pay bills. We pretty much agreed on everything, and we all had our little duties to do.

My best advice is to keep the accounts separate. Dad's retirement and Social Security check was electronically deposited into his account each month at a certain time, so I knew exactly how much was in there all the time, once we took the checkbook away from him.

If you're going through the same thing, talk to them while they are still healthy about what their wishes are. We often assume that one parent has discussed it with the other, but in our case, we had no idea if they had or not. We thought Dad had it under control, but we soon found out he didn't. He really didn't know how to cope with losing a spouse of 49 years. And it was apparent that he didn't like living alone, because he stayed on the road visiting folks.

Watch for a change in habits. To our surprise, Dad started dressing differently, staying on the road all the time, and drinking. He even did some remodeling on the house. Before Mom died he pretty much was a stay-at-home guy, working on the farm with the cows. But as soon as Mom passed away, he sold the cows and hit the road. He couldn't stay at home — I guess that was his way of coping. But it also cost him — he spent all the money, got in a wreck, and eventually got his license revoked. So watch for unusual changes; not all change is bad, but just keep a watchful eye.

Once you take control of the finances, be honest with them. Let them know, what you are spending it on (at least the big stuff) — so they don't feel like they are being taking advantage of. When Dad would ask for something extra, we were honest with him.

Most of all, let them know you still love and care about them — they are still your parents.

6 Helping Your Parents Live the Way They Want

In this chapter, we address the issues involved in the budgeting of another person's finances, as well as emergency financial planning and how your parents can maintain a comfortable lifestyle that the rest of the family can live with.

As we review these issues, you will hopefully find ways that allow your parents to keep their dreams and plans alive during the rest of their lives. You will find some guidance on budgeting for day-to-day living, food, utilities, and personal needs, as well as what to do when there is not enough income to meet expectations. We will also address other issues in this chapter such as investments and retirement income, investments with a fixed income, and what you should be aware of when your parents need to take money out of their retirement.

DREAMS AND PLANS FOR YOUR PARENTS' REMAINING YEARS

Before we explore the specifics of handling your parents' finances, keep two considerations in mind. The first is to remember that you are managing your parents' finances, not their entire life; hopefully, you will not have to manage more of their life than is needed. Ideally, your parents should still be able to decide what they want to do, where to live, and how to spend their money. The job you will have is to know what it will take to help them achieve their wishes, or in the worst-case scenario, to find what can be done to keep their finances straightened out. If you find yourself assuming authority during a crisis or temporary hospitalization, try to remember what they wanted or said about their goals from past conversations. Ask other family members to weigh in, if needed.

The other consideration, if you and your parents are working together before a crisis arises, is to gain as much information as possible about their financial goals and needs. Here are some questions you might want answers to:

- When do your parents plan on retiring? Do they want to continue working part-time?

- Is a return to college in future plans?

- Are they planning on keeping the house? Traveling cross-country in a motor home? Moving to an apartment?

- Are they considering volunteer work? If so, where? This could be anything from the local schools, libraries, or hospital, to working with the United Way, Habitat for Humanity, or Salvation Army.

- Do they see themselves living at home until the end? Are they planning to eventually move into an assisted-living facility?

- If they plan to travel, how often and how far?

- While being an uncomfortable notion to consider, knowing what one parent will do after the other dies is important. Will they move in with someone else? Will they live alone? Will they want to move closer to their children?

- If they enjoy gambling of some form, do they have an amount budgeted for that? Is there a limit to the amount they can spend before stopping?

Even if your parents have some sort of a retirement plan, if the date is still years away, they may not have definite answers to all your questions. Also, it is quite possible the answers will change with time. They may discover in another ten years that early retirement looks appealing, or the thought of not working at all is too boring to contemplate. Or they may have to take in one of their grandchildren to raise, which will force a life reevaluation. It is also possible that this conversation will bring a realization that your parents have not considered what they will do beyond "travel" or "volunteer." Also be aware that surprises cannot be factored completely out of the future.

Another consideration is what they want to do more or less of. Ideas of gardening, housecleaning, and hobbies will probably come to mind. Consider what they would like to accomplish and whether they want to stay near the family. If they have thought of leaving a legacy, a lasting accomplishment, what would they like that to be? Write down the results and ask which ones are top priorities.

Once you and they have a broad idea of where they want to be, you can help them figure out what that would take. Volunteering may require enough money that they can keep all the bills paid while they donate their time; regular international travel will require a lot more cash. If your parents are planning to live in a motor home for a few years, consider what the best financial situation will be; there will be the options of selling the house, renting it, or selling it and buying a smaller, downsized house instead.

Also consider that your parents may already have their retirement goals sketched out, money placed in a Keogh account, and a good investment portfolio. If that is the case, consider yourself lucky in that you may only need to help keep their goals on track. If they have plans for their retirement, they may not want or need you to go over their accounts and make sure everything is on track. You may have to settle for their assurance that they know what they are doing, though you should still encourage them to make all their financial papers and information available to you in the event of emergency.

BUDGETING — DAY-TO-DAY LIVING, FOOD, UTILITIES, AND PERSONAL NEEDS

If we assume your parents do not need your full attention or do not want it at this time, move on to the next step. After goal setting, the budgeting of daily expenses is the biggest issue to independent living.

The first thing you should do if you are having this conversation ahead of retirement or a crisis is to find out what the monthly income really is. Take a look at the categories listed below and add up the numbers. If you see a category that does not apply, move past it.

- **Earned Income** – This would include take-home pay, bonuses, commissions, overtime (if it is common), stock options, tips, side income from eBay, or any other regular income that they count on.

- **Self-Employment Income** – This would include any freelance or side business they have going; include income from partnerships, or rental payments. This must be separated because the IRS separates this as well.

- **Family Income** – This category includes alimony, child support, and money from a family trust or an inheritance.

- **Government Income** – This category includes any form of government assistance, disability payments, unemployment insurance, veterans benefits, Social Security, civil service benefits, or any income from any government agency.

- **Pensions** – This is any income from any retirement accounts they have.

- **Investment Income** – This is where you put interest from bank accounts, certificates of deposit, money market accounts, stock dividends, savings accounts, or interest on bonds.

- **Miscellaneous Income** – This category is used for anything that does not fall into the others listed above.

The next step is to find out what the opposite end of the financial situation looks like — the expenses. Again, take a look at the list below and add up the numbers. There may be categories that do not fit, so do not worry if you cannot fill in every one.

- **Automobile Expenses** – This includes car payments, gas, license fees, and regular maintenance costs; insurance premiums are in a category farther down the list.

- **Family Expenses** – This category includes support payments, alimony, food, and tuition.

- **Mortgage Payments** – This includes any monthly payments for their home; if your parents rent, then that number goes here.

- **Insurance Premiums** – This includes all insurance payments such as car, health, disability, dental, homeowners', life, property, and liability if they have it.

- **Utility Bills** – This is where you put the electric, gas, water, cable, sewer, and phone bills.

- **Loan Payments** – This is the category for any uncategorized loan payments not listed above.

- **Taxes** – This does not include deductions from any paychecks. These are the taxes due either quarterly, yearly, or back taxes due. Break these down into monthly amounts to be included in the budget.

- **Clothing** – This category not only includes new clothing but also upkeep, such as repair, dry cleaning, and special occasion clothing for events or day trips.

- **Children's Expenses** – This is the place for any allowances, babysitters, school supplies, day care, clothing, or tuition your parents handle.

- **Dues** – Any fees or dues for clubs, societies, or unions go here.

- **Gifts** – This is where the financial donations for charities, church, or politics go. If they are annual gifts, break them down into monthly amounts to work into the budget.

- **Equipment Costs** – This is where you include extended warranty payments, service contracts, replacement costs, maintenance, and rental agreements if your parents have them.

- **Financial or Legal Services** – This category is for any financial advisors, legal advisors, online investment accounts that charge a fee, or tax services your parents use.

- **Food** – This includes not only their monthly grocery bill, but also dining out and the bar tab.

- **Home Maintenance** – This is where you put the cleaning supplies, repairs, monthly maintenance, payments to the gardener, housekeeper, or other in-home help.

- **Pets** – This category covers the food, pet care, and veterinary bills.

- **Medical Care** – This is the category for the doctor, dentist, prescription medication, medical supplies, and any medical equipment purchases broken down into monthly amounts.

- **Recreation** – This is where you place the theater and concert tickets, movie nights (rental or theater), magazine subscriptions, book club memberships, and hobbies.

- **Travel** – This category not only covers vacation travel but also subways, bus fare, taxi fares, tolls, hotel bills, and vacation expenses.

The next step is to subtract the expenses from the income to get the current monthly cash flow. Then, multiply that by 12 for the annual cash flow. If your parents are already retired, this amount will give you an accurate picture of how financially stable they are.

If your parents are still working when you create the financial overview, there will be one more calculation to make. You will need to take their gross income, the amount they get before any deductions, and subtract their annual savings. The answer will be how much they spend currently in a year.

Assuming that your parents' spending habits stay the same, they will spend about 70 to 90 percent as much during retirement. This is because they will no longer have work-related expenses and their children will be independent. Keep in mind that some expenses now will not be a factor in another ten or 15 years. This is easily found by reviewing current expenses and crossing out those that will not be a factor once retirement is achieved. Some of these expenses will be replaced with medical costs, but others may increase over time.

If your parents are looking to retire in 16 years, multiply the retirement income by a figure based on the rate of inflation to see how much they will need to live in the style they want. You can also factor in how many years they expect to live after retirement to see how much they would need to keep the same style at the estimated end of their lives. You can also make the calculations online through a Web site like the one CalcXML uses (**www.calcxml.com**). If your parents' income is less than their expenses, you may need to cut living expenses, or consider the possibility of working beyond retirement. In today's society, it is not uncommon for older people to continue working part-time to supplement their income, if their health permits.

When looking at ways to cut spending, use the same basic logic you would use to work through your own spending. Keep in mind that unless you have guardianship of your parents' finances, you have no authority to control your parents' spending. They may see a need in having a Netflix account as well as several satellite movie channels, or a subscription to their five favorite magazines each month.

Once the budget is set, make sure your parents review it on a regular basis. It does not need to be monthly, but it should be at least quarterly. It is possible that the numbers did not work out in reality as they did on paper; an unforeseen expense could have popped up, or inflation increased. Once the facts are known, you can discuss changes to help your parents change spending amounts in different categories or find a way to avoid certain expenses.

What Next?

With a better view of the financial situation showing how much your parents have, or will have in retirement and what they spend now, you can translate this into a spending plan. If your parents are capable of making decisions, work on the plan together or have them make their own plan and allow you to look it over.

If you attempt to do this using "I" statements, or if you try to tell your parents you want to place them on a budget, you may be confronted with defensiveness or hostility. When dealing with one parent, especially if he or she is the one who never touched the finances, you could find that a parent can be uncomfortable seeing a spending "limit" set on paper. The overall feeling may be one of a cramped and confined lifestyle that he or she will not like.

Instead, emphasize that creating a budget is not meant to cut out their fun or ability to have their lifestyle, but a way to ensure they can afford their lifestyle. You would also be wise to stress that budgets are not cast in stone and can, when needed, be revised at any time. Also emphasize how using a budget can free them from the stress of knowing if there is enough money available to go around when they need it.

Pinching Pennies Not Needed

While the budget needs to be realistic, it does not need to be shaved down to the penny, or even the nearest dollar. Rounded-off figures will work just as well. Usually, a $5 error will not amount to much, but the figure should be watched to make sure it does not compound into a larger number. Simply put, this is budgeting; the exactness needed is not the same as handling a checkbook.

The next consideration you should help your parents with is figuring if there is enough money for them to live comfortably for the remainder of their lives. If there is not, what changes would they need to make to get comfortable? Assuming the money is there — meaning their living expenses are paid for — the next consideration is what to do with the extra money and what your parents would like to be doing in the next few years. This goes back to your parents' goals for their life. Are there goals for traveling, donating to charity, or buying the grandchildren a new car? These need to be planned for after the basics are handled.

What happens if basic expenses increase? Having a plan in place for this is also possible. Your parents do not need to cut back so far that it hurts. Perhaps they give less to the United Way, or they go to Florida on vacation instead of Mexico. Perhaps the grandchildren can get a used car, or accept a little less in their college fund. While the budget may become tighter, your parents do not have to scale back completely if there is a plan in place beforehand.

WHAT TO DO WHEN THERE IS NOT ENOUGH

Now you have figured out the income and expenses. What do you do if the situation shows there is not enough income to cover the expenses? What do you do if your parents' liabilities (the loans, fees, premiums) are a larger expense than first anticipated? The possibility of coming up short in income is another reason to have as much financial work in place as possible. While facing the fact that your parents cannot support themselves will not make the financial management any easier, the more you can do ahead of a financial crisis, the better off everyone will be.

With the knowledge of this alarming fact clear, you now have the option to improve the balance sheets for the better. It may not look possible, but it can be, at a minimum, partly accomplished.

The first option you have is cost-cutting and financial belt-tightening. Start by looking for ways to save money without causing significant strain. Taking a look at everything can usually help to find some way of cutting back costs without losing the advantage of having a particular item. For instance, you could try the following ideas:

- **Cell Phones** – Have your parents switch from a monthly plan to a pay-as-you-go-plan, or consider adding their phone onto your plan with set limits for airtime.

- **Vehicles** - If there are two vehicles but only one parent, or one parent does not drive, consider selling one of the cars. Also check the possibility of switching to a more economical vehicle.

- **Credit Cards** – Consider paying these off if possible. If they need to keep one for emergencies, consider finding a lower-interest card or a pre-paid card to save on interest charges. Also, completely paying off the current charges each month will help.

- **Utilities** – If you can, get your parents on a year-long equal payment schedule with the heating and electric bills. Consider sealing off the second floor or unused rooms to reduce charges, and make sure the residence is winterized for efficiency.

- **Automatic and Online Services** – Getting direct deposits, online banking, online bill-pay, and e-mail service can reduce the costs of using a car to visit the bank — and is most often free.

- **Refinancing** – While this is a more difficult option than it once was, it should still be considered; this is an especially good option if interest rates have decreased lately.

- **Fuel Providers** – Locking in prices in the summer or fall will help keep heating costs down.

The second option is to find books on home maintenance, then tour your parents' home for drafts, insulation problems, leaks, gaps in the foundation or chimney, and the age of furnaces and boilers. Here are a few things to look into:

- **Lighting** – Switch to energy-efficient lighting.

- **Furnaces and Boilers** – If either of these are more than five years old, serious consideration should be given to their replacement for new energy-saving models.

- **Hot Water** – Checking the temperature of the water heater, as well as the age of the heater, is essential. Turning down the temperature will save money, as will replacing older water heaters and pipe.

- **Insulation** – Houses without proper insulation can see a significant increase in heating and cooling costs; wrapping insulation around pipes and insulating attics and basements will also help.

- **Windows** – While it may seem expensive at first, replacing older windows does save enough over time to make this expense cost-effective.

A third option is to have your parents sell or rent out their home and move in with another member of the family. We get to this option in more detail in Chapter 7. And while it may seem to be a drastic measure, it is also one of the most economical measures if your parents' finances cannot stretch far enough to handle housing needs at the present time.

Another option, while not recommended by insurance agents, is to have your parents tap into their life insurance policy. This usually works well for whole life or universal life policies. This move should be seen as one of the last steps to take in resolving financial issues. But if this step is needed, here is how it could work:

- Your parents can tap into the accumulated cash value of the policy. This counts as a loan, and your parents will pay interest, but they will not have to pay it back until after death, when it will be deducted from the payment to the beneficiary.

- The beneficiary can be asked for a cash advance, to be paid back from the death benefit.

- Some insurers will give you money in return for steeper premiums or a lower cash payout to the beneficiary.

If your parents are terminally ill, another solution is a viatical settlement provider, something that originated as a way for terminal AIDS patients to find money. Under the settlement, the provider will pay your parents a percentage of the face value of the policy, on average 45 to 80 percent, in a lump sum. In return, they take all rights and obligations under the policy, which is frequently sold to an investor. The investor pays the premiums on the policy, then collects when your parents dies. If it is only a chronic illness, they will not have to pay if the money goes toward long-term care expenses.

The rules for using such a plan are typically set up such as the following:

- Your parents must own the policy for two years.

- The beneficiary signs a waiver or release of the funds.

- Your parents are not expected to live past two or four years.

- You sign a release allowing the provider access to medical records.

Providers have to be licensed in most states, and some states forbid the practice. Check with your state's insurance department to find out if it is allowed, under what rules, and whether there are complaints against any providers you may be looking at. Check out several providers and compare their rates. When you make a deal, insist the money be placed in an escrow account before your parents sign anything.

ABOUT THE INVESTMENTS AND RETIREMENT INCOME

If you turned to these pages seeking specific how-to advice on turning your parents' savings or income into a lush retirement portfolio, you will not find it. There are enough how-to books out there that offer tips, tricks, and secrets of beating the market. It is unclear which ones work, but here are some basic guidelines, principles, and some common errors to stay clear of.

The purpose of managing your parents' investments is not to "beat the Street" or score a huge success, but to give your parents a steady income stream in retirement, or to give them the option to retire even if they do not plan to stop working.

This is quite different than putting money into your kids' college fund or saving for the down payment on a new car. Those are one-time expenses, even though it may take a long time to save up for them; paying for retirement is an ongoing expense that will last as long as your parents are alive. Successful investing means building a nest egg that can support your parents even if they live through their 80s.

This requires your parents, and now you, to strike a balance. An ultraconservative portfolio that avoids stocks in favor of bonds, CDs, and Treasury bills is not likely to grow enough to support your parents over the long haul. But if you put everything into stocks and speculative investments, your parents could wind up with less money than they started with.

Fluctuations in the market are normal, and letting investments increase gradually over ten years will produce better results than actively speculating over ten months. Hot stocks can cool, and spectacular mutual funds can flatten out.

Of course, average growth does not guarantee anything about how the market will be doing at the time your parents retire. If your parents have to tap into their 401(k) or IRA when the market sinks, as many had to do in 2008 and 2009, long-term average growth will not make them feel better about a portfolio that may be worth less than the money they put into it.

This leads to the next warning: High gain usually has high risk associated with it. Speculative investments can pay off spectacularly, but they can also fall apart in your hands. A perfect example is the housing crash of 2008. Dozens of condos and town homes were bought by people who had no intention of living there but merely wanted to "flip" their investment and sell it to someone else— sometimes for double the price.

These warnings are not intended to keep you and your parents from investing, or to suggest they put all their cash in an old mattress. The point is, just like in poker, they should never invest more than they can afford to lose.

Even if your parents are already retired or disabled, the guidelines still apply until you have to sell their portfolio or liquidate their 401(k) to keep them in the black. The longer the investments can keep generating money, the better.

Here are a few tips to help maintain your parents' finances:

- Double-check their existing accounts. If your parents went with unbalanced checkbooks for a while before you took over, there may be money sitting in them that has not been recorded and could be placed in higher-yield accounts.

- Do not invest all your parents' money in a sole investment.

- Do not take on more than you can handle.

The guideline is that your parents' investments will do best if they are diverse. A mix of stocks, bonds, and cash instruments combines a certain amount of safe, stable investments with those that are more likely to rise, and also requires less scrutiny of individual stocks and, therefore, less time to manage.

The cautious course — converting all your parents' stocks to bonds as they age — could miss out on the benefits of a rise in the stock market. For someone approaching 60, a mix of 40 percent in stocks and 60 percent in bonds, Treasury bills, and other fixed-income investments is often recommended. Remember, the goal is a long-term source of income, not a one-time pool to be tapped at retirement and spent over a few years.

Financial experts recommend rebalancing the portfolio periodically. For example, if the stock market booms, that part of your parents' portfolio will be worth more than 40 percent of their assets, making it a good time to sell. If stocks drop, use the bond money to buy while they are cheap.

The more complicated your parents' investments, the more time it will take to manage them. Investing in individual stocks and deciding when to sell requires serious study and attention to the market to succeed. Simply put, if you do not have the time, do not take on the responsibility. To look for safe, high-yield stocks, consider a stock mutual fund, which provides an inflation hedge, ideally one investing in utilities, banking, oil, and insurance stocks.

Indexed mutual funds are good for "passive" investors who do not want to devote a lot of energy into managing their portfolio. Rather than trying to beat the market, indexed funds copy the mix of stocks in one of the major market benchmarks, such as the Standard & Poor's 500 or the Wilshire 5000. Benchmarks are selections of stocks that are either broad enough to reflect the performance of the whole market, or track the performance of a specific sector, such as tech stocks. That means indexed funds will perform just as well as the benchmark they track, with the only difference being the trading and management fees. While this may not sound like much of an accomplishment, index funds have consistently achieved higher returns than actively managed funds. If your parents have the money to spare and the desire to gamble it, putting 10 percent of their funds in higher-risk growth stocks is generally safe, provided they can live with losing the money.

INVESTMENTS WITH A FIXED INCOME

Fixed-income investments are the ones that provide interest payments at regular intervals. Examples of these would be certificates of deposit (CDs), which can be found at any bank and offer a higher rate of return than savings accounts, and money market funds, which involve holding short-term securities with high credit ratings. These have better interest rates than savings accounts, but not as good as CDs or bonds. There are also bonds that are issued by government agents and corporations; the best example, and most stable, are the U.S. Treasury bills, which are considered risk-free.

It should be noted that bonds have drawbacks. The purchasing power may not keep pace with inflation. Also, as interest rates rise, bond prices fall. Longer-term bonds have higher yields, but there is also the potential for larger price swings, and it may cost $1,000 or $5,000 to buy into a particular form of bond.

401(k) Plans

A 401(k) allows your parents to invest money directly from their paycheck before taxes, and many companies will make a matching contribution — for example if your parents put in 5 percent of their paycheck, the company will contribute 2.5 percent.

You may think it is ridiculous to bring this up with your parents because you think that they have invested in one already. In reality, 70 percent of Americans who have the choice to put money into a 401(k) do not do so.

One of the advantages of a 401(k) is your parents do not pay taxes on the money or the matching contributions. The fact is that interest and dividends compound and grow tax-free, and that money withdrawn on retirement is taxed at their post-retirement income rate, which will be lower. Because the money is not taxed, it is a smaller bite out of your parents' paycheck than it appears. If they put in $100 each pay period and they are paying 15 percent income tax, their paycheck would only shrink $85 because the other $15 would have gone to taxes anyway.

You do have to pay fees for the management of the 401(k), though you will not see them because they are taken out of the fund. If they are more than 1 percent, they may be too high. An option to consider suggesting to your parents is that they put the largest amount into the 401(k) that nets an employer match, and put the rest into an IRA.

You should also know the limits to a 401(k) plan as set by the IRS:

There is a limit on the amount of elective deferrals that you can contribute to your traditional or safe harbor 401(k) plan.

- The limit is $16,500 for 2009.
- The limit is subject to cost-of-living increases after 2009.

Generally, all elective deferrals that you make to all plans in which you participate must be considered to determine if the dollar limits are exceeded.

Limits on the amount of elective deferrals that you can contribute to a SIMPLE 401(k) plan are different from those in a traditional or safe harbor 401(k).

- The limit is $11,500 for 2009.
- The limit is subject to cost-of-living increases after 2009.

Although general rules for 401(k) plans provide for the dollar limit described above, that does not mean that you are entitled to defer that amount. Other limitations may come into play that would limit your elective deferrals to a lesser amount. For example, your plan document may provide a lower limit, or the plan may need to further limit your elective deferrals in order to meet nondiscrimination requirements.

Catch-Up Contributions

For tax years beginning after 2001, a plan may permit participants who are 50 years or older at the end of the calendar year to make additional elective deferral contributions. These additional contributions (commonly referred to as catch-up contributions) are not subject to the general limits that apply to 401(k) plans. An employer is not required to provide for catch-up contributions in any of its plans. However, if your plan does allow catch-up contributions, it must allow all eligible participants to make the same election with respect to catch-up contributions.

If you participate in a traditional or safe harbor 401(k) plan and you are age 50 or older:

- The elective deferral limit increases by $5,500 for 2009.
- The limit is subject to cost-of-living increases after 2009.

If you participate in a SIMPLE 401(k) plan and you are age 50 or older:

- The elective deferral limit increases by $2,500 for 2009.
- The limit is subject to cost-of-living increases after 2009

If your parents leave their jobs, they can take the money out — but the best choice is to roll the money over into a 401(k) at their new job or an IRA if they are retiring, thereby avoiding tax penalties.

Employers' matching contributions are not "vested" — meaning belonging to your parents, permanently — immediately. Some employers have everything in the plan become vested at three years. Others allow it at six, with gradual increases in the investment amount up to that. In cases of death, disability, or the employer shutting down the plan, they will become immediately fully vested.

One risk to be aware of is an employer who structures the 401(k) so your parents' investment is primarily or exclusively in the company stock. As employees of Enron found out when their company stock turned out worthless, this is potentially a bad deal. It is, at least, a good reason to think twice about putting in more than the employer is going to match.

It is possible that at some point in their working lives, your parents put money into a 401(k) and then lost track of it. The Web site **www.unclaimedretirementbenefits.com** can help you search for any leftover accounts.

Individual Retirement Accounts (IRAs)

IRAs, or individual retirement accounts, are another type of tax-deferred account the IRS allows. These accounts allow your parents to invest thousands of dollars each year. The exact amount allowed depends on factors such as age, income, and the law. You and your parents can visit the IRS Web site to find specific information about IRAs.

There are two types of IRAs most common to everyone: the traditional IRA and the Roth IRA. What is the difference? Roth IRAs gain no tax advantage until you begin to take money out of the account; traditional IRAs have tax advantages for simply contributing to the account.

The difference between an IRA and an employer's 401(k) is that there are no matching funds from your employer coming into an IRA. Also, if you have creditors, a 401(k) is protected if you show it is for retirement; an IRA is protected if you show the money is necessary for retirement, after factoring all your other funding sources.

You can set up an IRA to put money into a variety of investments, including stocks, bonds, or treasury bills. Some financial advisors recommend putting the 20 percent of your money devoted to stable investments into an IRA.

If your parents want to speculate, a self-directed IRA allows them to invest in anything, except for life insurance and collectibles; gold, business ventures, and real estate, for example. Despite the name, your parents do not have to manage the IRA themselves. Instead, the money is placed with a bank or trust that oversees the vehicle and invests as your parents request.

Even though the range of investments for a self-directed IRA is broad, specific investments may be prohibited by the IRS' complex rules for these funds. One requirement is that your parents do not benefit from the investment in any way other than by growing their IRA. Having the IRA buy their house and handle the taxes and mortgage payments while they keep living in it would be prohibited because it poses to a conflict of interest. Even if the IRA could benefit by selling the house, your parents would have a vested interest in the IRA hanging on to it.

It should be noted that an IRA is not protected from creditors like a 401(k) would be. So if your parents come into significant financial trouble, their IRA would be one of the first accounts taken to repay debts. This includes the IRS and back taxes, home mortgages, or even credit card debt. Anything tied in with the IRA is then subject to seizure, as well.

Keogh Plans

A Keogh plan or HR (10) is a retirement account for self-employed individuals. Contributions up to a certain limit are tax-exempt. Contributions can be based on regular payments or profit-sharing plans, where the contribution levels vary based on your self-employed income. Possible investments include stocks, bonds, CDs, and annuities; the age rules for withdrawing money are the same as for an IRA. You can set up a Keogh even if you also have a day job with its own retirement account.

Making Retirement Accounts Work

Now that you know what types of retirement accounts are out there, you should also have an idea as to how to make the most out of them. Here are some tips that might help you out:

- **Keep Costs Down** – Look for funds or investments with few fees. Use a fee-only financial advisor.

- **Use Direct Investments** – Many companies allow you to purchase stock directly without paying commissions. A good place to find this information is **www.dripinvestor.com**.

- **Mutual Funds** – Mutual funds invest in a range of stocks and bonds. There are usually several allocations available. Many mutual funds require initial investments of $500, but there are a few that go as low as $50. For a good list check out **www.mfea.com**.

- **Discount Brokers** – This type of brokerage offers a chance to buy shares with less than $100; many offer funds with no transaction fees.

One of the best ways to control costs and maintain income is to stick to an investment plan for years. The stocks may fluctuate at many times, and you may want to move money into growing stocks, or into a CD. If the plan your parents have is sound, stay with it to make it work. But, how do you know if it is working?

The plan should include regular reviews every six to 12 months. You might want to check the stocks every day — a lot of people do — but the drawback is that every time the market dips, you may feel nervous or doubtful, and on a daily basis, there will be a lot of dips. Over six months, those will smooth out and — hopefully — be outweighed by the growth.

How do you measure progress? Even if your parents have not invested in an index fund, you can compare their portfoilo to to the Standard & Poor's, or whichever benchmark resembles the portfolio most. If your parents' investments are performing as well, or better, they are in good shape; if not, consider changing the investments.

Other questions to consider are how much of your parents' stocks are small, medium, and large companies, and whether they are value stocks or growth stocks. Are they in different sectors of the economy such as health care, energy, and banking? How much is invested overseas? How much are the expenses?

If you or your parents need answers to questions, it is not a bad idea to find a financial advisor and go over their plan with someone who knows about investing.

TAKING THE MONEY OUT OF RETIREMENT

Retirement (or, less happily, disability) means it is time for your parents to enjoy the fruits of all that saving and investing in earlier years. It does not mean cashing in their investments and putting the proceeds in a bank account. The longer investments can go on producing money, the better; the quicker they take the money out, the less time the money will last.

If your parents have $100,000 in various investments, making 4 percent a year, they could withdraw $5,000 a year for more than 20 years before the fund is empty. Drawing out $15,000 a year would exhaust a fund, making 10 percent interest a year in just eight years.

How much do they have to take out? That depends on how much they have in other sources, and on the results of all that budgeting. The standard for keeping the funding going as long as possible is a 4 to 5 percent withdrawal; if they can stick to that level, great. As they grow older, they might consider increasing it, say 1 percent every decade. But in the first few years, withdraw as little as possible, and nothing beyond the safe level.

Once you and your parents decide how much to withdraw a year, set up a money-market fund within each brokerage account they own and channel any profit from the investments at the brokerage into a money-marketing account with free check-writing privileges. Keep three months' worth of living expense in the fund at all times. If there is an emergency, the fund will provide money faster than, say, selling the house will. It will also provide you with money to cover the tax on the dividends and interest.

Retirement Account Investments

Money in an investment account such as a Keogh, 401(k), or IRA is a special case. There are three considerations that must be taken into account with their use:

- Because the tax is deferred, every year that these accounts sit untapped is a year that your parents do not pay taxes on any of the money inside.

- If the money is withdrawn early, your parents will pay a tax penalty. Withdrawing money from an IRA before 59 ½, for instance, means you pay your normal income tax rate with a 10 percent tax on top of it.

- Some of the accounts have mandatory withdrawal dates after which the money has to start coming out. With an IRA, for instance, you have to begin withdrawing at 70 ½. These rules will a play a role in deciding how to pay for your parents' retirement planning.

If it reaches the point your parents cannot survive on the interest on their investments, they may have to sell them outright. Start by rebalancing: If their bonds or stocks have grown out of the percentage you assigned, sell to bring them back into the right percentage. Sell assets that do not bring on capital gains taxes; for example, selling stocks that have lost value, or selling bonds that generate minimal capital gains.

7

Thinking About Where Your Parents Will Live

You have chosen to take control over your parents' financial situation. You have gathered all the needed information, and you have figured out a rough yearly and monthly budget. Now you are faced with another possible problem: Where will your parents live? In this chapter, we will go over how financial situations relate to housing, and how a caregiver can handle any possible problems.

The primary concern is to ask yourself if your parents can safely live at home. If they can, there are financial methods that allow them to keep their homes. Home equity loans, reverse mortgages, and refinancing are options to generate income, and renting out the homestead is another possibility. There is also the potential issue of having to sell in a bad market.

What do you do if your parents must move because they could live with a smaller space, or they need to be closer to you? Some parents are willing to look for a new home, while others simply choose to rent out their retirement. There is the option of buying a mobile home to consider. If the income will not allow these options, you may have to consider the option of having your parents moving in with you. This can have both benefits and drawbacks. There are also alternative housing ideas, such as assisted independent living and senior apartment complexes. If your parent can no longer live completely independently, there are also other options short of placing them into a nursing home.

LIVING SAFELY AT HOME

Along with financial considerations, you will need to consider the physical limitations of the parent. Because of accidents, illness, or simply from age, your parents may find that their comfortable family home has become a challenge to navigate.

In extreme cases, there may be health problems, such as tube feeding, skin care, or physical inability to get out of bed, that may not make it possible for your parent to stay at home without help (Funding for home health care will be covered in the next chapter.). Even in better cases, frail bones, weak muscles, and deteriorating balance can make walking upstairs to their bedroom painful and exhausting, and a walk from the bathroom to the kitchen can be lined with unseen hazards.

Retrofitting the home for greater safety and comfort can make it possible for a parent to live independently for several years longer. Some of the improvements that can accomplish this include the following:

- Making sure the light is bright enough for them to see possible obstacles and ensuring there is a convenient light switch or lamp at the entrance to every room.

- Raising the height of their bed or installing grab bars to make it easier for them to get out of bed.

- Buying a bed or chair that will automatically push them up from a reclining position.

- Making sure there is a clear, obstacle-free path wherever they go.

- Having convenient tables or shelving so they do not have to deposit things on the floor.

- Installing ramps with handrails at the entrance steps.

- Installing an elevator to take them up stairs.

- Putting grab bars around the toilet to help them stand.

- Making sure faucets turn off easily and completely.

- Setting the water heater below 120 degrees to reduce the risk of scalding.

- Having the wiring checked.

- Widening doorways for wheelchairs or walkers.

- Lowering kitchen counters so someone in a wheelchair or stooped over can cut and chop atop them comfortably.

If a parent needs this kind of help and cannot afford the expenses, it is up to either you to do it or pay for a professional to do it for you. If the money is not there, do not hesitate to check out the senior centers and agencies on aging in your parents' area for charitable funding or services. Also research home-repair funds in your parents' state, and several of the suggestions below.

If there is no way you can afford to senior-proof your parents' home, it may be that even if they have the money to stay there, they will have to move. It is also possible that while they may have their mortgage paid off, and the value of their home is rising, they do not have any other substantial investments. Fortunately, there are several ways your parents can make the value of their home work for them.

HOME EQUITY LOANS

The equity in your parents' home is the worth of the house less the amount they owe on it. If they have $80,000 of mortgage debt on a $200,000 home, for instance, the equity is $120,000. Using that equity as collateral, your parents could take out a loan up to the value of the equity.

Home equity loans have a fixed term and interest rates, and some of the interest on the loan may be tax deductible. Financial planners recommend picking a loan that does not apply any penalties for paying off the loan early.

If your parent does not have an immediate need for cash, they might consider setting up a home equity line of credit for emergencies. A line of credit would enable them to borrow money against their equity any time that they need to, with the rate of interest depending on when they take the money out (usually tied to the prime rate).

With either case, home equity can be one source for money to make the repairs, maintenance, and retrofitting that will enable your parents to keep living in the family home, and possibly at a lower rate of interest than credit cards are offering.

The Downside

On the down side, borrowing against equity still means money spent every month paying back the loan, which will reduce financial flexibility; even if the interest rates are low, borrowing against equity to buy a new toy or trinket is not a wise choice. As always, though, as long as they are independent adults with control over their spending, you cannot dictate their financial choices, even if they make what you consider to be foolish decisions.

REVERSE MORTGAGES

A reverse mortgage is an option if the mortgage is paid off or close to being paid off. With a reverse mortgage, a lender takes money out of the equity and pays a monthly sum to your parents. Homeowners must be at least 62 to sign up for this, and the exact amount they receive will depend on the value of the house, the location, and current interest rates. Because they continue to hold title to the house, they will still be responsible for taxes, insurance, and repair costs.

Reverse mortgages offer monthly payments for a set number of years; monthly payments the rest of their life (usually smaller payments); a line of credit, which means the lender charges no interest until your parents withdraw some money; a single lump sum; or some combination of the above.

In addition to the interest payments, your parents will also have the same expenses as a regular mortgage: title search, appraisal fees, closing costs, and origination fee. Because of the up-front costs, a reverse mortgage does not make financial sense if your parents are planning to move within a couple of years.

One possible drawback is that reverse mortgage payments may boost your parents' income enough to disqualify them for need-based programs such as Medicaid or food stamps, or cut the amount of money they could receive. If they spend the reverse-mortgage payment during the month they receive it, it will not affect their qualifications. If some of the money carries over month to month, it will be treated as an asset.

A variation on the reverse mortgage is the reverse-annuity mortgage. With a regular reverse mortgage, your parents can only receive money as long as they live in the house; with a reverse-annuity mortgage, they keep receiving payment after they move. All reverse-annuity payments are treated as income when measuring your parents' assets, and the money is subject to taxes while a reverse mortgage is not.

A sales-leaseback arrangement or lifetime tenancy involves selling the home to a buyer who then leases it back to them with a written guarantee that they can keep staying in the house as long as they live. This provides the financial benefits of a reverse mortgage without the burdens of property taxes, insurance, and repairs — but also without the benefits of owning the home.

Family members who think the home is a good investment are the most likely source of a leaseback deal, as it allows the family to give parents money without it feeling like a handout. Charities that help seniors may also participate in such arrangements.

If your parents are interested in going this route, consult an attorney about the effects this will have on their taxes and their estate planning. The tax benefits for buyers are not as large as they used to be, so finding a non-family member willing to invest in such a deal may be difficult.

Here are some other options that fall under this category:

- With a charitable remainder trust, your parents donate their home to a charity in return for a lifetime annuity and possibly a tax deduction. Your parents remain responsible for taxes and maintenance on the home, and stay in the house until death.

- Under a life-estate deal, your parents sell their home but retain the right to live there until they die. The buyer can pay in a lump sum, monthly payments, or a mix of both, and your parents remain responsible for repairs and taxes.

- House-sharing means your parents or parent take a roommate. Your parent may open up their home to a student or a retiree who is willing to pay rent and some expenses, and provide help around the house that your parents cannot do. In return, the sharer receives the benefits of a cheap, comfortable place to stay.

Alternatively, if your parent cannot stay at home, they might consider house sharing with someone else.

Craigslist

Before advertising for a roommate on **www.craigslist.org**, check the zoning and land-use rules for your parents' community. Some cities restrict the number of unrelated adults who can share a house to prevent owners from turning single-family rental homes into boarding houses. You should also check with your local Department of Social Services to make sure sharing will not threaten your parents' benefits.

And, of course, exercise due diligence with the roommate: Ask for references and contacts and, once they move in, be alert to how your parents are coping, and ensure that everything is moving smoothly.

REFINANCING THE MORTGAGE

If your parents are not planning to move and still have a mortgage to pay off, refinancing is one possibility for obtaining a better interest rate, a smaller monthly payment, and a shorter-term loan. All of these can provide extra cash each month for home improvements, debt consolidation, or other purposes.

Reducing a 30-year loan to a 15-year loan — which means bigger payments, but less interest — or swapping a loan with flexible interest rates for one with a fixed percentage are among the reasons homeowners consider refinancing. The catch? Taking out a new loan means your parents will have to take out the same costs as their original mortgage, such as closing costs and origination fees.

When is refinancing worth it? A simple measure is the "break-even point," the moment at which your parents' total monthly savings have exceeded the costs of taking out the new mortgage. The more it costs in fees, the longer it will take to break even; the bigger the cut to the interest rate, the sooner the break-even point falls. If your parents are planning to move in two years, for example, and the break-even point for a particularly loan is three years, refinancing the loan is not worth it.

If your parents' monthly income barely covers the bills, cutting the monthly payment could give them more financial security. Money from refinancing could be used to make home repairs; put more money into a 401(k) retirement account at work or an IRA; go into a money-market fund or savings account for emergencies; or consolidate your parents' credit card debts into a single payment that is lower and tax-deductible.

If the problem is not that your parents have little income but that they do not manage it well, refinancing is only a short-term solution that will not fix an underlying problem.

RENTING OUT THE HOMESTEAD

Even in a good real estate market, renting — rather than selling the old home — is something for your parents to consider. Renting can be long-term, or short-term for properties in vacation areas, where the house might see a dozen different tenants over the course of the summer.

Renting out a house means a steady stream of income, and one that can keep coming, even if homes are not selling. If the rent covers whatever payments they are still making on the property, that leaves them in good shape financially and also gives you the option to pass on the property to heirs.

The downside is if neither you nor your parents live in town, or you do not have the time and energy, you will have to hire someone else to make credit-checks on prospective renters, handle repairs, answer any issues or complaints from the renter and neighbors, and deposit the rental checks. Also, some renters have no respect for property they do not own. After a renter moves out, owners or rental managers may find curtains torn down, furniture torn up, cigarette burns in the carpet, and the walls defaced. The damage deposit may not cover everything.

Hiring a rental manager will reduce the income your parents receive, but it can take a lot of the work involved in successful renting off their hands. Not all managers are diligent about their work, so ask for references and seek recommendations from friends.

To size up the pros and cons, look at what typical homes are renting for in your neighborhood. You may be able to learn from the "to rent" ads in the local paper, or you can talk to a property manager or real estate professional. Ask them how long a home might stay vacant because that will cut into the income.

SELLING IN A BAD MARKET

A few years ago, housing was touted as an guaranteed, sure-thing investment. Prices in many parts of the country were skyrocketing, and as long as it was a good house in a good neighborhood, owners could take it as a given that they could sell for a lot more than they paid for it.

The recent burst of the housing bubble proved once again that there are no sure things. Homeowners on the brink of relocating or retiring found themselves with a house they could not sell at the price they had budgeted for, sometimes not even for what they had paid for it. People who had picked up condominiums or homes as investments, intending to "flip" them quickly, found themselves with unsellable, dead weight on their hands. Some unlucky homeowners discovered the offers they were getting would not even cover what they owed on the mortgage.

If your parents are in this situation, you do not have to despair. Sooner or later, the housing market will pick up again in most areas, and homes that do not have any serious problems will sell for a good price. If your parents can afford to wait until then, it is clearly the better choice.

That may not be something they are willing to do. Maybe the neighborhood is going downhill and they no longer feel safe, or it has become gentrified with a younger crowd moving in and your parents do not like the added noise and activity. Maybe one of your parents died, and the survivor wants to get as far away as possible. Maybe the money from selling their house was the linchpin of their retirement plan.

If moving — in with you, into an RV, or into a cheap apartment — has been built into the retirement budget, then the sooner they can move, the sooner those savings will materialize. The longer they stay in their home, the longer they will pay property taxes and insurance on it.

If you need a feel for the current market, real-estate agents should be able to provide information about what comparable homes in the neighborhood or similar neighborhoods are selling for. Alternatively, you can have the house appraised; it is true that your property-tax appraiser will do that annually, but current market conditions may have changed since then.

Whatever information you gather, go over it with your parents and decide whether it is possible to wait on a market upturn. If selling is a priority and the market is not cooperating, you have several options.

WHEN PARENTS HAVE TO MOVE

If your parents have decided to move nearby, you and they already know what life is like in their community. If they intend to make a long-distance move, there is a lot more to consider.

Is there a single area they have their heart set on — the mountains, the beach, the lake, or somewhere warm? Are they looking to move abroad, to settle in the country, or to live in the city?

Fortunately, large numbers of relocation books are available that help set priorities for relocation — Is a low crime rate more important than the weather? Is the weather more important than the cost of living? — and compare various areas based on those figures.

The most important factor to watch for is that the area they pick offers the activities they want to do in retirement — walks in the country, opera performances, or mass transit — and that the cost of living is in line with their budget. Find out if there is an active senior community, and what sort of services will be available as they grow older and frailer.

Check to compare cost of living, including housing costs, food costs, and state taxes. If there is a big change, find out why. The house they are looking at may be cheap because it is in a rundown neighborhood, for instance. Also check moving costs, which could run several thousand dollars. Movers will provide you with an estimate.

PARENTS WHO PLAN ON A NEW HOME

The flip side of selling the old home is buying a new one. Your parents may already have a vacation home or rental property they intend to move into full-time once they retire. If not, here are the mortgage alternatives:

Fixed-Rate Mortgages

Like the name says, the monthly payment on a fixed-rate mortgage remains constant from the day they sign the note to the day it is paid off. The monthly payment will be less with a 30-year mortgage than a 15-year one, but they will also pay more interest, which means a higher total cost.

Adjustable Rate Mortgages

The interest rate on ARMs adjusts every year based on some outside measure; hybrid loans start out with a fixed rate, then fluctuate. There is usually a limit to how high an ARM can adjust annually.

When interest rates are low, an ARM can be a good deal, and it will usually start off with a lower rate than a fixed-rate mortgage. If interest rates go up, so will your parents' monthly payments. Sometimes rates can go up even when the market is flat and nobody wants to take the house off their hands.

If your parents are only planning to stay in the new home a short while, then an ARM with a low initial rate could be a good deal as they can plan to be gone by the time it rises high enough to be a problem. It would be wise, though, to ensure that if things do not work out as planned, and they wind up saddled with a higher rate, they could still afford to live there.

Balloon Rate Mortgages

With a balloon mortgage, after the initial fixed-rate period, the entire balance of the principal comes due, unless you refinance at current market rates.

If you had the time to do all the budget work before taking over your parents' finances, you have the information you need about how much of a house they can afford to buy. When looking at homes, match their budget against the PITI — monthly payments of principal and interest on the mortgage plus taxes and insurance — and see how they compare.

Do not forget that buying or selling a home means extra fees: Closing costs, taxes, and real-estate commissions may increase the sale price by 7 to 10 percent, something people often overlook.

The federal government allows your parents to exclude up to $500,000 ($250,000 for one person) of gain on the sale of their home from their taxable income, provided they have owned and used the home as their principal residence for the past five years. This means that if they move and rent out their house, however, that no longer applies.

Individual states may also offer a variety of breaks on property taxes. In Florida, taxes on an owner-occupied house cannot go up more than 3 percent in a year, and the first $50,000 is exempt from taxable value if the owner makes less than $20,000 a year. At press time, multiple other breaks are being debated by the Legislature, including a special tax cut for seniors. Like other items in tax law, these can grow quite complicated: For property taxes levied by school boards, for instance, the exemption is only $25,000.

RENTING AND RETIREMENT

If your parents have decided to downsize and rent an apartment, you should keep in mind a few potential problems:

- Rent may rise. Inflation alone will do that, and property tax increases or rising insurance rates may also be passed on to renters. This may not always happen — landlords who have had bad experiences with destructive tenants can be especially appreciative of good ones — but you should be prepared.

- The landlord makes the rules. Find out what they are before your parents move in.

- Definitely inspect everything about the apartment or house: Run all the appliances, flush the toilet a few times, and find out if the heating and air-conditioning work well. If there are problems with the apartment, make sure they be fixed before your parents move in. Promises can be forgotten.

- Find out if your parents or the landlord will be responsible for pest-control spraying and yard maintenance.

- Learn if any utility costs are included.

- Visit by day and by night to size up the neighbors and determine the noise levels.

- Remember that when calculating costs, landlords will usually want a damage deposit, and possibly two months' rent as a security deposit. This sum will likely be returned, less any expense on repairs and cleaning, when your parents leave.

- If your parents expect to rent for only a few months, a month-to-month arrangement is fine. If they expect to stay at least a year, it would be wiser to ask for a lease, which will keep the rent the same for the next 12 months.

- Property can be sold. Your parents could be told they have to move because someone else has taken over the property, or the landlord could decide to turn the apartments into condos, which will make it more expensive for your parents to stay.

MOBILE HOMES

For seniors (and many younger adults) on a tight budget, mobile homes are an affordable alternative to owning a house.

For many mobile homeowners of any age, if they do not own the land in the trailer park they live in, there is always the possibility that the park owners will sell and the park will be closed (Converting the land to a condo high rises or a luxury subdivision will usually yield greater profits).

Some states have set up funds to reimburse mobile homeowners if their park is closed. Depending on the circumstances, the fund, which is financed by park owners, will pay owners to relocate within a limited distance, or buy them out outright if there is no park closer that has an open space. In most cases, the money will not cover the cost of moving, but it will provide some money for whatever the next phase of your parents life is.

MOVING IN WITH YOU

There are several reasons why having a parent move in with you can be a viable option. Here are a few to consider.

Less Cost – It will be cheaper for them to live with you than any alternative. Even if they pay rent, you can afford to charge them less than the market rate. If you provide any sort of assistance other than living quarters — meals, transportation, or health care — you will undoubtedly be working for less than a professional would charge, and you will save on the gas it might have cost you to drive across town (or fly across the country) to help out.

Rent Out The House – If they cannot sell their home right now, they can stay with you and rent out their house. If they cannot afford to buy as seen when the housing bubble was at its peak — even the cheapest homes in some communities were not cheap — living with you is a chance to save money.

Ease of Care – Keeping your parents close at hand may draw them, you, and your family closer. It could also make it much easier to provide whatever help they need while fulfilling your duties to your spouse, your children, and your job.

ALTERNATIVE HOUSING

If you decide moving in with you is not a viable option — or they did move in, but their health makes it necessary to reconsider — what are the alternatives?

If your parents have already discussed their goals, you will know what they want. If they were determined to stay in their own home and that is no longer possible, you will need to switch gears. If they are unable to competently make a decision, you may have to make the call yourself.

The Family Caregivers Alliance (FCA) suggests you ask what level of care they need, how much independence and privacy they want or need, their level of impairment, and whether a smaller or larger place would suit them better.

Do not hesitate to ask your spouse or siblings for moral support. Moving your parent out of their home (or yours), can feel like you have betrayed or failed them, even if it is the best choice.

Remind yourself that you are not abandoning them. You will be checking to make sure the facility is suitable; you will check again if there are problems; and you are still your parents' advocate and chief caregiver.

Bobbye Sikes Wicke, a retired Florida nursing-home ombudsman, recommends listening and helping out with your parents' complaints, even if they appear trivial. As their level of frailty and dependence increases, Wicke says, "Their world contracts, and unsatisfactory meals or a lack of consideration from the staff can assume increasing importance in their world."

CASE STUDY: BOBBYE SIKES WICKE

Unfortunately, I did not become involved in my father's financial affairs before his death. He had always been open about his investments and plans for us and our children, and he had sent my brother and me copies of his wills annually, until five years before his death. He was diagnosed with Alzheimer's disease six years before his death, but this information was kept from us by his new, young third wife.

Upon learning that he died of malnutrition and dehydration, and his estate had been systematically transferred to his new wife during the four years before his death, I saw how my mistakes had enabled his misery — and ours.

I was concerned over his increasing short-term memory loss, inability to absorb new information, and increasing paranoia — all early signs of Alzheimer's disease. But I accepted the judgments of less analytical and critical people: "He's just getting old. He's under a lot of stress; he'll get better." However, he got worse after the stress was gone.

When my outgoing, hospitable, family-oriented father became isolated from family and friends — unreachable by phone, and not responding to mail during the eight years before his death — I let my pride, and his, keep me from investigating personally. I accepted my brother's comments — "He's fine, she's taking good care of him" — but later learned that my father and brother's conversations were always only about hunting, fishing, and the grandsons, and that my father forgot that he had just asked the same questions.

CASE STUDY: BOBBYE SIKES WICKE

My father and I always had extensive conversations about politics, current events, and people. I accepted the opinions of my adult children, who had been accustomed to frequent contact with him: "He's just busy; he's just having fun."

Things to keep in mind when you are concerned about a parent:

- Do not take changes in your parent from aging and disease personally; it's not about you. Remain objective, compassionate, and tactful, no matter how hurt your feelings are.

- Keep communications open, and go there personally if you have doubts about a situation. It's difficult to assess a situation when you live far away and depend upon casual opinions. Seek professional help.

- Fiduciary relationships must be based on protecting the best interests and wishes of the parent, and established in a timely and professional manner. As a Long-Term Care Ombudsman, I often observed that in the absence of a caring fiduciary relationship, after the death of a parent, all relationships dissolved into battles over money.

Complaining and protesting their problems may feel like the only control they can exert over their world.

Housing options vary widely, as do the official names. Whatever level of care you are looking for, here are some basic guidelines for the search:

- First, do not hesitate to ask friends who provide eldercare, or members of any support groups you belong to, for advice on finding a facility. You can also check with your community's eldercare-locator service (see the list of resources).

- Visit before a crisis hits, if possible, so you have time to think and make comparisons. Make an appointment with the administrator and bring lots of questions. If you like a particular facility, make a couple more visits at different times of the day. The FCA recommends visiting during a meal to check if the food is appetizing and healthy.

- Do not hesitate to tell the administrator if you anticipate problems: If your mother is incontinent but does not want to wear diapers, or has serious insomnia and plays music all night, let the administrator know and find out how he or she would deal with the problems.

- You might want to go with a supportive friend rather than alone. Seeing residents in various stages of incapacity can be jarring, even for someone who does not have to think about putting his or her parents in an assisted-living home.

Talk to the staff, as well as the administrators. Talk to some of the residents and their families, if you meet any. Find out what they like most and least about the place. Ask how long the staff have been there, and how many employees have stayed for more than one year. Try to get a feel for the atmosphere of a place, and whether it would be a good fit for your parents. Check as to your parents' specific needs: Will the facility accept your parents' cat? Does it offer meals that satisfy vegetarians or the lactose-intolerant?

Other items you will want to look into:

- Find out if the facility you are looking at is licensed, and what licensing regulations are in your parents' state.

- Find contact information for a long-term ombudsman. An ombudsman acts as a patient's advocate in nursing homes and other situations and will try to work out any problems the patient is having.

- Check the costs. Ask if rates are increasing and how often; how much notice is given; and how the administration determines that someone needs a higher and more expensive level of care.

- What is the staff-to-patient ratio?

- If you find a site you otherwise like that has a flaw, is it one you could fix? If there is no beauty shop on-site, for instance, can you take your parent out, or bring over movies and a DVD player one evening for entertainment?

- If only one of your parents needs increased care, will it be possible for both to move into the facility together?

- Make an unannounced visit.

- Check out **www.medicare.gov** for information about specific nursing homes (Click on the link to "Compare nursing homes in your area"), if it is a nursing home that you are looking for.

- Provide the staff with a typical description of your parents' day. Write down your parents' schedule. Let the staff know if your parents prefer a male or female caregiver. See how they respond.

Even if you make a good choice, adjusting to the new setting will be tough. After a few months, once you are satisfied that they are doing all right, you will feel relief. You may even enjoy visiting them more now that your feelings for them, and theirs for you, are not colored by the stresses of hands-on caregiving.

If it turns out after a while that you picked incorrectly and the site is not a good match, you can either work with staff to help your parents adjust, or you can look for a new place based on what you have learned about what your parents really need.

JUST SHORT OF A NURSING HOME

There is a common perception that the only alternative to living at home or with the kids is for a parent to go into a nursing home. Years ago, that was true, but today, there are a number of less extreme alternatives with varying levels of care, varying numbers of residents, and varying fees.

Which one is right for your parents? It depends. The ideal is they live in a place that gives them all the care they need and no more than that; one that does not impose any unnecessary restrictions on them; and one that can be relied on to treat them well — and not as a cheap source of funding.

Supportive Housing

Supportive Housing for the Elderly is a federal Housing and Urban Development program, also known as Section 202 housing. Typically this provides a studio or one-bedroom apartment with a small kitchen in buildings with senior-friendly features. Transportation, shopping, and laundry services are available for fees.

Applicants must be at least 52, and have less than 50 percent of the median income — meaning that half the people make more, half the people make less — for their area. A typical resident is a single woman in her mid-70s with an annual income of less than $10,000.

The rent is low, but the facility does not provide support for seniors who are unable to perform basic care for themselves. Also, the waiting list for these facilities is long, and it can take years to move up.

Assisted Living

Assisted living is a marketing term that covers a wide range of facilities, usually licensed, although the exact standards and regulations vary from state to state. Under this catch-all label, you may find large complexes with small apartments or shared bedrooms in a small group-housing arrangement. The level of service varies widely. Parents who require some help and support in daily activities but do not need medical oversight and still function well mentally, are the best candidates for assisted living

Assisted living has many benefits: It balances independence with aid, and it provides socialization for people who want it.

The downside? Medicare does not cover assisted living, and if your parents have a medical crisis, the level of supervision may not be adequate. If your parents' long-term insurance covers the facility, it might cost your parents funding that they may need for nursing home care later.

When checking out an assisted living facility, ask whether it is licensed, and what level of care and supervision is provided.

Find out how frequently residents are checked on, how big the night staff is, and whether staff will track and help them take medication. As your parents become more dependent, will the services available increase? Just how much are they charged, and for what? How many meals are included? How often are the rooms cleaned?

Boarding and Care Homes

Board and care homes are group living arrangements — typically a house with four to six residents and a few staff members, often in a regular neighborhood — that provide help for people who cannot live independently. The services and care levels available vary wildly, but they are usually cheaper than assisted living and commonly provide a room, meals, and help with daily activities. Check the homes carefully to make sure they are not substandard, and find out what your parents' state's licensing requirements are.

Some care homes are specialized, for example, caring for Alzheimer's patients only. Continuing-care communities are also called life-care or multilevel care. There is a fee to move in, and a monthly charge afterward; housing, meals, activities, housekeeping, and medical care are provided. Your parents have to be fully independent to qualify for admission, but once they move in, additional care will be provided as they go along, albeit sometimes with higher fees.

Continuing care costs quite a bit of money. Research the cost and go over the contract thoroughly before making a decision.

8 Your Parents' Medical Bills

In this chapter, we will address the medical details that a caregiver will need to understand and manage while handling parental finances.

Among these details is the detail of power of attorney, as well as how it relates to health care. There are also the issues of prescription drugs and the many insurance programs that you will need to possibly address. This chapter will provide an overview of the most common types of elder care insurance.

POWER OF ATTORNEY AND HEALTH CARE

If your parent is incapacitated, a health care power of attorney, whether durable or springing, works the same way a financial power of attorney does, but for health care decisions.

As the attorney-in-fact for health care, once your parents are incapacitated, you will have the power to hire and fire their doctors; consent to surgery; move your parents into and out of hospitals, nursing homes, or assisted living; and make medical decisions, other than end-of-life decisions. For those, you still need an advance directive or a living will.

Just like a financial power of attorney, this is something you need to set up well in advance of any problems. Without it, you will have to apply as your parents' guardian or conservator to make medical decisions.

PRESCRIPTION DRUGS

Most people over the age of 65 take about four or five prescription drugs and two over-the-counter drugs a day. Some have to be taken with food, and some must not be taken with food. Some are taken every day, some twice a day and some every few hours.

Keeping track of what to take and when can be hard enough; even younger people are prone to misuse their medications; for example, stopping antibiotics when they decide they feel better and saving the rest for later. Adding an over-the-counter drug to the mix and not telling the doctor is another common issue.

In addition to the side effects of any individual drugs, drug interactions may also be clouding your parents' minds.

These are all problems you may need to discuss and deal with at some point. However, how do you pay for them?

MEDICARE

This federal insurance program covers most, but not all, of the health care costs for people 65 and older. It has been revised several times in recent years and will certainly undergo more changes over the next few years.

Medicare coverage comes through traditional fee-for-service in which your parents see the health care provider of their choice if the provider accepts Medicare. Alternatively, they may go with a managed-care provider such as an HMO for smaller monthly premiums, but they will have to restrict their medical care to doctors in the HMO program.

If your parents are 65 and have applied for Social Security benefits, enrollment in Medicare parts A and B (described below) is automatic (part D must be signed up for). If they have reached 65 and are not applying for Social Security yet, they will need to file a written application for Medicare. If your parents are not eligible for Social Security, part A will require a premium. Part B requires a monthly premium either way.

Some people younger than 65 can also enroll in Medicare; for example, those who have received two years of Social Security disability or have been on dialysis for two years.

Along with premiums, your parents will have to pay deductibles like most other forms of insurance. They may also have to pay coinsurance (a percentage of the total cost of a service) or a co-payment (a fixed amount for a service).

Most hospitals and nursing homes, and many home health agencies, accept Medicare. Doctors may accept or reject Medicare patients on a case-by-case basis, but if your parents are in Medicare, the doctors will be limited in what they can charge, even if they do not accept Medicare.

Part A covers inpatient hospital care, hospice care, and some skilled nursing facilities and home health care. On the first day of inpatient care, your parents will be billed for an initial deductible, and they will be covered for the next 60 days. For the 61st through 90th day, you will have to pay a fee. From the 91st day on, your parents can pay the full costs themselves, or they can use their "lifetime reserve days" — 60 days of extra coverage that a Medicare patient can use once in their lifetime — and only pay a coinsurance payment.

If your parents leave the hospital and go back in within 60 days, the benefit-period clock will resume ticking: If they spent 45 days on the first stay, they have another 15 days of full coverage. If they spend 60 days without skilled-care services, the clock resets: When they go in, they will have to pay another deductible, then they will have another 60 days of full pay.

Part A will cover their room (with two to four beds), general nursing, meals, drugs provided during their stay, treatment by special services (such as the intensive-care unit), lab tests and X-rays, medical supplies, operating room costs, and rehabilitation, including physical and speech therapy. It does not cover private rooms (unless they are medically necessary), private-duty nurses, and personal conveniences, such as a phone or a television.

If your parents are admitted to a hospital for three days, Medicare will cover inpatient care at a "skilled nursing facility" afterwards, provided your parents need skilled nursing or rehabilitation care (this must be based on a doctor's orders) and that they go into the facility fairly soon (usually within 30 days of the hospital stay). Medicare pays all covered charges for the first 20 days and part of the costs for the next 80 days, then coverage stops until the next benefits period.

The covered charges include your parents' rooms, meals, nursing services, physical and speech therapy, drugs, medical supplies, and personal items (soap, toothbrushes, and so forth).

Skilled care is care that requires the services of a licensed nurse or a physical rehab specialist — for example, changing sterile dressings, administering intravenous injections, or speech therapy. Custodial care covers daily living needs — feeding patients, dressing them, bathing them, and reminding them to take their medicine. The latter is not covered by Medicare.

If your parents are looking at a nursing home after their hospital stay, ask if it qualifies as a skilled-nursing facility by Medicare standards. If your hospital recommends a facility, it does not mean your parents must pick that one. Check it out first: If they move in and it turns out to be a bad fit, they will have to pay for transportation to a new place, even if it is in an ambulance. Medicare only covers transport if it is medically necessary.

Also, if your parents are recovering in a skilled-nursing facility or at home, they must show continuous improvement. When they are as well as they are going to get, Medicare will classify their care as custodial, which will not be covered.

Part A also covers some sorts of home health care: physical, occupational, and speech therapy; part-time or intermittent skilled nursing; part-time care from a home health aide; and medical equipment for home use. It does not cover your parents' medicines, or any custodial services they require, but there is no charge to them for the services that are covered.

Your parents do not have to be released from a hospital before qualifying for home care, but they do have to meet four standards:

- The care must be ordered by a doctor.
- Your parents must be homebound and only able to leave the house infrequently. (Some absences such as doctor visits or religious services are acceptable)
- They must be receiving skilled nursing or physical or speech therapy.
- These services must be performed by a Medicare-qualified home health agency.

If your parents need a home health care agency after they are discharged from a hospital, Medicare will only pay if the agency is certified. Ask, or check the Medicare Web site; do not assume or trust that whomever recommended you to them knew for sure. If you are wrong, either you or your parents will be responsible for possibly thousands of dollars.

Not having certification does not mean a particular facility is bad; it may just mean their plans provide services that are not insured by Medicare.

If your parents' doctor certifies they have less than six months to live, your parents can accept hospice care (from a Medicare-sanctioned hospice service) from Medicare instead of the standard benefits. Hospice can include painkillers and other drugs, inpatient stays if necessary, and visiting nurse or physician care. It may also include respite care, under which your parent will be taken to stay for up to five days in a respite facility so you and your family can get a break from caregiving. Your parents' costs will be up to $5 per outpatient prescription, and 5 percent of the cost of any respite care.

If your parents need hospitalization, it should continue as long as they keep providing the co-payment. Do not hesitate to fight if the hospital tells you otherwise. If your parents are ready to be discharged to a skilled-nursing facility, but there is not a bed available, the hospital is also required to keep them.

If there is a limit to the improvement from physical, occupational, or speech therapy, providers or Medicare may try to discontinue it, but if it will prevent further deterioration, your parents are entitled to it.

If your parents are Medicare patients, hospitals cannot discharge them immediately, no matter what the administrator tells you. Your parents must receive a written "notice of noncoverage," after which they have three days before they have to leave. If the hospital has told your parents they have to leave but has not given them the notice yet, insist on it.

There are special rules that Medicare uses to keep patients from being put out of a hospital too soon. No matter what anyone says, a patient cannot be discharged until three days after he or she has received a notice of noncoverage. If you do not receive this notice, insist on getting it. This is a legal thing for you to do, and it will also give you added time to find a rehab facility that is best for your parent.

In today's economy, hospitals are quick to discharge Medicare patients faster than ever. In 1968, someone 65 or older had a hospital stay of 14 days. In 1982, this was down to 10 days. Today this has been reduced to 6 days.

Why? With Medicare under constant pressure from Congress to cut costs, Medicare benefits pay hospitals a fixed fee for each patient with a set medical condition, no matter how severe the level of that condition. If a patient has an extended stay, the hospital pays from its own profit. If a patient has a shorter-than-average stay, the hospital keeps the unused funds. How bad has the situation become? *The Wall Street Journal* reported that "Nearly one in five people admitted to hospitals with broken hips are discharged before all of their vital signs are stable…those patients are far more likely to die or be readmitted to the hospital within two months."

Medicare guarantees certain rights to patients if they think they are being asked to leave the hospital too soon. The problem is that the written form of these rights is usually given to the patient along with the other paperwork they sign when admitted. Most people do not even realize this paper is included with the forms, or how important these rights are. This form is titled "An Important Message from Medicare: Your Rights While You Are a Medicare Hospital Patient." This form must be supplied to the patient upon being admitted to any hospital.

Here is a brief overview of the form for reference:

If your doctor or hospital informs you about being discharged, and you think you need further care, you have three options you can use.

Option 1

You immediately ask a hospital representative for a written explanation for the reason of your discharge. This is called a Hospital Issued Notice of Non-Coverage and must be given to you at least three days prior to discharge. This notice tells you if a peer review organization (PRO) agrees with the hospital decision to release you.

If you decide not to appeal the hospital decision, you still pay nothing for these last three days. The time frame for these three days does not begin until you have this notice in your hand. Here is a tip to make the best use of this three-day rule: If the hospital wants to send you to a rehab facility for recovery, you do not have to go to the one they use; instead, use the three days to find a rehab unit certified by Medicare. This ensures continued coverage. Otherwise, Medicare will not cover the cost of any rehabilitation.

Option 2

If you appeal the discharge and your doctor agrees with your appeal, you must ask the hospital's PRO to review the decision to discharge. You can contact the PRO using either phone or written method. You must use this option before noon on the first work day after notice of discharge is given.

If the PRO agrees with the discharge, you might be billed for the cost of the hospital care on the day after the PRO decision. The time between the appeal and the PRO decision will not be billed. If the PRO sides against the hospital, Medicare continues to pay for the hospital stay.

Option 3

When your doctor disagrees with the hospital, the hospital can ask the PRO to review the discharge. If the PRO agrees with the hospital, and you still think differently, you can ask the PRO to reconsider. This must be done immediately after receiving their notice, either by phone or in writing.

The decision of the PRO can take three working days to be completed. You will be informed in writing. But you should remember that the PRO has already seen your case before they issued their original decision.

In this situation, the hospital can bill you for care as of the third calendar day after the notice is given, even if the review is not complete. If the PRO still agrees with the hospital after the appeal, you will probably pay for at least one day in the hospital.

Do not be afraid to stand up to the doctors or the hospital staff if you have to. Some of them may not know the Medicare rules, while others may be hoping to trim costs by bumping your parents out the door early. Ask questions, make objections, and expect reasonable responses. Your parent has the right to be informed and involved in the decisions about their health care. They also have the right to receive as much care needed for proper treatment of their health problems.

You have the right to appeal any Medicare decisions, including denials or partial denials. The first step is to insist on a written determination from Medicare, not an oral one. After the notice, you will usually have 60 days to appeal a Part A or B determination; if they deny your parents again, you can file another appeal.

If a nursing home or home-care provider tells you they do not think Medicare will cover a particular service, request (again) a formal notice of noncoverage. Before noon on the last day of coverage, ask for a peer review of the decision by the home's Quality Improvement Organization (QIO). As with hospitals, if the QIO sides with the provider, your parents will be paying for care from the moment noncoverage began.

You can appeal the decision within 120 days, asking the Medicare contractor to review and make a redetermination. If the first appeal fails, you have the option to appeal further; check out Medicare's Web site for details.

Medicare Part B

Medicare Part B covers "medically necessary" outpatient services such as doctors' visits, emergency room trips, diagnostic tests such as X-rays, medically necessary equipment like wheelchairs and oxygen tanks, outpatient rehab, dialysis, ambulance trips to the hospital, and some other services. It also covers some preventive services, such as prostate cancer screenings and flu vaccinations.

It does not cover routine checkups, routine dental care, eye exams for fitting glasses, cosmetic surgery, and any services not considered "reasonable and necessary."

If you have specific questions about certain services, check with your Medicare provider or **www.medicare.gov**.

If you want to appeal a refusal of coverage by your Part B provider, once again request that the Medicare contractor make a redetermination.

All plans must cover emergency care when there is a situation where waiting until your parents reach a covered doctor or hospital would pose a serious risk, and urgent care, when they are outside the plan's coverage area. If payments are turned down, consider appealing them.

Medicare Part D

Part D provides outpatient prescription drug benefits, but only through HMOs or similar programs. Your parents can keep regular Part A and B coverage and go with a stand-alone prescription plan, or they can enroll in an HMO completely.

Medicare may provide extra help on Part D for beneficiaries whose income is only 150 percent of the poverty level (or less) and have income less than $16,245 (individuals) or $21,855 (married) in 2009.

There are a variety of plans that may appear somewhat confusing, so if you are helping your parents pick one, look at the overall costs, whether their drugs are in the formulary, and how many of their doctors and pharmacies are in-plan providers.

If your parents want an "exception request" for a drug that is not in the formulary, or to appeal denial of a particular drug, they need a statement from their doctor that the drug is necessary. Armed with that, they can request the HMO reconsider, which the program has to do within 72 hours. If the plan denies your request, your parents can request a redetermination that must be made within 60 days (The time limits for both steps can be shortened if the need for medication is life-threatening).

Medicare's Web site offers more details on the plans and guidance for choosing between them.

Medicare Savings Plans

Medicare Savings Programs (MSPs) provide help to seriously low-income people in paying Medicare premiums and co-pays.

The Qualified Medical Beneficiary program covers premiums, deductibles, and co-insurance for income around the poverty line and limited assets.

The Specified Low-Income Medicare Beneficiary Program covers Part B premiums for people with incomes between 100 and 120 percent of the poverty level. The Qualifying Individual program covers Part B premiums for people between 120 and 135 percent of the poverty-level income.

Medicare's "extra help" benefit will pick up some of the costs of Part D for low-income seniors.

Even if none of these apply to your parents' situation, there may be new programs or state programs that will help. Visit **www.benefitscheckup.org**, a Web site run by the National Council on Aging, which can help you figure out Medicare benefits your parents may qualify for, as well as research other federal and state programs.

COBRA

If your parents are fired from a job or the company shuts its doors, they can retain their health insurance if they are still working — including if they are self-employed — under the Consolidated Omnibus Budget Reconciliation Act (COBRA). COBRA allows them to pay the same premiums as their old employer's health plan (which will be more expensive for them without the employer's contribution, but cheaper than if they bought insurance themselves).

Medigap

Your parents may also want Supplemental Medicare insurance (Medigap) from a private insurance company, which plugs most of the holes left by Medicare A and B (it does not apply to C). If Medicaid or a Medicare Savings Program covers your parents, they probably do not need Medigap. If they have retiree insurance from their employer or their union, they may not need it, but compare the benefits of each to decide.

To avoid confusion, federal law has defined 12 standardized plans, but not all states allow all 12, and not all companies offer all 12 (and a few states have different rules).

Premiums may be uniform for everyone, based on your parents' age and rising as they grow older, or based on the age at which they signed up. If they signed up at 64, for example, they would pay the 64-year-old premium, which could go up for all 64-year-olds if the company decides. Obviously, a uniform benefit is a good deal for older buyers.

The first six months that your parents are both 65 and enrolled in Medicare is the best time to buy a Medigap policy because they cannot be refused or charged a higher rate because of preexisting health conditions.

TRICARE

If you or your spouse is in the military, including the National Guard or the Reserves, or if one of your parents is a military retiree, they may be able to use the military's TRICARE health plan.

In TRICARE-speak, beneficiaries are either sponsors (active-duty military or retirees) or family members. TRICARE covers "medically necessary" and "proven" care (meaning it will not cover treatments TRICARE considers experimental and untested). Some services require prior authorization and coverage, and out-of-pocket costs depend on your eligibility and your program.

TRICARE is a big, complicated system with multiple different programs, offerings, and benefits, to the point that the TRICARE Web site says, "Our surveys have found that most service members and their families are confused by TRICARE."

Active duty, National Guard and Reserve members, and their families are automatically enrolled in TRICARE Prime, which relies on military facilities as the health care provider. Retirees under 65 and their families must choose among TRICARE Prime, TRICARE Standard, and TRICARE Extra.

TRICARE Prime has no annual deductible, though there is an enrollment fee for retirees, and there are fees for inpatient and outpatient care and skilled-nursing facilities. Most of the care will come through military hospitals, but retirees take a back seat to active-duty military if there is a shortage of space. Beneficiaries enrolled in any program other than TRICARE Prime take a back seat if seeking care at military hospitals.

In TRICARE Standard, there is no enrollment fee, and beneficiaries can see any authorized provider on a fee-for-service basis; patients' co-payments usually run to around 25 percent of allowable fees or a preset limit, whichever is less (the limit is set anew each fiscal year). There is also a "catastrophic cap" on covered services in a given year. If the bill from a provider exceeds what TRICARE considers an acceptable fee, your parents must pay the balance, and the extra is not included under the catastrophic cap. It will be up to you and your parents to fill out all the paperwork for TRICARE Standard.

TRICARE Extra works much the same as TRICARE Standard, but if your parents use a TRICARE Extra network provider, they do not have to file the claim themselves, and the co-pay is lower. TRICARE Extra is not a program they have to enroll in; they simply have the option to use Extra providers if one is available, on a case-by-case basis.

If your parents are older than 65 and qualify for TRICARE and Medicare, they can enroll in TRICARE for Life (unlike some TRICARE programs, dependent parents are not eligible), which will pick up the remaining tab after Medicare and private insurance — though for Medicare-covered services that TRICARE does not pay for, such as chiropractors, TRICARE for Life will not pay anything.

If your parents are registered with Medicare Part B, the TRICARE Senior Pharmacy program offers them several choices for cutting the costs of medicine: Filling prescriptions for free at military pharmacies, if one is available; through a mail-order program that currently charges $9 for a three-month supply of brand-name medications, less for generic; or an in-network pharmacy, where the cost will be three times mail-order.

MEDICAID

Medicaid is a separate program from Medicare that can cover seniors, the poor, children, pregnant women, and people with disabilities. Medicaid is paid for by the federal government and the states together, and administered by state governments, each of which sets its own rules for eligibility and coverage. There are no premiums or deductibles (there may be a small co-pay for some services), and doctors cannot charge you fees above the Medicaid payment. There are no limits on coverage, and Medicaid can provide substantial help with nursing-home costs.

The downside? The program is complicated and bureaucratic, and your parents will have to be close to insolvent before you can take advantage of it. Many doctors will not take Medicaid patients; Medicaid-qualified nursing home slots are hard to find; and if your parents go into a nursing home, their state of residence will seek to recoup nursing-home costs from the states.

Find which of your state's government agencies handles Medicaid — your local elder services or a look at the state's Web site should be able to do that. Or you can contact a senior-center benefits counselor or an attorney experienced in these issues, which might be a good thing to do in any case, given how complex Medicaid rules can be.

Your parents will need to prove their state of residence and document their financial situation in detail. Unlike Medicare, which kicks in at 65, Medicaid benefits are linked to the date your parents apply and may even be retroactive so the sooner they file the papers the better. Even if they do not complete the complex forms immediately, a signed request with their name on it can establish their application date.

Federal law requires that Medicaid programs in all 50 states cover hospital services (including outpatient care), doctor and nurse-practitioner care, nursing home care, rural health-clinic services, home-health care fees, laboratory tests and X-rays, and transportation to and from health care providers. Services that may be covered include physical therapy, eyeglasses, dental care, mental-health services, and private-duty nursing. Your parents will have to obtain their medicines through Medicare Part D. The providers bill Medicaid and Medicaid sends the money directly to them. Most states have a waiver program that allows some people access to services not otherwise covered.

Many states offer a Home and Community-Based Services program (HCBS) that pays for personal care services, respite care, adult day care, and "habilitation," which is training that helps your parents improve their mobility, social behaviors, health care, safety, hygiene, and so on. If your state participates in this program, HCBS might allow your parent to receive paid-for care at home, rather than in a nursing home.

Qualifying

To qualify for Medicaid, your parents have to be 65 or older (or blind or disabled) and meet the Medicaid financial tests. In most states, most people eligible for Supplemental Security Income qualify for Medicare, as do people who "spend down" a certain percentage of their income on medical bills (the percentages and amounts are based on Medicaid's formula). The rules vary among states, so your parents might be ineligible in one state and qualify in another.

Nursing home benefits, in a number of states, require your parents' income fall below the Medicaid cap. In others, medically needy people who have spent down their assets will also qualify for help.

Your parents must also have assets less than a certain amount (in 2007, $2,000 for a single person, $3,000 for couples), but exempting some assets, such as some of their home equity (up to $500,000 in 2007), their car, trade, and business property needed to support themselves, their wedding rings, items that are not currently available (your parents won a lawsuit, but the defendant has not paid yet), and other things.

The rules on assets can become quite technical. For example, your parents' home is no longer excluded if they move into a nursing home permanently, but will be excluded if they declare that as soon as they get better, they will move back home — even if the chance of that is unlikely. If they sell the home, the proceeds must be reinvested in another excluded home within three months or the money will become a countable asset.

If Medicaid rules your parents do not qualify, or are denied a particular service, they are entitled to an appeals hearing before a case officer. The written notice turning them down will include instructions on how to appeal.

If your parents require nursing home care, meet Medicaid's financial standards, and the home is Medicaid-certified, Medicaid will cover the first 20 days of care completely, then 80 more days with a large co-payment on their part.

If they are not eligible, that could change before long: A single person with $1,500 a month income and $50,000 in savings would qualify for Medicaid after a year in a facility that costs $5,000 a month.

If your parents need to spend down to qualify, try to put the money they have to spend to good use. Paying down mortgage debt and building up equity (which is protected) makes great sense. Paying off credit card bills, car payments, or any other recurring debt also does double duty, spending down while eliminating the debt that could haunt your parents when nursing home care has depleted their resources. Spending down by putting money into home repair and renovation will also benefit your parents by increasing the value of their home and putting money into an exempt resource. Other possibilities include making your home more handicapped-accessible, buying a new car if yours is somewhat old, and prepaying funeral and burial expenses.

Giving away money to you and your siblings (or anyone else) is not a good way to pay down your parents' resources. When they apply, they will be required to disclose any gifts they have made in the previous five years, and spending down by gifts will render them ineligible for several months, based on the size of the gifts and the rules of their state.

If your parents can prove that they made the gift for some non-Medicaid reason such as it was made while they were in excellent health and did not think they would need to apply or that ineligibility poses a serious health risk, the penalty will be waived. But that is a big "if," and the burden of proof is on you. For this reason, some sources recommend you wait as long as possible after making such gifts before applying for Medicaid, so if the government decides the gifts were not legitimate, your penalties will be less.

Legitimate Exemptions

You might think the best solution is for your parents to give you or your siblings the money and not tell anyone, or to come up with some other scheme to hide their assets, but this is also a mistake. Anyone found guilty of Medicaid fraud is liable for penalties, damages of two to three times the amount of the fraud, and possible prison time, and those are just the federal penalties — the state your parents live in will have punishment to add on top of that.

Here are a few legitimate ideas that might help:

- Personal property and furnishings are exempt, so investing in these would be a productive use of assets. The rules of Medicaid state that the government will not go into your parents house and assess everything, but if the government becomes aware of an investment in gold or $10,000 worth of jewelry, then they have the right to call it an investment.

- The current rules, as of 2009, exempt one family car of any size or value (although buying a Ferrari might bring a warning flag), so trading in an old car for a newer model makes sense, as long as your parents use it. This includes having you drive them around in it (an example of this is the 1989 movie *Driving Miss Daisy*, where the car owner used the car but did not drive). Buying a mini-van or wheelchair-accessible van is a good move here.

- Your parents can hire you as a caregiver. There must be a contract, and your pay and services must be in line with what the professional standard is at the time. Medicaid will look closely at this idea. You cannot collect retroactive pay for past services.

- If your parents move into your house, they can purchase a life estate in your house, which is similar to the life estate they would be allowed in their own home if they sold it. This puts cash into your hands, provides a living space for them, and brings down their assets.

- If you live in a state with a Medicaid income cap, and your parent's income is too high, you could try a Miller Trust. This is composed solely of Social Security, a pension, or other income. This trust will pay your parent a monthly stipend that falls just under the income cap, and thus your parents now qualify for Medicaid. The drawback to this is that when your parents pass away, any remaining money left in the trust goes straight to Medicaid.

- As we discussed earlier, an irrevocable trust can also be used to put assets and income off-limits when qualifying for Medicaid. By allowing only a small part of your parents' income from trust assets (rental income, stocks, interest on CDs, etc.), you can keep their income low enough to get nursing home aid from Medicaid. When your parents are in the nursing home, you can consider cutting back the income further, and Medicaid will pick up more of the expense.

The vast majority of nursing home residents do not engage in this kind of asset depletion: most of the elderly in nursing homes, according to a Georgetown University study, are genuinely broke, and a large number of the elderly pay their way through nursing home care as long as they can. The Georgetown report found that seniors who expect to go into a nursing home at some point will usually save more than seniors who do not. The Georgetown University study was part of the Long-Term Care Financing Project from 2006. The project and study can be found at **http://ltc.georgetown.edu**.

So you may not need any strategies to qualify your parents for Medicaid. And if your parents still have a say in their affairs, they may choose to pay, even if it does drain their bank account.

If your parents have substantial assets and you do decide go to ahead and reduce them, do not forget that these decisions may affect estate planning and tax strategies, as well as pose other legal complications. Plus, specific strategies may not work in specific states.

Your parents' state may also offer Medicaid-waiver programs that allow people to receive care at home — personal care, adult day care, or housekeeping — and thereby avoid having to go into a nursing home. The waiting list for waiver programs can be long.

The Community Spouse

If only one of your parents is in a nursing home, the "community spouse" who lives outside can keep all the income that is exclusively his or hers, including any checks for pensions, annuities, or royalties that have her name as the payee. Some, possibly all, of your parents' joint income will go to nursing home care, as will the parent in the home — though if the community spouse's income is low enough, some of the nursing home parent's income may be provided to them.

In some states, if the community spouse formally refuses to support the nursing home spouse, the community spouse's assets will not be a factor in figuring Medicaid eligibility. Otherwise, the community spouse's assets will be figured in along with joint assets and the nursing home parent's assets. If the state resource allowance matches the federal maximum allowance, the community spouse may keep up to the federal maximum; if the state has a lower allowance, the community spouse can keep half your parents' total resources (this does not mean your other parent has lost their share; this is a legal determination only).

Once the nursing home parent is approved for Medicaid, changes in the community spouse's income will not affect that, according to a 2004 court decision. Growth in their investment or a rush of royalties when a book becomes a best-seller will not disqualify the nursing home spouse from coverage.

If the community spouse dies first, and their assets pass to the nursing-home spouse, that could disqualify the latter spouse from Medicaid and make all the assets eligible when the government tries to recover its Medicaid spending from the nursing-home spouse's estate. The community spouse cannot, however, cut the nursing home spouse out of the will (as noted above, they have a minimum entitlement), so this is another issue where an attorney's help would be advisable.

In some states, nursing homes may favor private patients over Medicaid patients when allocating beds. In other states, this is illegal.

Family Finances and Cost Recovery

You and your siblings are not legally required to pay for nursing home care, though that is an option if you have the money (which gets around the shortage of Medicaid beds). Homes are prohibited from requiring you kick in for your parents' care or insisting you guarantee that you will pay the homes' charges. If you have power of attorney, however, you can be required to put in your parents' money as their agent.

After your parents die, states are required to try recovering some of the Medicaid money your parents spent from their estate, for example nursing facility costs and adult day care. Legally, this includes property that goes through probate, but some states can include a variety of nonprobated assets such as life estates, joint accounts, joint tenancy, life estate, and living trusts. If your parents' state changes the rules after your parents enter a nursing home, assets that you all thought were protected may no longer be so. A state can also file a lien against the deceased's house.

There are exceptions to the recovery rule: For example, if a Medicaid recipient is survived by their spouse. It is also possible to avoid the impact of estate-recovery by transferring ownership of the house to the community spouse. Once again, the exact details should be worked out with an elder-law attorney who knows Medicaid. Transferring the house may also have tax and estate-planning drawbacks unrelated to Medicaid.

Long-Term Care Insurance

Long-term care insurance is a relatively new idea that covers the cost of prolonged periods of nursing home care (that is, two years and up) and may also cover assisted living, home care, and adult day care.

Most policies pay a preset amount or percentage for each day of care. The best policies cover all levels of care from intensive nursing home care down to assisted living, and also home care. When looking at the policy, compare several side-by-side to judge which offers the best benefits.

Length of care is not necessarily crucial. Four years of nursing home care coverage will be enough, and — if cost is an issue — your parents may be able to get by on three.

Of particular importance is whether the per-day payments will be adjusted for inflation and whether the policy allows "alternate plans of care" that meet your needs and that the insurer approves. This could be important because changes in the health care system may create new options or requirements 10 or 20 years from now that we cannot yet imagine. A policy that does not require prior hospitalization before nursing home care is preferable.

Many attorneys are against policies that pay only for "medically necessary" care because the standard gives insurers too much flexibility. A better and more common standard is that the policy kicks in when your parents have trouble with at least two daily activities such as bathing, eating, or taking medication

To obtain a policy, your parents will need to undergo medical screening, and might be excluded for a preexisting condition.

If your parents are in a low enough income bracket to qualify for Medicaid and other help, this kind of insurance might not be necessary. Premiums vary with the age of purchase and are set for life, unless the insurer raises premiums for everyone across the board.

Because this policy will not be needed until years after your parents take it out, evaluate companies as well as individual policies. You do not want to take out a policy from a company with less than a B+ rating by financial services — a sign that it is financially solvent.

CHAPTER 9

Taxes

With this chapter, you will get an overview of the tax issues that a caregiver responsible for parental finances will face. We will also look at donations, estate taxes, and common mistakes that can cause problems with the Internal Revenue Service.

In this chapter, you will find tips on keeping parents' income taxes low. You will also find guidelines on how to access tax-deferred retirement accounts, as well as what to do about capital gains taxes. We have also included a section on how to deal with taxes when a parent passes away, as well as the issue of gifting. Finally, we will look at some common tax errors and myths that should be avoided.

Keeping the Parents' Income Tax Low

You may have heard that the only things that are certain in life are death and taxes. But it is possible that, for your parents, income tax is not a certainty. The standard deduction is greater for someone older than 65, so if your parents have an income under $8,950 for the 2008 tax year, the deductions would have wiped out any tax obligation (the exact amount is adjusted annually). If your parent is entitled to a refund, they should file to receive it. Here are some guidelines to help figure this out.

If your parent do not have much in the way of retirement income, that may be all you need to know about taxes. If they own rental property, have a sizable stock portfolio, or you sold their house this year, then the tax picture becomes more complicated. If it exceeds what you are comfortable dealing with, do not hesitate to hire an accountant to advise you.

If your parent is still working but making very little, they may be entitled to an Earned Income Tax Credit. In 2008, a single person with no dependent children would have had to make $12,880 or less to qualify.

If your parents' medical expenses add up to more than 7.5 percent of their adjusted gross income, they can deduct them off their taxes.

If you provide more than half your parents' support in a given year, and their income was less than the standard exemption, you may be able to claim them as a dependent, which would allow you to take a deduction for them. If they live in your home, you may also be able to deduct services that allow you to keep working, such as adult day care.

Your parent's charitable donations above a certain percentage of your parents' income are also deductible.

HOW TO ACCESS TAX-DEFERRED RETIREMENT ACCOUNTS

If your parent has a tax-deferred account, sooner or later they will need to access it. Even if they are doing well financially, they have to take out monthly minimum withdrawals from a 401(k) or IRA eventually, unless they are still working. They can keep those withdrawals to the monthly minimum (whatever that is when the withdraw becomes mandatory), and if they are doing well otherwise, they should stick to the minimum. The longer the money sits in a tax-deferred account, the longer it has to accumulate with no taxes paid.

Your parent can withdraw money from a 401(k) after the parent who earned the account reaches 59 ½ years old. Your parent have to start making monthly minimum withdrawals after 70 ½, unless they are still working for their employer.

You may be able to access the money early in the case of "hardships," such as medical expenses, college tuition, or covering the mortgage payment before foreclosure. Your parent will have to pay taxes on the withdrawn money, plus a 10 percent extra tax early-withdrawal fee (they may take extra money out to cover the taxes). The year after you take out the money, your contribution limit will be reduced by the size of the withdrawal; an example of this would be $9,000 rather than $15,000.

Your parent may also be able to take up to 50 percent (typically) of the account's value in the form of a loan at 1 or 2 percent over prime. You repay the loan, usually within five years, but out of post-tax dollars, so the repayments do not give the same tax benefits as contributing money in the first place did.

If your parent is in the high-income range, be warned that there is a limit to how much they can invest in a given year.

Individual Retirement Accounts and Roth IRAs

Like a 401(k), your parents will have to start withdrawing from their IRA at 70 ½, and they will pay a penalty if they withdraw money before 59 ½. With a Roth IRA, there is no tax penalty when the money is withdrawn.

CAPITAL GAINS TAX

Capital gains are paid when your parents sell investments or collectibles, whether they be stocks, bonds, jewelry, art, real estate, or rare coins. Generally, your parents will be taxed on the difference between the purchase price (and the cost of any upgrades or improvements, such as a new kitchen in a house) and the sale price of items that have been owned for more than a year. For less than a year, they will be taxed at the regular rate. At present, the capital-gains tax is lower than the regular income tax for many Americans.

Many items, such as your parents' primary residence, may be exempt from capital gains taxes, at least up to a certain amount.

If your parents have an investment that has sharply increased in value since they bought it, they might be better off keeping it in the estate than selling it while they are alive. Passing it to you (or anyone else) resets the capital gains clock. When you sell the item, the capital gains are calculated from the moment you inherited it, wiping out all the years it grew in your parents' possession. Of course, keeping the asset means a larger estate, which may not fit your plans for minimizing estate tax.

If an asset has lost value when your parents sell it, they can use that as a tax deduction. This is why investors often sell off money-losing assets late in the year: to benefit from a last-minute loss.

If your parents have a lot of investments or collectibles (the exact definition of which is somewhat subjective) that have accrued (or lost) value, consider contacting a tax specialist, who can help you figure out the best financial moves to make.

THE POST-DEATH CHALLENGE

In contradiction to the belief that family farms, small businesses, and households are wiped out by estate taxes every day, the fact is that this is an extremely rare event. Estates do pay taxes though, and the more an estate pays in taxes, the less will be passed on to beneficiaries.

Your parent's estate may be subject to income tax if the estate passes the income limit guidelines, as well as any tax on their income if they received money the year they passed on. There are also state and federal taxes if the estate exceeds a certain income limit; as well as the inheritance tax that is paid by the beneficiaries.

The largest single regulation that all estates must comply with is that all taxes must be paid before any money or assets can be handed off. If there is not enough cash available to pay the taxes, the executor of the estate will be forced to sell whatever assets are needed to cover the remaining tax owed.

If you are able, here are some ways to help minimize the tax bills.

Unified Tax

As of 2009, this tax credit has a $3.5 million income limit. Assets under this level are not subject to estate tax under the unified tax credit, which is what protects most people from losing their entire estate. If your parents fall under this tax rule, you do not need to worry about any other tricks or loopholes to search for. This tax credit was scheduled for elimination in 2010, but will be restored in 2011.

Assets Passed Between Parents

One parent can leave everything they own to their spouse, and there will be no tax penalties. The drawback to this trick is that the surviving spouse may end up with growing assets that can exceed the income limitations of the unified tax credit, which make the assets a target for estate taxes.

The Marital Deduction and Bypass Trust (A/B Tool)

This tool functions as a revocable trust during the lives of your parents. When one parent passes, this trust splits in half with the trustee (usually the surviving parent) deciding how the property in trust is divided. The "B" trust is irrevocable, and the property placed in this trust is sheltered from estate taxes. While the surviving parent can retain much control over the assets in the "B" trust, it does not count as part of their estate. This means that when it comes time to settle their estate, there is less in the "A" trust subject to estate tax.

Yearly Planned Giving

Your parents can give away a certain amount of their assets every year without triggering gift taxes on their giving. If they use this tool, remember that big gifts need to be given at least three years before their death to avoid being counted as part of the estate, which is taxable. If any paperwork is involved, such as title transfers or stock transfers, the papers must be filled out to show that the transfer is irrevocable. If gifts are given to a person listed in your parent's will, a written document is needed to state that the gift was not intended as an advance on the inheritance.

Charitable Remainders and Gift Annuities

These two types of gifts work very similarly. With a charitable gift annuity, an investment property such as stocks or real estate are given to a nonprofit organization. Your parents then receive a set payment each month, in return for the nonprofit's keeping the donation. Such gifts are often used for when hospitals or schools purchase property and allow the original owner to remain in the home until their death. The hospital or school then uses the property to expand later on. The donated property is not included in the taxable estate.

The other gift idea is the charitable remainder. A sum of money is placed into a trust by your parents, who collect payments from the trust during their lifetime. After death, a nonprofit organization gets the remaining assets of the trust. The payments for this trust can be set dollar amounts or a percent of the trust assets. This tool avoids not only the estate tax, but also capital gains that increase in value.

Life Insurance Trusts

This method is used so that your parents receive the proceeds of their life insurance policy that otherwise would be a part of their estate. If the money is placed in a trust, it avoids estate tax and also probate. The proceeds can be given out to beneficiaries immediately or over several years.

Using Limited Liability Corporations (LLCs)

Putting property under the control of an LLC (limited liability corporation) or partnership can be an efficient way to hand out large assets over time. Rather than giving a part of a real estate investment each year, the parent can give interest in the LLC. The one drawback to this is that the IRS may look closely at this type of setup.

GIFTS

Regular gifts that fall under the maximum allowed by the IRS can be a way to whittle down the size of your parents' estate over the years. If they give away more than the maximum, the gift-tax will hit the estate just as hard as the estate tax does.

COMMON TAX ERRORS AND MYTHS

As the manager of the finances, your first priority to your parents should be their happiness and comfort. Making sure there is enough proper medical care, a good place to live, and the ability to enjoy live as much as possible is your goal for your mother's or father's life. Even if there are huge financial advantages to selling off their house, moving in with you, and giving away everything they own, the question remains: Is this what they want to do? Is it financially essential that they do these things?

If they feel content working a second job during retirement and it does not cause financial problems, such as making them ineligible for Medicaid, then the job is worth having. This is true even if the income from the job is canceled out by the cost of gas or other expenses.

Paying taxes and tax evasion seem to occupy more of the financial landscape than anything else. Most people must pay taxes each year, or find a way to not pay taxes, with estate planning and probate being infrequent experiences left mainly to legal and financial professionals.

This does not mean that you or your parents should base either long-term or short-term planning around lowering the taxes owed, even in a crisis. Depending on the wants and needs of your parents, lowering the tax bill may be one of the lesser concerns as opposed to keeping as much of the estate as possible out of probate, or keeping it away from creditors. Keeping the income down below the Medicaid limits also would be more important than reducing the tax bill.

There are many schemes and theories that will supposedly help lower or escape income tax completely. Remember, if the idea sounds dubious or illegal, check with a professional first. The con artist will say he or she has information about avoiding taxes that lawyers, bankers, and the IRS do not want the general public to know about. He or she may claim these professionals do not want you to know about this information because it would put people out of business. Do not listen to them; this is just a way for them to take your parents' money.

You can also find people who will argue, at length, on why the income tax is illegal and the government cannot actually force you to pay it. Some have claimed their religion does not permit them to pay income tax. Or consider the man who argued that to meet the original intent of the Constitution, solid gold coins were the only legitimate currency and because there were none in circulation, he had no legal tender to pay his taxes. The courts disagreed with both of them.

10 Scams, Undue Influence, and Abuse

There is one area of handling parental finances that has become all too common in the media in the last decade: The issue of financial scams and abuse. While everyone would love to say they will never become a victim of a financial scam, most often, the people affected are those who are unprepared or who are not aware of the signs of a scam or abuse. This chapter will address scams, issues of abuse, and fraud that can affect parental finances. It will show how to not only recover from these, but also possibly avoid these issues.

We will look at the faces of fraud and what to do when your parent is the victim. We will also address ways to fight back against fraud and scams.

THE FACES OF FRAUD

Telemarketers

According to the American Association for Retired Persons, 56 percent of telemarketing victims are older than 50. Older Americans are targets because they are more likely to be at home to take calls; they have more time to talk; and many of them are willing to listen respectfully (though that may change as the Baby Boomers age).

Police say that many seniors, precisely because they feel less control and less independence in their lives, may jump at a chance to prove they can make a lot of money in a fantastic, cannot-miss stock deal.

And, of course, many con artists are good at their job: If your parents turn them down, scam artists, like any other good sales person, will have a list of counter responses, such as:

- Your parents have to act immediately to take advantage of this amazing offer.

- They have won a free gift, but must pay for shipping.

- They have to send a money order, or give a credit card or bank account number.

- They are told not to bother checking out the company or the offer with anyone else, either family, attorneys, or the Better Business Bureau, and that there is no need for any written information about the company or the charity. One scam operation used to tell male victims that yes, they could provide all that information — but a real man would show guts and make a decision immediately. Some people fell for it.

You can work with your parents to develop responses such as "I do not do business with people I do not know," or "Please send me everything in writing before I consider it," or "No thank you" followed by a swift hang-up. Remind them that they should never give out personal information over the phone, and that anyone who calls and asks for it is a con artist.

An obvious solution, of course, is to put your parents (if they consent) on the national Do Not Call Registry, which restricts telemarketing to companies they already do business with. You can sign them up at **http://donotcall.gov**. This may not stop scam artists from calling, but with a few exceptions, anyone your parents do not already do business with — charities they give to regularly, their credit card company — who calls with a "Do Not Call" in place is a crook.

Phishing

This is a situation in which your parent gets an e-mail telling them that their has been a billing error or an unauthorized attempt to hack their online account and, unless they update their account information immediately, their account will be frozen. If they click on the link in the e-mail, it will take them to a dummy site. The creators will then use your parents' information to raid their account, send spam e-mails, or pull off a full-scale identity theft.

If your parent still has the authority to make investments and spend money, your best bet here is to remind them of some basic rules:

- Any e-mail from a site they do business with, such as eBay or America Online, that does not identify them specifically by user name, e-mail address, or name is a fake.

- If an e-mail tells them their account is going to be frozen or suspended, or that someone has made unauthorized attempts to withdraw money, it is usually be a scam. Instead of clicking on the links in the e-mail, they can check for problems by logging onto the site in the regular way and checking there.

- E-mails that ask for information — bank account numbers, Social Security numbers — are scams.

If the e-mail threatens to suspend accounts they do not have — online banking services they do not use, for instance — they need not even bother checking. The e-mail is a phish.

One solution that may cut down on the spread of information on the Internet is to always opt out of any information-sharing when your parent does business with a Web site. Another idea is to always empty the e-mail of any deleted files before leaving the e-mail service.

Basic Fraud

Even in the age of the spam e-mail, a lot of fraud is still conducted face-to-face. "Contractors" will show up and offer to mow your parents' yard, fix their roof, or repair the front ramp and do it all off-the-books, for cash, so nobody has to pay taxes or worry about immigration officials checking on the contractor's crew. If the contractor receives the money up front, he or she may disappear without doing the work, or do a roofing job that looks solid but will not stand up to a strong breeze.

These scam artists are particularly prevalent after hurricanes and other disasters, when legitimate contractors are backlogged and your parents may have to wait weeks or months for someone to make necessary repairs.

Another classic scam is for a salesperson to contact one parent after the death of the other and claim that the deceased ordered something expensive — furniture, a new bed, or a set of new china — as a gift for the survivor, but never paid for it. The story is a lie and the merchandise usually garbage, but a great many grieving people have shelled out money rather than let their spouse's "last gift" be thrown away.

Your parents' mail presents a different set of problems. There really are people who will pore through sacks of garbage looking for discarded pre-approved credit-card offers — which they then take out, using their own address and your parents' name — and an assortment of bills with Social Security numbers, credit card numbers, and other information that crooks can exploit.

Even your medical bills and reports from your parents' insurer can be exploited. Someone could use the account and personal information to put their medical expenses on your parents' insurance. Not only will this cause financial problems for your parents until the confusion is straightened out, but the thief's medical information could also contaminate your parents' files.

The simple solution is to use a shredder. If you have one, take your parents' leftover bills and records to your house. If you do not, you can buy your parents a cheap one for less than $20. Shred bills, credit card offers, credit-card slips, medical records, and other similar items. Shred financial records when your parents no longer need them. Bank statements can be safely shredded after 12 months, and tax returns after seven years. Another solution, if the local code allows it, is to burn any papers mentioned above.

Another useful precaution is for you or your parents to contact the major credit bureaus (Experian, Equifax, and TransUnion) and ask for a copy of their report on your parents. Under the Fair Credit Reporting Act, every American is entitled to a free copy from each agency once every year; there is no need to turn to **www.freecreditreport.com** and other services that offer the information for a fee.

If you believe your parents are the victims of identity theft, you can ask the reporting agencies to place fraud alerts in their file, though that may delay the ability of your parents to obtain credit. You can call any one of the three agencies, and they will report it to the other two. Your parents will have to provide proof of their identity, which may include their Social Security number.

The Fair Credit Reporting Act also gives your parents the option to block information in their credit files that results from identity theft, such as an identity thief running up bills and not paying them. This will require an identity theft report and proof of identity.

Some states will also allow your parents to place a security freeze on their credit report, which prevents credit agencies from releasing information without authorization. The freeze can be removed later. While it is in effect, it may delay any credit-related actions your parents take such as new loans or taking out a second mortgage.

Charitable Donations

Genuine charities will be registered with any state they operate in as nonprofit organizations; that list will be available online at your state government Web site. If the charity that called, e-mailed, or wrote to your parents is not listed, your parents should not give them money.

Many charities, while meeting the letter of the law, spend a great deal of the money donated, sometimes most of it, on administrative expenses and fundraising rather than carrying out the charity's supposed mission. The Charity Navigator Web site (**www.charitynavigator.org**), which rates the performance of various charities, says that any organization that spends less than a third of its money on programs is not a success. Other charity review groups recommend donating to charities that put 70 percent of their money into their programs.

If your parents want to give to worthwhile causes, research such as this will help them get the most charitable bang for the buck. Another idea is to locate local agencies or churches that could also use the donations, or donate non-monetary items.

WHEN YOUR PARENT IS THE VICTIM

Warning signs, according to the National Consumers League, include the following:

- Junk mail for contests, free trips, prizes, and sweepstakes. This could indicate someone has successfully bilked them.

- Frequent calls from strangers offering great moneymaking opportunities, valuable awards, or asking for donations.

- Repeated payments to out-of-state companies, particularly large payments.

- Payments picked up by courier.

- Receiving lots of cheap items (costume jewelry, beauty products, pens, and pencils) in the mail. These may have been purchased to qualify them for a big prize (supposedly) or these could be the prizes they entered to win.

Remember, if your parents have been scammed out of money, they may feel foolish, pathetic, and old. Rather than let anyone know, they may not admit it if you confront them.

If any sort of fraud or manipulation becomes a recurrent problem, consider steps to prevent it: Confiscate your parents' credit cards and debit cards; keep a minimal amount of money in their bank account every month; and tell the bank not to use money from your parents' other accounts to cover any overdrafts. This will limit the damage that can be done, assuming your parents will accept it.

FIGHT BACK

If you suspect someone is taking advantage of your parent, insist on a private visit where they will be free to talk, or take them to a social worker with experience handling elder-abuse cases. You can also contact police or your state's agency for the elderly to report the problem.

In some cases, such as if a credit card is stolen, your parent are not legally liable for the expenses the thief ran up. If someone simply took money out of your parents' wallet, it may be gone by the time the police catch up with the thief. In the case of fraud or theft, your parents may not want to go on the record about what happened, or press charges against the culprit. They may have decided it was their own fault they were taken or trusted the wrong person, or they may be too embarrassed to file charges. If the culprit is a close friend or family member, they may not want to hurt them, or may be afraid of losing their affection.

Remind them that jailing the thief may prevent him (or her) from victimizing someone else down the line. They may make up excuses for why a family member acted against them; do not accept the excuse. If they absolutely refuse to take action or testify against someone they care about, make sure that whomever it is never gets the chance to repeat the crime.

Issues of Abuse

THE SIGNS OF ELDER ABUSE AND WHAT TO DO

As your parents age, they may become tempting targets for abusers for the same reason that children are vulnerable. Your parents may be under someone else's supervision; they may be isolated; they may depend on someone else providing care for them; and, physically, they may be in no shape to fight back. Even if they are in good shape and fairly independent, however, they could still become victims of abuse.

A large percentage of elder abuse is actually spousal abuse. A husband or wife who has been inflicting violence on his or her spouse for most of their lives may continue inflicting abuse, even in their senior years.

Other abusers share a home with the victim, which makes it easier to cover up the abuse and to isolate the victim. Caregivers in a professional setting, such as a nursing home, may also commit abuse, but a greater percentage of abuse happens in a family setting.

If you cannot imagine your parents doing anything to bring out abuse, or not telling you if it happened, remember that victims do not cause abuse, even though the abuser may blame them (the "If you would just do what I tell you, I would not have to punish you" rationalization) and that like victims of any age, your parents may be intimidated into silence ("If you tell anyone I will tell the cops you are senile and have you committed," for instance), unwilling to report a family member to the police, or terrified that if they report their caregiver — especially if they are living in a family member's home — they will have nowhere to go and no one to help them. Like many abuse victims, they may accept the idea that it really is their fault that their caregiver hits them.

Abuse is not always physical. There is verbal abuse, such as yelling, threatening, humiliating, and belittling or blaming them; nonverbal emotional abuse, including ignoring or isolating them; and sexual abuse, which can include forcing your parents to look at porn.

Neglect constitutes more than half the reported cases of elder abuse. This can include failure to provide food and water, clothing, or medicine; refusing to give your parents the assistance they need with daily activities or personal hygiene; or, in the case of financial caregiving, refusing to pay the bills or manage the money responsibly.

Here are warning signs of abuse to watch for:

- Unexplained bruises, pressure marks, broken bones, abrasions, or burns.

- Unexplained withdrawal from family or social activities.

- Bedsores, unattended medical needs, and poor hygiene are all indicators of possible neglect.

- Strained, tense relationships and frequent arguments between your parents and the caregiver.

- Broken eyeglasses.

- Marks on the wrists that could indicate that your parents have been tied up.

- You see or hear a caregiver verbally belittle or threaten your parents.

- Your parents show signs of dementia, such as rocking, sucking their thumb, or talking to themselves.

- Unexplained genital or anal bleeding, or an unexplained STD.

If you see signs, do not tell yourself that it cannot possibly be what you fear it is. You may find it unimaginable that someone at the nursing home has raped your parents, but most rape is not about sex as much as it is about aggression and a sense of power. Sexual abuse of a senior is no different.

Do not assume that if your parents live with you and your spouse, or with one of your siblings, that there has to be another explanation. Even if there is no history of abuse in your family, caregiving can become a high-stress situation, particularly if your parent has slipped into dementia.

Among the triggers that can touch off abuse from a caregiver are inability to cope with stress, depression, lack of support from other potential caregivers, substance abuse, and the feeling that taking care of the parents is tiresome and unrewarding. Painful life events such as death, illness, or a job loss may push a caregiver to the breaking point and have them taking out their frustration on your parents.

Authorities receive from 500,000 to a million reports of elder abuse a year, and most of them turn out to be true. Some states estimate that 12 times as many cases happen as are actually reported. Even if the abuser is a family member, you cannot ignore the abuse.

The first priority, if the abuse is ongoing, is to get your parents to safety. If you are in a position to act immediately, get them away from the abuser to somewhere safe. Do not confront the abuser or try to intervene personally if you cannot get your parent away from them. A confrontation will only make your parent more vulnerable and more of a target afterward.

Instead, report the abuse (which you should do after you have them in safety). You can find a toll-free elder-abuse hotline in any state. Call the national Eldercare Locator at 1-800-677-1116 for information on the number for your parents' state.

FINANCIAL ABUSE

Financial abuse is a term that includes the frauds described earlier in this book — your parents paid for a service, but did not receive what they bought — but also misuse of a power of attorney or other authority over your parents' finances, using your parents' credit cards to make purchases; open credit accounts using their name; changing their will or other documents for the abuser's benefit; refusing to pay back a loan from your parents when due, or when asked to do so; or undue influence, which will be described in the next section.

Financial abusers can include family members, professional caregivers, financial planners or accountants, a housekeeper or employee, or someone new who has wormed their way into your parents' life, like a new husband or a much-younger girlfriend.

Signs to watch for include changes in beneficiaries; check signatures that do not match your parents' signatures; large cash withdrawals, particularly in round numbers; withdrawals from an ATM when your parent is confined at home; missing money or checks; a new check card that cannot be explained; a new name on your parents' account; changes in the will, or beneficiaries on insurance policies or retirement accounts; or using power of attorney to appoint a new agent, particularly someone whom no one in the family knows.

Nonfinancial signs could include your parents suddenly not wanting to discuss matters that would usually be routine; your parent seeming tired or depressed; a girlfriend or caregiver telling you your parents are not able to see you or talk to you; a caregiver who speaks for your parents, even when they are present; or a caregiver or new friend who has no means of support other than your parents' income.

"Undue influence" is the specific form of financial abuse that occurs when someone is in a position to exert control over your parents and make them carry out the influencer's wishes instead of their own. While this can include threats and intimidation, it is often more subtle. Abusers will attempt to isolate your parents by keeping the family away while simultaneously convincing your parents that the family has rejected them and is not interested in visiting, and that the abuser is the only friend they have. Abusers may use a caregiving position to keep your parents overmedicated and unable to think clearly. In some cases, your parents may act out of helplessness and bond to their abuser to create a feeling of security.

Some exploiters will actually scan obituaries to spot a senior who has suffered recent bereavement in order to move in and take advantage of them at their lowest point. Almost all exploiters will have a close, trusted relationship with the victim. Most cases of undue influence involve family members, but accountants, attorneys, doctors, housekeepers, and neighbors can do it, too.

Warning signs can be missed, partly because bankers and others dealing with your parent may assume that caregivers and friends are operating out of altruistic motives.

A SPECIAL CASE: ABUSIVE PARENTS

It is one thing to bring this up with parents if your relationship with them was good, or even all right. But what if the parents you are asked to care for are abusive, physically or sexually?

You might think that would put caregiving out of the question: What goes around comes around, and a parent who gave no love to his or her children cannot expect to be loved back.

In practice, even after years of abuse, some adult children still feel the need to help their parents when age and illness take their toll. Some adults with strong religious convictions believe they have an obligation to forgive and to care for their parents. Some see it as a chance to attain closure, or even to win their parents' love.

Others may feel pressured to offer care because they know people expect it of them. This is particularly true if the abuse has stayed secret. The parents' Social Security caseworker, their friends, and possibly even family members may wonder why the abused child refuses to do her duty and care for the parents.

If you or any member of your family is in this position, here are some points to consider:

- Abuse may continue in some form: Unreasonable demands on the caregiver's time, efforts to control them, or verbal abuse ("You do not love me! You would be happier if I were dead!").

- Do not make yourself vulnerable. If you think your parents will become belligerent or belittling if you talk with them about money, make sure you have someone with you.

- Do not do more than you can handle. Maybe the most you can bear is to arrange for assisted living. Maybe you can handle the financial affairs, but not being in the same room with your parents, or you provide financial support for the sibling who does give care. Do not beat yourself up for not doing more.

- Do not deny what took place or how you feel. If talking about the abuse is the only way to make people understand why you refuse to help your parents, you are not required to keep silent, even if you concealed the abuse for years.

- Some families find it easier to support the abuser than admit what the abuser did. Do not let their disbelief push you into offering more help to your parents than you can live with.

- Do not let your children near a potential abuser if you believe there is any risk of more abuse.

- Do not imagine that by being good to your parents now, it will finally win their love.

- When the stress builds up, abused adult children have been known to relieve it by becoming abusers in turn. If you feel yourself going down that road, stop before you cross the line, even if you feel justice is on your side. Elder abuse defeats the purpose of becoming your parents' caregiver. It is also a crime, and past abuse is not a legal excuse for doing the same.

12 Wills, Trusts, Executors, and Burials

While you will do everything possible as a caregiver to make your parents' final years as pleasant as possible, no one can avoid the inevitable when a parent comes to the end of their life. Because of this fact, here is a chapter on what issues and problems need to be addressed when a parent is at the end of his or her life, and what to do when the parent passes on.

Many financial and health issues will need to be addressed and worked out. As caregiver, you will need to handle issues such as end-of-life medical decisions and advance directives if there are any. There is also the possibility of what to do when there is no direction, and you must make all kinds of decisions. Some of these decisions will include your parent's funeral plans, as well as dealing with estate planning, wills, executors, and probate.

END OF LIFE MEDICAL DECISIONS AND ADVANCE DIRECTIVES

A health care directive is a common provision in the legal profession that enables a person or persons you have chosen to make any final medical decisions for you when you cannot speak for yourself. Usually this is a written statement that clearly lays out what wishes you want when you no longer have the ability to tell anyone. Such is the case of an elder parent who is faced with ongoing medical treatment to stay alive. Or, in the case of a comatose person, their wish to continue receiving life-saving measures when there is no evidence that the person will ever recover. Living wills and health care power of attorney are types of this legal tool. All states, including the District of Columbia, have recognized these types of directives as normal legal procedures.

When the time comes when your parents can no longer make the medical decisions required for themselves, the advance directive will help greatly ease any confusion and wondering by others if they are making the right decision for your parents. The problem is that, unless you take the initiative well in advance, you will never know what your parents' wishes are for their final days. Another problem is that wishes do change over time, so it will be important to continue an ongoing conversation over time about your parent's current wishes. Advance directives, like wills, can be changed at any time. By starting the conversation — and doing so early enough and going forward — your parents will realize that you are willing to abide by their wishes to the end of their lives.

There is no possible way to know every possible circumstance that could happen, especially with science and technology advancing every year. The more informed you are about what your parents' wishes are, the easier it will be to have them carried out when it is time. Making sure the entire family and the physicians involved know what these wishes are will also ensure less conflict in the end.

There are three general types of advance health care directives: the living will, the health care power of attorney, and the comprehensive health care directive. Here is how each one is summed up briefly. For a more comprehensive look into each type of directive, you should consult a lawyer knowledgeable in health care directives.

Living Will

Living wills are also known by the terms "directive to physicians," or medical directive. Simply put, they are basic legal documents stating exactly what your parents will want to be done in case they are unable to make the decision for themselves. Most states allow this type of directive, with the exception of California, which calls this a health care directive.

What does a living will cover, and when are they placed into effect? Living wills are used in situations when there is no hope of recovery by the patient. Such situations include being in a vegetative state, terminal illness, and advanced progressive illness in which no treatment can create an option other than painful last days.

Living wills are most often general in nature, as there is no way to know what specific issues will bring them into use. And while an advanced directive such as this should ensure compliance by everyone involved, most states insist on two physicians to agree that the conditions of the will have been met before being put into place.

Health Care Power of Attorney

This is simply another version of power of attorney in which a person is appointed to make decisions for them, in this case health care. In general terms, this allows the appointed person to weigh out all medical options and choose one as he or she thinks the appointer would want. Health care power of attorney has more flexibility than a living will, as it gives the appointed person as much, or as little, power over medical decisions as you allow.

Your parents can limit what options you would have if you are chosen as their appointed agent. They can stipulate that certain treatments are not allowed, or that certain decisions will require a doctor's consent.

If you are given this appointment, you will be allowed to authorize any medical treatment, hire or discharge medical personnel for your parents' medical needs, and decide where your parents will receive treatment. You are also allowed access to their medical records, any authorizations to obtain treatment, and to sign waivers or release information. You are allowed to question doctors and get second opinions.

Comprehensive Health Care Advance Directive

This is the combination of the above two directives. This directive can also include other directives and orders, such as:

- **Do-not-resuscitate** – This states that if your parent's heart stops, he or she does not want CPR in any form, including electric shock, chest compressions, or medicine.

- **Organ Donation** – This states which organs your parents want to donate. It also can limit where the organ goes.

- **Where and How They Choose to Live** – This normally covers convalescent care or treatment if they are temporarily incapacitated. It can also cover hospice and home care.

If your parents do create one of these directives, be sure they understand the importance of being completely clear in both the word and action laid out within these documents. There are attorneys who will recommend the comprehensive approach because of the flexibility that it offers, while others will advise against it simply because courts read these directives as concrete rules instead of guidelines.

Be sure that any form your parents sign has two witnesses sign with them. While state laws vary, in most cases, the witnesses cannot be related to your parents, or cannot be their physicians or hospital staff. They also cannot use anyone who will be responsible for their medical bills.

Once the document is signed, make copies for yourself, your immediate family, and any doctors, attorneys, and ministers your parents have. Then take the original and store it in a safe place where you can reach it quickly.

If your parents revoke the directive, they can do it orally, but they should also do so in writing, contacting their agent and everyone else who received a copy. Amending the directive will have to be done in writing also. Executing a new directive would be just as simple because amendments require the same witnessing procedures. The directive should be reviewed every few years; shortly after any major life change, such as the death of a spouse or a remarriage; and in the event a terminal illness is diagnosed, or your parents' physical health declines steeply.

What does all this have to do with parental finance? If you do or do not become the appointed person for this type of legal issue, you certainly will be in charge of the financial handling of the directive. The costs for carrying out the directive will be dealt with by the caregiver, and the estate will handle the medical costs during probate.

Knowing the legal status of the directive in your state will be helpful for both the appointee and the caregiver. The laws in some states will allow hospitals to stop life-sustaining treatment if they believe recovery is not an option and if the money to pay for the treatment has been exhausted. Also take notice of the definition of "life support" within your state or your parents' state of residence. This can be different for many facilities and states. Some laws take the meaning of "no use of extraordinary measures" to include food and water while the patient is comatose. There is the possibility that a family member can challenge the directive when it is enforced with the theory that the parent was forced into signing it, or that your parents revoked their order, even if there is no written proof. Having two physicians who disagree on the criteria of the terms in the directive can also complicate the issue. All of these facts can cause legal and financial problems that can quickly drain resources and wipe out an estate.

The best option if an advance directive is issued is to have everyone who handles medical and financial situations on the same page. If you are given the task of managing both, you have both a blessing and a curse. You will know where the money is going, but you must also decide if the treatment is worth getting. If you are not the appointed person, make sure you are in agreement as to what would happen if the day were to come when the directive was needed.

WHAT TO DO WHEN THERE IS NO DIRECTION

What happens when your parents have not signed a health care directive of any kind? The ability you, or your family, have to make health care decisions for them varies with each state. The best scenario here would be that you know what your parents would want; the family agrees with you; and the doctor is supportive of everyone's decision. But there are cases where this just does not happen.

A classic case for example is that of Terri Schiavo. This mother and wife fell into a permanent vegetative state without giving any direction for what the family should do if this were to occur. Her husband, Michael, and the family generally agreed on what her condition was and how to handle her health care. Then, Michael Schiavo stated that his wife would want life-saving measures suspended, rather than living in the condition she was in.

It was at this point where the dispute began between the husband and the remaining family as to what Terri would have wanted.

The family stated that she had responded to them opposite of what Michael had said where her wishes. The battle over this last wish took years before the husband won in court. Then, right-to-life activists convinced then Gov. Jeb Bush to push the Florida legislature into passing a bill that kept Terri Schiavo alive longer. Eventually, her life support ended after years of hardship and infighting.

Most states allow for a default surrogate to handle health care decisions if there is no advance directive. Usually the spouse is given first option, followed by the adult children, then other family members, and finally close friends if there is no one else available. State laws and regulations will determine the exact power or limitations a surrogate has in health care decisions. You could be given full authority or limited to specific decisions. Some or all decisions may require the agreement of a majority, or all, of the immediate family as well.

MAKING DECISIONS

Let us assume that you are the surrogate in charge of health care decisions. You will be called upon to use your authority. There are steps that you need to take to ensure you make the proper decision in each case.

First, find out exactly what the problem is. Ask questions if there is anything you do not fully understand. Do not stop asking for explanations until you are satisfied and understand the entire situation.

Some questions you should ask include questions about:

- Your parents' condition
- What the cause of the medical problem is
- What the chances of a full recovery are
- If the chance is low, what the most likely outcome of the problem would be

If the cause of the problem is unknown, you should ask about:

- The chances of a proper diagnosis
- If more tests are requested, the chances that those tests will produce useful information

A common issue raised between caregivers and physicians is the level and amount of testing given to a patient. While it does raise costs, doctors conduct multiple tests to prove they have done everything possible (to avoid a malpractice suit), instead of needing these tests for usable information.

If the cause is known, some questions to ask would include the following:

- What the treatment options are, and their chances for success
- Any drawbacks, risks, or side effects
- What the doctor would recommend as the best option

If death is inevitable, then the following options should be discussed:

- Would the treatment make death less painful?
- Would the treatment allow home care or hospitalization?

- Would hospice be an alternative care option?

While these questions may seem unrelated to parental finances, they are related to the responsibilities of a caregiver who is in charge of another person's health care. In that regard, you are financially responsible for your parents' medical treatment as well, and because of this, you will need to ask the same questions as anyone else who would handle this task.

YOUR PARENTS' FUNERAL PLANS

Death and taxes are two items many people do not like to openly discuss. For those who find discussing your parents' finances and health difficult, discussing how they want to be buried will be no easier.

The best tip is to talk to them about this issue. Let them know that their last wishes will be honored — it will make them happier. And it will be one less issue you will have to contend with when that day arrives, as this is not a task you want to work on at the last moment.

The way to do this is to ask them about their wishes: how do they want to be buried? Where? Do they want cremation? If so, what do they want done with the ashes? Another consideration is a possible wish for organ donation, as well as the type of funeral service they may want. There are ways to avoid financial problems and disasters once you know what your parents want in their funeral. Once you know their plans, try these tips to ensure they are carried out:

- Consider paying for as much as possible in advance, if they have not done this already

- Consider all options for both funerals and internment. Things can change in the final years. Having planned alternatives will save a lot of money and stress.

- Take advantage of several trust accounts that can help with funeral expenses. An example of this would be a Totten trust that invests money in a certificate of deposit, or money market account and holds the money in trust for the funeral.

- If the parents want to donate organs, get them organ donor cards from their state Department of Motor Vehicles. They need to sign this card and always carry it with them. These wishes should also be made public with the doctors and the family.

- As you collect certain documents such as cemetery deeds and advance directives, keep them in a secure container where you can always access them.

Funerals can get very expensive without proper advance planning. The farther ahead you begin planning this task, the more likely the cost and the stress will be considerably diminished.

ESTATE PLANNING: WILLS AND EXECUTORS

Before naming a person to act as executor to your parents' estate, be sure to ask them if they want to handle the responsibility of this position, as executors have a great deal of significant duties to fulfill.

There are some key elements to estate planning. You must arrange your parents' affairs to make sure their wishes are honored, and that everyone in the family (along with friends, employees, and charities) receives what your parents wanted them to have. Also ensure the estate will be disposed of as swiftly and smoothly as possible with minimal time in probate. You should take advantage of financial planning that guarantees your parents' estate be passed on with as little loss to the IRS as possible. This requires a different set of plans: A living trust will pass property immediately to the other trustees and avoid probate, but it will not protect the trust contents from the IRS. Financial planning includes preparing for the losses that you know will occur. The estate plan should include ensuring that there is enough cash available to cover any taxes that your parents' estate incurs to avoid having to sell property or stocks to pay for them. The estate may also have to put up a bond against the executor committing any financial malfeasance. Appoint an executor to carry out the provisions of the will and trustees to administer any trusts they set up. The executor could be you, one of your siblings, or a trusted family friend.

The Will

If your parents have not made out a will, talk to them about this to ensure it gets done. While this is not the only essential part of estate planning, it is one of the most important pieces. Someone will need to notify anyone paying your parents' benefits, and the IRS will want a tax return for the last year of their life, even if no taxes were paid. Any contracts signed by your parents will need to be settled and completed.

Many bookstores have a range of self-help books written about writing wills for a certain state. The more assets your parents have, the more complex the will is going to become. This is also true of the final tax return, as this will become more complex with more assets. If there are a large amount of assets, consider bringing in a lawyer for assistance.

The will needs to cover the disposal of all property that your parents own; this includes not only the cars, residence, and china, but also the stocks, bonds, books, clothing, pictures, and family papers. Wills do not cover anything placed in a living trust that automatically is handed over to the trustees. Another item not put into a will is the beneficiary to life insurance policies or pension accounts. Financial accounts should never be put into your parents' will, as this has no legal standing.

There are some states that allow a will to be signed without a witness being present, but many states require at least two witnesses be present who also sign the document as evidence of their participation. In any case, the witness legally cannot be anyone who would benefit from the outcome of the will, such as heirs, trustees, health care providers, caregivers, or financial caretakers. If a witness were to inherit an item from the will, that portion of the will and the inheritance automatically becomes invalid by law.

If your parents are thinking of giving — or not giving — a certain item to a certain person, this should be spelled out in the will so that there is no confusion. Another area that may bring confusion is clarity in the will. When a will is written, it must state clearly, without a doubt, where, when, and how much property will go to each heir. Again, this is the best way to avoid confusion.

It is good practice to have your parents review their will every five to seven years to make sure it is still accurate. While this takes only a few minutes' time, it saves countless hours — and sometimes months — of delay and legal issues when the will is needed.

Potential Issues

Another issue your parents may face is the effect of living in a community property state, if they live in such a state. This means that everything acquired during a marriage is divided equally among both spouses, no matter what a will says. The only way around this is if one parent acquired property outside of the marriage.

The next issue, which is an absolute must if your parent is in either a same-sex partnership or has taken on a partner after their spouse has died, is to place the partner into the will. In most states, this is essential if anything is to be left to the partner because there is no legal standing for the partnership outside of the will.

In today's society, divorce and remarriage are common. If this has happened in your parents' history, they need to make sure their will is updated to reflect this. If one of the heirs dies before the parent, this also will require an update to the estate planning. If your parent moves to another state after creating the will, the will may have to be updated to reflect the laws of that state.

In regard to parental finances and caregivers: If you are in charge of your parents' finances and are forced to sell property or deplete bank or retirement accounts, this must also be changed in the will.

When editing a will, if the changes are minor, your parents can use a written appendix to the original will, called a codicil. If the changes are more extensive, or happen multiple times, it is usually better to rewrite the entire document from scratch.

What happens if your parent dies without leaving a will? Laws of their state of residence will decide where the property goes and when, regardless of what your parent — or the family — wanted. Most states award up to half of the property to the surviving spouse, then divide the remainder among everyone else. If your parent is single, the state divides the assets equally among surviving children. If one of the children dies, then their children inherit that portion of the estate.

There is also the possibility that your parents can leave assets in a testamentary trust, or living trust, where the property transfer only occurs after their death. While this does not leave out the involvement of the IRS, it does give more control to your parents in regard to who can have what and when. It should be noted that trusts can also be revoked or adjusted at any time, and should also be reviewed every five to seven years to make sure they are up-to-date.

PROBATE

Probate is required with or without a will. Depending on the size of the estate, the speed of the process can move very quickly. In most cases, estates of up to $100,000 or uncomplicated, larger estates can be handled by a streamlined process.

Two states that have restrictive probate guidelines are California and Florida. Both states require that lawyers represent every person represented in the estate, including the executor. There are set fee schedules that lawyers in both states stick to and can increase the cost of probate considerably for smaller estates needing little legal work.

Steps involved with probate:

1. Take probate inventory and management of the estate
2. Pay off all lawful debts and taxes of the estate
3. Distribute the remaining probate estate according to the will or state law, if there is no will

In the case of no will, the probate court appoints an administrator, usually a family member. In the case of family disagreement, the court can appoint a public administrator or a knowledgeable attorney. Public administrators must be paid from the estate funds.

What is probate court? Probate court is a lower court within the court system, commonly referred to as surrogate court. Use the county clerk's office to get information pertaining to this court.

Once you petition the court to grant power of executor, you must wait for the probate court to accept the petition. When the petition is accepted, the court then appoints an executor. If you are appointed executor of your parents estate, the court will provide documents that you will then present to any financial institutions involved such as banks, investment agents, or insurance agents.

When you become the executor, open a checking account in the name of the estate to pay bills for the estate and make deposits for any items the estate sells. You will be required to protect the estate property in any way possible, including keeping up insurance and loan payments, and paying off claims on the estate.

Probate is a term used for a court process that totals up all assets of a deceased person, ensures that any outstanding debts are paid, and then divides up the remainder according to a will, if one is available. If no will is available, the laws of the state where your parents resided will take effect. You should be able to find further guidance online by referencing the Web site for the state your parents lived in.

As a general guideline, here are a few things to do when a parent passes away:

- File a petition with the probate court where your parents lived, requesting probate and asking for the appointment of an executor. Most often you can get the forms for this from the local county courthouse.

- If you are named executor, gather your parents' financial information. If you are missing information, look back on Chapter 3 to help you in your search. List every asset your parents owned, including bank accounts, physical property, and stocks. Make a note as to how they were owned (by trust, jointly, business partnership, sole owner, etc.).

- You will need multiple copies of your parent's death certificate, which will be used as proof of death and may be needed as part of a file.

- Start to notify everyone involved in the financial end of this process. This includes the Social Security Administration, insurance companies, retirement account holders, banks, lenders, and any others. Be prepared to take out a legal ad in the newspaper so that any creditors who have claims can file them against the estate.

- Make any arrangements needed to pay off debts or taxes your parents owe.

- Finally, transfer the remaining assets to the beneficiaries and heirs to the estate.

As the executor, you have the right to claim a fee for your work. This fee is set by state law where you filed as executor and is paid from the estate. You can refuse the fee, but the work you do will more than make up for the fee.

As executor of a parent's estate, your duties are guided by many of the same rules you use when you are the caregiver or guardian for your parent. Family and outside disputes can occur, and it will be your duty to settle the issue in the best interest of your parents. Your duties can include any or all of the following tasks: the selling of real estate; the payment of valid debts after you have verified they are valid; paying taxes; transferring funds into and out of the estate account, settling with insurance agents, banks and other financial concerns; maintaining the property of the estate; and taking care of any unfinished business left behind by your parents.

If your parents had property in more than one state, you may need to handle probate procedure in each state. Putting property in a trust will help greatly. If your parents owned business or rental units, try to continue these operations until probate is completed and you can most likely deal with these in one bulk task when the estate is settled.

Depending on the state your parents' estate is probated in and the size of the estate, you may be able to avoid full-scale probate. Some states make it optional, unless the will or the executor's abilities have been challenged. Small estates in some states ("small" being defined by state law) may bypass probate completely. Whoever inherits will file an affidavit stating what they believe they are entitled to, and the executor distributes property accordingly.

There are two levels of probate you should be aware of, simply because of the amount of legal and financial involvement of the executor of an estate:

Informal Probate
Informal probate is used for estates that require no court involvement because of either their undisputed nature and simplicity, or their small size. This probate allows the executor to take responsibility to promptly, completely, and legally discharge the estate with the probate court needed only to give final approval to the entire

process. The downside to this is that the executor is legally liable for any mistakes and charges made because of their actions.

Formal Probate

This type of probate is used when more complex estates and disputes require court supervision for distribution. The court must approve of each legal step taken by the administrator of the estate, which adds a lot of time and cost to the process. With formal probate, the court intervenes to hear conflicting claims, find heirs when they are missing, and handles approval for asset distribution. If a person dies with a large family, large financial debts, or bankruptcy, having the court involved can prove very beneficial in the end.

Most often, the executor of an estate will hire a lawyer to serve as a consultant to ensure that some of the duties are properly handled. The time that an estate administrator spends in court can be substantial, depending on the amount of work involved.

Not every part of an estate is subject to probate. Here are some examples of what is and is not an asset liable to probate.

Examples of Probate Assets

- Deceased's property inherited upon the deaths of his/her parents, as his/her separate property.

- Deceased's home, as to his/her one-half interest in community property.

- Deceased's interest in a vacation home, a boat, or an airplane, as a tenant-in-common (i.e., not joint tenancy) with other joint owners.

- A life insurance policy owned by the deceased on his/her life and whose named beneficiary is his/her estate.

- Deceased's IRA or a Keogh Plan for his/her benefit and whose named beneficiary upon his/her death is his/her estate.

Examples of Nonprobate Assets

- Deceased's car, as a joint tenant (i.e., with right of survivorship).

- Deceased's bank account, payable on death ("POD") to one of deceased's children.

- Deceased's securities account, transferable on death ("TOD") to deceased's trustee.

- Property subject to a valid community property agreement, transferable to the deceased's surviving spouse.

- A life insurance policy owned by the deceased on his/her life and whose named beneficiary is other than his/her estate (i.e., his/her spouse or children).

- Decedent's IRA or Keogh Plan for his/her benefit and whose named beneficiary upon his/her death is other than his/her estate (i.e., his/her spouse or children).

- Property held in trust for the benefit of deceased and whose named beneficiary upon his/her death is other than his/her estate (i.e., deceased's revocable living trust held for a. his/her benefit during his/her life and b. his/her spouse or children following his/her death).

Nonprobate assets pass upon death to the named survivor or beneficiary outside of probate. The methods for making nonprobate assets (i.e., joint tenancies, POD or TOD accounts, community property agreements, living trusts, etc.) are sometimes called will substitutes. Source: **www.wa-probate.com/instructions/Probate-FAQ.htm**

CONCLUSION

Whether you have read this book cover to cover or cherry-picked the parts you really need to know about, by this point, you should have learned what you need to know about helping your parents during these difficult times. You also have some idea of the emotional and practical obstacles you can run into while trying to help, and of the steps you can take to avoid them. There is no guarantee this will make your decisions easy or painless, but you have the knowledge to make informed decisions.

Keep this book handy as you plunge into the world of caregiving. Even if all you need to know right now is how to run a family meeting, you may have questions later about Medicaid, guardianship, or living trusts that the book can answer.

Do not forget that the laws on Medicaid, living wills, gay marriage, and estate taxes — and pretty much everything else in this book — can change and, in many cases, will definitely change. When it comes time to draft a document or apply for Medicaid, this book cannot replace the expertise of a fully trained professional, but it will give a good idea of where you need to head.

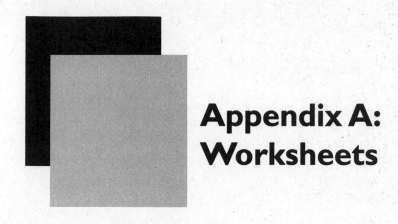

Appendix A: Worksheets

ASSETS AND LIABILITIES WORKSHEET

A look at what your parents have on hand, and what their debts are.

Assets

Current assets   Value

   Checking account: _____

   Checking account: _____

   Savings account: _____

   Savings account: _____

   Money-market account: _____

   CDs: _____

Savings bonds: _____

Bonuses due: _____

Commissions due: _____

Tax refunds due: _____

Total: _____ = _____

Securities

Treasury bonds: _____

Municipal bonds: _____

Corporate bonds: _____

Bond mutual funds

_____ : _____

_____ : _____

Stocks

_____ : _____

_____ : _____

Stock mutual funds

_____ : _____

_____ : _____

Futures

_____ : _____

_____ : _____

Stock options

_____ : _____

_____ : _____

Total: _____ = _____

Real estate

Primary home: _____

Second home: _____

Retirement home: _____

Rental property: _____

Rental property: _____

Rental property: _____

Total: _____ = _____

Business

Your parents' business: _____

Partnership in a business: _____

Total: _____ = _____

Retirement funds

IRAs: _____

Annuities: _____

Keogh plan: _____

401(k) plan: _____

403(b) plan: _____

457 plan: _____

Roth IRA: _____

Pension: _____

Civil service pension: _____

Military pension: _____

Total: _____ = _____

Personal property

Antiques: _____

Appliances: _____

Art: _____

Books: _____

Clothes: _____

Computer equipment: _____

Collectibles: _____

Furniture: _____

Electronics: _____

Jewelry: _____

Home fixtures: _____

Vehicles: _____

Total: _____ = _____

Total Assets: _____

Liabilities

Current liabilities *Amount owed*

Alimony: _____

Child support: _____

Utility bills due: _____

Medical bills due: _____

Total: _____ = _____

Unpaid taxes

Federal income tax: _____

State income tax: _____

City income tax: _____

Capital gains tax: _____

Property taxes: _____

Social Security (self employed): _____

Total: _____ = _____

Real estate

Primary home

First mortgage: _____

Second mortgage: _____

Home equity loan: _____

Second home

First mortgage: _____

Second mortgage: _____

Home equity loan: _____

Rental property

First mortgage: _____

Second mortgage: _____

Rental property

First mortgage: _____

Second mortgage: _____

Total: _____ = _____

Installment debt

Credit card debt: _____

Vehicle loans: _____

Student loans: _____

Debt consolidation loans: _____

Bank loans: _____

Furniture loans: _____

Home improvement loans: _____

Life insurance loans: _____

Retirement plan loans: _____

Total: _____ = _____

Net worth (assets - liabilities): _____

CASH FLOW

How much money is coming in? How much is coming out?

Annual income

Earned income   **Amount**

Take home pay: _____

Self-employment: _____

Tips: _____

Bonuses: _____

Commissions: _____

Royalties: _____

Rental income: _____

Total: _____ = _____

Family income

Alimony: _____

Child support: _____

Trust fund income: _____

Total: _____ = _____

Government income

Veterans' benefits: _____

Civil service benefit _____

Food stamps: _____

Disability income: _____

Unemployment: _____

Workers compensation: _____

Other: _____

Total: _____ = _____

Retirement income

IRAs: _____

Annuities: _____

Keogh plan: _____

401(k) plan: _____

403(b) plan: _____

457 plan : _____

Roth IRA: _____

Pension: _____

Social Security: _____

Total: _____ = _____

Investments:

Interest on savings accounts: _____

CD interest: _____

Money market interest: _____

Bond dividends: _____

Bond interest: _____

Stock dividends: _____

Total: _____ = _____

Other income (specify)

_____ : _____

_____ : _____

_____ : _____

_____ : _____

Total: _____ = _____

Total income: _____

Annual expenses

Taxes

Income tax: _____

State income tax: _____

Property tax: _____

Self-employment tax: _____

Total: _____ = _____

Insurance premiums

Automobile: _____

Property: _____

Health: _____

Life: _____

Renters: _____

Long-term care: _____

Total: _____ = _____

Utilities

Electricity: _____

Water: _____

Gas: _____

Telephone: _____

Cable: _____

Internet: _____

Total: _____ = _____

Vehicle expenses

Gasoline: _____

Car payment: _____

Tolls: _____

Repairs/maintenance: _____

License fees: _____

Train/bus fees: _____

Automobile rentals: _____

Total: _____ = _____

Divorce expenses

Alimony: _____

Child support: _____

Total: _____ = _____

Total Assets: _____

House expenses

Mortgage payments: _____

Rent: _____

Yard maintenance: _____

Repairs: _____

Housekeeping: _____

Total: _____ = _____

Family/child expenses

Food: _____

Clothing: _____

Tuition: _____

School supplies: _____

Other school expenses: _____

Shoes: _____

Day care: _____

Pet care: _____

Food: _____

Gifts: _____

Other: _____

Total: _____ = _____

Recreation expenses

Toys: _____

Games: _____

Books: _____

Movies: _____

Video rentals: _____

Concerts/plays: _____

Sporting events: _____

Club/organization dues: _____

Dining out: _____

Vacation (travel): _____

Vacation (lodging): _____

Vacation (food): _____

Vacation (other): _____

Total: _____ = _____

Donations

Charity: _____

Tithing: _____

Political: _____

Total: _____ = _____

Medical expenses

Copayment: _____

Dental care: _____

Medicine: _____

Eye care: _____

Hospital fees: _____

Alternative living: _____

(assisted living, nursing homes)

At-home care: _____

Medical equipment: _____

Total: _____ = _____

Investment expenses:

Bank fees: _____

Investment account fees: _____

Total: _____ = _____

Net cash flow (income - expenses): _____

INFORMATION YOU WILL NEED TO KNOW OR FIND

Parents' address: _____

Phone number: _____

Work number: _____

Cell phone numbers: _____

Place of birth: _____

Social Security numbers: _____

Medicaid number: _____

Location:

File of financial information: _____

File of medical information: _____

Birth certificate: _____

Marriage certificate: _____

Divorce papers: _____

Passports: _____

Business records: _____

Financial file: _____

Military records: _____

Durable power of attorney: _____

Power of attorney for health care: _____

Health care directive: _____

Living will: _____

DNR: _____

Checkbooks: _____

Insurance documents: _____

Bank statements: _____

Will: _____

Deeds: _____

Keys: _____

Safety deposit boxes: _____

Web sites   User names   Passwords

Web sites	User names	Passwords

A CONTACT LIST FOR YOUR PARENTS:

Medical

Primary care physician: _____

Phone number: _____

Hours: _____

Address: _____

Specialist: _____

Contacted for: _____

Phone number: _____

Hours: _____

Address: _____

Specialist: _____

Contacted for: _____

Phone number: _____

Hours: _____

Address: _____

Specialist: _____

Contacted for: _____

Phone number: _____

Hours: _____

Address: _____

Pharmacy: _____

Address: _____

Phone number: _____

Hours: _____

Legal

Attorney: _____

Address: _____

Phone number: _____

Hours: _____

Executor: _____

Address: _____

Phone number: _____

Hours: _____

Financial

Accountant: _____

Address: _____

Phone number: _____

Hours: _____

Banker: _____

Address: _____

Phone number: _____

Hours: _____

Financial planner: _____

Address: _____

Phone number: _____

Hours: _____

Investment manager: _____

Address: _____

Phone number: _____

Hours: _____

Stockbroker: _____

Address: _____

Phone number: _____

Hours: _____

Insurance agent: _____

Address: _____

Phone number: _____

Hours: _____

Employee benefits counselor: _____

Address: _____

Phone number: _____

Hours: _____

Miscellaneous

Religious advisor: _____

House of worship: _____

Address: _____

Phone number: _____

Hours: _____

Social Security counselor: _____

Address: _____

Phone number: _____

Hours: _____

Medicaid counselor: _____

Address: _____

Phone number: _____

Hours: _____

Medicare counselor: _____

Address: _____

Phone number: _____

Hours: _____

Address: _____

Phone number: _____

Hours: _____

Address: _____

Phone number: _____

Hours: _____

Address: _____

Phone number: _____

Hours: _____

Address: _____

Phone number: _____

Hours: _____

Address: _____

Phone number: _____

Hours: _____

Address: _____

Phone number: _____

Hours: _____

Address: _____

Phone number: _____

Hours: _____

Address: _____

Phone number: _____

Hours: _____

Address: _____

Phone number: _____

Hours: _____

Address: _____

Phone number: _____

Hours: _____

Address: _____

Phone number: _____

Hours: _____

Appendix B:
Case Studies

If you want to know first-hand what coping with these problems is like, here are the stories of people who have been through — and in some cases, still are — handling their parents' finances. There are also two case studies by financial planners with experience working with seniors and eldercare givers.

CASE STUDY: P.J. COLDREN

P.J. Coldren

My father, twice a widower, moved from Baltimore to West Branch, Michigan, to be closer to me. At the time, he was living independently in a senior citizen complex in Catonsville, Maryland; now, he lives alone in an assisted living facility, in a one-bedroom apartment.

There was no need for me to get involved in his finances at the time and I did not have to bring it up with him: He chose to get me involved before the need arose. In Baltimore, he already had my brother on his checking accounts with a durable power of attorney for both financial and medical issues. He transferred those POAs to me, and I am on his checking account.

CASE STUDY: P.J. COLDREN

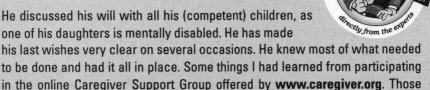

He was very blasé about it: He is an engineer, a very pragmatic man, and had lived in the senior-citizen complex long enough to see what happened when one was (or was not) prepared for major life changes.

He discussed his will with all his (competent) children, as one of his daughters is mentally disabled. He has made his last wishes very clear on several occasions. He knew most of what needed to be done and had it all in place. Some things I had learned from participating in the online Caregiver Support Group offered by **www.caregiver.org**. Those people are a wealth of information, both on the site and in the support group.

He is very up-front about where the money comes from and what he wants done with it. He lives a simple life with few luxuries, and seems to be handling his money just fine. I knew before he moved out here what his sources of income were; what I have learned since then is the exact amounts of those sources.

He was very blasé about it: He is an engineer, a very pragmatic man, and had lived in the senior-citizen complex long enough to see what happened when one was (or was not) prepared for major life changes.

He discussed his will with all his (competent) children, as one of his daughters is mentally disabled. He has made his last wishes very clear on several occasions. He knew most of what needed to be done and had it all in place. Some things I had learned from participating in the online Caregiver Support Group offered by **www.caregiver.org**. Those people are a wealth of information, both on the site and in the support group.

He is very up-front about where the money comes from and what he wants done with it. He lives a simple life with few luxuries, and seems to be handling his money just fine. I knew before he moved out here what his sources of income were; what I have learned since then is the exact amounts of those sources.

The hardest past of assuming responsibility was getting used to the fact he was not pinching pennies any more. There were five children and a single income, and I am just getting used to him not asking me how much change there was from the grocery store, or how much I spent on his new bed. Looking at his resources, he can afford to be that way, and so I am slowly adjusting.

My fear is that his mind will start to go, and I have no idea how that will change his attitudes about money. I guess I'll play that hand when it is dealt me.

Spending money on major purchases, such as the bed, without input from Dad made me uncomfortable.

CASE STUDY: P.J. COLDREN

I've never enjoyed being responsible for the checkbook.

I don't think we have set any financial goals, jointly or separately. There is a set amount of money available to him and, right now, it is more than enough for his expenses. If it ever is not enough, my siblings and I will sit down and figure out what to do next.

I think his priority is to live comfortably for as long as he can. This goal probably has more to do with his health than with his finances, since the former is more likely to change than the latter. It has been very easy to meet these goals so far, since the money is there for him.

We haven't called in anyone other than someone to prepare his income taxes. The people already "on his team," such as stockbrokers, predate my involvement; I think they came with his second wife and her money.

I keep copies of any financial and medical paperwork and the standard stuff for taxes, checking, CDs, and so on. I have a notebook for all his medical information, which makes it easy to keep track of things and keep his health care providers up-to-date. I haven't used any tools for his finances separated from what I, as a "regular" person, have on-hand.

He is not on my personal/family checkbooks and accounts. I am on his checking account, but my husband is not. I am listed as the primary on some CDs that he provided the money for. I pay the taxes on them and get to keep any interest they earn. This is some compensation for the caretaking I am doing, and it was his suggestion. I owe him some money, and I write him a check every two weeks on the balance due. He cashes the checks and sometimes gives me the cash back for what he calls the "slush fund," to buy toilet paper with, put gas in the car, and so forth.

This is still fairly new: Dad moved here about three months ago. So far, my stress level has gone up a bit, but not more than I expected. As we work out the routines, the stress is decreasing somewhat. I cope by not dealing with Dad issues every single day — I take days off from Dad duty. So far, the duties are not onerous, so this has worked.

I have no idea how anyone else can avoid being overwhelmed: One person's tolerance level may be quite different from another person's; the demands placed on someone else with a different situation, a different level of parental involvement, and functionality.

CASE STUDY: P.J. COLDREN

Make time for yourself. Decide what you can and can't, will or won't do, and stick to it. Get help; you haven't failed if someone else does it for you. You've just delegated, which is the mark of a good manager.

So far, disagreement among us siblings hasn't been an issue. Of my four siblings, one is not capable of being involved; one is dead; one lives out of the country; and one is very glad to have passed the baton on to me. What we've done in the past is discuss possible problems with each other when Dad wasn't around, come to whatever decision we needed to get to, and present a united front to Dad. That has worked so far. Dad is very clear on what he wants, so the ultimate authority is still "Dad said."

When Dad makes a major financial decision, I ask him if he's discussed it with my sister and brother and if he has not, he does. I have been very clear that I want full disclosure. It's working so far.

Dad lives alone in a facility that offers both independent and assisted-living apartments. He is in a one-bedroom assisted apartment, on the waiting list for independent. He is not a very social animal, so he has not made any friends, although he is cordial and polite to other residents when at meals. He does not participate in any of the activities offered by the facility. He has recently been diagnosed with early-stage macular degeneration in both eyes; this is a major problem because his favorite pastimes are reading and watching sports on television.

Dad spends more time sleeping than I would like. He is eagerly awaiting the arrival of consistently warm weather so he can go outside to smoke his cigars; smoking is only permitted in the independent living area — another reason for him to be on the waiting list. We go out to a local restaurant once or twice a week, where he enjoys the good food and his private stock of 18-year-old single-malt scotch. He is trying to, as he phrases it, "get off my dead butt," and get his museum settled. His social interaction consists of time spent with the aides at the facility, time spent in the dining area when he goes to meals, and time spent with me and my husband.

My advice to others:

- Take care of yourself! If you aren't well, you can't deal with anyone else's problems. Take time for yourself: Social time, time off, and time with friends.

CASE STUDY: P.J. COLDREN

Do not give up your entire life for someone else because, when that someone else is gone, you better have something left of yourself!

- Do not be afraid to ask for help. Asking for help is not weakness — it is a sign of personal strength to know when you cannot handle something. Getting help is a good thing; do it often.

- If you have the misfortune to be an only child with siblings (if this is you, you'll know exactly what I mean), get all the legal paperwork done early. Get that durable medical power of attorney. Get that financial power of attorney. If you need to get guardianship, do it! If you want to be in charge of things you will, sooner or later, need that paperwork, especially if there is dissension in the family. It may not make your emotional life any easier, but at least you will know what your father or mother wanted done, and that they wanted you to do it. That will make it possible for you to do what needs to be done.

The rest of the family can say whatever they want and can be as hurtful as they like, but if you've got the paperwork, you can do what needs to be done.

CASE STUDY: JIMMY RICH

President
AUS Manufacturing Company
704 West Hwy 90
Bonifay, FL 32425
Phone: 850-547-1660
Fax: 850-5471216
Cell: 850-415-0300
E-mail: jimmy@ausmanufacturing.com
See Us On The Web:
www.ausmanufacturing.com

Everyone's case would work differently, depending upon economical and health factors of your parents when we get to this time in life. In my case, I ended up with both father and mother to see after at almost the same time, but in their case, they have actually been separate entities who divorced and remarried other people back in the mid-'70s. Another factor in our case is that Father and Mother are different in the way they need to be treated.

CASE STUDY: JIMMY RICH

In Father's case, he is 80-years-old, dementia is setting in, and his mind just can't keep up with the routine of keeping his bill paying organized. He also had strange ideas about not using a checkbook, and going the long way around to pay things with cash when he was able. I'm sure he had bad experiences with the stepmom that made using a checkbook painful.

Mother's health: Being a COPD patient is the result of two packs a day since she was 14. She's now 75, so she has 61 years of heavy smoking, which is taking its toll. She just had a six-week hospital stay that she almost didn't survive. That made it necessary to get her checkbook and go to her house and get the bills paid so her world would continue. Keep in mind that she was a bookkeeper for years and a stickler about keeping her own numbers organized. She had an automatic irritation in the background that someone else was in her checkbook, even though it was obvious I had to do it.

Dad was still married but had to be partially convinced that he was unable to mentally keep up with the heavy maintenance of a diabetic step-mom. Obvious situations were developing that were showing that they were too old and unable to see after her health. Since the first of this year, she went into a nursing home. Two weeks ago she died, which makes him now widowed.

The stepmom's health helped make this inevitable; a diabetic's diet as well as the medication (insulin three times a day) is a lot to stay on top of with young people, much less the elderly.

I need to mention at this point that the stepmom has six children — six stepbrothers and sisters to me — that I had to sit with to come up with the decisions that needed to be made. They needed my help with my father to help him to understand what the future was about to be, and that was hard, even in a case with a very agreeable old man. You're having to tell them that they can't keep up housekeeping the way they were used to.

Mother's health and hospital stay made this actually easier in her case. She's got the tougher mind to convince, but the conditions were taking care of themselves.

After things got started, Father was actually OK with everything I had to suggest, a step to setting him up to live alone, which he is barely able to do. His physical health is great, but there are simple things, like cleaning out his refrigerator last night so he is not sitting on health hazards that he might eat.

CASE STUDY: JIMMY RICH

Mother almost died three days after being at the hospital. She went for about two weeks not really coherent as to what and who was doing for her. As soon as she started getting her wits, she wanted to know about all her financial details; they started worrying her a lot.

The only prior discussions we'd had, in his case, was where to be buried, due to him being transplanted out of the area for about 20 years and wanting to come back home when the time came.

He has been reduced down to almost nothing when it comes to assets, and the home where they lived belonged to one of the stepbrothers. This made for the decisions on his move back home here easy, to cut the ties of that situation.

In Mother's case, we have already deeded her house, which is all she has, to us kids and given her a life estate.
I am listed on her bank account, so there is not much left to do when it comes to dealing with her assets. The reason for doing this was to give me borrowing power, using her house as collateral, to spend more money before she goes. At the same time, even though we were able to take care of some of the big issues in that manner, due to the way she thinks about keeping control, she has funny ideas about doing the needed POAs for health care. It does not make good sense, but that's what we are dealing with.

I scanned through any mail my father was receiving; had a change of address made due to his relocating; and took each subject a step at a time. He moved from Alabama to Florida, which meant we had to deal with changing Medicaid and Medicare, which I did online and on the phone. I got him subsidized housing, which was an in-depth application process, but very worthwhile.

I have probably been very fortunate that there hasn't been a tremendous amount of financial problems or surprises. I deal with a lot of subjects, but I am a business owner and haven't been surprised with too much. The largest and most important thing is, they are both actually poor in most respects — just a Social Security income — and making that work.

I have made a definite point to keep all the records clean and separate. That works best for yourself, parents, and other concerned friends and family who want to check in on things, if you know what I mean. There will never be a problem over where the money went.

CASE STUDY: JIMMY RICH

There's no question that it has been very tough. I've had times when I didn't think I would get to everything quickly and efficiently enough. But, again, I've run a business for years, hired and fired several people, and I have always made a point of staying cool, calm, and collected. I have had some help from my siblings.

I have always made it a point to get along with the "steps," so I haven't had much problem there. It's worth mentioning that I have an older brother who hasn't handled it as well as I, in either getting along with the steps or taking care of our own parents, now that the time has come. He'll have to live with his decisions.

My sister and I are on target on everything; we both don't understand the aforementioned brother.

I wish I'd checked with both my parents on what they have in the ways of life insurance — in both cases, none. It's too late now.

Father's actually faring wonderfully in his new little apartment; it works well for him. His physical health is good, but he's just starting to lose memory. He has good days and bad days in this area. Mother's barely able to be home alone — we have home health coming, hauling her meals. It takes a lot of going by and calls to keep her there, and the future doesn't look too good. She'll easily be back at the hospital or nursing home situation, which will be a bad subject for the little independent woman who wants to sit home and smoke.

My advice: Keep yourself in a flexible state; let family and friends help where they will; and use each step of information and the professionals you get it from to help you to the next step.

CASE STUDY: JOE CHASE

My father passed away, and my mother was not able to manage her affairs due to dementia. My parents were still living together after 60 years of marriage when my dad died. My mom lived alone at their home for several months, then moved into assisted living near me.

CASE STUDY: JOE CHASE

My mother was aware of her situation. We had to meet with the lawyer who had written their wills, and her stock broker. I had them broach the subject. There was no resistance. She knew she couldn't do it and trusted me. We'd had no other discussion of her wishes, other than cremation.

I brought my father's two-drawer file cabinet and the contents of their safety deposit box home and went through the contents. A small amount of consultation with the lawyer was necessary. I did as much as possible through the stockbroker. The hardest part was reading through two file drawers of material. The only unexpected resources I encountered were stocks my dad had bought independently of his broker. I gave the broker permission to do buying and selling of them.

Dad's trust and directions to his broker had pretty well taken care of setting financial goals. Their properties were divided into two trusts: one in her name and one in his estate. His was untouchable and set up as an income generator for her. Hers was to take care of her in any way necessary.

Little help was needed from the lawyer. The broker did the work to set up the two trusts. I was able to rely on my parents' long-term relationship with both. I did hire a CPA to do their taxes that, with two trusts and her personal taxes, were way over my head. I continued the files my dad had going, mostly keeping records of stock transformations. It wasn't really very hard. I created a couple of spreadsheets to track things, but they were my preference, not essential.

I kept their files in a separate file cabinet from my own. I also established checking accounts for the trusts, a personal checking account for my mother, and another for their home, which was transferred to my brother and me. I viewed this as doing what needed to be done. My friends and family saw more stress than I felt. The greater stress was dealing with my mother's dementia on a daily basis.

I moved my mother into assisted living near me as quickly as possible. That allowed me to visit her on a nearly daily basis. I kept her as informed as possible about what was going on, but the dementia limited the need and ability to do so.

My brother pressed me to become the trustee of the estate, even though he was older. The only serious disagreement was whether to sell the home, which had been deeded to us. I simply reminded that he had wanted me to be the trustee and that the decisions were mine. He reluctantly agreed. In retrospect, the process went fairly smoothly.

CASE STUDY: JOE CHASE

My mother has since passed away. Her last two and a half years were lonely, but the basic personality never changed. All who knew her spoke highly of her. My advice: You'll get through it. Keep good records. Have an accountant do their taxes, which avoids IRS red flags.

CASE STUDY: J. BRIAN VERCHOT

www.verchotbaxter.com
bverchot@verchotbaxter.com
205.970.5203 direct office
1.800.409.9476 toll-free
205.970.5240 fax

Brian Verchot is the founder of Verchot, Baxter & Associates LLP, a financial advisory firm in Birmingham, Alabama. His firm specializes in addressing concerns centered on retirement investing and legacy planning. He graduated from Birmingham-Southern College in 1991 and has been in the financial advisory business for 17 years.

J. Brian Verchot offers securities through AXA Advisors, LLC (NY, NY 10104) Member FINRA/SIPC and insurance and annuity products through AXA Network, LLC and its subsidiaries. Mr. Verchot's answers are for general informational purposes only and do not constitute a recommendation or advise. Neither AXA Advisors nor its employees give tax or legal advice. Please consult with your professional tax and legal advisors regarding your particular circumstances.

People may encounter resistance and reluctance from the parent when it comes to turning over control and being forthcoming with information about their finances. In most cases, the child(ren) will have to take the lead, assume the role of responsibility, and "sell" the parent(s) on how it benefits the family as a whole. It takes real commitment from the child(ren) to assume the role of financial caretaker.

Have the discussion with the parent(s) early on. For most families, when the parent(s) approaches retirement age is a good time to begin the dialogue. At that point in time, the parent(s) is thinking about financial matters; for example, Social Security, Medicare, company retirement plan, life insurance, long term care insurance, and so forth, so it is an easier time to initiate the discussion.

CASE STUDY: J. BRIAN VERCHOT

Write down all aspects of the parent(s)' financial situation: Safe deposit box location, who is on the signature card for it, long-term care insurance, medical insurance information, location of the will, medical directives, credit card and bank account information, and so forth.

Changes in past patterns relating to finance are always a good, early sign that discussions should be had: suddenly not paying bills on time, not being able to remember if bills have been paid, not being sure if a will, medical directive, or Power of Attorney has been written or its location.

In many cases, having the input or involvement of a professional can make the process easier on all family members. One can serve as "quarterback" of the situation, seeing things from a more objective point of view. This person or team becomes the trusted family advisor. Additionally, being a non-family member can make it easier for the reluctant parent(s) to open up.

Referrals are a great source for finding professionals. Ask friends and other family members whom they have used. There are financial advisors, CPAs, and attorneys who have a niche in this marketplace.

Many times, the child(ren) is tentative about making tough decisions. If the situation merits or warrants you stepping in, you are stepping in to not only make the easy decisions, but the tough ones, as well. Paying the bills may be easy, while deciding on health care matters and guardianship issues may not be. One must also understand that the responsibility is not to appease other members of the family, but to do what is in the best interest for the parent(s).

Sometimes, the wife is not given full disclosure by the husband and is unable to help in the process, discovering that one spouse was uninformed regarding household finances. Both spouses have to be well-informed prior to an adverse health event occurring. The non-disclosure can run the gamut from not knowing what the true debt picture is, not knowing if there is a survivorship benefit on retirement plans, what companies the insurances are with, and so forth.

No dollars there? This has happened within my own family. It takes having a very frank discussion about what the new financial reality is. Moreover, it takes more family guidance and collaboration because every decision comes with greater potential adverse consequence. Strict budgeting is a must.

The no. 1 regret expressed by the parents is that they did not open up and share with the family early on.

CASE STUDY: J. BRIAN VERCHOT

Second is not following through on their intentions to purchase long-term care insurance. It can provide tremendous financial and emotional relief knowing that certain expenses and needs can be provided for.

Additionally, having a professional in the relationship who can offer objective, third-party advice can be critical to the decision-making process.

Different people handle stress in different ways and can tolerate different levels; this is a very sensitive and personal issue. Whatever your threshold or method of handling stress (hobbies, meditation, medically, or spiritually) know when you need to take care of yourself. If you are an emotional wreck, you can't make good decisions, and you definitely can't take care of someone else. I have found that the more open the family has been about the parental financial situation, the better all parties handle the inevitable stress.

Stress heightens everyone's sensitivity. As family members, all want their opinion and thoughts to matter. Those opinions and thoughts are not always going to run parallel to one another. Again, having a professional, trusted advisor, involved can be critical to having uniformity in decisions and harmony in the family. As emotions enter the equation, rationality and objectivity tend to be diminished.

Before having the first conversation with your parent(s), be strong and be committed. You will need strength to deal with the stress and emotions that will come up. Your judgment may come into question, your motives may be questioned, and the person(s) you would least expect it from may question them. Those you think will provide support may not. Commitment needs to be there, as the process is rarely a short one, nor an easy one. Remembering that your parent(s) may need you to provide for them, as they provided for you when you could not, is a worthwhile mantra.

Glossary of Terms

A/B trust: A trust that allows your parents to split their estate and pass on the two halves separately, which can keep the halves small enough to avoid estate taxes.

Activities of daily living (ADL): Bathing, dressing, eating, taking medication, and other routine activities.

Adjustable rate mortgage: A mortgage where the rate adjusts every year.

Adult day care: A center that provides social involvement and activity to the elderly, and perhaps also some health services.

Agent: The person named by a power of attorney to handle health care, legal, and financial matters for someone else.

Annuity: Regular fixed payments provided by some forms of investments.

Assisted living facilities: Homes for people whose minds are still sharp but need some support with everyday activities.

Attorney-in-fact: The person named by a power of attorney to handle health care, legal, and financial matters for someone else.

Balloon mortgage: A mortgage that starts with low rates, then the entire loan amount becomes due.

Benchmarks: A set of stocks that track the performance of the whole stock market, or a specific sector, such as tech stocks.

Beneficiary: Someone who inherits under a will, or receives money from a trust or a life insurance policy.

Board and care homes: Group living for people who cannot live independently.

Break-even point: The point at which the savings from refinancing a mortgage have paid off all the lender's fees and closing costs.

CD: Certificates of deposit, which you buy for less than the face value, hold for a set period of time, then cash in at full value. The rate of return is higher than savings accounts.

Charitable remainder trust: Your parents donate their home to a charity in return for a lifetime annuity. Alternatively, your parents put money into a trust and collect a payment every month, then the remainder goes to charity at their deaths.

Community property: Property one spouse acquires during a marriage becomes 50 percent the property of the other spouse in community-property states.

Community spouse: The spouse of a nursing-home resident receiving Medicaid.

Comprehensive health care directive: A document that

combines a health care power of attorney with a living will.

Conservatee or ward: The incapacitated person for whom a conservatorship or guardianship has been established.

Conservator/guardian: Someone appointed by the court to act for an incapacitated or incompetent person, making either health care or financial decisions. The terms have different meaning in different states.

Co-payment: The amount insurers and Medicare will require you to pay for certain services, such as X-rays or doctor visits.

Continuing care community: A home that provides increasing levels of care as your parents age and require more help.

Custodial care: Help with daily activities such as bathing or eating, and some medical care, such as taking medicine or using eye drops.

Do-not-resuscitate order (DNR): A directive forbidding the use of CPR if someone's heart stops.

Durable power of attorney: A document by a principal authorizing an agent to make decisions on their behalf. A power of attorney can apply to financial and legal matters, or to health care decisions.

Estate: The assets a person leaves behind at death.

Estate taxes: Payable on estates if they exceed a certain dollar value at the time of death.

Executor: The individual named in a will who administers the estate during probate, makes sure taxes and debts are paid, and distributes the estate to the beneficiaries.

Fiduciary responsibility: The obligation of trustees and agents to use their authority for the good of the principal and not to enrich themselves.

Fixed income annuities: Issued by insurance companies, these investments pay back a sum every month after they are purchased.

401(k): A retirement account provided by employers. Employees pay no taxes on money placed in a 401(k) until they take it out at retirement. Employers may add matching funds to the account.

Guardian: Someone who has full authority over the health or financial decisions of another individual, whom the courts have decided cannot take care of themselves.

Health care advance directive: A comprehensive directive that combines a health care

power of attorney with a living will.

Health care power of attorney: A document signed by your parents giving you the authority to make medical decisions when they are incapacitated.

Health Insurance Portability and Accountability Act of 1996 (HIPAA): Federal legislation that limits the informal communication of information from doctors and other health care providers.

Home equity loans: Equity is the worth of a house minus the amount the owner owes on it. A home equity loan uses the equity as security for the loan.

Index funds: Funds holding a mix of stocks picked to match the performance of the stock market, so that investors in the fund will do as well as the market.

IRA: Individual retirement accounts that allow people to put money in and not pay taxes on it until they take it out at retirement.

Irrevocable trust: A trust that has terms and provisions that cannot be changed.

Joint tenancy: A form of ownership by two or more people. A joint checking account is a typical example.

Keogh account: A tax-exempt retirement account for self-employed people.

Life-care community: A home that provides increasing levels of care as your parents age and require more help.

Life estate: Selling a home while retaining the right to live in it until death.

Life tenancy: Selling a home to a buyer who leases it back, guaranteeing that the seller can live there until death.

Living trust: A trust created while your parents are alive that controls some or all of their assets.

Living will: A document that spells out what medical care your parents will accept if they are incapacitated or incompetent.

Long-term care insurance: Private insurance that, depending on the terms of the policy, can pay for home care, care in an assisted-living facility, or a skilled nursing facility.

Marital deduction and bypass trust: A trust that allows your parents to split their estate and pass on the two halves separately, which can keep the halves small enough to avoid estate taxes.

Medicaid: A state and federally financed program that provides medical care to low income people.

Medicare: A federal program providing medical coverage for persons who are 65 years old or disabled.

Medicare savings programs: Aid programs that help some low-income individuals cover Medicare's premiums and co-pays.

Medigap: Insurance that covers the gaps in Medicare, such as the deductible.

Miller's trust: A trust that pays your parents a small enough monthly income that they qualify for Medicaid.

Money market mutual funds: Safe, short-term investments that pay less than CDs but more than savings accounts.

Multilevel care community: A home that provides increasing levels of care as your parents age and require more help.

Notice of noncoverage: Advance notice that a hospital or nursing facility intends to send a Medicare patient home.

Nursing home: A facility that provides your parents with room, board, and custodial care. It may provide a high-enough level of nursing care to qualify as a Medicaid skilled-nursing facility.

Nursing-home spouse: The spouse living in a nursing home with Medicaid support.

Peer review organization (PRO): A body of medical professionals reviewing the quality of care delivered to patients.

Power of attorney: A document in which someone authorizes an agent to make legal or medical decisions on their behalf.

Power of attorney subject to disability: A power of attorney that kicks in when the principal is disabled or incapacitated.

Principal: The person who signs a power of attorney, authorizing an agent to make decisions on their behalf.

Probate: The court proceeding which oversees the administration of a deceased person's estate, whether he or she has a will or not.

Quality Improvement Organization: A group of health professionals employed by the federal government to review and improve the care provided by Medicare.

Reverse-annuity mortgage: A reverse mortgage that keeps paying your parents' money, even if they no longer live in the home.

Reverse mortgage: A lender takes money out of the equity in a home and pays it back to your parents in monthly installments.

Revocable Living Trust: A device that describes certain property, names a trustee (who manages the property), and names a beneficiary who receives benefit from the trust. A living trust is an effective means of avoiding probate and providing for management of assets. It can be revoked by the person who created it during that person's lifetime.

Roth IRA: An individual retirement account that offers your parents no tax advantage now, but they can withdraw the money tax-free in retirement tax.

Sales leaseback: A life tenancy.

Skilled nursing facility: A facility that provides the services of licensed nurses or physical rehabilitation specialists who provide patients with services such as intravenous injections or speech therapy.

Springing power of attorney: A power of attorney that only functions when a preset condition is met. A power of attorney subject to disability is a good example.

Supplemental Security Income (SSI): A federal program that provides cash assistance to the aged, blind, and disabled who have limited income and resources.

Supportive Housing for the Elderly: A federal program that provides studio and one-bedroom apartments for seniors who can still function independently.

Testamentary trust: A trust that receives some of your parents property at their death. Testamentary trusts do not escape probate, but they can be used to control how the estate is distributed to your parents' heirs.

Testator: The person who writes a will.

Totten trust: A trust that invests money for funeral expenses.

TRICARE: A health care program for the military, veterans, and their families.

Viatical settlement provider: A company that pays your parents a percentage of the face value of their life insurance, in return for the rights to all proceeds when they die.

Will: A legal document directing the disposition of property, which is to be operable at the time of death of the person who created the document.

Resources

Finding help:

Eldercare Locator: 1-800-677-1116 or **www.eldercare.gov**

Information and links to support groups

The National Alliance of Caregiving
www.caregiver.org

The Family Caregiver Alliance
www.thesandwichgeneration.com

Credit reports:
www.ftc.gov/credit

Equifax: 1-800-525-6285
www.equifax.com

Experian: 1-888-397-3742
www.experian.com

TransUnion, 1-800-680-7289
www.transunion.com

For researching a move:

Places Rated Almanac: The Classic Guide for Finding Your Best Places to Live in America (Places Rated) by David Savageau

Calculating retirement expenses:

http://moneycentral.msn.com/personal-finance/calculators/
Retirement_Income_Calculator/home.aspx
www.irs.gov/retirement/participant/article/0,,id=151786,00.html

Appraising attorneys:

www.lawyers.com
www.martindale.com

Medicare

www.medicare.gov

Medicaid

www.cms.hhs.gov

Elder care

www.eldercare.gov

The government's Administration on Aging

www.aoa.gov

Extra help

www.unclaimedretirementbenefits.com
www.benefitscheckup.org
www.donotcall.gov.

Bibliography

Here are some additional books on financing, investing, retirement, and elder care you might find of use:

Aging Parents and Common Sense. AXA Consumer Insight Series, New York, NY (1996).

The American Bar Association Legal Guide for Americans Over 50. Random House, New York, NY (2006).

Carnot, Edward J. *Is Your Parent in Good Hands?* Capitol Books, Herndon, VA (2004).

Garrett, Sheryl. *Just Give Me The Answer$.* Dearborn Trade Publishing, Chicago, IL (2004).

Garrett, Sheryl. *On The Road: Caring for an Aging Parent.* Dearborn Financial Publishing, Chicago, IL (2006).

Garrett, Sheryl. *On The Road: Planning an Estate*. Dearborn Financial Publishing, Chicago, IL (2006).

Hamm, Allen. *Long-Term Care Planning*. Plan Ahead, Inc., USA (2007).

Heiser, K. Gabriel. *How to Protect Your Family's Assets from Devastating Nursing Home Costs*. Phylius Press, Superior, CO (2008).

"Miles Away: The MetLife Study of Long Distance Caregiving." MetLife Mature Market Institute, New York, NY (2004)

Newman, Brenda Watson and Benna, Ted. *401(k)s for Dummies*. Wiley Publishing, Indianapolis, IN (2008).

Palermo, Michael. *AARP Crash Course in Estate Planning*. Sterling Publishing, New York, NY (2005).

Randall, Richard L. and Overdorft, Scot W. *Ways and Means*. Esperti Peterson Institute Incorporated, Denver, CO. (1999).

Tyson, Eric and Brown, Ray. *House Selling for Dummies*. Wiley Publishing, Indianapolis, IN (2008).

Weisman, Steve. *Boomer or Bust*. Prentice Hall, Upper Saddle River, NJ (2006).

Weisman, Steve. *The Truth About Avoiding Scams*. FT Press, Upper Saddle River, NJ (2008).

Zukerman, Rachelle. *Eldercare for Dummies*. Wiley Publishing, Indianapolis, IN (2003).

Index

Q

R

S

T

V

Praise for *The Warrior Diet*

"Nothing tugs at your purse strings like the promise of a fat-burning miracle, but let's face it: the weight-loss industry is $35 billion fat, and sometimes it seems that the only thing getting thinner is our wallets. Well, we've had it. We've spent the entire year searching, researching, tasting, and testing so you don't have to waste precious time or money. We're so convinced that we've found 2002's 25 best (the fastest, easiest, cheapest, and most effective) get-fit solutions, that we are awarding them a prize.... FIRST'S first annual Slimmys for weight-loss excellence. When it comes to diets, we weed the godsends from the gimmicks and give you the very best every issue. But our pick for best of the best? The Slimmy goes to ... the Warrior Diet."

—*First For Women* magazine, December 2002

"Women everywhere are raving about the super-effective 'warrior' diet—eating lightly during the day, feasting after dark, and losing weight at record speeds."

—*Woman's World,* November 2002

"An original, distinctive, and highly satisfying diet plan, the Warrior Diet is meant especially for those who pursue an active lifestyle."

—*Midwest Book Review*

"In my quest for a lean, muscular body, I have seen practically every diet and suffered through most of them. It is also my business to help others with their fat-loss programs. I am supremely skeptical of any eating plan or 'diet' book that can't tell me how and why it works in simple language. Ori Hofmekler's *The Warrior Diet* does just this, with a logical, readable approach that provides grounding for his claims and never asks the reader to take a leap of faith. *The Warrior Diet* can be a very valuable weapon in the personal arsenal of any woman."

—DC MAXWELL, two-time Women's Brazilian Jiu-Jitsu World Champion;
Co-Owner, Maxercise Sports/Fitness Training Center
and Relson Gracie Jiu-Jitsu Academy East

"I refuse to graze all day, I have better things to do. I choose *The Warrior Diet.*"

—PAVEL TSATSOULINE, author of *Power to the People!*
and *The Russian Kettlebell Challenge*

"In a era of decadence, where wants and desires are virtually limitless, Ori's vision recalls an age of warriors, where success meant survival and survival was the only option. A diet of the utmost challenge from which users will reap tremendous benefits."

—JOHN DAVIES, Olympic and professional sports strength/speed coach

"The credo that has served me well in my life and that which I tell my patients is that I only take advice from those who practice what they preach. To me, there is nothing more pathetic and laughable than to see the terrible physical condition of many of the self-proclaimed diet and fitness experts of today. Those hypocrites who do not live by their own words are not worth your time, or mine.

"At the other extreme, Ori Hofmekler is the living, breathing example of a warrior. There is real strength in the sinews of his muscle. There is wisdom and power in his words. His passion for living honestly is intense and reflective of the toil of a tough army life. Yet in a fascinating and true Spartan way, his physical nature is tempered by an equal reveling in the love of art, knowledge of the classic poets, and in the drinking of fine wine with good conversation.

"Welcome *The Warrior Diet* into your life and you usher in the honest and real values of a man who has truly walked the walk. He has tread the dirt of the path that lies before you, and is thus a formidable guide to a new beginning. He is your shepherd of integrity that will lead you out of the bondage of misinformation. His approach is what I call 'revolutionarily de-evolutionary.' In other words, your freedom from excess body fat, flat energy levels, and poor physical performance begins with unlearning the modern ways, which have failed you, and forging a new understanding steeped in the secret traditions of the ancient Roman warrior."

—CARLON M. COLKER, MD, FACN, author of
The Greenwich Diet; CEO and Medical Director, Peak Wellness, Inc.

"*The Warrior Diet* certainly defies so-called modern nutritional and training dogmas. Having met Ori on several occasions, I can certainly attest that he is the living proof that his system works. He maintains a ripped muscular body year round despite juggling extreme workloads and family life. His take on supplementation is refreshing, as he promotes an integrated and timed approach. *The Warrior Diet* is a must-read for the nutrition and training enthusiast who wishes to expand his horizons."

—CHARLES POLIQUIN, author of *The Poliquin Principles* and
Modern Trends in Strength Training; three-time Olympic Strength Coach

"Ori Hofmekler has his finger on a deep, ancient, and very visceral pulse—one that too many of us have all but forgotten. Part warrior-athlete, part philosopher-romantic, Ori not only reminds us what this innate, instinctive rhythm is all about, he also shows us how to detect and rekindle it in our own bodies. His program challenges and guides each of us to fully reclaim for ourselves the strength, sinew, energy, and spirit that humans have always been meant to possess."

—PILAR GERASIMO, Editor in Chief, *Experience Life* magazine

"I think of myself as a modern-day warrior: businessman, family man, and competitive athlete. In the two years that I have been following the Warrior Diet, I have enjoyed the predators' advantage of freedom from the necessity of frequent feedings. I also benefit from the competitive edge of being a fat-burning machine. My twelve-year-old son, who is also a competitive athlete, has naturally gravitated towards the Warrior Diet. He is growing up lean, strong, and healthy, unlike many of his peers, who even in this land of plenty are overweight and frequently sick. Thank you, Ori, for writing *The Warrior Diet*."

—STEPHEN MAXWELL, MS; two-time Brazilian Jiu-Jitsu
World Champion; Co-Owner, Maxercise Sports/Fitness
Training Center and Relson Gracie Jiu-Jitsu Academy East

"At a certain age, I began to notice a change in my pre-competition training. The intense physical stress I put my body under started to leave me feeling burnt out after my work-outs. I also suffered from frequent sugar crashes due to my hypoglycemia. I would become irritated, light-headed, and physically weak. I often became angry after train-ing, and I could not explain why. I was having a difficult time trying to figure out what and when to eat. This became a serious problem. When competing on an international level, proper diet and training are the bare necessities for peak performance. Upon meeting Ori, I was advised on what and when to eat. Once I modified my diet, my energy levels changed immediately. I was able to work harder throughout my workouts. I no longer felt total fatigue after training. Ori and I are of one mind when it comes to func-tional training. In martial arts you must train every aspect of movement in order to perform well. Ori's advice had a direct effect on the way I trained for my two interna-tional titles this year. The information in *The Warrior Diet* will help you achieve the next level in training for the twenty-first century. It is the physical training along with the diet that will make a lasting impact on your life. I am deeply grateful for Ori's advice and the friendship we have established over the years."

—SIFU JOHN R. SALGADO, World Champion,
Chinese Wrestling and Taiji Push Hands

"Despite its name, *The Warrior Diet* isn't about leading a Spartan lifestyle, although it is about improving quality of life. With a uniquely compelling approach, the book guides you towards the body you want by re-awakening primal instinct and biofeedback—the things that have allowed us to evolve this far. Ironically, in a comfortable world of overindulgence, your survival may still be determined by natural selection. If this is the case, *The Warrior Diet* will be the only tool you'll need."

—BRIAN BATCHELDOR, science writer/researcher;
National Coach, British Powerlifting Team

"Ori and I became friends and colleagues in 1997 when he so graciously took me under his wing as a writer for *Penthouse* magazine and *Mind and Muscle Power*. When I received *The Warrior Diet* in the mail I nearly burst with pride. Not only because my dear friend had finally reached his particular goal of helping others be the best they can be physically, but because I had a small role in the creation of the book. Ori enlisted my help in researching topics such as the benefits of fasting, the perfect protein, and glycogen loading. I believe in Ori's concepts because I trust him wholeheartedly and because I helped uncover the scientific data that proves them. I also live by *The Warrior Diet*, although not to the extreme that Ori does. My body continues to get tighter and more toned in all of the right places . . . and people marvel at my eating practices.

"Read *The Warrior Diet* with an open mind. Digest the information at your own pace. Assimilate the knowledge to make it fit into your current lifestyle. You will be amazed at how much more productive and energetic you will be. Be a warrior in your own right. Your body will thank you for it."

—LAURA MOORE, science writer, *Penthouse* magazine,
IronMan Magazine's Body of the Month for IronMan, September 2001;
Radio Talk Show Host, *The Health Nuts*; author of *Sex Heals*

THE
WARRIOR
DIET

OTHER BOOKS BY ORI HOFMEKLER

Hofmekler's People
Hofmekler's Gallery
The Anti-Estrogenic Diet
Maximum Muscle, Minimum Fat (2008)

THE
WARRIOR
DIET

Switch on Your Biological Powerhouse– For High Energy, Explosive Strength, and a Leaner, Harder Body

ORI HOFMEKLER

BLUE SNAKE BOOKS
BERKELEY, CALIFORNIA

Published by Blue Snake Books
Blue Snake Books' publications are distributed by
North Atlantic Books
P.O. Box 12327
Berkeley, California 94712

Interior photographs by Don Pitlik and
 Rick Osborn (CFT Photos)
Cover and book design by Suzanne Albertson

Printed in the United States of America

Blue Snake Books' publications are available through most bookstores. For further information, call 800-337-2665 or visit our websites at www.northatlanticbooks.com or www.bluesnakebooks.com.

Substantial discounts on bulk quantities are available to corporations, professional associations, and other organizations. For details and discount information, contact our special sales department.

The Warrior Diet: Switch on Your Biological Powerhouse—For High Energy, Explosive Strength, and a Leaner, Harder Body, Second Edition is sponsored by the Society for the Study of Native Arts and Sciences, a nonprofit educational corporation whose goals are to develop an educational and crosscultural perspective linking various scientific, social, and artistic fields; to nurture a holistic view of arts, sciences, humanities, and healing; and to publish and distribute literature on the relationship of mind, body, and nature.

PLEASE NOTE: The creators and publishers of this book are not and will not be responsible, in any way whatsoever, for any improper use made by anyone of the information contained in this book. All use of the aforementioned information must be made in accordance with what is permitted by law, and any damage liable to be caused as a result thereof will be the exclusive responsibility of the user. In addition, he or she must adhere strictly to the safety rules contained in the book, both in training and in actual implementation of the information presented herein. This book is intended for use in conjunction with ongoing lessons and personal training with an authorized expert. It is not a substitute for formal training. It is the sole responsibility of every person planning to train in the techniques described in this book to consult a licensed physician in order to obtain complete medical information on his or her personal ability and limitations. The instructions and advice printed in this book are not in any way intended as a substitute for medical, mental, or emotional counseling with a licensed physician or healthcare provider.

Library of Congress Cataloging-in-Publication Data

Hofmekler, Ori, 1952–
      Warrior diet : switch on your biological powerhouse for high energy, explosive strength, and a leaner, harder body / Ori Hofmeckler. — 2nd ed.
      Warrior diet : switch on your biological powerhouse for high energy, explosive strength, and a leaner, harder body / Ori Hofmeckler. — 2nd ed.
            p. cm.
      Includes bibliographical references and index.
      ISBN 978-1-58394-200-0 (trade paper)
1. Nutrition. 2. Food habits. 3. Circadian rhythms. 4. Weight loss. 5. Physical fitness. I. Title.
RA784.H575 2007
613.2'5—dc22   2007038652

2 3 4 5 6 7 8 9 Data 14 13 12 11 10 09 08 07

DEDICATION

In loving memory of my parents Rina and Daniel Hofmekler, I'd like to dedicate this book to my sons Nehemiah and Daniel, to my daughters Nadia and Shira, to their grandparents Ronald and Josephine, and especially to their most beautiful mother, my wife Natasha.

TABLE OF CONTENTS

ACKNOWLEDGMENTS

I'd like to thank my family, especially my wife Natasha, for all her loving care and advice.

In moments of truth you know who your real friends are. I want to thank Zvika Elgat, the godfather of my son Nehemiah, for his friendship and support. I want to thank my friend Billi Rosenzweig for his honesty and generosity. I also would like to acknowledge Erich Bumgardner for his persistent encouragement and true friendship.

I'd like to thank Diana Holtzberg for helping me edit me the first edition of this book. I also want to acknowledge Karen McCorkle for her professional contribution. A special thanks to my literary agent Bill Stranger for his commitment to this project.

I owe thanks to a few others who took part in creating this book project: Marc Salzman for his ongoing professional support, Gary Choma and Rick Osborn for their awesome creative contributions, and Barry Bragg and Barry Seneri for being great warriors and mentors to their community.

I'd like to acknowledge the late Bill Lauren, who initially offered to assist me with the writing of *The Warrior Diet*. Bill was a wonderful writer, and it was my privilege to have worked with him on a health column that I used to edit. I'd like to acknowledge Linda Gail for her genius talent and incredible support.

I'd also like to thank all those that follow the Warrior Diet, who send me streams of letters telling me of their progress and testifying that the Warrior Diet really works.

Finally, as strange as it sounds, I'd like to acknowledge my cat Junior. Watching him always gives me inspiration—for his modeling of grace, agility, and instinctual power.

—Ori Hofmekler, 2007

FOREWORD

By Harvey Diamond, author of *Fit For Life*

I met Ori Hofmekler a couple of years ago in a Japanese restaurant. It stunned me how much he ate that night. I had never seen anyone so lean eat like that. At the time, he was editor in chief of *Mind & Muscle POWER* magazine. I had known of Ori's art for quite a while. His political satirical paintings always struck me as unique, bold, and thought-provoking. They are often very funny. His images have stuck in my mind for years. To quote the late, great Joseph Heller, author of *Catch-22* and numerous other classics: "Ori Hofmekler is a painter of great merit with tremendous wit, intelligence, and imagination. He is better at satirical political art than any other artist I know of at this time. His work deserves to be much better known and more widely enjoyed and treasured."

Breaking taboos, exposing lies, and punching holes in political "balloons" are all essential qualities for strong, effective satire. Real satire makes us laugh every time we're shown the naked (and often ugly) truth.

The Warrior Diet isn't satirical art, but the uncompromising integrity of its creator is evidenced here as well. This book is about the art of raw living. I find the concept of *The Warrior Diet* unique, and although it's quite controversial, I believe it will create a revolution in people's lives. *The Warrior Diet* triggers and unleashes primal instincts within us, many of which have been inhibited or dulled. It endorses virtues such as feeling a sense of freedom, alertness, and possessing optimum mental and physical strength. It also redefines what it means to be a warrior, to be tough, and to be romantic. In other words, this isn't just a diet. It's a way of life, a renaissance of the spirit of raw living. Ori and I share a similar vision. We both believe that detoxification activates a natural self-healing process and should, therefore, be a top priority.

We both believe that there is a wisdom deep within us all that can guide us to live better, healthier lives. We both agree that consuming live [raw] foods and live enzymes is essential for your health, and it affects the way you feel. While we naturally have our differences, they do not detract in any way from the overall effectiveness of Ori's approach. Besides, all you have to do is meet Ori and you will quickly see that the man is definitely onto something.

While reading Ori's *The Warrior Diet,* I realized that it all makes sense. Concepts such as the Warrior Cycle, the energy cycle—and his explanation of the interplay between materialism and dematerialism—shed new light on how we operate around the circadian clock. Time is an essential factor in the Warrior Diet. Ori calls this "the lost dimension," since the concept of time and cycles doesn't play an important role in most other diets. (My original *Fit For Life* book was based on the circadian clock.)

"Unleashing the power of your instincts" is a refrain that appears through-out the book. Ori is at his fascinating best when discussing our human primal instincts, be it the hunter/predator instinct versus the scavenger instinct, the instincts to survive and multiply, or the romantic instinct. Ori demonstrates how each instinct connects to the other and how they all relate to the Warrior Instinct.

This book is akin to a new "manifesto." It covers all aspects of life, including the instinctual connection between food and sex—a connection that penetrates to the core of human existence. Beyond all the unique and intriguing philosophy, vision, and ideas set forth, there is a very clearly defined diet here that I find to be most effective. "Lessons from History" explains how the Warrior Diet is based on the old traditions of ancient warriors, yet has been updated to be effective for the modern world. It's designed to allow for creativity and individuality, so you can follow its principles in your own unique way. I find this diet to be as effective for women as it is for men, in spite of all the macho references. As a final note, I believe strongly in "what you see is what you get." Ori is living proof that the Warrior Diet works.

FOREWORD

By Udo Erasmus, author of *Fats That Heal, Fats That Kill*

*T*he *Warrior Diet* is an unusual book. It is a book without measurements, but with feeling. A book that encourages you to break rules to find passion. A book not written by academics who analyze everything, but by someone who trusts life and questions stupidity, and encourages you to do the same. This alone is reason to read *The Warrior Diet.*

Something in you already knows a lot about how you should live. Find, and listen to, and trust that instinct, author Ori Hofmekler tells you.

Experts have a nasty tendency to make what's natural and simple more complicated. They make their living by collecting rent on the insecurity they create by undermining your common sense. To do that, they snow you with big words.

In that regard, luckily for you, Ori is not an expert. He encourages you to live by an inner wisdom born of 3.5 billion years of development of creatures made from food and for activity—survival, reproduction, discovery, and joy.

You are endowed with a genetic program that knows how to build a healthy body. Do not poison that program with toxic synthetic manmade molecules that have never been present in nature. Provide it with the building blocks it needs to build that body. How do you do that? Without getting technical, Ori encourages you to get there through interesting information, through tasty recipes for health, through exercise, through lifestyle, through ways of thinking, and through calling the sleeping warrior within you to awaken. *Some of my favorite topics:*

- Ori's description of the daily sympathetic-parasympathetic rhythm: light food during the day, when energy goes to external pursuits; the big meal in the evening, relaxation with friends, when the day's work is done.

I love the simple logic of it, and it works in practice. Do big meals during the day make you feel lazy? Does light food during waking hours keep you from getting tired while you need alertness for work? Does eating when you're hungry make food taste better? While you read, ask yourself such questions.

- The Warrior Instinct. Whatever you call it, this instinct within us is more reliable than thousands of half-baked rules imposed by half-alive, double-blind theoreticians. Rules serve the need to control, but most are out of line with your need for freedom to discover the truths of your own life.

Your life is a warrior's path. Whether it is to hunt for food, protect your family, village, or country, or to conquer lies and establish truth, the full life has always been a warrior's life.

The warrior's life involves goals. It has commitment. There is passion. It is heart-felt. It is conscious. You use your creativity. You question, and you build.

A warrior's life gives expression to the basic, in-built striving to get better. Its confidence comes not from memorizing but from doing, observing, examining, arguing, learning, and improving. It is not nine to five, but goes an extra mile or an extra hour, inspired to accomplish goals because they are worthwhile.

- Romanticism: it is much more than a way to get other people to satisfy your sexual urges. It includes that, but also all that you do with passion and care for life.

Rare in books about foods, there is wisdom in the pages of *The Warrior Diet*. Technicians write most food books, and Ori knows the techniques, but he shows you a possibility—a platform for living your life as well.

Ori's style is easygoing. His sense of history is interesting. His psychology is common sense. His stories are simple and they flow. He is flexible and learns from all his activities. He does not judge.

Ori talks about food, about ambience, about activity (exercise), about friendship, about lifestyle, about romanticism, and he provides some great recipes.

The Warrior Diet is a book that talks to all of you—the whole person hidden inside. Read the book, think about what he says, try it, find out how it works for you, argue with him if you want, and discover more of who you are.

AUTHOR'S PREFACE

I've been practicing the Warrior Diet on and off for many years. During this time I've discovered that being on the Warrior Diet has made me more energetic, alert, instinctive, ambitious, and in control than those times when I have been off the diet. My metabolism has accelerated to the point that I find it difficult to keep my weight from dropping. I'm naturally lean. I don't count calories, and I eat as much as I want of all the food groups: protein, fat, and carbohydrates. When sitting at dinner with friends or family, I used to apologize in advance for the amount of food that I consume. A few still think that something must be wrong with me, but by now most of my friends and even some family members also practice the Warrior Diet. I've heard people say, "How can anyone eat so much late at night and still be so lean?" or "It's all genetics," "He is crazy," or "Ori, how come everyone is finished and you're still eating?" I've noticed that those who are on weight-loss diets usually enjoy watching others who can eat unlimited amounts of food. For them, it's a vicarious experience—a dream come true.

Since "The Warrior Diet" column began running in *Mind & Muscle Power* magazine, many who have read it, or just heard about it from others, have been trying to jump in, often without enough knowledge or information. I've been blitzed with so many letters and phone calls from people who want advice or guidance that it became impossible to answer everyone. That is why I've written this book. Reading it should guide you to practice the Warrior Diet on your own. This is not just a diet. It's a way of life. It involves your body and mind, and gives you a sense of freedom—a sense that, in my opinion, many people lack today.

I hope you will find this book intriguing enough to try practicing my diet plan. If you do, I believe that you'll notice significant changes in the way you look and feel, and even in the way you think. It may, in short, change your life.

Those who want information regarding specific food and supplements will find it in the "Undereating Phase," "Overeating Phase," and "Warrior Meals and Recipes" chapters. The historical component of this book, "Lessons from History," is limited to basic research that shows how the Warrior Diet is actually based on a very old tradition, yet is still quite relevant, pertinent, and practical for the twenty-first century.

Life is a struggle. You either win or lose. For a warrior, survival is just not good enough. Warriors want to win. To be a warrior, you don't need a war. All you need is the spirit, which is hidden inside you. This spirit is what I call the "Warrior Instinct." Once unleashed, it will guide you to greater health and your own sense of freedom. And nothing tastes sweeter than freedom.

INTRODUCTION TO
THE SECOND EDITION

Since the initial publication of *The Warrior Diet* in 2002, I have received numerous testimonials with enthusiastic reports on fat loss, increased energy, improvements in health conditions, and increased feelings of well-being. Nonetheless, I've been routinely addressing requests for consultation coming from readers who love *The Warrior Diet* but yet have been confused as to how to fully take advantage of its principles and apply them for various needs and lifestyles. I've also learned that some people have misinterpreted the applications of the diet's eating cycle.

This revised edition of *The Warrior Diet* incorporates lots of new information that I hope will clear common misunderstandings and help address different needs.

The Warrior Diet principles haven't changed; nonetheless, a large part of the text was adjusted and re-edited in order to elucidate the various applications of the diet.

Overall, the new edition expands in areas that have drawn the most interest. These include topics such as stubborn fat, male potency, female disorders, physical performance, and sport nutrition.

Statistically, all current diets virtually fail to help people lose weight or sustain health in the long run. People today are getting more and more skeptical of dieting. The current epidemics of obesity, diabetes, hypertension, and sterility bear witness to the fact that something is wrong in the way people are dieting.

I believe the Warrior Diet is the right alternative. Based on science, epidemiology, and real life experience, it provides viable solutions while applying critical elements that are missing in other diets. As controversial as it may appear, the Warrior Diet has been endorsed by health experts, researchers, champion athletes, coaches, military instructors, soldiers, policemen and firemen, as well as men and women of all ages and different ethnic groups.

Recent studies (2003) on intermittent fasting by Dr. Mark Mattson and colleagues at the National Institute on Aging have caught the attention of researchers worldwide as to the awesome biological benefits of feeding cycles, similar to those featured in the Warrior Diet.

There are many speculations as to how humans should eat and live. More studies are needed to clarify these issues. Nonetheless, there is emerging evidence that humans have primarily adapted to better survive on certain feeding cycles, foods, and exercise. Some researchers speculate that the question isn't how beneficial these elements are for our survival, but rather how damaging it would be without them.

The Warrior Diet's goal is to reintroduce and restore the way people are supposed to eat and exercise and thus help people today live in the way that they're predestined to live. I hope you'll enjoy this book.

—Ori Hofmekler, 2007

INTRODUCTION

I'm about to commit dietary heresy. What I'm about to propose will cause an army of doctors, nutritionists, and self-proclaimed dietary experts to wail and gnash their teeth. They'll call me ignorant. They'll read about my revolutionary diet plan—one that can create a society of lean, muscular, modern warriors—and they'll smack their foreheads as they dismiss all my theories. No matter.

It's always been that way since the dawn of civilization. Whenever something revolutionary is proposed, society is loathe to accept it. Picasso dealt with it and eventually won. Einstein grappled with it and came out on top. So did thousands of others throughout history. I'm not putting myself in their class, but regardless, they give me inspiration.

The Warrior Diet is unlike any other modern diet plan. Every other modern eating plan is based on restraint. You count calories; you're careful about fat intake; you avoid carbohydrates. They tell you not to overeat or undereat. Well, I'm here to tell you that it doesn't have to be that way. The Warrior Diet is simple, effective, and ultimately, instinctual. It involves using the body's innate ability to burn fat and build muscle through the release of natural hormones and other growth factors. It doesn't involve any drugs. And it breaks all the rules. But that's what warriors do—they break the rules and shallow-minded restrictions placed on them by society.

Given that this mode of eating is so different from anything you've probably considered, I feel it necessary to offer some background before you learn the simple facts behind the Warrior Diet. After all, to accept anything merely on faith would be patently "un-warrior-like."

Ancient Warriors vs. Modern Man

About ten thousand years ago, modern man reached his current state of evolution. At that point his body, his genes, and his instincts pretty much reached their peak. The main thing that's really changed since then is how we now live—in a much more crowded, civilized world. Initially we had to live by our instincts. Now they've been all but choked out of us. There's a reason, of course: following one's natural instincts is often dangerous to society. You can't very well let people go around doing every and anything they please.

In other words, in order to control people you have to control their most primitive instincts or desires.

Still, there are those who break rules. They are the true romantics of the world. They are the spiritual warriors, and their actions often change the way we all live. Children start out as such romantics, but this instinct is usually beaten out of them by the time they reach adulthood. Consequently, there are very few modern warriors. Thousands of years ago, these warriors were common. They lived entirely by instincts. In fact, whole societies were made up of warriors. They spent their days defending their lives and their families' lives. They moved from place to place, never stopping long enough to settle down. Generally, they only sat down to eat one meal a day, and that was always at night after the battles had been fought. Consequently, their bodies were lean and hard, and their instincts were honed to perfection.

You can even see these body types illustrated in ancient art. If you take a look at examples of Minoan art, the people depicted are lean, muscular, and heroic-looking. So, too, were the ancient Greeks and Romans. They were nomadic, eating one meal a day—mostly seasonal fresh food, meats, fish, legumes and whole grains, olive oil, and wine. However, if you look a little farther south to Egypt, long-revered for their magnificent civilization, you see something altogether different. Much of their art depicts a people very soft, almost feminine. The difference? They weren't nomads; they instead settled down and farmed the land. They had fewer battles to fight. They were a "rich" society, and consequently many of it members lived an aristocratic life, eating many meals throughout the day, much of which consisted of refined wheat and other grains, breads, and cakes.

The early Roman and Greek art reflected a warrior race. Soon after, though, decadence set in and they began living much the same way as modern man: with frequent meals, a sedentary life, and dulled instincts. Predictably they began to look like modern man and suffer the same ailments. (Until Nero, there wasn't one emperor who was obese.)

Clearly, the dietary habits of civilized modern man are very, very different from those of the ancient warrior. Civilized man lives largely off refined grains; eats often; and is reluctant to engage in intense physical pursuits.

Contrast that with the warrior who consumed fresh, seasonal, and fermented food; ate sparingly during the day but filled himself up at night; and toiled during the day. Civilized man has grown fat, and much of his unused muscle has atrophied. He lives by the clock, eating at predetermined times. The warrior, however, remained lean, hard, and muscular, living off his instincts and eating when necessary or when the workday was done.

One Meal A Day

By now you've probably gotten an inkling of what kind of eating plan I've practiced for years and the one that's the subject of this book. The gist of the Warrior Diet is to eat a meal only once a day, preferably at night, and without any restriction of calories or macronutrient content.

It involves retraining the body and the mind. If you try it for a few weeks, I maintain that your hunger will diminish during the day. And when you eat at night, you'll know exactly what to eat and how much to eat. Your body may, in fact, tell you to eat a considerable amount—no matter, listen to it. During the day you'll likely want to nibble on things. This is okay, as long as your snack consists of fresh vegetables, fruits, and a little protein if desired, and doesn't include carbohydrates like breads or grains.

Yes, this runs against current theory. Yes, it runs against modern-day common sense. But there's a body of science to support it. We already know that exercising on an empty stomach supports our sympathetic nervous system and promotes more weight loss than if we had eaten beforehand. This diet guarantees you several hours a day of fat-burning hormones percolating through your body.

During these daily hours your body is at a peak capacity to remove toxins and generate energy, while staying alert, resisting fatigue and stress. Long periods of undereating increase protein efficiency. If you refrain from eating large amounts of protein at arbitrary times, your body will become more efficient at recycling proteins, so when you do eat protein, it'll be utilized much more efficiently. Not eating for long periods also improves insulin sensitivity, so when you do eat, your blood sugar doesn't fluctuate wildly and your body won't store the carbohydrate calories as fat.

The list of potential benefits is staggering. Taking in certain types of protein on an empty stomach can increase testosterone levels and growth hormone levels, and you can't do that on a full stomach. Long periods of fasting also allow certain beneficial amino acids to act favorably on the brain. How many conventional diets do that? Naysayers might argue that the body needs large reserves of glycogen to compete in athletic events. This may be true, but the Warrior Diet trains the body to stretch glycogen reserves so that athletic endurance doesn't become a problem. Others might point out that this type of diet may induce the production of the catabolic hormone cortisol, which may have negative effects on muscle growth and fat deposition. Ordinarily, yes, but this diet is not about water fasting. By ingesting the right nutrients during the Undereating Phase you will be able to block the cortisol effect.

Just to make sure we're on the same page, let's recap the essentials of the Warrior Diet. The main "trick" is to retrain your body; teach it to become more instinctive. You can do this by avoiding most foods during the day, although I do recommend that you eat vegetables and fruits (mainly as freshly squeezed juices). It's also okay to have a little protein during the day, such as eggs, cheese, yogurt, or high quality whey. As you get used to eating this way, your cravings should disappear. And once you're done "fighting the battles" of the day, you can eat as much protein, vegetables, and carbs as you want—even if it means eating the equivalent of three meals in one seating.

The Warrior Diet Advantage

Make no mistake about it. This is not a three-week program or "get in shape for summer" plan. It is a lifestyle. As you continue to do it, hunger pangs during the day will likely disappear. Simultaneously, you'll find yourself getting leaner and more muscular. Furthermore, your thoughts should become clearer and more focused. You will, in short, become a warrior.

Remember, genetically we humans are hunter/gatherers, as are predators in the forest. Wild animals, which practice "free feeding," stay lean and athletic, but when you put them in captivity they begin to eat like most modern human beings—nonstop. Their natural instincts wane and so they eat and eat, and eventually die.

Most people habitually eat between three to six small meals per day. Unfortunately, many are not satisfied with these small meals.

Additionally, eating meals during the day leaves many people feeling sluggish and exhausted due to uncontrolled hormonal and neurotransmitter changes. On the other hand, when you practice the Warrior Diet, you can let your hormones and neurotransmitters work for you. In other words, instead of the hormones clashing against the diet, your diet will work in synergy with your hormones.

Although it may seem difficult to accept at first, the Warrior Diet allows you an incredible sense of freedom. Once your natural instincts kick in, you'll want to eat only one large meal per day, at night. You'll fully enjoy it and will get even more satisfaction knowing that you can eat to your heart's content. I believe that every time you fulfill an instinct there's a feeling of intense pleasure, a kind of high. We get this feeling from food, sex, and even after completing a workout. Could it be that the drive to exercise intensely is part of the "Warrior Instinct," and that people are drawn to bodybuilding or other sports because we're so deprived of this instinct in our modern lives?

I think so. It's all part of being a warrior.

"Warrior"—A New Definition

When I refer to the term "warrior," it is to an instinct that is deep within us all—men, women, and children alike—and which can be triggered by practicing the Warrior Diet.

The "Stubborn Fat" Syndrome

"Stubborn fat" is a major problem for many people today. Those who suffer from this "stubborn fat syndrome" know that it's almost impossible to get rid of it. And they realize that even when they lose some body fat through diet and exercise, the fat they lose is not the stubborn fat. That's why it's called stubborn fat. This stubborn fat usually remains around the belly or chest area, making men look soft. On women, it usually hits their hips, butt, and thighs.

Stubborn fat is caused by an excess of the female hormone estrogen in both women and men. There is evidence that stubborn fat is a modern-man problem due to exposure to estrogenic chemicals in the environment, food, and water. These chemicals affect the body like estrogen, causing fat gain, sterility, and various disorders, including cancer. Besides *The Anti-Estrogenic Diet,* my recent book dedicated to this topic (North Atlantic Books, 2006), I'm not aware of any diet that seriously addresses this problem. It isn't a simple issue. Excess estrogen—which increases the size of estrogen-sensitive fat tissues—comes from various foods and chemicals that mimic the effects of the hormone in our body. The result can be metabolic disorders, fat gain, and mortal disease in men, women, and children.

One needs to understand what stubborn fat is, what the reasons are for having it, how to avoid it, why it's so hard to burn if you have it, and most importantly, how to remove it. In Chapter 7 I explain how to deal with this syndrome. It's all part of the Warrior Diet.

Some Practical Advice for Utilizing This Book

The Warrior Diet is simple and practical. However, since this book details a lot of information and ideas, it may seem a bit overwhelming at first. While I think it is essential to ultimately read the whole book to fully understand all the concepts behind the Warrior Diet, you don't need to read it in its entirety before starting to practice it!

For those who want to begin the Warrior Diet without first breaking their teeth on all that's included, here is my advice:

Read the introduction to each chapter (as well as my preface and introduction at the beginning of the book). This will give you a clear indication of what it's about. Once you understand the goals and follow the principles of the diet, you'll be able to start practicing it. I believe that shortly after you begin the Warrior Diet you'll naturally be driven to learn more and more details because the effects of it may change your life. So, breaking the ice will, in time, come easily.

The goals and principles of the two main phases of the diet, Undereating and Overeating, are at the beginning of their respective chapters. "Warrior Meals and Recipes" offers some great meals and recipes to prepare. Reading these chapters should make it easy for anyone to follow the Warrior Diet.

To sum up, I think any diet is practical if:

First: One understands the goals.

Second: One understands the principles.

Third: One has access to the right nutritional foods.

Fourth: One is able to follow it on a daily basis, enjoy it, and feel satisfied.

It's all here!

The Warrior Diet Principle

- The Warrior Diet is based on a daily cycle of undereating and overeating.

The Warrior Diet Goals

1. Trigger the Warrior Instinct
2. Burn Fat
3. Gain Strength
4. Accelerate Metabolism
5. Boost Virility
6. Detoxify
7. Slow the Aging Process
8. Attain a Sense of Freedom
9. Reach Satisfaction
10. Live Instinctively

CHAPTER 1

THE WARRIOR INSTINCT

THERE'S A PRIMAL INSTINCT DEEP INSIDE YOU that may be triggered in moments of truth. This instinct spontaneously guides how you act, react, compete, fight, or hunt when faced with different situations or events that require an action or reaction in order to survive—without compromising your freedom to be what and who you really are. I call this the "Warrior Instinct."

The question remains: What really triggers this "Warrior Instinct"? My answer, all through this book, is the Warrior Diet. Once you get on the "Warrior Cycle" you trigger this awesome instinct.

This chapter is devoted to all aspects of this primal force, including how the "Warrior Instinct" manifests itself through three other human instincts:

- The Instinct to Survive and Multiply
- The Hunter/Predator Instinct
- The Scavenger Instinct

I believe strongly that the Warrior Instinct, the Instinct to Survive and Multiply, the Hunter/Predator Instinct, and the Scavenger Instinct are all related and come from the same source, and that they're all eventually connected to the Warrior Diet. Another instinct, which I call the Romantic Instinct, is discussed in Chapter 10, the "Warrior Diet Idea," as I believe it is also a manifestation of the Warrior Instinct.

There's much more to all this, so please keep reading.

The Instinct to Survive and Multiply

Two basic instincts guide us throughout our lives, and the Warrior Instinct controls and allows them to manifest. The Instinct to Survive ensures that we keep ourselves alive, by protecting ourselves and hunting for food. Human beings are hunter/gatherers, and the fact that we are hunters by nature places us in the category of predators. This Hunter Instinct is part of our survival instinct, and with it comes the aggression to do two things: protect our lives and kill, if necessary. The Instinct to Multiply gives the human species, like any other species, the desire to engage in sex and produce offspring in order to keep the race alive and well, and to ensure future generations.

There is also competition among males and females to select the best mate. This involves the Warrior Instinct. When triggered, you try to demonstrate your superiority and uniqueness, continually improving yourself to be able to compete for the best mate so that you can produce the best possible offspring to carry your genes. Throughout history, this has been the case with both humans and animals. Humans, civilized creatures that we are, control and repress these primal instincts. I believe, however, that people cannot inhibit them completely, since they remain deep in the subconscious—like a volcano about to explode.

By now you're probably asking yourself why I'm talking about this in a diet book. It all ties together and relates to the Warrior Diet. It will all make sense soon.

The Hunter/Predator Instinct

Hunters have always intrigued and fascinated me. The Warrior Diet mimics the way classical hunters cycled between phases of undereating (controlled fasting) and overeating (compensation).

We all know that in the past humans had to hunt for food in order to survive. Hunting gave the hunter an adrenal rush, as it should, and a whole culture of ritualistic behavior. For instance, when stalking large animals, hunters usually went in groups. At the end of the day, when the mission was accomplished, there was a ritual of compensation—cutting the meat, creating a feast, and compensating all who took part, including the animals that helped, like the dogs. (British hunters dipped a piece of bread in the quarry's blood and gave this to the dogs as a reward for their hard work.)

So, the day consisted of two periods, hunting and compensation. Most of the day was devoted to the hardship of hunting and then preparing the meal, and at the end of the day all were compensated. The entire cycle is important. Nothing can be missing. Today, when we no longer need to hunt for food and the Warrior Instinct is inhibited by its aggressive, antiestablishment connotations, many people still find ways to feel and experience their Warrior Instinct. This is evident in most competitive sports, which closely mimic the experience of hunting.

Following is another example of hunting that is closely related to the Warrior Diet.

Falconry

In the ancient tradition of falconry, falcons are taught how to hunt. They learn to fly above their trainers, who follow on horseback until the falcon catches a bird and drops him down.

Falconry is still practiced in the British Islands, other parts of Europe, and especially in the Mediterranean and the Middle East. Hunters in these regions of the world adore falcons and think of them as "the ultimate bird." Some even compare them to humans in a positive way (or at least with a positive aspect). The eagle, which is within the same family of hunting birds, has been and is today a symbol of many nations.

The methods used to train falcons are worth noting. In order to keep this bird in captivity without losing its Predator Instinct, trainers created what I call a "cycling diet": the falcon is deprived of food for most of the day and is then fed fresh meat, just enough to give them the taste of blood. This deprivation of food keeps their Warrior Instinct alive, and their Hunter Instinct sharp. The cycling diet keeps them strong and aggressive enough to catch their prey.

Cycling the falcons' diet with fasting and then feeding mimics the way that they eat in the wild, hunting whenever hungry and fasting when not. If you feed a falcon even a little bit too much, he loses the desire to hunt, loses his vitality, and loses his alertness. A hungry falcon is in his best shape. So, they are trained to hunt on an empty stomach. The other key element in training falcons consists of playing with them, using a stick with fresh, raw meat on top, which the trainers move in the air, allowing the falcons to fly and catch it. The distance of the play is gradually increased. It is like a "virtual reality" game of hunting birds in flight. And this is how the bird exercises.

I feel empathy toward this beautiful bird, and I believe that falconry not only symbolizes but also parallels how human beings are supposed to live. Yet most of us no longer live in the woods, hunting and gathering food. Instead we live in crowded urban environments, in the suburbs, or even rural communities, with busy schedules, working in offices, carrying briefcases, with around-the-clock routines, far from a purely natural lifestyle. And most of our primal instincts are crushed on a daily basis. We are basically living in a very unwarrior-like, almost captive situation.

But, like a falcon, if you want to you can turn this virtual reality into reality and trigger your Warrior Instinct—without going to war, needing to kill anything, or even changing jobs. All you must do is keep a cycling diet, which is built on the essence of extremes:

undereating, which I call controlled fasting; and feeding/overeating, which I call compensation. When following a cycling diet you'll get both feelings—hunger and satiety, deprivation and compensation. Another key component of the Warrior Diet is exercise. This will be discussed in "The Warrior Workout" (Chapter 14).

As mentioned before, I believe that human beings by nature are hunters, and that many successful people have similarities to predators. Therefore, it's interesting to look at what happens to wild animals when they are caged for an extended period of time.

Predators in the Wild vs. Predators in Captivity

A lot can be learned when looking at the differences in behavior between predators in the wild and those that live in captivity. When a wild predator such as a lion hunts and eats its kill, it eats in safety and only to the point of satiety. Then it leaves and the surviving prey know that the lion is no longer a threat, at least for the time being, simply because lions don't hunt when they are not hungry. They become peaceful. They lie on their back, enjoy the sun, and sleep. However, when you put predators in a cage they often eat and eat (bingeing) and usually don't stop until they get sick. They will eventually die if their captors don't control their feedings.

I give this example because I feel there are also some similarities between human beings and caged predators. Too many of us, for instance, eat several meals throughout the day and evening, sometimes even when full—without reaching satisfaction. If this continues unabated, it'll likely cause sickness.

I've come to the conclusion there are two main reasons why people eat like this:

1. They feel liked caged predators.
2. They've lost their instinct.

Sadly, most of us are not aware that our eating habits, and what we consume, are major reasons why we become sick, overweight, age prematurely, etc., or of the fact that we have the power to choose whether to live like a free predator or a caged animal.

Let's look at the opposite spectrum, what I call the Scavenger Instinct.

The Scavenger Instinct

There are several distinct differences between hunters and scavengers. Hunters/predators work in order to get their food. They make a selection. They know exactly what they are after. Wild cats do not hunt cucumbers. They hunt rabbits and deer. They eat only when hungry. They have a sense of priority—and a sense of time. This is very important. When a hunter/predator is about to eat his kill, he may be in danger if there are other animals around. If this is the case, he'll tear it apart, taking the best chunk and running with it to a safe place to eat. When necessary, he'll fight for the first bite. Hunters/predators like to eat when it's safe and they can relax. Some animals, like wolves or mountain lions, will take the food, bury it, and come back at night (when it's safe) to dig it out. Their instincts are sharp.

The scavenger is exactly the opposite. While hunters work hard to get their food, scavengers don't. They pick up leftovers. While hunters have a sense of priority and know exactly what they need, scavengers have no clear sense of priority. While hunters will make a selection, choosing their food, scavengers eat whatever is available. While hunters eat only when hungry, scavengers eat all the time. While hunters eat warm, fresh, live food, the scavenger often eats cold, dead food. While hunters like to eat when it's safe so they can relax, scavengers eat "on the go." These comparisons might make you wonder what kind of person you are. Are you a hunter/predator or a scavenger? Be honest with yourself. Which do you want to be?

Can You Be a Hunter Without Hunting?

You may ask, "Are we all forced scavengers?" The answer is mostly yes. "Are there really hunters anymore?" My answer is that even though most of us no longer hunt in a traditional sense for our food, the Hunter Instinct is within us all—and you can easily switch it on. "Can you be a hunter if you choose your food but purchase it in advance?"

Good question.

With awareness, by choosing your own food you're already working for it and making priorities. Once you reach the peak—by designing your meals, cooking your food, and understanding what tastes do for you—you are living like a hunter. You understand what you want, set your priorities, acquire your food and, as necessary, prepare it, all of which requires effort. You sit down for your meals and relax. Then when you eat you're satisfied and you don't need to eat more. People who shop in health food stores, even if they don't understand exactly what they're doing, are already a big step ahead because they at least have awareness and are making priorities and choices. The scavenger, by contrast, is like an idiot. An idiot is someone who doesn't think about what he's doing. A scavenger will pick up any food, not knowing its nutritional value or where it came from, nor care if it's fresh, and eat it—just for the sake of eating.

Thousands of years ago, hunting and eating fresh kill were a necessary part of life in order to survive. The later development of raising animals on farms, which dominates the way we eat meat today, crushes the "traditional" Hunter Instinct.

Today, the vast majority of these farm-raised animals are given hormones in order to gain weight rapidly. For the meat industry, time is money and, yes, we are the victims. We are forced to scavenge what's available in the supermarket, most of which is drugged (loaded with chemicals) and is therefore contaminated meat. I believe that the mainstream food industry has been largely responsible for turning people into scavengers by supplying and heavily promoting overly processed foods with aggressive tastes, lacking freshness and nutritional value.

You can mimic your Hunter Instinct by refusing to buy meat filled with hormones or other drugs, or fed rendered feed. Instead, seek out and buy organic meat that comes from animals that were treated in a humane way, fed freely on grass and grain, and were not injected with estrogen, growth hormones, or antibiotics. It might be more expensive, but your body will be healthier and your life more expansive. Don't ever think otherwise.

Hopefully I've put this all in perspective and you're now in touch with (or at least aware of) this deep primal instinct within you, and within all of us—the Warrior Instinct.

CHAPTER 2

THE WARRIOR CYCLE

WE NATURALLY DO EVERYTHING IN CYCLES: EAT, drink, go to the bathroom, sleep and awaken. Our body is cycling nonstop, things going in, things going out. When one of these processes is blocked you become imbalanced, sick, and you may eventually die if it's not corrected. Our brains react to the cycle of day and night, especially through the pineal and the pituitary glands, which secrete hormones. I believe awareness of these cycles is instinctual, that everyone has his or her own cycle, and each time you break it, you're going to feel it.

Some even believe that life itself is a cycle—that once you die your soul is going to recycle to another life, and that the people you knew in this life were part of your former life and will be again in your next. Whether this is true is beside the point. I'll try to illustrate in this chapter that there is indeed a human feeding cycle and that it's built on extremes.

The Warrior Diet is built on the principle of cycling between periods of undereating and overeating, based on an instinct deep within us to undereat and overeat. The combination of undereating and overeating is not endorsed by mainstream diets; they recommend against this practice and oppose the principle. Yet I truly believe that the "Warrior Cycle" is the only biological cycle that we are built for and are naturally meant to live by. Any other method compromises our true nature.

The distinguishing aspects of the Warrior Cycle are:

- The Energetic Cycle
- The Cycle of Materialism and Dematerialism
- The Healing Process of the Cycle
- Finding the Right Cycle for Optimum Results: Timing

Each is discussed in this chapter, as well as how they relate to the Warrior Diet.

The Energetic Cycle

When Einstein introduced his theory of relativity, it was just that: a theory. It wasn't proven until years later. When asked what he'd say if his theory was not correct, he replied that he would feel sorry for God Almighty if such a beautiful theory didn't work.

Today we know that there is unity between matter and energy, that material can turn into energy, and energy can turn into material. The exact connection between quantum mechanics and macro-mechanics is still not known, but such a connection is acknowledged. Whether our spirit and soul are pure energy, and our body pure material, is not known. One thing for sure is that without energy we are dead, so we are not just material. Even though we think of the world in a materialistic way, we actually sense it through energy. All our cells are built to survive and function through quantum mechanic principles.

Moreover, people throughout the world believe that material can move into spirit and spirit into material. They believe that when we die all we lose is the material, our body, but the spirit will go on. They believe in past lives, future lives, and in cycles. No matter what your belief, it's clear that the role energy plays in the universe is quite predominant.

How does this connect to the Warrior Diet?

The Cycle of Materialism and Dematerialism

What happens in your body during the "Undereating Phase" of the Warrior Diet is what I call dematerialization, meaning that you remove/eliminate more material than you put inside. Basically, burned material turns into energy. Once you learn how to undereat and begin to practice it, you'll find that you have more energy, are more productive, more creative, more ambitious, and hungrier for life. This expanded "hunger for life" occurs when your body and mind are in a state of turning material into energy.

On the other hand, when feeding is frequent (between three and six meals) throughout the day, the opposite may occur and many people may gain weight. Why? When material (food) is continually added to the body, much of our energy must be devoted to digesting and eliminating it. The body often doesn't produce enough energy to eliminate it all. When this is the case, one becomes "overmaterialized" and the body is overwhelmed. Lethargy, exhaustion, and bloating are the result. Additionally, the excess material is deposited as body fat and stored as toxins. On top of all this, some undigested material eventually reaches the bloodstream, which can trigger allergic reactions and may lead to full-blown diseases.

The Healing Process of the Cycle

A most important aspect of the Warrior Diet is the healing process. What does this really mean? And how do you prevent illnesses and keep your mind and body healthy? To me, you can't truly understand what health and healing are unless you understand what illness is and are able to recognize its symptoms. Philosophically speaking, perhaps illness was sent to us in order to understand how to be healthy.

Just as a warrior must anticipate his enemy's behavior and reactions and understand the dangers, and just as a hunter must know the behavior patterns of animals that he hunts, in order for us to heal, to achieve and maintain a state of mental and physical health, we must be in touch with our body and be aware of the symptoms of illness. Our ability to heal, and the healing process itself, should never be taken for granted. Vanity often keeps us from accepting that we'll all inevitably face cycles of being weaker and stronger, sicker and healthier. This isn't just a slogan. Look at it like this: When you want to build muscle and get strong, you first have to break the fiber. Only then is the body tricked into a healing process to rebuild the tissue. This is similar to how the immune system is built after being exposed to colds, viruses, infections, etc.

Acupuncture heals by inserting tiny needles into certain places on the body that are energy sensors and pathways. The tiny incisions that penetrate the skin and the energy currents they stimulate create a healing process.

Similarly, every time you undereat by following the Warrior Diet rules, your body has the potential to heal. Undereating (controlled fasting) triggers healing in two major ways: first, you will have more energy available since it's not being used for digestion; and second, a detoxification process occurs during this phase that is part of healing and staying healthy. Then when you eat a meal, it completes the compensation process and gives you a sense of freedom and satisfaction. On the other hand, when you eat several meals throughout the day, you don't give your body a chance to go through the processes of detoxification and healing or deprivation and satisfaction.

The Undereating Phase of the Warrior Diet empowers you both physically and mentally to finish the day with compensation. Every day has a happy end. So, you go through two extreme periods: first the Undereating Phase, when you are very alert, energetic, active, productive, "hungry for life," and then the Overeating Phase, when you cool out, calm down, and are fully compensated.

All in the Timing: Finding Your Cycle

It's crucial to determine the right cycle, and to find harmony when moving between undereating and overeating. The Undereating Phase should not last longer than necessary. If it goes beyond twenty-four hours, the body usually starts to draw from its lean tissues because the available material used for energy has been completely depleted. Your potential energy will decrease when fasting or undereating for too long. This is self-destructive and dangerous to your health. You'll become weak, and possibly anorexic. That's why it's the art of controlled fasting that keeps your metabolism high. Once you find the right eating cycle, all will be balanced and you'll see your body become stronger, leaner, cleaner, and healthier.

Moreover, an integral component of the Undereating Phase of the Warrior Diet is that it should be done while you are awake. This is the time to produce energy out of matter. Because your body is not being burdened with breaking down and digesting food, you'll have lots of energy to think, create, produce, be ambitious, and, figuratively, to "go for the hunt." This is also when the sympathetic nervous system is dominant—the system that controls the "fight or flight" instincts. The sleeping hours are when your body needs to rejuvenate, recuperate, and rebuild. This is the time when the parasympathetic nervous system dominates—the system that controls digestion, relaxation, and sleep. Your body will serve you better if you follow the Warrior Cycle.

CHAPTER 3

THE UNDEREATING PHASE

"Yond Cassius has a lean and hungry look; He thinks too much:
such men are dangerous."

—WILLIAM SHAKESPEARE, *Julius Caesar,* Act I, Scene 2

FOR MOST PEOPLE, UNDEREATING MEANS not eating enough. Actually, what it really means for you is not eating as much as you used to eat during the day. This may sound so simple, and maybe it is, but there is much more to it. This chapter explains what controlled fasting is, why it's so essential for optimizing your energy and performance, and how exactly to put it into practice. The key to maintaining the Warrior Diet is found in this phase, so please bear with me.

The Undereating Phase is the first part of the Warrior Cycle, lasting most of the day. It's the time that requires more energy—physical, mental, and spiritual. This is when you are working, learning, creating, competing, doing physical activities, and often struggling through the hardships of your day. The Undereating Phase, as you'll see, nourishes your brain while accelerating fat-burning hour by hour, on a daily basis.

The first part of this chapter covers the different aspects of controlled fasting, including:

- What happens to your body during fasting
- The fear of hunger
- How to deal with hunger
- How fasting is defined on the Warrior Diet

Following that, this chapter covers the subject of daily detoxification, which is a major goal of the Warrior Diet. It also explains how by manipulating your hormones you naturally guarantee hours of fat-burning, day by day.

At the end of this chapter you'll find some practical information on the adaptation period and the changes you will experience with the Warrior Diet.

Once you review this chapter, I think you'll find that my concept makes sense. By practicing the Undereating Phase, you should discover that you'll become leaner, more vigorous, and, I believe, more focused.

Before you begin to practice this phase, it's necessary to understand two fundamentals, the Undereating Principle and the Undereating Goals.

The Undereating Principle

The Undereating Phase is built on the principle of controlled fasting. It lasts during the daily hours, from the time you wake up until the evening meal. During this phase, you can consume "live": fresh, raw fruits and vegetables, and some light fresh protein.

The Undereating Goals

- Detoxify and cleanse
- Manipulate your hormones to reach maximum metabolic efficiency
- Burn fat

Controlled Fasting

The Undereating Phase can be followed by not eating anything. Some people like water fasts, while others prefer to drink coffee or tea and water. This is okay if it's what you like to do. However, these are extreme methods that won't appeal to most people. Moreover, I believe that the best way of going through the Undereating Phase is by following a controlled fast, not a water fast. Controlled fasting is easier to follow and it accelerates detoxification and overall well-being.

To practice the Undereating Phase, it's crucial to understand what controlled fasting and hunger are, as well as their different aspects. This is essential information (required reading) for following the Warrior Diet. Here is briefly what happens:

When you fast, insulin drops and the hormone glucagon increases, to ensure a steady supply of energy to the body. When glucagon dominates, most of the body's energy is derived from glycogen reserves and fat stores. Also, the drop in insulin allows the growth hormone (GH) to peak. Elevation of

GH increases the body's capacity to rejuvenate, repair tissues, and burn fat. A natural elevation of GH on a daily basis, I believe, should help slow the aging process. Unfortunately, GH is generally inhibited during the daily hours. Chronic low GH levels are also associated with sluggish metabolism, high insulin levels, and aging. Most people suffer from a sluggish metabolism as a result of over-consumption of chemical-loaded processed foods, a lack of digestive enzymes, mineral deficiencies, and physical or mental exhaustion.

The advantage of controlled fasting is the detoxifying effect that "live" fruits and vegetables, and their juices, have on the body, which is further enhanced by minimizing overall food intake. Under this metabolic environment, GH is elevated and most likely will reach its maximum metabolic efficiency.

Next we'll look at the different aspects of hunger and fasting.

What happens to your body during controlled fasting?
- Detoxification occurs (a cleansing).
- The body's enzyme pool is reloaded (which accelerates fat-burning and creates an anti-aging effect).
- Insulin drops and is stabilized (efficient metabolism of carbs and fats).
- Glucagon increases (a fat-burning hormone).
- Growth hormone increases (tissue repair and fat burning)

The Fear of Hunger

Many people today have an irrational—almost phobic—fear of hunger. We live in a society that teaches us that it isn't ever good to be hungry, and that hunger can even be dangerous. Of course, this is partly true since everyone needs to eat, and when you're hungry it triggers the *reactive* part of the survival instinct (which says "I must eat in order to survive"). Nonetheless, when you know how to manipulate hunger *correctly*, it will serve you in many positive ways. Hunger will trigger the *active* part of the survival instinct—that which makes you more alert, ambitious, competitive, and creative.

Throughout history, humans have had to contend with hunger, and not just because they were unable to afford food or suffered from drought and famine. Learning to deal with hunger was also practiced intentionally, to make people tougher and stronger, thereby more resilient to life's hardships.

The historical correlation between hunger and freedom is quite evident. During the period when the Bible was written, and later, during the Roman Empire, hunger and fasting were considered an integral part of life for free people, warriors, and those who wandered. Slaves, on the other hand, were fed frequently throughout the day. The Israelite slaves' first complaint after leaving Egypt was of hunger, and they wandered in the desert for forty years, adapting and eventually becoming a free nation. Only the second generation of those escaped from Egypt reached the Promised Land.

I firmly believe that hunger triggers the Warrior Instinct, and if it's under control it will give you a "sense of freedom." I also believe that frequently feeding—due to a fear of hunger—may, to put it strongly, create a "slave mentality," because when fed continually, people tend to become more lethargic and submissive—and thus easily controlled. One could almost consider food abundance a less drastic or obvious form of "opiates for the masses."

How to Deal with Hunger

First, you should know that when you control hunger, it isn't going to harm you, and you shouldn't be afraid of it. During a controlled fast the hunger sensations usually don't last more than a few minutes, after which there is an adaptation in the body to the stress of hunger—and the feeling should dissipate.

The second thing you should understand is that hunger is a sign of vitality and health. It is now known that the hunger sensation involves production of certain proteins (neuropeptides) that stimulate growth hormones, which then promote tissue regeneration and fat-burning. Third, when you do feel hungry, go ahead and have a piece of fruit, or a freshly squeezed vegetable or fruit juice. If you crave protein, eat a small portion of light, fresh protein food (such as yogurt, kefir, or boiled eggs), which can be consumed with small amounts of raw green vegetables. (See Chapter 4, "What to Consume During the Undereating Phase," for more detail on this.) Take advantage of your energy and alertness. In time you should adapt, find that you no longer suffer during this phase, and you will enjoy a general feeling of well-being.

All that said, excruciating hunger is a different story. When your body is chronically depleted of essential nutrients, such as when you fast for more than twenty-four hours or feel starving with extreme sensation, almost like a pain, you should listen to your body and eat. Regardless, it's always good to break a fast with fresh vegetable or fruit juice.

What Does "Fasting" Mean on the Warrior Diet?

Fasting means different things to different people. Islamic people, for instance, fast during the holy period of Ramadan. To them, this means not eating during the day, and eating only at night. Roman Catholics fast during Lent, avoiding meat. Orthodox Jews completely avoid all foods and drink, including water, for virtually twenty-four hours during the Yom Kippur fast. In the past, Jewish spiritual leaders went on a mono diet. They lived solely on figs and carob fruits. In the East, spiritual leaders used to practice water fasting—some for short periods of time, and others for a couple of months. During the era of the Roman Empire, Romans fasted, eating only peas. Today fasting is becoming popular in mainstream America, especially among people who want to lose weight or do a natural cleanse.

On the Warrior Diet, the principle of fasting is based on not eating a full meal during the day. Since the Undereating Phase lasts for most of the day, you can consume certain "live" foods and should drink a lot of water. Naturally stimulating beverages, such as coffee and tea, are allowed, and a few nutritional supplements are suggested. You must, however, minimize the amount of food to mostly live (raw) food, in the form of fruit and veggies and their natural juices—and small portions of light fresh protein food such as yogurt, kefir, poached or boiled eggs, or a whey protein shake if needed. This will keep your digestive system untaxed and manipulate your hormones to the optimum balance.

Choose your food and beverages carefully, to accelerate detoxification. Processed carbs and sugars should be avoided during this phase, so as not to boost your insulin levels.

Fasting vs. Starvation

There is a *significant difference* between fasting and starvation. Fasting is the art of manipulating the metabolic system; it is controlled, and for a limited time. When you reach this peak time period, and then eat a large meal, your body will compensate and your metabolism will be boosted higher than it was before.

Conversely, with starvation, the fasting is not controlled. The body is forced to slow down its metabolic rate and start to "cannibalize" muscles and lean tissues. Starvation, if done chronically, may lead to death.

The Spiritual Side of Fasting

Many different religions, including Hinduism, Islam, Christianity, and Judaism, consider adult fasting a way to reach a deeper spiritual level. There also seems to be a natural connection between controlled fasting and becoming less materialistic. During a fast, material in the body is turned into energy, and I believe this alone makes one less materialistic and more spiritual.

The Hunger for Life

As I've mentioned before, during this time you're moving from the material world into an energetic, creative one. On the scientific side, the hormonal balance is different when you fast than it is after you eat. After you eat a full meal, including carbs, the insulin system is dominant. Insulin promotes buildup of material (both protein and fat) in your tissues.

On the other hand, during a controlled fast, the glucagon system takes over from the insulin system and removes material from your body, turning fat into energy. So, during the controlled fasting time, you move away from a "materialistic metabolism" to an "energetic metabolism." Once you adapt to controlled fasting, you should experience a "hunger for life." Your Warrior Instinct will kick in and you'll become sharper, more alert, more energetic, more creative, and more adventurous.

A Few Words on Fasting to Heal

Children fast instinctively when they are sick; so do animals. And for many years, when people wanted to heal, they incorporated a fast as a natural therapeutic method. Overall mind-body energy is increased with fasting. This healing force throws off accumulated toxins, clears dead cells, and rebalances and rejuvenates the body. Paul Bragg, author of *The Miracle of Fasting*, states: "The greatest discovery by modern man is the power to rejuvenate himself physically, mentally, and spiritually with rational fasting."

Researchers believe that cancerous cells die in alkaline environments. Theoretically, manipulating the correct pH through fasting can help accelerate the destruction of sick cells and tumors, which thrive in acid environments. There is also a great deal of research on the anti-cancerous properties of nutrients in fruits, vegetables, and herbs, as well as natural toxin elimination. Fasting can be analogous to "the burning of rubbish." I'll touch on these subjects in more detail soon.

Daily Detoxification (Elimination of Toxins, Burning Fat, Anti-Aging)

The accumulation of material in your body, especially undigested foods and toxins, makes you sick. To begin with, avoiding toxins is very important, but it's at least as important to give your body the chance to detoxify itself. This is key for your health. When you follow traditional diets, eating three to six meals a day, your body doesn't have enough time to get rid of all the waste material. Detoxification, in my opinion, is the most important thing you can do to live longer and have a healthier, more attractive body.

When you detoxify, a cleansing takes effect. There is a natural wisdom of the body to remove toxins. Unfortunately, when too many toxins are ingested, the overwhelmed body can't get rid of them all. And when toxins remain, building up over time, it leads to ever-greater health risks. Since we consume, breathe, and absorb so many contaminants and pollutants through our skin, lungs, and gastrointestinal tract every day, I firmly believe it's important to detoxify on a daily basis. We're commonly exposed to estrogenic chemicals in the environment, food and water that have shown the capacity to bind to estrogen receptors in the body and cause fat gain, metabolic disorders, and cancer. We can protect ourselves by applying a daily detox regimen and nourishing ourselves with food and herbs that have been shown to have anti-estrogenic and detoxifying properties.

We'll cover here the different aspects of daily detoxification, as well as three awesome properties of the Undereating Phase:

- Anti-Aging (Through Nutrients Loading)
- Fat-Burning (Through Hormonal Manipulation)
- Destroying Tumors and Cancerous Cells (Through Detoxification)

What Is Detoxification?

Detoxification is literally the neutralizing, breaking down, and elimination of waste and toxins from the body. Every organism and cell has "anabolic and catabolic processes." The anabolic process deposits material—whether good or bad, protein, fat, or toxins—into the tissues. The catabolic process destroys and takes material away from the body, whether it's through burning fat, eliminating waste or removing toxins. *This cycle of depositing material and removing material should be done on a daily basis. If one of these processes does not happen properly, you will eventually get sick.* Detoxification ensures the elimination of waste and removal of toxins. This is an essential part of the life cycle. Unfortunately, most people today do not eliminate enough. To be brutally honest, I would say that many people are in fact constipated and chronically loaded with toxins. And it's not just because they eat the wrong food. It's also because they don't give their bodies enough time to detoxify. Time is a very important factor in the Warrior Diet—indeed it is one of the factors that makes this diet so special and unique.

The Warrior Diet is the only diet I'm aware of that's based on daily detoxification—without, as I've said before, deprivation. There is no other diet that includes these two elements: detoxification, and then eating as much as you want.

Elimination

Elimination is integral to detoxification. It's also a vital part of the daily human cycle, or the Warrior Cycle. It is believed that constipation and other elimination-related disorders are the main causes of most disease, as well as of premature aging. Such failures of elimination create an acidic condition in the body, which is the precursor to most chronic disease. The Warrior Diet promotes a natural, healthy elimination cycle.

Destroying Sick Cells and Tumors

More and more evidence shows that fasting and detoxification help attack and kill sick cells and tumors. Cancer cells thrive on sugar and acid environments. Daily fasting helps lower blood sugar levels, and the alkalizing effect of live fruits and veggies (and their juices) aids in rejuvenating healthy cells while helping to destroy sick cells. Enzyme loading accelerates the healing process. More on this is found in the next chapter under "Enzymes."

Your immune system is naturally boosted during fasting and detoxification. When the immune system is intact, the body recognizes sick cells as "foreign invaders" and will try to destroy them. The body produces special enzymes that digest and recycle broken proteins, sick cells, and tumors. Daily detoxification and fasting are key to activating this immune response. In my opinion, fasting daily works like a natural chemotherapy, and detoxifying daily is the best natural way to let the body defend itself. It takes time to detoxify, and the Warrior Diet gives your body this vital time through the Undereating Phase.

Detoxification and the Healing Process

Detoxification brings on a healing process. Most people that I know who have gone through this process have done so with no side effects. However, when the body is overburdened with toxins, it may sometimes produce temporary and uncomfortable symptoms as toxins are eliminated. For instance, you may get allergic reactions, like a runny nose or skin rashes, or experience flu-like symptoms. People don't usually realize that these symptoms are the body's way of naturally activating the immune system to help heal and cleanse itself by getting rid of toxins in any available way. Instead of letting nature do its job, many people today try to eliminate these symptoms by taking drugs. The mainstream pharmaceutical and medical communities compound this problem by advocating, promoting, and selling quick-fix medicines to mask the effects or reduce these symptoms, making a fortune in the process.

If, for instance, you have a fever and let it do its natural course without taking drugs, in most cases the fever will kill the bacteria or other pathogens, thus helping the body to detoxify and heal. Taking drugs cuts short this process, so your body may not have the chance to finish the healing cycle. It's important to realize that some unpleasant symptoms are normal, and you should try to overcome them without interference. There are also natural ways to reduce them such as taking minerals, vitamins, and antioxidants (we'll discuss these later). The cleaner your body is, the fewer symptoms you will get. As noted, most people I know who have gone on the Warrior Diet did not face any unpleasant symptoms; in fact, quite the opposite. Most felt better and almost immediately experienced a greater increase in energy.

Manipulating Hormones and Neurotransmitters to Reach Maximum Metabolic Efficiency

During the Undereating Phase, growth hormone, insulin, glucagon, and the stress hormone cortisol are all manipulated naturally to optimum balance. You may ask why you want to manipulate these hormones. My answer: to reach a peak metabolic efficiency, to burn fat, and to rejuvenate your body overall.

Manipulating your hormones has certain important benefits, including the following:

- Anti-Aging: Elevation of growth hormone (GH), removal of toxins, and enhancement of sex hormones can help provide anti-aging effects.
- Burning Fat: This occurs when the hormones and enzymes that burn fat are working at an accelerated rate (through elevation of GH and glucagon, and the decline of the insulin hormone).
- Vigor: You will feel potent, powerful, and more positive (by opening the "brain barrier," boosting brain neurotransmitters through improved blood circulation and increased production of cellular proteins that promote energy, alertness and vigor). When you know how to naturally manipulate your hormones and brain neurotransmitters, which are the best energy controllers in your body, you can reach your most energetic state.
- Ability to resist fatigue and stress: Under a high energetic state and a low metabolic stress, cortisol is gradually controlled while the body gets more resilient to fatigue and stress.

The Adaptation Period

Adapting to the Warrior Cycle is a necessary component of the Undereating Phase. During this time your body will get stronger and tougher. The adaptation period usually lasts for the first few weeks when beginning the Warrior Diet. Some people adapt immediately, but it normally takes between one to three weeks.

In the past, our ancestors adapted more easily to different situations because they were forced to face times of real hardship and pressure, like famines, and so had no choice but to adapt to changes in order to survive. All changes in lifestyles, careers, etc., are necessary in order to evolve, acquire new skills, and grow wiser and stronger. Adaptation is necessary. Adaptation relates to the Warrior Instinct (see Chapter 1) because part of the Warrior Instinct involves taking chances.

Once you have adapted, you should feel great and full of energy during this phase—not to mention how exhilarated you'll feel once you've liberated yourself from old habits. And, you can look forward to true satiety because you will soon be eating as much as you want. The Overeating Phase is just around the corner.

If You Find It Difficult to Adapt

Some people find it difficult to jump right into the Warrior Diet all at once. If this is your case, I recommend that you begin to practice it gradually. Here are two suggestions:

Gradually increase the undereating time.
Start by undereating from morning until noon, and then add an hour or two per day. In a matter of a few weeks, you'll get used to it and will probably enjoy it. Remember, you're allowed to consume certain foods during the Undereating Phase. The Warrior Diet is not a water fast.

Gradually increase the days that you practice the Warrior Diet.
Start by practicing the Warrior Diet one or two days per week. Increase to three or four days the following week, then to five or six the week after that, and so on until you're fully adapted.

As I said, it's better for some people to ease in gradually than to jump in cold turkey, so take your time with the adaptation period if this is what you need.

Many of those who tried the Warrior Diet have said that they almost immediately experienced such tremendous improvement, both physically and mentally, that they felt confident they were on the right track and found it quite easy to change their eating habits. Do what's good for you.

CHAPTER 4

WHAT TO CONSUME DURING THE UNDEREATING PHASE

THIS CHAPTER COVERS THE DIFFERENT FOODS and nutritional supplements you can consume during the Undereating Phase. At the end of the chapter I offer my review of protein powders, for those who like to consume them during the day.

As already mentioned, detoxification and keeping insulin at a minimal level are of prime importance during the Undereating Phase.

"Living" Foods

It's most important to consume live (raw) foods on a daily basis during the Undereating Phase. Live foods contain vital nutrients, enzymes, vitamins, and minerals that aid in daily detoxification. The importance of live foods goes beyond the vitamins and minerals you get from them.

"Living" foods are fresh, raw fruits and vegetables, as well as freshly squeezed fruit and vegetable juices. I mean really fresh fruits, really fresh vegetables, and really fresh juices, not those sold pre-made.

Living foods contain many vital live ingredients. They are the highest source of food enzymes, vitamins, minerals, and other phytonutrients in their most active state. They are critical for your health. When you ingest raw fruits and veggies, or freshly squeezed veggie and fruit juices, you reload your body with living enzymes. And every time you reload your body with living enzymes, you optimize your body to:

1. Detoxify and create an anti-aging effect.
2. Reduce inflammation, congestion, and pain.
3. Better digest the food that you will eat later during the Overeating Phase.
4. Replenish your body with nature's life forces.

Processed Foods vs. Live Food

Most processing—including many cooking methods, heat, acid processing, and pasteurization—destroys the food's enzymes and probiotics (the friendly bacteria that colonizes your gastrointestinal system). Processing can denature protein and fats. However, special processing techniques, like controlled low-temperature, freeze-dried, or air-dried techniques, can preserve much of the vitality and integrity of living foods. You could say that the term "living food" is a relative matter. Fresh, raw foods are most alive, and from there it begins a downhill slide until food is technically dead. The processed-food industry does a wonderful job wrapping up and selling dead food in a way that makes it look alive and attractive. But, as a warrior, you should be able to tell the difference between what's alive and what's dead.

What To Drink

It's extremely important to drink a lot of fluids throughout the day, primarily water. Vegetable juices that are freshly prepared in a juicer are the best choice to complement your water intake throughout the day. Fruit juices, made in a blender with no additives, are also good. However, because of their sugar content, fruit juices should be your second choice. Minimize or avoid using fruits with a high glycemic index, like grapes or watermelon, because they contain too much sugar.

Natural stimulants like coffee are allowed, and you can add a trace of milk or milk-foam. Most teas are okay. Make sure that the coffee and tea are not made with sugar or sugar substitutes to avoid over-triggering an insulin response or forcing your body to work harder as it attempts to detoxify chemical sweeteners. Every time you overtrigger insulin response during the day, you may block the benefits of undereating and can jeopardize the whole plan. Stay clear of all soft drinks.

I personally like to drink carrot and ginger juice. Sometimes I add beets or parsley to the mixture. It's delicious, detoxifying, and a very good source of minerals, vitamins, phytonutrients, and food enzymes. The naturally occurring sugars in veggies (like carrots) are not simple processed carbs; they're naturally bound to other compounds including fiber particles, vitamins, trace minerals, and phytonutrients, all of which play important roles in sustaining a healthy metabolism. You can have veggie juices every few hours. Drink them slowly, but within ten minutes after they are prepared to ensure that you'll receive all their live nutrients.

What To Eat

Fruits

Eating whole fruits is allowed and recommended (in moderation) during the Undereating Phase. Since you don't want to spike insulin, it is best to consume low-glycemic fruits that provide a lot of nutrition, such as berries (blueberries, blackberries, raspberries, strawberries, etc.). I highly recommend berries because they have a good ratio of vital nutrition to sugar—meaning they contain a lot of minerals, vitamins, and phytonutrients, but not much sugar. Some berries, such as blueberries, raspberries, and amla berries, have healing properties and contain potent antioxidant as well as anticancerous properties. Note that amla berries are the highest natural source of vitamin C and also are a rich source of alagic acid, which has shown the capacity to destroy cancer cells. Berries can complement the digestion of high-protein meals. Warriors ate berries seasonally during the day.

Eating an "apple a day" is another good choice during detoxification, as are pears. Tropical fruits like papayas, mangoes, pineapples, as well as grapefruits, oranges, and kiwis are good, too. They are very dense fruits and contain lots of vitamins and enzymes. Citrus fruits are rich in flavonones, which have protective properties against estrogenic chemicals.

"Live" (Raw) Vegetables

During the Undereating Phase you can eat raw green vegetables of any variety. They will detoxify without taxing too much insulin. Save the cooked vegetables for the Overeating Phase. If you really want to have cooked vegetables once in a while, it's best to have them steamed. Don't eat many because they can overload your system.

Live Enzymes—Rule of Nature

There's a rule in nature that all living foods contain their own self-digesting enzymes. When you process food, enzymes are destroyed, so the food moves through your system without digestive help, and it robs the natural enzyme pool of your body.

When the body is depleted of enzymes, it starts to compromise digestion. And when digestion is compromised, your health is compromised.

Live Minerals

The best and most accessible minerals are those naturally derived from live foods. These minerals are more potent, naturally ionized, and better assimilated by your body. For example, carrot juice is a wonderful natural supplier of live potent minerals and electrolytes, which alkalize and nourish your system instantly.

Natural minerals should taste good when you put them in your mouth. Wild animals lick salty rocks to ingest the minerals as they need them. In the past, people did, too. You'll be able to know whether you need minerals or not by your taste buds. As long as you're depleted of minerals, they'll taste good. Once enough is ingested, they no longer will. Synthetic minerals are another story. They taste like chemicals; therefore, you can't taste and balance them orally.

Having the right amount and balance of minerals in your system prevents food cravings. A deficiency of even one mineral may create a craving for a certain food. For instance, a zinc deficiency may create a craving (or even a deep, excruciating hunger) for protein, like meat and dairy, which are naturally high in zinc. Some people crave something—but they don't know what. It may well be due to a mineral deficiency.

Protein

If you feel it's necessary, you can eat small protein meals made with light, preferably fast-assimilating proteins such as yogurt, kefir, or whey protein. Remember, though, that you're detoxifying your body, so it's important to let your digestive system rest—this is why I recommend minimizing protein intake/per serving during the Undereating Phase. To minimize the stress on your digestive system, use good-quality lean protein that is easily digested, such as plain yogurt, kefir, cottage cheese or whey protein, poached or boiled eggs, or sashimi. Don't mix proteins; and limit the amount to no more than

8 ounces per serving. You can also choose to have a handful of raw nuts, such as almonds, instead of lean protein, preferably starting in the afternoon hours.

I like to use my own protein powder, made from a proprietary blend of pesticide-free whey and milk protein with air-dried organic colostrum that has been taken from the first milk of lactating cows. Colostrum is the first fluid secreted by the mammary of a lactating mammal, just after a birth. Colostrum is believed to mimic the nutritional composition of human mother's milk and thus contains some unique immune supportive properties and tissue-repairing properties which regular milk doesn't.

Recovery Meals

Active individuals who exercise during the day should have a recovery meal after training, made from fresh fast-assimilating proteins such as whey or milk proteins (15–30g), together with low-glycemic carbs such as rice or oats (10–25g). After exercise, the body is in a peak metabolic potential to absorb amino acids and other nutrients into the working muscles. This highly anabolic potential diminishes within three to four hours after exercise. Timing of recovery meals is therefore critically important for overall recuperation, muscular development, and strength gain.

Protein Utilization

It's important for everyone who eats protein to understand protein utilization—especially so for athletes and bodybuilders who ingest so much protein to build their muscles.

The Undereating Phase of the Warrior Diet should potentiate your body to handle the Overeating Phase. One of the top priorities of the Warrior evening meal is protein, and proper protein assimilation is vital for your health.

Many athletes and bodybuilders reach a plateau, even though they exercise intensely and consume large amounts of protein daily. In my opinion, malabsorption of protein is one of the main reasons for this. With all the ads and information blitzed by the media, there's still a lot of confusion regarding protein utilization. Without it, you cannot reach the peak anabolic state you need to build muscle and repair tissues. There's more to this, so bear with me. Let's now cover these two essential issues regarding protein: I am referring to protein utilization and the quality of protein consumed.

Principles of Protein Utilization

The principal rule for protein utilization appears as a triangle. The top point is protein. On the lower left point of the triangle are enzymes and probiotics (the friendly bacteria in your intestinal tract), and on the right side is the live-food factor (which gives protein its integral structure). In this case I am referring to un-denatured protein (which has not been denatured, broken, or twisted). Protein should be minimally processed and sustain its integral composition of amino acids. The "triangle" is an organic structure, and each of the angles needs the other to be complete. Protein can never be fully digested without the help of enzymes, and enzymes cannot be completely potentiated without probiotics. To fully utilize protein you must optimize all three factors: enzymes, probiotics, and the live-food factor.

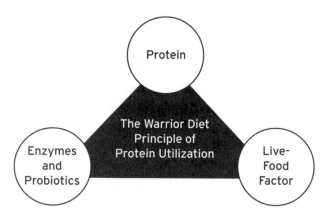

Protein Digestion (How It Works)

Protein, as you now know, needs digestive enzymes to be broken down. Letting your body reload its enzyme pool during the Undereating Phase is therefore critical for protein utilization and digestion, especially if you ingest large amounts of protein during the evening meal. Finally, probiotics help complete digestion and allow protein to be utilized more efficiently by breaking down waste toxins and undigested protein particles into harmless substances.

Carbohydrates

No carbohydrates, other than fresh vegetables and fruits, should be ingested during the Undereating Phase. This includes bread, cereals, muffins, pastas, corn, potatoes, rice, barley, any other starchy foods, as well as candy, pastries, and all other sweets. None of these are allowed during the Undereating Phase.

Note that endurance athletes and individuals engaged in prolonged drills can have a bowl of oatmeal or barley an hour before training.

Professional Athletes and Extremely Active People: Go to Chapter 6, the section titled "The Warrior Diet Daily Food Cycle," and also the end of Chapter 9, the section titled "Conclusions for the Modern Warrior / The Historical Role of Nutritional Carbohydrates" for information tailored to your specific needs.

Enzymes

Enzyme-Loading for Anti-Aging

There's a connection between your body's pool of enzymes and your health. When your enzyme pool is loaded, enzymes run directly to your blood from the digestive tract and induce beneficial health effects, including anti-inflammatory and antioxidant effects. A negative correlation has been found between the body's enzyme pool and aging. In other words, the fewer enzymes you have in your body, the faster you age.

So, by reloading your body with enzymes, you may slow the aging process, rejuvenate your skin, and even recycle muscle tissues. Enzyme reloading means letting your body recycle and synthesize its own enzymes as well as ingest enzymes from food, thereby having more potent available enzymes than are actually needed for digestion, preferably on an empty stomach.

Enzymes act also as a cellular intermediary in hormonal synthesis. They regulate numerous functions that sustain the integrity of the cell and the whole body. In conclusion, undereating during the day while reloading your body with live food enzymes will give you more vitality and will accelerate healing.

Burn Fat by Loading Your Body with Good Fat

There is a link between a lipase deficiency (enzymes which break down fat) and obesity. Loading your body with lipase derived from live food—like raw avocados, raw nuts, and raw seeds—may help ensure proper fat metabolism. The fat content in nuts and seeds is rich in phytosterols, known for enhancing sex hormone production in men and women. Don't listen to those who tell you to avoid avocados or nuts because of their high-calorie, high-fat content. Quite the opposite. These foods in their raw state may help accelerate fat burning, increase libido, and resist aging.

Note: It is best to consume high-fat raw foods, such as avocados and nuts, at night during the main meal so as not to overtax your digestive system during the Undereating Phase. Do not combine nuts and seeds with grains or sugar. These high-fat foods work best in a low-glycemic environment.

Enzyme Loading

I believe strongly in the importance of enzyme loading and even supplementation, particularly for people who suffer from enzyme deficiencies or digestive problems. Young people usually don't need enzyme supplements as much, but the older one gets, the more necessary they often become. They're also helpful for athletes who eat more (usually protein) than the average person. Digestive enzymes are vital to your health on a variety of levels:

Immuno-Protective

In addition to breaking down food, digestive enzymes work as a first defense against pathogenic invaders in the stomach, destroying bacteria and fungus.

Anti-Inflammatory

Protease enzymes (enzymes that break down protein) have anti-inflammatory properties. People suffering from injuries or arthritis can benefit from them, as can those who experience inflammation in muscle tissue after a workout. Enzymes (like bromelain) can counteract inflammation and may help reduce water retention.

Anti-Allergenic

Many people suffer from food allergies and allergic reactions due to undigested food particles in the colon and blood. Undigested food causes toxicity, inflammation, and water retention, often leading to a total metabolic decline. Your body recognizes it as a foreign invader, thus triggering an allergic reaction. Digestive enzymes may help combat these problems, preventing leakage of undigested food particles into the circulation.

Metabolism
Loading your body with enzymes may help enhance fat and carb utilization for energy and thereby help sustain your energy, strength, and health.

Supplements for the Undereating Phase

During the Undereating Phase you shouldn't overload your body with synthetic vitamins and minerals. If you choose to take supplements, make sure they're from a natural source and made by a reliable company. Do your own research to make informed choices because taking the wrong supplements can hurt you. Some can be toxic just because they're not assimilated, and may be deposited in the wrong places. For example, taking excessive synthetic B vitamins may cause high metabolic stress, adversely affecting organs such as the liver and kidneys. Ideally, you can live quite well with proper nutrition and minimum supplements.

Nevertheless, there are some supplements that I often recommend for people during the Undereating Phase.

Probiotics

Probiotics are the friendly beneficial bacteria in your digestive tract. They're necessary for healthy digestion and may be the first line of defense in disease prevention.

The main function of probiotics is to aid in the efficient absorption of food, vitamins, and minerals. They secrete antibiotic substances that destroy harmful pathogenic bacteria, yeast, and parasites, and thereby help you digest and assimilate your food (and thus use protein optimally).

The human gastrointestinal (GI) tract is supposed to contain 85% "good" bacteria and 15% "bad" bacteria. Unfortunately, many Westerners today have the opposite ratio. When our ancestors consumed fresh plant life thousands of years ago, they unknowingly ingested large amounts of these beneficial microorganisms. However, with the advent of modern farming techniques, which use chemicals such as pesticides, herbicides, and fungicides, these essential microorganisms have been greatly depleted from our food supply. Therefore, supplementation is often needed. Probiotics are abundantly found in naturally fermented foods including sauerkraut, miso, yogurt, and kefir.

Minerals

The most important supplements are minerals, especially if you exercise during the day or are under stress. During the Undereating Phase, especially when burning fat, toxins are released into the blood. Essential minerals will chelate (bond to and transport) a lot of the toxins out of your body and keep your hormonal levels intact. Live, potent minerals are also the first defense against radiation.

Unfortunately, mineral supplements don't seem to be a priority for most people, and the ignorance of them is stunning. Research indicates that many athletes and bodybuilders are deficient in several essential minerals like magnesium, potassium, calcium, and zinc. Sometimes a deficiency occurs due to a mineral imbalance in the body. For example, if you take too much calcium, you may actually deplete your body of magnesium and zinc, and vice versa. Each mineral is essential for different bodily functions, and a deficiency in even one of them might lead to unpleasant symptoms and metabolic disorders.

Magnesium deficiency is one of the main causes for tension headaches and nervousness. Zinc deficiency can cause chronic food cravings; copper deficiency might rob you of your sex drive. Chromium deficiency could cause insulin insensitivity that might lead to hyperglycemia, and possibly even diabetes in a later stage. The list of mineral deficiencies is a long one. Most importantly, active people can deplete themselves of minerals in a matter of hours, especially during the summer months. When you practice controlled fasting, it's important to "max up" your minerals. Warriors in the past were aware of the essential role of minerals. Salt was a precious commodity and people used to trade mineral salts for gold.

I usually recommend taking a multivitamin and minerals supplement that contains the right balance of minerals. Magnesium is essential not just for relaxing muscles and therefore avoiding muscle cramps and spasms, it's also necessary for maintaining hormonal levels, especially testosterone. Zinc is important for your glandular, reproductive, and immune systems. Active people especially need it. It's best to take the multimineral supplement before or right after your workout. Minerals help alkalize your body and thus protect it from the acidic side effects of physical and mental stress.

Note: Minerals should not make you nauseated if you use ones that are derived from a natural source.

Vitamins/Antioxidants/Herbs/Brain Boosters

For extra protection against free radicals and to accelerate detoxification, there are certain vitamins and antioxidants that should be taken in the morning or during the day:

- Natural amla C with bioflavonoids. Amla C is the best source of natural vitamin C with bioflavonoids and alagic acid. Natural vitamin C is believed to be hundreds of times more bioactive than synthetic C and therefore requires lower dosages. It is best to take vitamin C in the morning (100–500 milligrams).
- Grapeseed extract is an antioxidant that is believed to help aid in the detoxification process, elimination of free radicals, and rejuvenation of tissues (100–300 milligrams).
- Multivitamins: Many people suffer from vitamin deficiencies. Stress, excessive alcohol consumption, smoking, and intense physical exercise may deplete your body of its B vitamins and vitamin C, E, and A. Taking a good-quality multivitamin each day is a way to ensure an adequate vitamin supply in your body. Nevertheless, I recommend that people take a few extras as well, simply because the dosage amounts of certain vitamins (such as vitamin C) in some multivitamins are too low. You can take the multivitamin in the morning or at night with your main meal. Those who work out in the morning or during the day may want to take a multivitamin and minerals afterwards, because exercise depletes essential vitamins and minerals from the body. The best vitamins and minerals are those derived from natural sources rather than synthetic sources.

Antioxidant Treat

Another option is to take bilberry, blueberry, or elderberry powder out of the capsule and mix it with a half teaspoon of raw honey. You can then mix this paste with water or chew it as is first thing in the morning. The purple pigment in berries like bilberries, blueberries, blackberries, or elderberries is a most effective antioxidant. This is a natural alternative to popping grapeseed or pignogenol capsules, is much cheaper, and you can enjoy it while benefiting from it at the same time.

Ginseng (Panax and Siberian)

Ginseng is an adaptogenic herb, meaning an herb that helps you adapt to stress. I find ginseng to be a good natural stimulator and substitute for caffeine (for those who are sensitive to caffeine). I like to alternate between these two natural stimulants (ginseng and caffeine) so that I don't overdo either of them. Please note that all of my suggestions for supplemental stimulants and herbs are optional.

Ginseng could be especially helpful during the Undereating Phase. Besides being a great aid against stress, it contains antioxidant and healing properties. Both ginseng and ginkgo biloba are believed to be aphrodisiac herbs. They boost the body's own production of nitric oxide, which plays a vital role in regulating blood pressure. Nitric oxide is also essential for getting and maintaining erections and for sexual potency. Ginseng has been used for thousands of years. Today scientists believe it contains more beneficial properties that still need to be researched.

I like to mix ginseng with a half teaspoon of raw honey. I use panax during the day or Siberian ginseng at night. I enjoy the taste and aroma of this bittersweet herb. The honey makes it more edible and I believe it helps in the delivery of its nutrients. (Panax is a pick-up herb, while Siberian ginseng is more of a sedative.)

Ginger

Ginger is a warming thermogenic herb with anti-inflammatory properties, and one of the best natural digestive aids. Gingerol, the active ingredient in ginger, possesses natural antibiotic properties, which makes it a most viable herb for detoxification. I mix ginger powder (200–500 milligrams) with a half teaspoon of rice syrup. It tastes like a hot candy, freshens your breath, cleans your mouth, and warms your body. I have this during the day. I also like to add fresh ginger to veggie juices that I drink during the Undereating Phase.

Liver Detoxifiers

Herbal detoxifiers for the liver include *Picrorhiza kurroa, Bacopa monniera,* amla, chicory, *Gotu kola, Boerhaavia diffusa, Eclipta alba,* and *Andrographis paniculata.* These herbs have been used traditionally as liver tonics for cleansing, jaundice, and protection against ethanol (alcohol) toxicity. There is growing evidence of their therapeutic properties. For instance, studies reveal that certain phenolic compounds in chicory (esculetin) were found to inhibit oxidative degradation of DNA. Amla contains a most unique spectrum of antioxidants, believed to be two hundred times more powerful than synthetic vitamin C. Gotu kola has been important in the medicinal system of central Asia for centuries. *Boerhaavia diffusa* has been used traditionally as a diuretic and also for detoxification. Other liver detoxifiers including *Eclipta alba* and *Andrographis paniculata* have shown substantial hepatoprotective properties against chemicals and alcohol as well as substantial enhancement of bile flow, which is critical for fat metabolism.

Male Virility Enhancers

These include *mucuna* and various estrogen inhibitors. Mucuna has been mostly used to enhance male virility, yet it also has anti-inflammatory properties. The seeds contain L-dopha, which has been studied for use in Parkinson's disease. L-dopha promotes dopamine production, which in turn enhances testosterone activity and overall feelings of vigor and well-being. For estrogen inhibitors, see the section below.

Kidney Detoxifiers

Shilijit, *Tribulus terrestris* (the fruit), *Boerhaavia diffusa* (root), cardamom (fruit), and triphala (fruit) are plant substances that have been used traditionally to maintain kidney health. Some of them have diuretic and detoxifying properties (boerhaavia, tribulus), whereas others help enhance digestion, elimination, and rejuvenation, thereby lowering the overall metabolic stress on the kidneys (cardamom, triphala).

Shilijit

One of the Himalayan herbs with a long history of use, shilijit has been a traditional treatment for various ailments and injuries, as well as immune support. Shilijit is a great source of trace minerals. It is also rich in essential acids, all of which work as potent anti-inflammatory agents. Shilijit can be beneficial in cases of injury, muscle soreness, or inflammatory disease. It has been traditionally used to enhance liver and kidney detoxification.

Ashwagandha

This plant has long been used medicinally in India and Africa as an adaptogen, anti-inflammatory, fever relief agent, and as a first defense against infections. It is also believed to enhance brain functions, aid in memory, and increase resiliency to fatigue. The active ingredients in ashwagandha, including anolides and flavonoids, were found to induce anti- inflammatory, antioxidant, anti-tumor, and brain boosting effects. Ashwagandha can be used as a general adaptogen (tonic), as a brain "pick up" agent, and also as an anti-inflammatory and adrenal supportive aid to enhance recuperation from physical exercise or injury.

Prostate Healing Herbs

Prostate healing herbs have been traditionally used to alleviate prostate enlargement symptoms and reduce the risk of cancer. Prostate healing herbs work systematically on the detoxifying organs—the liver and the kidneys; they also support a healthy hormonal balance and help enhance the body's defenses against harmful inflammatory substances. These herbs include: Triphala fruit, guggul gum, wild yam root, neem leaves, coriander seeds, milk thistle seed, sandalwood, pumpkin seeds, garlic rhizome, and *Embilica officinalis* fruit.

Blood Sugar Stabilizers

The following herbs have been traditionally used to stabilize blood sugar by enhancing insulin sensitivity and supporting utilization of carbohydrates for energy: asphaltum gum, neem leaves, *Gymnema sylvestre* leaves, cinnamon, and fenugreek seeds.

Brain Boosters

There are natural ways to boost brain neurotransmitters throughout the Undereating Phase. The "empty-stomach factor" can accelerate the delivery of certain amino acids and nutrients to the brain. By crossing the brain barrier, these nutrients can boost mood, alleviate depression, and give you a feeling of well-being. Following are some of these brain booster supplements.

Glutamine

Glutamine is a free-form amino acid that nourishes the brain as a daily fuel. The main fuel for the brain is glucose, but when glucose supply is short, the brain converts glutamine into glucose and uses it as a reserve fuel. Glutamine also works as a neurotransmitter, boosting the feeling of well-being and assertiveness.

The Undereating Phase is the best time to take glutamine supplements. When you take this amino acid on an empty stomach, it will cross the brain barrier and do its job as a brain booster. However, when glutamine is taken with food, it won't reach the brain. The body will use it as fuel, or to replenish the lining of the digestive tract.

Glutamine is believed to be a stress-hormone blocker. On top of all this, glutamine is essential for the anabolic process. This amino acid is found in very high concentration in the muscle tissue. Every time you are under physical stress, your muscles lose glutamine. Maintaining a proper diet should be adequate to supply your body's demand for glutamine. Most protein foods are rich in glutamic acid, which converts to glutamine in the body. Nevertheless, it's worth considering glutamine supplementation during the day if you want to boost your mind and muscle performance. Use the advantage of the empty-stomach factor through the Undereating Phase to ensure maximum glutamine absorption.

Tyrosine and SAM-e (s-adenosyl methionine)

Tyrosine and SAM-e (an active metabolite of the amino acid methionine) may boost your dopamine and acetylcholine (major brain neurotransmitters) if you take them on an empty stomach. Boosting your dopamine will improve your mood, making you more alert and excited to face the day. High dopamine is linked to an increase of growth hormone. In an indirect way, dopamine keeps testosterone levels high by blocking prolactin (the female hormone that stimulates milk production, which adversely affects men's virility).

Estrogen Inhibitors

Certain compounds in food and plants have shown the capacity to inhibit estrogen and protect the body from the harmful effects of estrogenic chemicals in the environment, food, and water. The most potent anti-estrogenic foods are cruciferous vegetables, omega-3 oils, citrus fruits, onion, garlic, and dairy products made from grass-fed animals. The most potent anti-estrogenic herbs are indoles derived from crucifers, apigenine derived from chamomile flower, and chrysine (5,7 dihydroxy flavone) derived from passion flower.

(For more information on this topic, see *The Anti-Estrogenic Diet,* North Atlantic Books, 2007.)

Protein Powders: A Review

For athletes or bodybuilders interested in keeping their protein consumption high during the day, protein powders could be an instant alternative to cooked meals. However, it's very important to choose the right one. Protein powders are divided into three groups: dairy, soy, and egg.

Whey Protein

Whey (a dairy protein) is considered by many nutritionists to be one of the best powders for its immuno-supportive properties. It's also a complete protein food. A good whey protein powder should contain two factors to make it viable and potent:

1. *Immunoglobulins*—proteins that support the immune system by containing compounds that trigger immunity antigenic activity against pathogens and infections.
2. *Growth factors*—these translate in your body as growth hormone derivatives, promoting tissue repair, muscular development, and rejuvenation.

Commercial Whey Protein

Unfortunately, most commercial whey protein manufacturers compromise on the immunoglobulins (the protein that supports the immune system). And, as far as I know, none contain any growth factors. Growth factors (especially IGF-1) are bound to the fat globules of the raw dairy. High-temperature processing, pasteurization, and removal of the fat completely eviscerates commercial whey powders of their natural healing properties.

To top it all, many of these powders are loaded with estrogenic chemicals. The beef and dairy industries use estrogenic hormones to increase cattle weight and tenderize the meat with layers of fat. Prolactin (a milk-producing hormone) is often added to the drug mixture to stimulate milk production. Prolactin has a devastating blocking effect on testosterone. Derivatives of all these toxins may appear in the milk and products that are derived from milk, unless they're made from organic milk.

Do your own research. Look for products made from pesticide-free, hormone-free dairy and check the processing methods and ingredients used.

Lactoferrin, the Magic Bullet

Lactoferrin is a major immune-supportive protein in mother's milk that protects babies from bacterial infections. It's also the best iron scavenger. Lactoferrin is abundant in good-quality colostrums and whey protein, but it rarely appears in commercial dairy protein powders. Lactoferrin can be beneficial in more than one way. In addition to its iron scavenging abilities, lactoferrin deposits iron in places where the body really needs it.

Iron oxidation is a tremendous problem, not just because it can toxify the tissues, but also because it feeds the bad bacteria in your intestinal tract, such as the pathogenic bacteria that cause yeast infections.

Some researchers believe that lactoferrin has anticancerous properties, and scientists surmise that lactoferrin contains other healing properties, including the possibility that it may eventually combat chronic diseases such as AIDS and cancer. These issues need further research. Nonetheless, based on current data, lactoferrin could be one of the most promising "dairy derivative" healing aids in the future.

Dairy Protein Powders

Regrettably, whey protein powders are not the only protein powders with problems. Most dairy protein powders on the market today are just not "clean." For instance, dairy protein powders (the most highly consumed protein powders) are generally produced cheaply with overaggressive processing methods. As a result, they often contain damaged protein and toxic byproducts.

This can have a terrible effect on your body. Besides being toxic, what's possibly most upsetting is that some of their damaged or twisted protein is deposited in body tissues, compromising the integrity of the tissue fibers. Such products may eventually damage lean tissues in your muscles or skin. Pasteurization alone can potentiate negative side effects. The process separates the milk from the friendly bacteria within it, which is killed by the heat. The acidity of pasteurized dairy also increases to the point that it's no longer natural (raw milk has neutral to alkaline pH). Since raw (unpasteurized) milk is illegal in many states, the only alternative I know of is low-temperature processed, freeze- or air-dried pasteurized dairy powders, which retain most ingredients in their natural state.

Soy Protein Powders

I don't use soy protein powders. There are several reasons why:

- Pasteurized processed soy powder loses a lot of its nutritional value when compared to the whole soybeans.
- Soy protein is high in protein-inhibitor substances, like phytates, which may also inhibit mineral digestion and iodine absorption, thereby impairing thyroid hormone production. (An under-active thyroid leads to slow metabolism, fatigue, and impotence.) The Undereating Phase requires that you eat only protein that's easily assimilated, which does not include soy.
- Soy protein contains isoflavones that may accelerate an already existing estrogenic disorder in some people. Soy isoflavones are estrogen-like substances that have been shown to bind to estrogen receptors in the body and mimic the actions of the hormone estrogen.
- Many people are sensitive to soy. Soy is one of the most allergenic foods, especially when it's highly processed.
- Most soy powder supplements are loaded with fillers and gums that may irritate your guts and cause bloating and pain.
- The fiber in textured vegetable soy protein is harsh and tough. I don't recommend it for anyone who has a sensitive digestive tract. This said, sometimes I like to have whole soybeans (edamame) during the

Overeating Phase as a complementary source of protein from whole food. The isoflavones in whole soybeans are less bioactive than those in soy protein isolate or tofu, and thus can be neutralized by the liver before inducing any estrogenic effects.

Egg-Protein Powders

I personally do not consume commercial egg-protein powders. However, whole fertile or organic eggs are a very good source of protein, minerals, vitamins, nucleotides, and essential fatty acids. Unlike sterile eggs, fertile eggs carry both X and Y chromosomes.

Therefore, I recommend consuming eggs, preferably fertile, mainly for the Overeating Phase, but once in a while it's okay to eat eggs during the Undereating Phase. Make sure that you consume the whole egg, with the yolk. Those who like to consume egg whites only as a source of protein should try to keep a ratio of about four egg whites to one yolk. The yolk contains many vital nutrients, so don't skip it.

Summary of the Undereating Phase

Once you have finished the Undereating Phase, you've kept to the priorities of detoxification. You let your body reload its enzyme pool, optimized your glandular and hormonal systems, and stabilized your insulin. You turned your body—naturally—into a highly energetic, fat-burning machine.

It's best to exercise now to accelerate these effects even further. But, since the Warrior Diet is, after all, a diet, I'll complete the diet section first, and we will deal with exercise in the "Warrior Workout" chapter. Besides, you may only wish to incorporate the diet components into your life. I strongly believe that a very good way to start on the Warrior Diet is by following the diet elements first. This alone will probably do the job. Moreover, it may stimulate even sedentary people to begin some kind of physical activity, due to all the extra energy people generally feel when they become warriors.

In the next chapter you'll learn how to practice the Overeating Phase of the Warrior Diet.

Foods and Supplements for the Undereating Phase

- Live (raw) fruits and vegetables
- Freshly prepared fruit and vegetable juices
- Yogurt, kefir, pesticide-free whey and milk protein shakes, poached or boiled eggs

Optional:

- Handful of raw almonds (starting in the afternoon hours)

Supplements Recommended:

- Multivitamin and minerals
- Amla C
- Probiotics
- Estrogen inhibitors
- Liver detoxifiers
- Blood sugar stabilizers

Optional:

- Grapeseed extract
- Ginseng
- Gingko biloba
- Ginger
- Glutamine
- Tyrosine
- SAM-e
- Enzymes
- Prostate healing herbs

CHAPTER 5

THE OVEREATING PHASE

OVEREATING GENERALLY MEANS EATING MORE than normal. But what is "normal"? When people refer to the term "normal" they usually think it relates to a standard that all should live by. However, what many people call "sensible eating" doesn't always make sense to me. And today "normal" certainly isn't a clear-cut indication of quality. I feel it's high time to reconsider and reevaluate the concept of overeating. I'll explain why and how overeating can work for you in short order.

You've now reached the point that it's time to eat your main meal. Your body is conditionally depleted of carbohydrates. Your hormonal levels are at their height, and their effects are accelerated even more if you've just exercised. Your growth hormone has picked up, and your enzyme pool is fully loaded. Most important, your insulin level is at peak sensitivity, which is one of the biggest advantages of the Warrior Diet.

Put simply, your body is ready now to consume large amounts of food without gaining fat. This is the best time to eat as much as you need and enjoy this wonderful sense of freedom.

The Overeating Principles

Overeating sounds like a lot of fun. As a matter of fact, it is! But there is an order to this "piggin' out" thing. You need to know *how to overeat* during your main meal. The Overeating Principles are based on Three Rules of Eating:

Rule #1: Always start with subtle-tasting foods and move to the more aggressive.
Rule #2: Include as many tastes, textures, colors, and aromas as possible in your main meal.
Rule #3: Stop eating when you feel much more thirsty than hungry.

I highly recommend that you start with raw veggies, and then move to cooked food including vegetables, protein, and carbs. Another option is to substitute carbs with high-fat foods such as raw nuts and seeds. To fully enjoy your meal, try to prepare the food in a way that will incorporate as many tastes, textures, colors, and aromas as possible.

Finally, you should be able to stop eating instinctively—either when you feel pleasantly satisfied, or when you become significantly more thirsty than hungry.

There is of course much more to it, but once you understand these basic rules, you can practice overeating and reach the goals of this phase of the diet. The second part of this chapter goes into more detail on these three rules.

Instinctual Eating

The Overeating Phase does not involve guilt or obsessive self-control. You should find that by following the rules you'll create a way of eating that is more instinctive. By trusting your instincts, you'll experience a sense of freedom and real satisfaction. Having a sense of freedom is necessary to be truly happy.

The Goals of Overeating
- Enhance your recuperation (repairing tissues and building muscles)
- Boost your metabolism
- Replenish your energy reserves
- Nourish your body and mind while providing a sense of pleasure and full satisfaction
- Experience a sense of freedom (guilt-free)
- Retrain to eat instinctively

Controlled Overeating

The Science Behind Overeating

I'd like to address the issue of overeating. This is a controversial topic, so please bear with me.

Briefly, when people practice overeating after undereating, their body changes to a more thermogenic and highly metabolized state. The brain receives a signal that it should elevate metabolism in order to burn the extra energy coming from food. On the whole, when one overeats after a controlled fast, nutrients are assimilated at a greater rate, there is an acceleration of the anabolic process of repairing tissues and building muscles; a replenishment of depleted glycogen reserves and intramuscular triglycerides (special high-octane fat fuel in the muscle); and there's an increased secretion of dopamine, thyroid hormones, and sex hormones. If overeating is practiced regularly, your body's metabolism will remember this, and while adapting to these daily big meals, it will most likely become metabolically faster and more efficient than before.

Many people have lost the capacity to enjoy the subtle taste of whole food; if you're one of them, you should know that it's fairly simple to retrain your taste buds. As noted, after the Undereating Phase, your taste buds are very fresh and sensitive, so that's the best time to train yourself to acquire subtle tastes.

Exploring the Advantages of Overeating: Metabolic Acceleration Per Meal

Scientific studies indicate that there's a correlation between our metabolism and how many calories are consumed per day. However, as far as I know, no studies have been conducted on the correlation between our metabolism and the amount of calories consumed per meal. I truly believe that the amount of calories consumed per meal is the bottom line.

The Fasting-Overeating Cycle

Studies by Dr. Mark Mattson, Professor in the Department of Neuroscience, Johns Hopkins University, and colleagues at the National Institute on Aging (2003) have shown that mice who followed intermittent fasting (one day fasting followed by overeating twice the amount of daily calories the next day) were surprisingly provided with substantial benefits, including increased life span, reversal of diabetes, and increased resilience to age-related brain damage. Researchers speculated that the cycle of fasting-overeating affects the brain similar to the way physical exercise affects muscles.

Adaptation to Big Meals

Let me give you an example of how adaptation works. People can walk for two hours every day without noticing any improvement in muscle, strength, or speed, but if they sprint for only five minutes a day, they will most likely notice improvement in both strength and speed. So, it's not necessarily the length of time spent exercising, it's the intensity of the exercise. Coming back to the subject of diet, the question remains: Is it the intensity of the meal that will dictate your body's metabolism? My answer is yes. That's the way I experience it.

Overeating: A Primal Instinct

The Warrior Diet is the only diet that explores the advantages of overeating. Let me say something to all those who overeat and then feel guilty. You feel guilty because you didn't know that a deep, primal instinct drove you to overeat—an instinct that we have most likely inherited from our late Paleolithic ancestors who were night eaters, cycling between periods of famine and feast (undereating and overeating). Many people binge late at night when exhausted from a rigid, obsessive, daily self-control. That's usually the time when inhibitions are broken down and the alleged "demons" come out. But these are not demons. If you know how to use this instinct in the right way, it can work for you instead of against you.

The Three Rules of Eating

First Rule: Always Start with Subtle-Tasting Foods and Move to More Aggressive-Tasting Foods

Start with raw veggies, then move to protein and cooked veggies, and finish with carbohydrates, or alternatively, high-fat foods such as nuts and seeds.

Subtle Tastes

The first rule of eating is to start with subtle tastes (the tastes that nature gave us—free of processing, fried foods, and sugar). If you start with food that has more aggressive taste and then move back to a more subtle one, your body won't react as well.

Everyone can develop a subtle taste, and it's very important to do so. After a controlled fast, you already start to develop a subtle taste, and the foods that possess the subtlest tastes are actually raw vegetables. Soon after starting the Warrior Diet, you should find that you'll begin to enjoy eating raw (live) vegetables.

The American diet is too aggressive—too much sugar, salt, fried fats, and overly processed foods. It's hard to enjoy natural food when one is used to aggressive tastes. In the past, food was more natural and subtle. People didn't have access to refined sugar. Honey was scarce. I believe the human body is basically built for subtle, whole-food tastes. But taste buds today have been dulled from being fed an aggressive, overly processed diet from an early age.

It's okay to combine protein and carbohydrates. However, if your goal is to lose weight, have the carbohydrates at the end of your meal. Following this method can also prove effective for those who like to rotate between high-fat days and high-carbohydrate days.

Note: People who suffer from blood sugar problems should shift from carb to fat-fuel foods until their blood sugar stabilizes.

If you choose to consume more natural food, you'll develop a subtle taste rather quickly and will begin to find it unappealing to eat foods that are too aggressive. Even after just a few months people tell me that they no longer crave fast-food meals. This is the truth; they say that they'd rather have salad greens, steamed veggies, a stew, broiled fish, chicken, or a steak.

How to Begin the Overeating Phase and Follow the First Rule

Begin the Overeating Phase with live (raw), leafy green vegetables. The greener they are, the better they are, and the denser they are, the better it is. Starting with a mixed green salad is a good choice. A handful of parsley, a cucumber, and some endive leaves can be added to your salad as well as other vegetables such as tomatoes, raw onion, scallions, and olives. They'll enhance flavor, texture, and the salad's nutritional composition. The amount to consume is optional. Use your instincts.

There are several reasons to start the meal with live food (raw vegetables):

- Your stomach lining is very sensitive, and when you first ingest dead food, it doesn't react so well.
- Vitamins and minerals are absorbed more quickly when live (raw) greens are the first thing to reach the stomach.

- It's also healthy for the digestive system since raw foods are high in food enzymes, which are vital for optimum digestion and elimination.

If you prefer to have a low-glycemic fruit, such as berries, or a tropical fruit such as a papaya, mango, or pineapple as an appetizer, this is also allowed. Tropical fruits are good because they're very dense and contain a lot of digestive enzymes. As a general rule though, I'd rather you begin the Overeating Phase with leafy greens.

Second Rule: Include As Many Tastes, Textures, Colors, and Aromas As Possible in Your Main Meal

It's my strong belief that you should try to include as many different tastes, textures, colors, and aromas as possible in your main meal because doing so will deliver a complete feeling of satiety. If you miss even one of them on a regular basis, after a while you'll probably develop food cravings.

Aside from hot and cold, warm and cool, sweet and sour, salty and bitter, spicy and plain, tart, pungent, and astringent (the sharp, biting or harsh taste in foods, such as that in ginger and hot radishes), we know there are other factors, including aromas, colors, and textures, which also relate to and affect taste, and are vital to feeling satiety. The more variety you introduce in your diet, the better off you'll be. There are enormous possibilities. When preparing meals, you should try to incorporate this huge variety as much as possible. Combining them in the right balance is the art of cooking. Traditionally, meals were prepared like this. (See Chapter 9, "Lessons From History," for more on this topic.)

- *Tastes:* sweet, sour, salty, bitter, spicy, astringent, pungent, smoked
- *Textures:* hard, soft, crunchy, sticky, grainy, chunky, smooth, chewy, jelly, gummy, light, heavy, thick, thin, wet, and dry
- *Aromas:* related to all of the above, such as sweet, sharp, smoked, rich, aged—like cheeses or wine
- *Colors:* green, orange, red, yellow, purple, brown, white, black, blue
- *Temperatures:* hot, warm, room-temperature, cool, cold, frozen

Sensing Essential Nutrients

Different foods contain different essential nutrients. Your body can instinctively sense essential nutrients by sight, smell, taste, and touch (texture), and they activate pleasure sensors in your brain. There is a connection between cravings and nutrient deficiencies. For example, people who suffer from a mineral deficiency often crave salty foods, and those on a very low-carbohydrate diet often develop cravings for sweet foods.

Some natural foods, such as mother's milk, contain all the tastes necessary to satisfy a newborn baby. Natural foods that contain all the tastes are usually the most nourishing. The main idea here is to prepare a meal that contains as many tastes, aromas, colors, and textures as possible, so one can reach full satisfaction and at the same time be nourished with all the essential nutrients.

Colors and Nutrition

The pigmentation in foods marks the presence of vital nutrients, flavonoids, minerals, or vitamins. There are different theories about how to combine food colors. Some suggest starting the day with bright colors, such as yellow, orange, and red, and finishing the day with purple, black, and brown. Others believe that there's a correlation between the color of food and different inner energies. According to this theory, red stimulates sexual energy, while yellow and orange are spiritual energizers. Regardless, colors should never be taken for granted. This is one way of evaluating the nutritional quality of whole foods. Introducing a variety of colors in a meal will enhance the nutritional composition. It's also aesthetically pleasing and helps you reach satiety.

Saying all that, the most essential color is green. I believe that if a main meal has no green color, it is nutritionally inadequate.

Third Rule: Stop Eating When You Feel Much More Thirsty Than Hungry

How Do You Know When You Reach Satiety?

A lot of people say, "I eat and eat and never reach satiety." On the Warrior Diet you're going to gradually gain a sense of satiety. And the more you practice it, the more you will feel satisfied.

Generally, you're allowed to eat as much as you want, so you don't eat feeling guilty. And, the minute you start to become more thirsty than hungry, that's the first indication that satisfaction is coming. It means that you now need more water than food, and it's time to start thinking about finishing. Allowing your thirst to become a parameter for controlling your satiety is an instinctual matter. When you drink after dinner, you probably won't want to eat after that, because you'll feel like you gave your body exactly what it desired, and any more is unnecessary. Take a 20-minute break. See how that affects your hunger. It takes about that amount of time for satiety signals to reach your brain.

But if you're still hungry, you can eat again. There is no rule to stop. You're not going to gain body fat because, as I said, your insulin is at peak sensitivity, and your body is busy replenishing your depleted energy reserves.

You might get tired after eating your meal. Use this time for relaxation—read, watch TV, wash dishes, or do nothing, just as long as it makes you feel peaceful. However, it's best to wait at least two hours after finishing the meal before going to bed.

A Few Words on Hunger and Thirst
Your body has more sensitivity, in general, to hunger than to thirst. There is a common presumption that there's a sort of defect in our sense of thirst, so we often don't drink as much as we need to. In my opinion, one of the reasons why some people lack thirst-sensitivity is because of the following: if we were thirsty all the time, we simply wouldn't eat as much as we need to. And for active people this could be fatal.

Regardless, people who lack the ability to sense thirst are in constant danger of dehydration. Dehydration, as most know, can lead to headaches, fever, kidney stones, high-blood pressure, and even death.

It is believed that when you force yourself to drink on a daily basis, it helps develop a greater sense of actual thirst. Soldiers in the army go through this. When I was in the army, I remember being told to stand in line and drink a couple of liters of water before training. Let me note here that those who fail to supply their bodies with enough water put themselves in danger of compromising all metabolic systems. Without enough water, nutrient assimilation plummets, toxins are not eliminated, and the fat-burning process slows down. It's commonly recommended that adults drink at least 6–8 glasses of water per day; however, in my opinion you should try to gradually increase your intake beyond this amount, especially throughout the day, and during and after a workout. (I personally drink about one liter of water total during and after my workout.) Starting your day with a glass or two of pure water (with lemon, if you like it) is a great way to begin the detoxification and elimination process.

How to Instinctively Stop Eating

If you're one of those who has a large appetite and doesn't instinctively know when to stop eating, here's what you should do: once you reach the point that you feel significantly more thirsty than hungry, that's when you should start drinking and consider stopping eating. I'm probably the first one to tell you that the time to stop eating is not when you count your calories and say, "If I eat more I'm going to gain weight." And it's not because somebody told you to count the macro and micro nutrition. Stay away from all this guilt. You can eat unlimited amounts from all the groups discussed. But when your body tells you that it's more thirsty than hungry (and it will tell you more and more as you practice the Warrior Diet), this is the time to stop. Take a break and drink a glass of water or cup of tea. If after 15 or 20 minutes you still feel hungry, you can eat again. You probably won't be, but if you still are, go ahead and eat again. No other diet will give you this freedom.

What to Drink After the Main Meal

In addition to water, any tea that stimulates digestion is good. Herb teas such as peppermint, ginger, and chamomile, as well as green tea, are highly recommended. I often like to drink ginger tea or green tea mixed with ginger tea. On the nights when my main meal is largely protein, I like to sweeten my tea with a natural sweetener such as raw honey or maple syrup. Sweetened teas may help stop sugar cravings and enhance your feeling of satiety.

Other beverages such as regular or decaf coffee, cappuccino, latte, espresso, or even hot chocolate are also okay to have. Nonetheless, treat them like a dessert on days of high-protein, low-carb meals. Coming up in the next chapter, you'll learn "everything you wanted to know but were afraid to ask" about the main evening meal.

CHAPTER 6

THE MAIN MEAL: FOOD PREPARATIONS FOR THE OVEREATING PHASE

THIS CHAPTER IS ALL ABOUT THE MAIN MEAL. It covers every aspect—from choosing foods and food preparations to food reviews. Also included: what's good, what's bad, and what's ugly (meaning not so bad, but not so good either).

The Importance of Choosing Fresh Foods

Choosing fresh foods is part of the "Warrior Instinct." Predators are very conscientious about the food they eat. A wild cat first smells, licks, and then eats its food. If the food doesn't smell or taste right, the cat won't eat it. The survival of these animals depends upon their ability to distinguish between fresh viable and stale decomposing foods, and the same could be said about warriors.

Cooking Your Own Meals

I'm a big believer in cooking your own meals. It makes it much easier not only to ensure that you eat fresh foods but also to follow the second rule of eating (see previous chapter), which advises incorporating as many colors, tastes, textures, and aromas as possible into one's meal. Beyond those benefits, I feel that cooking celebrates self-respect, and it's especially important on the Warrior Diet. Through cooking, you can control exactly what you put inside your body. It's a creative process, where you use trial and error to determine what you like. You can use different herbs and spices to increase or balance flavors, aromas, and textures. You're not a scavenger on the Warrior Diet. You work to purchase (gather) the food, prepare, and cook it. Controlling the entire process is very important. For more on Warrior recipes, see Chapter 15, "Warrior Meals and Recipes."

Advantages of Eating Cooked, Warm Food

People have consumed warm food since the discovery of fire. Yet there's a lack of awareness today about the important role of temperature in relation to our food.

The main meal of the Warrior Diet encourages consumption of cooked, warm food, especially since the Undereating Phase is based mostly on raw (live) uncooked foods. There are people who adamantly believe that we should eat only raw food. With all due respect, I disagree with them.

There are several advantages to consuming cooked, warm food:

- Eating warm food often brings more satisfaction than cold food. The thermogenic (warming) effect slightly increases the temperature in your brain, so you feel more satisfied and happy with your meal.
- Warm temperatures are beneficial for your digestive tract, which reacts much more efficiently to warm than to cold food. Food is easier to digest when warm.
- Some people are sensitive to cold foods; others suffer from overacidity. Well-cooked warm food may help ease these discomforts.
- Warm food stimulates the immune system.
- More of the flavonoids, indoles, and other phytonutrients bound to the fiber of many veggies and fruits are released and can be better absorbed when they're cooked.

I strongly believe that eating warm food mimics the effect of a fresh kill. A predator's first bite of its prey always tastes warm. Scavengers, on the other hand, who eat leftover corpses, experience the cold taste of the animal that was killed some time ago by a predator. It's my belief that when you eat and enjoy warm food, it triggers the Predator Instinct, and those people who settle for cold leftovers may trigger the Scavenger Instinct.

Napoleon and the Predator Instinct

Eating chicken with your hands can indicate a Predator Instinct. Napoleon was notorious during his war campaigns for tearing apart a whole, cooked chicken and eating it with his hands. It's interesting to note that the night before Waterloo, Napoleon changed this habit and ate fried potatoes. As you probably know, Napoleon lost that battle.

Go and Kill a Pizza

Please bear with me for a moment and let's look at hot pizza in a completely different way. The crust is dry and, to me, it resembles the skin of a hunted animal; the inside is soft and warm, with melted cheese and red tomato sauce that's like the warm blood and flesh of a fresh kill. The way pizza is eaten mimics the way people used to hold fresh meat in their hands and, yes, bite the bloody thing. To continue with this line of thinking, I could even argue that eating fresh pizza is like virtual reality of a bloody kill. This may sound appalling to you. Or appealing. In either case, next time you're in the mood, go and hunt for a fresh pizza. The Warrior Diet doesn't recommend eating pizza often, but once in a while it's okay to have a slice or two.

Cooking Vegetables to Optimize Flavors and Flavones

Cooked vegetables possess different tastes, textures, and aromas. Certain veggies like parsley, celery, and cilantro work like herbs and spices to enhance the flavors and nutritional composition of a meal.

Vegetables are like water in the sense that you can have as much of them as you want. These calories don't count.

Now let's be specific. Other than leafy greens and salad foods, for the main course, the veggies should be cooked. Besides the advantages listed above of eating warm food, cooking also frees more of the fiber-bound nutrients from the veggies.

Tomatoes

Only a small percentage of the lycopene (an important carotene flavone) in tomatoes is absorbed when eating raw tomatoes. That doesn't mean it's bad to eat fresh tomatoes, but when you cook them you greatly increase lycopene absorption.

Broccoli and Cauliflower

Indole-3 carbinol, indole-3 acetate, and diindolymethane (DIM)—found in broccoli, cauliflower, and all other cruciferous vegetables—are very important phytonutrients which are bound to the fiber. When you eat cruciferous vegetables in their raw state, these indoles can hardly be absorbed. Cruciferous vegetables need to be cooked in order to potentiate nutrient assimilation, whether they're inside the veggie or on the fiber. Moreover, many people think vegetables such as broccoli and cauliflower taste better when cooked.

Cruciferous indoles help both men and women protect against estrogenic effects of chemicals (xenoestrogens). A large intake of cruciferous indoles was found to help the liver detoxify estrogen derivatives, protect against cancer, and may even enhance fat loss.

Berries

Cooking berries potentiates their flavones to a much higher degree. However, it will destroy live enzymes as well as some vitamins. The natural balance of nutrients is changed when you cook the raw fruit.

Legumes and Grains

Another substance that has warranted extensive recent study is IP6, inositol hexaphosphate. Researchers believe today that IP6, found in the fiber of legumes and grains, is the major ingredient responsible for preventing colon cancer and other cancers. Food must be well cooked in order to free IP6 from the fiber and enable it to be absorbed in the system.

IP6 seldom appears in soluble fiber. It's usually attached to the bran, the hard (insoluble) fiber, which is difficult to digest. IP6 is found in legumes, peas, wheat, barley, and oats.

Raw vs. Cooked Veggies in the Main Meal

Ideally, leafy green veggies should be eaten raw. They should cause no problem with digestion even if you consume a fair amount of them. But, as just stated, cruciferous vegetables such as broccoli, cauliflower, kale, and Brussels sprouts should be cooked. There's no reason to eat them raw. You won't be able to assimilate as many nutrients if you eat them raw, and they're not going to taste as good either. Moreover, when eating them raw, you'll likely suffer from unpleasant symptoms like gas and bloating.

Some raw plants may cause toxicity. Most sprouts, for instance, need to be soaked and washed well to remove toxins or other substances that may block nutrient absorption. Alfalfa sprouts should be eaten only when the sprouts reach maturity of at least three days. They should look green. If eaten prematurely, alfalfa sprouts may be toxic. Note that both alfalfa and clover contain active phytoestrogens and should be avoided by individuals suffering from excess of estrogen.

High-Sulfur Foods

Some foods are high in sulfur-containing proteins. As mentioned before, high-sulfur proteins like cysteine work as antioxidants, and they can be helpful as a defense against cancer and radiation. Cysteine is necessary for optimum metabolism, and is destroyed by aggressive processing and heat.

Sulfur is a mineral and a gas-forming substance. Be aware of how you combine high-sulfur foods when cooking. For example, eggs are high-sulfur protein. When you eat eggs and cabbage together, you may suffer from bloating and gas because both eggs and cabbage are high-sulfur foods, and you may be consuming too much at once. So be careful about combinations and quantities, and try to incorporate different types of foods, not only one group at a time. If you really want to combine high-sulfur foods, let your body adjust slowly to this.

If you suffer from sulfite sensitivity, you should consider supplementing with molybdenum, a trace mineral, which is involved in sulfite metabolism.

Eggplant

Cooked eggplant goes very well with protein meals, such as meat and fish. The soft, oily texture of peeled, cooked eggplant balances the harder, meaty texture of the protein. When mixed together it gives the protein natural tenderness and moisture.

Squash

I highly recommend eating all of the squash family. They contain numerous nutrients and minerals, and are highly beneficial for the digestive tract. I actually think the squash family is among the very best for the digestive tract. Squashes of all varieties aid in the elimination process without gas or bloating. They should be cooked well. There's no reason to eat squash raw.

Foods Containing High-Sulfur Proteins
Eggs
Raw milk
Raw cheese
Colostrum
Low-temperature-processed whey

High-Sulfur Vegetables
Broccoli
Cabbage
Cauliflower
Kale
Brussels sprouts

Soups and Stews

I'm a big believer in soups and stews, not just during the cold season, but in warm weather too. I think having veggies and soup is one of the best ways to start a meal. Hearty vegetable soups and stews, where everything is cooked together—often veggies, roots, eggs, fish or seafood, and whole grains—have a great advantage in that many tastes, textures, and aromas combine in one hearty, hot meal. This thousands-of-years-old tradition is extremely good for your satiety. Fermented soups (like miso soup) are also great. Miso is a natural alkalizer. Fermented foods are helpful for your digestion and the balance of healthy bacteria in your guts.

Protein

Proteins bear different tastes, textures, colors, and aromas. Dominant textures are chewy, wet, dry, hard, soft, or creamy. Dominant tastes are sweet, salty, and pungent. After veggies, what the body needs most (second among the subtle tastes) is protein. When you're hungry, starving, or lost in the jungle, the first thing that your body needs is protein. Human beings can survive without carbohydrates, yet cannot survive without complete protein. "Complete" protein foods contain all the essential amino acids. The body can synthesize carbohydrates from protein or fat; however, the body can't produce essential amino acids without ingesting it from outside sources. Therefore, in order to survive, the body needs complete protein. Both women and men should make protein quality their top priority.

Fish, Meat, and Poultry

While on the Warrior Diet, you're going to crave exactly the things you need most. After going through the Undereating Phase, people crave protein. It doesn't have to be meat or fish. It may be beans, nuts, legumes, or cheese. For active men particularly, I feel there's no substitute for whole protein that comes from wild-catch fish, organic fresh eggs (preferably fertile), or organic dairy (preferably raw milk products from grass-fed animals).

In principle, fish oils are essential to the body. Nevertheless, I do have some concern regarding conventional fish. A lot of fish today are contaminated due by polluted waters, and most of the toxins, including mercury, are in their fat tissues. Fish, however, is a fine source of protein. It's high in iodine, and as noted is an excellent natural source of essential fatty acids (EFAs) in their most bioactive form, EPA and DHA. These EFA derivatives are essential for brain development and maintenance, and they are the building blocks for prostaglandins, which help regulate the hormonal system. The least-contaminated fish, I believe, are wild-catch fish, as well as low-fat white fish such as flounder, sole, and turbot.

As for meat, let me say it upfront: *Humans haven't fully adapted to eating meat.* Unlike other predators, we lack enzymes that convert degraded "D" proteins into live "L" proteins. All life forms on this planet are made from "L" proteins. Nonetheless, upon the death of an organism, "L" proteins convert spontaneously into "D" proteins. This process, known as racemization, typically occurs during the decomposition (rotting) of meat. The racemization/degradation of proteins is a reaction that occurs during the death/decomposition cycle of all living things including plants, animals, and humans.

Meat has one of the highest rates of racemization. Improper storage or exposure to high temperatures increases the level of raceant proteins, rendering the meat rancid and unsuitable for human consumption. Our bodies are virtually defenseless against the intake of "D" proteins. Accumulation of these degraded proteins in the body's tissues, particularly the brain, is associated with aging and disease. Racemization isn't the only problem with meat consumption. Due to inhumane treatment of livestock animals, they produce a highly toxic byproduct of stress—an adrenaline metabolite called adrenochrome, which catabolizes (wastes and destroys) muscles and other tissues in the body. This metabolite occurs in high concentrations in the meat that we eat, along with antibiotics, hormones, and other substances fed to the animals.

Meat is known to be a good source of protein, iron, and zinc. Nonetheless, one should always be aware of the downside of eating it.

Organic Proteins—Say No To Drugs!

I recommend buying organic proteins to avoid the hazardous effects of hormones, antibiotics, pesticides, and other toxins such as rendered feed (ground-up remains of dead animals, including "road kill") that some meat growers use. Organic proteins also taste better. They're accessible today and, granted, cost a little more, but it's worth it. As for farm-raised fish, they may also contain toxins from polluted water and artificial feed. So right now, wild-catch fish is your best choice.

To Eat or Not to Eat Meat?

Research continues to show that, statistically, men who are meat eaters are more virile, compared to those who are purely vegan. Part of the reason for this is that many vegans simply don't know how to practice food combining and suffer from protein deficiency as well as deficiencies of essential oils, certain vitamins such as B12, and vital minerals such as zinc, calcium, and iron. Adding dairy to the diet can solve the problem. Some of the healthiest societies on this planet have followed lactovegetarian diets. Nonetheless, just to put things in perspective, compared statistically to meat eaters, vegans live longer, with lower rates of mortality from cardiovascular disease or cancer.

Nuts and Seeds

Humans used nuts and seeds as primary fuel food long before grains. It is very likely that the human body is better adapted to these low-glycemic, high-fat fuel foods.

Nuts and seeds have different tastes, textures, and aromas. They add a crunchy texture and different nutty aromas and flavors to meals.

A variety of nuts is allowed and suggested on the Warrior Diet. Raw and lightly roasted nuts are both good, but raw nuts are highly superior to roasted nuts since they nourish the body with healthy oil, live enzymes, and phytosterols, which the roasting process destroys. Eating raw, high-fat foods such as nuts and seeds is a natural way to load your body with hormonal-supportive nutrients such as sterols and sterolines, which are capable of enhancing sex hormone production in men and women.

On the Warrior Diet you can actually consume as many raw nuts as you'd like and still not gain weight. Just follow this rule: Do not consume nuts with grain carbohydrates. Nuts work very well with a small amount of protein and with an abundant amount of veggies. You can basically live on nuts and veggies, eating as much as you want of them, and still not gain weight. Actually I believe you're going to lose some weight. Try this for a couple of days and see for yourself. Just make sure you chew the nuts extremely well to ensure maximum digestibility. For a "nut-and-veggie" diet, the best nuts are almonds. An almond-veggie diet will give you a nice body odor, almost like a vanilla-almond scent. Sounds too good to be true? Well, that's the way life should be.

Almonds

Almonds are highly recommended. They are a great source of protein, minerals, vitamins, monounsaturated fats, and an excellent natural source of zinc. Almonds have long been considered to be an aphrodisiac food. Ancient Hindus, Hebrews, and Romans saw the almond as a symbol of female as well as male genitals. I truly believe that almonds are an aphrodisiac food, partly because of their mineral composition, partly because of their fat content, and partly due to their alkalizing effect. Edgar Cayce, among other holistic healers, considered almonds to possess anti-cancerous properties. It's interesting to note that almonds are believed to be a homeopathic remedy since they contain a minuscule amount of cyanide, which some say works like a natural chemotherapy agent in the body that destroys sick cells and tumors.

Almonds ideally should be eaten raw. In their raw state they're the only nut that alkalizes your body. It is okay, however, to occasionally eat lightly roasted almonds. They're still good for you, and some prefer their taste. It's best to eat roasted almonds right after you roast them to avoid rancidity.

Peanuts

Peanuts aren't really nuts. They belong to the legume family. According to Dr. Peter D'Adamo, author of *Eat Right for Your Type*, research shows that peanuts have anti-cancerous properties, especially the red skin around them. Just make sure you're not allergic to them! I personally like to eat peanuts in moderation because over-consumption is acidic, and for some this may make the peanuts harder to digest. Also, peanuts may contain mold toxin, which is believed to be cancerous.

On a positive note, peanuts are high in protein and contain essential fatty acids (mainly omega-6). The oil is relatively stable, which is why peanuts, their butter, and oils are used so often throughout the world in various dishes, sauces, and even protein bars.

Cashews

Cashews are one of the least allergenic nuts. They are naturally high in iron. If you like them raw, that's the best. To be on the safe side, seek out organic cashews. Note: Most cashews come from India and go through a fumigating process before they can be exported. So, it's unlikely that you'll find unprocessed raw cashews.

Walnuts

Walnuts are one of the most nutritious nuts, and they contain omega-3 essential fatty acid. Since their fat content is very high, you shouldn't eat more than a handful or two at any one time. To avoid indigestion, eat walnuts in moderation.

Pine Nuts

Pine nuts do not contain the ideal fat but are a good supplemental nut because of their antioxidant properties. Ancient Romans and Greeks used them often as a supplemental food, adding them mainly to grains to enhance taste and density. Pine nuts continue to be used in this way today, particularly in the Mediterranean.

Pistachios

One of the biggest advantages of the pistachio, besides the fact that it tastes so good, is that it's one of the least allergenic nuts. Very few people have reactions to pistachios, even if they react to all other nuts. Pistachios were popular all throughout the Roman Empire, especially in the Middle East and North Africa, and they remain popular in many regions of the world today.

Thoughts on Salted Nuts

Although they're allowed on the Warrior Diet, I think salted nuts aren't always the best choice, because salty means processed, which means less natural properties. Salted and roasted nuts can, however, accelerate satiety simply because they'll make you thirsty sooner than unsalted nuts, and some people prefer their taste.

Seeds

Seeds belong to the same high-fat food group as nuts. They are highly nutritious. To avoid indigestion, don't consume too many seeds at any one time; a half handful will do. I think of seeds as a supplemental food. It's best to eat them alone as a snack, or with protein meals. Seeds contain a higher content of fat than nuts. Sesame, pumpkin, and sunflower seeds are all good sources of oils, phytosterols, vitamins, minerals, and other nutrients that support and maintain optimum health. Pumpkin seeds, for example, are one of the highest natural sources of zinc. Seeds such as pumpkin and sunflower are thought to help protect your hormonal system and are considered to be aphrodisiac foods. Sunflower seeds are very sensitive to light and ideally should be kept in a dark container to avoid rancidity. Seeds are rich in plant sterols and sterolines, which are oil substances that, as previously mentioned, are believed to support the hormonal system and have cholesterol-lowering properties.

My thoughts on raw versus roasted seeds are the same as those for nuts. Both are good, but raw is always better.

Lecithin

Lecithin is a natural source of phospholipids, which are the building blocks of cell membranes. Lecithin has a nutty, buttery taste. Besides being a good source of phospholipids, it's also high in choline and inositol, which are building blocks for brain neurotransmitters. Lecithin is a natural emulsifier, helping the liver to metabolize triglycerides. Thus, lecithin is a great aid for liver detoxification and fat metabolism.

I usually put a tablespoon or two on top of my protein meals just before eating. Lecithin occurs naturally in egg yolks and soybeans.

Eggs

Another good source of protein, eggs have different tastes and textures. The dominant tastes are sweet and salty, and textures soft, smooth, wet, or oily. Don't be afraid to eat the egg yolk. It's a natural source of vitamins A to E, DNA, RNA, and the essential sulfur-containing protein cysteine. The yellow pigment of the yolk is a vital carotene, so don't eat just the egg whites. For those who consume many eggs in one meal, I think it's best to keep a balance between the yolk and the whites. I personally keep a ratio of about four egg whites to one yolk. As far as cholesterol is concerned, more and more research suggests that eggs do not raise cholesterol. Eggs contain natural lecithin and, as just mentioned, are one of the highest sources of the natural protein cysteine. Cysteine is crucial for our metabolism and immunity. It's a sensitive protein, though, and is often destroyed when processed. For instance, cysteine is destroyed in most commercial whey protein powders; however, whey and colostrum that are processed well do retain it. Eating egg yolks is one of the best ways to supply your body with cysteine. Egg whites are said to be a complete protein, but I feel that egg whites alone are an inadequate source of protein and at least some yolk is necessary to enhance the egg's protein composition and enable you to derive all the benefits of its nutrients. Nature created a white and yellow egg. There are no mistakes in nature, so use both to your advantage. I believe it also tastes better when the whole egg is eaten.

Dairy

Dairy contains a wide variety of tastes, textures, and aromas. Dominant tastes are salty, sour, sweet, pungent, and smoked. Textures are smooth, creamy, buttery, milky, oily, soft, hard, chunky, and chewy. Dairy is a very good whole source of complete protein, and often tastes great. Try to buy organic dairy products. The best sources of dairy protein, and those I highly recommend, are aged raw milk cheese as well as minimally processed fresh, white nonfat or low-fat cheeses like farmer, ricotta, and cottage cheese, and plain yogurt and kefir. Consuming moderate amounts of high-fat dairy can be highly beneficial, particularly if it's made from grass-fed animals or organic raw milk. Certain compounds in milk fat, called conjugated linoleic acid (CLA), were found to have anti-estrogenic and anti-cancerous properties. It's great to indulge sometimes in eating aged cheeses, such as a chunk of Parmesan, as an appetizer. Like wine, Parmesan has most of the tastes within it. Goat, sheep, and buffalo cheeses and yogurt have unique tastes and aromas. They can be great alternatives to cow milk products. Generally speaking, goat, sheep, and buffalo dairy products are less allergenic than cow milk products.

Dairy products that are made from raw, organic, non-homogenized, and non-pasteurized milk are thought to be the best, but these are hard to find due to current governmental regulations for aggressive pasteurization, which kills beneficial as well as potentially harmful bacteria in dairy products.

If you're not allergic to dairy, that's wonderful, but never take this for granted because if you overeat it you may become sensitive or allergic. So rotate your dairy and don't eat it every day.

Whey Protein

Whey is one of the best sources of fast-assimilating proteins. If processed right, it's a most viable protein powder, and a great alternative to other protein foods. I believe when taken on an empty stomach, whey protein will nourish your digestive tract, muscles, and also your brain. Whey is great for recovery after a workout, as a light meal during the Undereating Phase, or as a dessert. I don't think whey should be part of the main meal itself since it's a processed powder and doesn't contain the combination of tastes, aromas, and different textures that whole foods do. And, as mentioned before, you need to experience this sensual array to be truly satisfied. You should chew real food for the main meal and enjoy it. Whey is dairy, so some people are sensitive to it. Monitor yourself.

Legumes, Beans, and Peas—The Gladiator Protein

I highly recommend consuming beans and peas, not just because of the fiber and IP6, but also because they're a very good source of protein that's balanced well with complex carbohydrates. And they taste pretty good, too.

The most accessible IP6 is generally found in legumes, beans, and especially peas. A study conducted on Finnish people found that although they consume one-third as much fiber as the Swedish, they have much less cancer, especially colon cancer. Researchers attribute this to the fact that in Finland the main source of fiber is legumes and peas, with their abundant IP6.

Beans contain high natural quantities of the protein L-DOPA, which boosts dopamine (a major neurotransmitter) in your brain. Dopamine plays an important role in regulating testosterone and virility. Ancient Romans were aware of the aphrodisiac effects of beans.

For thousands of years, peas, lentils, and beans were a main source of protein for Greek and Roman civilians as well as the Roman legions. Beans were also the main source of protein for the gladiators. The Greeks and Romans hated feeling bloated, so they were very careful when selecting beans and utilizing cooking methods. Even given the high consumption of beans at that time, people were ambiguous about them. The full story is quite intriguing. I discuss it at greater length in Chapter 9, "Lessons from History."

Cooking Protein

History has taught us how to best prepare beef, fish, and fowl. Ancient Romans cooked protein foods in broth. They often mixed fish or meat with veggies, grain, and beans all together in one pot. The popular practice today of barbecuing or grilling meat, which caramelizes or burns its surface, damages the protein and creates toxins that are widely believed to be carcinogenic. Some processing and cooking methods are less damaging to the food than others. "Warrior Meals and Recipes" (Chapter 15) discusses how to prepare protein meals.

Rotating Protein to Avoid Sensitivities and Allergies

Rotating and varying protein works best. Try not to eat the same group of protein foods on an everyday basis. If you do, you may develop sensitivity or an allergic reaction to it.

Eggs, for instance, are considered to be an allergenic food. I believe that sensitivity to eggs often occurs due to high and frequent consumption of egg white omelets. I personally have never had a problem with eggs, but I don't consume egg whites alone. I have eggs a few times per week, and generally rotate them with dairy, fish, and seafood. Everyone is different, so experiment to see what works best for you.

Oils

Oils and fats have a variety of tastes, textures, aromas, and colors. In general, oils add richness to meals as well as a characteristically smooth texture.

- Fat is Essential
- Essential Fatty Acids—Yes
- Monounsaturated Oils—Yes
- Hydrogenated, Partially Hydrogenated Oils—No
- Butter—Yes
- Margarine—No
- Cocoa Butter and Chocolate—Yes

Essential Fatty Acids

Essential fatty acids (EFA) are the most important oils. Since our bodies cannot produce them, we have to ingest them. They should be part of your main meal. These oils belong to the "raw food" group. They should be cold-pressed, minimally processed, and applied on the top of food, never cooked or heated. Some great organic essential fatty acid oils are now available in the United States, and they can be found in the refrigerated section of health food and vitamin stores. Ideally your diet should contain a ratio of 2:1 (or higher) omega-3 to omega-6 oils. Many people suffer from an omega-3 deficiency. This essential fatty acid appears only in fatty fishes such as salmon, tuna, mackerel, and sardines; plant sources include flax seeds, hemp seeds, and walnuts, though the latter is not a rich source of omega-3 oil. For those who don't consume enough omega-3-rich foods, supplementation is necessary (preferably in the form of flaxseed oil, in which omega-3 is present in higher quantities than omega-6). Omega-6 is abundant in many foods such as grains, nuts, seeds, vegetable oils, animal protein, dairy, and eggs. Primrose and borage oils are good sources of omega-6 GLA (gamma linoleic acid). GLA is an omega-6 bioactive derivative, a building block for prostaglandins, which regulate blood pressure, inflammation, and pain.

It is best to consume essential fatty acids with protein and unsweetened carbohydrate meals. Never heat these oils. Fresh flax seed oil (an omega-3) has a pleasant nutty taste. Hemp oil contains both omega-3 and -6 and is very aromatic. Primrose oil, which is high in omega-6 GLA, has a light, neutral taste.

Essential fatty acids should be carefully processed and handled. Check the expiration date before purchasing and keep the bottle refrigerated. As mentioned before, use your senses. Smell oils before you use them. If they have a paint-like smell, it's time to throw them away. Taste them too. You should enjoy these oils. If they don't taste good to you, don't use them. As mentioned, EFA deficiencies, especially of omega-3, may create serious metabolic problems, including insulin insensitivity, chronic inflammation, hypertension, estrogen disorders, and increased risk for cancer.

On the Warrior Diet, healthy fats are unlimited. Use your instinct and trial and error to determine how much EFA oil you need. I generally recommend using 1–3 tablespoons per day.

Monounsaturated Oils

Monounsaturated oils are generally considered to be the safest oils since they don't oxidize so quickly, being less sensitive to light and heat. In their raw state, these oils have pleasant natural aromas and are great additions to meals, especially to dry or grainy foods. Olive oil is the least sensitive to light and heat, and is therefore the best monounsaturated oil to use for cooking. It's also great for dressings and flavoring. Use cold-pressed extra-virgin olive oil to obtain maximum nutritional value.

Avocados, nuts, and seeds contain monounsaturated oils. I highly recommend that you consume them as whole foods. The naturally occurring oil is in its most biologically viable state in avocados, almonds, pecans, walnuts, and seeds such as pumpkin and sesame. Processing these foods into oils may take away much of their live properties. When consumed in their raw state, avocados and almonds are alkalizing. Nuts and seeds are rich in lipase (the enzyme that breaks down fat) and other nutrients, including phytosterols that support the hormonal system.

Polyunsaturated Oils

Despite what many health practitioners say, people should be concerned about using polyunsaturated oils/fatty acids such as canola, soy, safflower, and corn oil. Most of these oils don't have enough omega-3 essential fatty acids and can be destroyed (go rancid) very quickly when heated, exposed to air, etc. High consumption of these oils may lead to an imbalance of essential fatty acids, and a deficiency of omega-3 may eventually lead to serious metabolic problems, including excess of estrogen, weight gain, and related disorders.

Hydrogenated and Saturated Oils

These oils have a solid texture at room temperature. They contain different tastes and aromas. When added to meals they usually enrich flavors and add a smooth, oily texture.

I think it's best to stay away from hydrogenated oils like margarine and the processed oils that are found in many commercial foods. Saturated tropical oils like palm or coconut oil are good as long as they're raw and unprocessed. Regarding butter, while I don't recommend using it extensively, it's okay to have once in a while. Butter is high in saturated fatty acid; however, it does contain a balanced ratio (1:1) of omega-6 to omega-3 essential fatty acid, and it is rich in vitamins A and E as well as the anti-estrogenic compound CLA. Butter is preferable to margarine. Saturated oils are more stable than polyunsaturated oils, so there's less risk of them becoming rancid.

Some saturated oils may actually be good for you. It is believed that chocolate might indeed be an aphrodisiac, and cocoa butter, which is high in stearic acid, may naturally convert in the body to monounsaturated fatty acids, which have a neutral-to-lowering effect on cholesterol. So, in addition to other surprises, the Warrior Diet allows you to indulge in—yes—chocolate (preferably dark), following low-carb protein meals.

The worst oils to consume are transfatty acids. These damaged (by high temperatures) fatty compounds are abundant in margarine, hydrogenated oils, and many processed foods.

Carbohydrates

Carbohydrates offer different tastes, with sweet or starchy being most dominant. They have different aromas and textures: light, heavy, grainy, smooth, chewy, creamy, and crunchy.

Complex and Simple Carbs

Most people know that there are two kinds of carbohydrates, complex and simple. Consuming complex carbohydrates (whole grains) is usually much more beneficial than consuming simple carbohydrates, but not always. Sometimes simple natural carbohydrate-rich foods, such as papaya or pineapple, can be the best complement to a meal. Adding more flavors and textures is partly why, but the main reason is that meat is usually digested more easily when eaten with certain fruits. Combining meat with fruit is a very old tradition. Hunter-gatherers hunted meat and also gathered berries, and often ate them together. In tropical areas people like to marinate meats with papaya or pineapple juices. The protease enzymes found in these tropical fruits predigest and tenderize the meat. Whole grains are best to eat when they're fully cooked. Soaking, rinsing, and cooking removes toxins and makes the fiber soft and more edible.

Pleasure, Satiety, and Relaxation

Carbohydrates create satiety since they naturally boost serotonin production in your brain. Serotonin is a protein neurotransmitter that makes you feel calmer, happier, more satisfied, and able to sleep better since serotonin is also a building block for the hormone melatonin.

Here are some reasons why it's good to eat carbohydrates as the last component of your meal:

Control Your Insulin: It is unhealthy to unnecessarily overspike insulin. High insulin spikes are associated with blood sugar fluctuations and insulin resistance. It's better to consume a meal with the lowest glycemic index. The higher the glycemic index, the more pressure is placed on your body to produce insulin. When veggies are eaten first, followed by protein and fat, the glycemic index of any carb that is consumed afterwards is automatically reduced.

Follow the First Rule of Eating: Carbohydrate-rich foods such as bread and pasta generally have more dominant, aggressive tastes than veggies or protein, and the more processed they are, the more aggressive they become. Since the first rule of eating is to begin with subtle tastes and move to the more aggressive, carbohydrates should in general be eaten last. You can skip carbs entirely if you reach full satiety after eating the veggies and protein part of the meal. You don't have to eat carbohydrates every day. It's also good to rotate between relatively low and relatively moderate carb days.

Lose Body Fat: Overconsumption of carbs may cause oversecretion of insulin, which inhibits fat breakdown. If you want to lose body fat, have carbohydrates as the last component of your meal (after protein). This method naturally minimizes the amount of carbs that you eat without a feeling of deprivation. The fewer carbs you ingest, the more fat you burn.

Choosing Carbohydrates—What Are the Best Carbs to Eat?

Plants and Roots

The safest sources of carbohydrates (meaning the least reactive, and with minimal insulin response) come from plants and roots, including beans, carrots, beets, pumpkin, and all the squash family. Potatoes, corn, plantains, and cassava are more starchy and dense, and have a higher glycemic index. Therefore, they're somewhat more reactive with insulin. All these plant foods are rich in vital nutrients such as minerals, phytonutrients, and fiber, and most of them need to be cooked.

The Problem with Refined Carbohydrates

It is my opinion that consuming whole-food carbohydrates is the best way to reach satisfaction instinctually, largely because of the mineral and fiber content of these foods. When one eats foods that are high in naturally occurring minerals and fiber, it triggers an instinctive feedback mechanism in the body that recognizes full nourishment and satisfaction. Conversely, eating refined, processed carbohydrate foods, which lack minerals and fiber, leads to feelings of deprivation, and this often manifests as compulsive bingeing.

Fruits

Fruits aren't necessarily a good choice of carbohydrate for the main meal, as they digest better on an empty stomach. However, fruits are loaded with phytonutrients, vitamins, minerals, and living enzymes in their most potent form. Since the Undereating Phase is based on ingesting live fruits and veggies, with their detoxifying, catabolic, alkalizing qualities, I believe that in order to balance the body into more of an acidic, anabolic state later in the day, and to reach full satisfaction from your meal, you should minimize fruits during the main meal and instead consume more plants, roots, and grains. There are, however, exceptions. As noted, you can complement high-protein meals with berries, tropical fruits, and fermented fruits, which are lower in sugar than other fruits and high in enzymes.

Grains

Next to plants and roots, the best source of carbohydrates comes from grains such as rice, oats, barley, quinoa, and millet.

Rice

Rice is a highly nutritious grain, and very few people are sensitive to it. Ideally you should develop a taste for whole-grain wild or brown rice, with the fiber. (Wild rice is actually a grass seed, not rice grains. Some grains are actually seeds and some are actually fruits, like quinoa.) Whole-grain rice is rich in B vitamins, rice bran, and a complex of vital nutrients, including tocopherols, which are believed to be the most potent form of vitamin E. But if you'd rather have white rice at times, this is also fine. I sometimes prefer white rice. Let your taste and mood be your guide.

Oats

Oats are another very good grain. I like oatmeal and sometimes include it as part of my main meal. With fish or other seafood, I prefer to have plant carbohydrates, rice, or other grains. Fish and rice simply works better for me than fish and oatmeal.

I know that most people like to have oatmeal in the morning, but the Warrior Diet does not suggest having grain carbs during the Undereating Phase (unless you are an extremely physically active person). In Chapter 10, "The Warrior Diet Idea," I discuss how you can alternate the Warrior Diet with days of high fat and days of high carbs. You can basically live on oatmeal on high-carb days.

I think oatmeal goes very well with certain proteins, like eggs or yogurt. Oatmeal is very high in water-soluble fiber and B vitamins, which are essential for your health. Oat fiber is rich is proteoglucans, known for lowering blood cholesterol and blood pressure while enhancing the immune system.

Barley—The Gladiator Grain

Barley is one of the most ancient grains. In addition to its high protein content, it has one of the lowest glycemic indexes. Barley was a major grain and ingredient in bread for both the ancient Romans and Greeks, and a main food of the gladiators (who were sometimes called "Barley Carriers" in mocking reference to the animals used to transport barley).

Barley is often used in soups but can also be eaten as porridge or as part of a cooked meal, just as you'd serve rice. Barley broth is believed to help detoxify the liver.

Quinoa

Quinoa isn't really a grain; it's actually the fruit of an herb native to the Andes. It's high in protein and contains all eight essential amino acids plus potassium, iron, and zinc. Quinoa requires only a short cooking time. It has a mild flavor and a fluffy, slightly sticky texture. It's one of the safest grains to ingest, and one of the most alkalizing.

Millet

Another alkaline grain, millet has a protein content higher than that found in wheat, corn, or rice. It's popular in India, Africa, China, and Russia. Millet is the least allergenic of all grains.

Amaranth

Another choice is amaranth. It is high in protein and is actually a complete protein with a roughly equivalent protein composition to that found in red meat. Like quinoa, amaranth is not really a grain; it's a fruit. There are different ways to eat amaranth, including toasting it so it pops like popcorn. It tastes pretty earthy when prepared other ways. Those who've never eaten it should prepare themselves for something completely different. Some people find its taste to be too strong and aromatic. You've got to try it to determine if you like it. Amaranth was the food of the Aztecs and their gods. Amaranth can be found in many forms in most health food stores.

Wheat and Buckwheat

The least desirable grain is wheat. A lot of people have allergic reactions to it or are sensitive to the gluten inside, and wheat is one of the most acidic grains.

The wheat we eat today is not the same as it was in the past; modern wheat contains a higher percentage of gluten. So be cautious with it.

According to Dr. Peter D'Adamo, author of *Eat Right for Your Type,* people with blood type O should avoid wheat, and those with blood type B and AB should avoid buckwheat. On a positive note, since buckwheat doesn't belong to the wheat family, it doesn't contain gluten. Buckwheat is also high in complete protein.

You can find gluten-free breads, cereals, and pastas in many health food stores.

Sprouted Wheat

Sprouted wheat is different from regular wheat. The sprouting destroys most of the gluten. It's also less acidic than common wheat, and a good source of enzymes and bran. Sprouted wheat breads are available in health food stores. Check the ingredients to make sure that sprouted wheat is the main ingredient in the flour.

Kamut and Spelt

Members of the wheat family, these grains are more ancient than wheat. Many people who eat them experience more or less similar but usually milder symptoms than with common wheat. These grains can be eaten as porridge or as part of a whole-grain meal. You can also find them in puffed and other dry cereals, and as puffed cakes (like rice cakes).

Dry Cereals

Carbohydrates are generally best to ingest when they're fresh, cooked, warm, and somewhat moist. But there's an alternative way to eat them—"chewing dry cereal." There are some very good, unsweetened dry cereals on the market today, usually sold in health food stores or the health-food section of supermarkets. The best ones are organic. I like cereals made from puffed rice, corn, or a combination of corn and amaranth, but there's a whole host of other options as well. The ideal time to eat dry cereals is toward the end of the meal, right after protein. Dry cereals add a crunchy texture to the meal. If you add essential fatty acids on top of these cereals it will lower the glycemic index, enrich the nutritional value, and might even make them taste better.

The advantage of dry cereal is that you use a lot of your saliva, which helps pre-digest the food. When you eat wet cereal, you don't chew it as much as when it's dry. The more you chew, the better you're going to digest the food, and I believe the more satiety you'll experience.

If you like eating your cereal with milk, note that you may miss the whole point of chewing dry cereal. However, if you like to add milk, check how it affects your digestion and satiety. If you're trying to lose body fat, stick to unsweetened dry cereal. Think of it as similar to eating popcorn.

Sweet Meals for a "Sweet Tooth"

The carbohydrate stage of the Warrior Diet is one of choice. You must select either a sweet meal or starchy one. Sweet meals are not the preferred choice. But for those who like to have something sweet for dessert, here's a suggestion.

Have a high-protein meal with veggies (such as zucchini, broccoli, spinach, Swiss chard, string beans, eggplant, or cauliflower). Avoid starches altogether, and minimize even starchy vegetables. Moderate your fat intake on these days as well—fat and sugar aren't an ideal combination because sugar may disturb optimum EFA (essential fatty acid) metabolism. At the end of the meal you can indulge in a sweet dessert. But try to avoid simple (common processed) sugars, and hydrogenated and partially hydrogenated fats. They're always bad for you.

In these pages I suggest and explain how to prepare some dessert recipes, such as pumpkin cheesecake and fruit gelatin, which contain minimal carbohydrates yet taste like a sweet, delicious dessert (see Chapter 15, "Warrior Meals and Recipes"). And, as noted earlier, it's okay to eat chocolate at the end of the meal if you want to. Just make sure that you treat it as a condiment.

Sugar Tip:
Natural sweeteners like raw honey or brown rice syrup can be mixed with protein (like whey powder). It'll add texture and taste, and may stop sugar cravings at the end of your meal. Moreover, especially for athletes, this is a good way to add protein to your diet.

Sample Sweet Meal
First Course—Salad
Main Course—Fish and Eggplant
Dessert—Pumpkin Cheesecake

Starchy Meals

The second choice, which I generally prefer, is to consume complex carbohydrates (starches) in my main meal and no sweet dessert. Remember, even though carbs are unlimited, it's best that they come at the end of the meal, particularly for those whose goal is to lose body fat. If you like to mix carbohydrates with protein, that's okay. As noted earlier, eating carbs alone, without protein or fat accompanying it, often causes overstimulation of insulin, which eventually leads to insulin insensitivity, blood-sugar fluctuations, and fat gain.

Sample Starchy Meal
First course: Salad
Second course: Grilled fish and cooked vegetables
Third course: Rice or pasta (third course can be eaten together
with the second course)

Fiber

Fiber contains different textures: pectins, mucilage, and gums are soft and gummy, while cellulose and bran are solid, coarse, and crumbly. Having fiber in your diet is critical for your health. Fiber helps keep insulin in balance, feeds healthy gut bacteria, helps prevent constipation, reduces cholesterol, and protects against cancer.

Unfortunately, when many people eat fibrous food they become bloated and gassy. Those who experience this should monitor themselves and eliminate from their diet those fibers to which they're sensitive. It's not unusual for people to react poorly to one kind of fiber, and better to others. Note that loading your body with enzymes may help digest fibrous foods and alleviate undesirable side effects. In my opinion, if you take a high-quality probiotic supplement, you can reduce your fiber consumption somewhat and should still keep your digestion and elimination systems intact.

Fermented Foods

Fermented foods contain a variety of tastes, textures, and aromas. They enhance the composition of the meal and thus fall within the second rule of eating. ("Include as many tastes, textures, colors, and aromas as possible in your main meal.") The dominant taste of fermented food is sour. Textures and aromas vary according to the food.

Naturally fermented foods are high in lactic acid-producing bacteria. This helps the digestive process and optimizes metabolism.

Fermentation helps protect food from spoiling. Warriors used to carry fermented foods with them during war campaigns, or under extreme conditions when fresh food wasn't accessible. The lactic acid-producing bacteria within naturally fermented foods is what prevents spoilage; and this good bacterium destroys pathogenic bacteria. In fact, consumption of naturally fermented foods is one of the best ways to help eliminate yeast infections, which affect much of the Western population today. Yeast infections are the result of a chronic imbalance of gut flora, and they are usually caused by the continual consumption of sugar, overly processed and junk foods, as well as taking antibiotics.

Naturally fermented foods are great aids in the supply of certain B vitamins, as well as vitamin D. They are probiotics, which support digestion. The lactic acid-forming bacteria within fermented foods complete the final digestion of amino acids, thereby improving protein efficiency. Traditionally, fermented food accompanied high-protein meals. This fact is extremely important for athletes, who usually consume much more protein than the general population. Lactic acid-producing bacteria optimize the pH in the colon, which protects against bacterial infections and cancer.

The Japanese traditionally pickle a variety of exotic vegetables, roots, and even fruits. In India, mangos and papayas are pickled and used as a chutney relish, often served with meat or fish. Mediterranean food is enriched with pickles, olives, and sauerkraut. Indonesian cuisine is also full of relishes and fermented foods. Ancient Romans used to pickle almost anything, including fish and dairy. Let me note here that not every sour food is naturally fermented. Real fermentation requires lactic acid-producing bacteria as a natural catalyst.

Fermented foods can be eaten at any stage of the meal. It's preferable to eat them before or with protein. You should monitor the amount of fermented food that you consume. Start with small amounts and increase gradually in order to avoid unpleasant symptoms, like bloating.

Fermentation destroys sugar by converting it to lactic acid. For those who are lactose-intolerant, eating fermented dairy (such as plain yogurt or kefir) may be of benefit, because under fermentation most of the lactose sugar is destroyed.

Examples of Fermented Foods
(that when naturally fermented are good sources of beneficial bacteria)

  Pickles
  Olives
  Sauerkraut
  Miso
  Apple Cider Vinegar
  Yogurt (preferably plain)
  Kefir (preferably plain)

Apple Cider Vinegar

Apple cider vinegar is a good source of food enzymes and minerals, and thus could be a good live supplement for your digestion and overall health. I'm not, however, a big fan of vinegar in general because it also feeds bad bacteria and may cause yeast. And, vinegar increases acidity, sometimes in an uncontrolled manner. If your diet is too alkaline, vinegar (in moderation) could be helpful. It has a balancing factor. But if you're too acidic, stay away from all vinegars.

Wine

Wine contains most of the tastes (with a dominance of sour, sweet, dry, and pungent), different aromas, and a smooth texture. Wine is a live fermented food. When you sense its taste, your brain already starts to achieve a certain level of satiety.

Wine is good for digestion of protein since it contains enzymes. It can also help combat free radicals, and studies have shown that the flavones in red wine may protect against heart attacks. Drinking wine in moderation may help keep you healthy.

A lot of people drink a glass of wine just before, or with, their dinner. This is acceptable on the Warrior Diet, as I believe, speaking generally, that drinking a glass of good wine just before or with dinner enriches a meal. Wine works well with protein food, veggies, and nuts. Nonetheless, wine should not be combined with sweets or with carb meals such as pasta or bread to avoid high insulin spikes, blood-sugar fluctuation, and fat gain.

Wine can have some negative side effects, including:

- It may tax the liver.
- The alcohol content may have an estrogenic effect on the body.
- Some people are sensitive (allergic) to the sulfites that are in most wines.
- Drinking wine may exacerbate overacidity in those who already suffer from it.
- If you suffer from toxicity, drinking alcohol will make this worse.
- Pregnant women should avoid all alcohol.

The Acid-Base Balancing Factor

In addition to balancing tastes, textures, aromas, and temperatures, it's important to reach a healthy acid-base balance of your meal in order to keep the second rule of eating intact. ("Include as many tastes, textures, colors, and aromas as possible in your main meal.")

You can control your acid-alkaline balance on the Warrior Diet without compromising the quality of food or the amount you eat. Since the Undereating Phase is based on consumption of living foods including fruits, vegetables, and their freshly prepared juices, which are potent alkalizers, you actually pre-potentiate your body's pH and your enzyme pool for the Overeating Phase, which is based on more acid-forming foods such as eggs, fish, meat, and certain grains.

Consuming a lot of vegetables with the main meal, in addition to the advantages mentioned earlier, is alkalizing. Regarding grains, some are less acidic. For example, millet and quinoa are alkalizing grains. All the grains that belong to the wheat family are more acidic.

People Whose System Is Too Alkaline

Those people whose systems are too alkaline can use vinegar (rice vinegar or organic apple cider vinegar are good choices) in order to instantly acidify the overalkaline system. Eating high-protein meals naturally acidifies the body. All animal proteins (besides raw milk) are acid-forming foods.

People Who Suffer from Overacidity

Those who suffer from overacidity, which is the case for the majority of people, should consume more live and cooked vegetables, since they are alkalizing, and avoid all vinegars. I also recommend consuming foods that are high in minerals, such as miso, which is made from nonpasteurized, fermented soybeans. Miso is a great alkalizer that's rich in minerals and naturally occurring sodium. It can be consumed as a soup or as a sauce. Another way to instantly alkalize the body is supplementing with good-quality minerals, in particular calcium.

Glycemic Index

The glycemic index (GI) shows how much insulin your body secretes when a food or beverage is introduced into your blood. Although this sounds simple, it's actually quite complex. For instance, the same food can have a different GI depending on how it's cooked. Pasta *al dente* (pasta that's cooked for a short time and so remains slightly hard) has a lower glycemic index than well-cooked soft pasta. Baked potatoes have a higher glycemic index than mashed potatoes because of a difference in the macrostructure of the carbohydrate.

When you add butter, milk, monounsaturated oil, or essential fatty acids to food, it usually lowers the GI. So, if you eat a baked potato with oil, for instance, it has a lower glycemic index than eating a plain baked potato. Fiber slows carbohydrate absorption and therefore may help reduce the glycemic index of the carbs ingested. Whole grains have a lower glycemic index than refined grains.

Even though many people consider the glycemic index to be the parameter for selecting carbs, I don't believe that the GI is always as critical a factor as it's projected to be. Fructose, for example, has a lower GI than white rice. But in my opinion, commercial fructose, which appears in many commercial foods, processed foods, and health bars, is one of the most dangerous and destructive sources of carbohydrate. The liver has a limited enzymatic capacity to utilize fructose. Any excess, particularly when fructose is ingested in a pure refined form, may overwhelm the liver, leading to elevated blood lipids, insulin resistance, and weight gain. White rice, with its higher GI, is a far superior choice. When mixed with fiber, protein, and fat, white rice can be effectively utilized without any adverse effects. Fruit juices and certain vegetable juices (like carrot juice) have a relatively high GI, but since they come from natural, live (raw) foods (I'm referring to juices that are freshly squeezed), the body can usually handle them very well. Freshly prepared juices contain digestive enzymes that load the body with essential nutrients to support overall metabolism. So, even though fruits and certain veggies have a relatively high GI, it's not something to worry about, unless you are diabetic or hypoglycemic.

The Case Against Grapes

The exception to not worrying about the high glycemic index of healthy fruits and vegetables is grapes. They're high in glucose (not fructose), and glucose causes rapid rises in blood sugar and therefore may trigger undesirable insulin spikes. As noted, grapes should be avoided or eaten in moderation during the day. I sometimes have grapes for dessert after a high-protein evening meal. It's essential to source organic grapes if you like them, since grapes are heavily treated with pesticides and herbicides and are consistently found to retain the highest amounts of toxic residue of any foods in the supermarket.

Salt Restriction

I question the effectiveness of salt restriction. When you restrict sodium, in the beginning you might lose some water weight, but if you reintroduce it, you may suffer from water retention. This is because sodium restriction triggers a spike in the hormone aldosterone (one of the adrenocortex hormones secreted by the adrenal glands), which works to preserve sodium inside the tissue cells, and this process creates water retention when sodium intake suddenly increases. As long as you keep sodium intake fairly consistent and in a normal ratio (which, of course, should be slightly higher in warmer weather and after extensive exercise), you won't over-secrete this hormone or trigger the "aldosterone syndrome."

Healthy people who routinely consume sodium generally don't experience ill effects by increasing it somewhat. It's those who restrict sodium consumption and then suddenly increase it who usually suffer from water retention. This is unfortunately what happens to bodybuilders and other athletes who need to "make weight" before competition. During the competitive season, when sodium is restricted, they look leaner, but sometimes hours after the first meal that's no longer sodium-restricted—boom—they can blow up like a balloon.

Keeping the Sodium Pump Intact

Balancing sodium intake has a lot to do with the ratio of sodium to potassium and magnesium. Natural foods—fruits and veggies, whole grains, and roots—have a high ratio of potassium to sodium (up to 200:1). Unfortunately, the typical American overly processed diet has an opposite ratio in which sodium is higher than potassium. To say this simply, in order to regulate your sodium intake, make sure that you balance your potassium-to-sodium ratio. Ideally your potassium intake should be higher than your sodium intake. Potassium is antagonistic to sodium. It drives excessive sodium out of the cells and thus keeps your sodium-potassium pump intact, helping protect against water retention and high blood pressure.

The best salts to consume are sea salts. My favorites are those that come from the Dead Sea.

Iodized salt is a fair option for those who suffer from an iodine deficiency. However, the best sources of organic iodine are fish, seafood, and sea vegetables.

Note: This advice relates to healthy people. Those who suffer from high or low blood pressure, arthritis, or heart problems should first consult their physician about sodium consumption.

The Most Allergenic Foods

The most allergenic foods are wheat, soy, peanuts, yeast, corn, dairy, and sugar—and all the foods made with them. There are many other foods that people are allergic to as well, including shellfish, chocolate, potatoes and other nightshades, aspartame, citrus fruits, coffee, chamomile tea, MSG, additives, and a host of other substances. Monitor yourself. Those who feel sensitivity to certain foods should avoid them and consider seeing an allergist. In any case, it's always a wise idea to rotate all the foods you consume to avoid developing sensitivities and allergies from over-consuming any one item.

What Is Not Allowed on the Warrior Diet

Almost everything is allowed on the Warrior Diet, but there are a few exceptions:

- Refined sugar
- Refined, processed pastries

Combining starch with excessive sugar does not work, never has, and never will. I think that if the sugar content per 2-ounce serving of a starchy treat (such as cereals or bread) is less than 2 grams, then it's okay. I don't recommend more than this because it may place unnecessary pressure on your pancreatic system to rapidly increase insulin production. You should read the ingredients to check the quality of the leavening, as well as the chemicals and preservatives used in baked products. If they contain aluminum-based leavening, artificial sweeteners, sugar alcohol, nitrites, sulfites, hydrogenated or partially hydrogenated oils, or simple sugars, stay away from these highly polluted treats. Also, avoid eating chemical-laden protein bars. If you choose to consume them, you may suffer the consequences, such as nausea, bloating, allergic reactions, and undesirable weight gain.

END NOTE:

If you're completing this chapter and still find the information confusing or a bit overwhelming, just remember to follow the Warrior Diet's Three Rules of Eating. This is a great way to ease in and begin experimenting.

> Rule #1: Always start with subtle-tasting foods and move to the more aggressive foods.
> Rule #2: Include as many tastes, textures, colors, and aromas as possible in your main meal.
> Rule #3: Stop eating when you feel much more thirsty than hungry.

By practicing this diet, you'll gradually remember more of the details, which will help you to define and reach your goals. This is a very personal and creative diet. As long as you follow the above rules, you'll soon find your own unique diet, the one that works best for you. Trust your instincts.

The Warrior Diet Daily Food Cycle: What and When to Eat and Drink

This is for all those guys who ask me, "Just tell me what I can eat during the day and what I can eat at night."

- Eat raw fruits, vegetables, and light fresh protein (yogurt, kefir, eggs, nuts and seeds, protein shakes) during the day; all food groups at night.
- Drink plenty of clean, pure water throughout the day.

Mornings through noon:
- Water—drink at least one glass of water upon awakening (plain or with lemon).
- Coffee or tea
- Fruits—fresh and raw
- Juices—freshly prepared from raw vegetables or fruits. I mean really

fresh, those made to order in a blender or juicer, not prepared or bottled juices.
- Small servings of light fresh protein food, such as plain yogurt, kefir,
poached or boiled eggs, as well as whey and milk protein shakes.

Noon through end of day:
- Coffee or tea
- Small serving of protein
- Fruits—fresh, raw fruits
- Juices—freshly prepared from raw vegetables (such as carrot, beet,
parsley) or raw fruits (such as oranges, grapefruits, strawberries, blue-
berries)
- Miso soup

During the adaptation period, and days that you feel deprived:
- Green salad, with little or no dressing
- Protein—pesticide-free whey and milk protein shake would be the
best protein of choice during the day.
- Or you can opt for lean protein (no more than 6 ounces) such as
sashimi, eggs, plain yogurt or kefir (low-fat or nonfat), cottage cheese,
or whey ricotta cheese. Don't mix proteins; have only one per snack.
- Raw nuts: A handful of raw nuts, preferably almonds, instead of lean
protein during the afternoon hours.

Evenings:
The Warrior Diet is based on the principle of eating one large meal per day,
preferably at night. During this meal you can eat as much as you want from
all food groups (protein, fat, and carbohydrates), as long as you follow the
Warrior Diet rules of eating:

1. Start with *leafy green vegetables* (such as romaine lettuce, red leaf lettuce, arugula, parsley, endives).
2. Continue with *protein* (such as fish, seafood, eggs, beans, cheese),
cooked vegetables (such as broccoli, cauliflower, zucchini, carrots,
squash, mushrooms, eggplant, beet greens, kale, collard greens), and
fat (such as essential fatty acid oils, olive oil, almonds, avocado,
butter).

3. Finish with *carbohydrates* (such as rice, potatoes, corn, yams, quinoa, barley) or alternatively, finish with raw nuts or seeds (such as almonds, pecans, walnuts, pumpkin seeds).
4. Stop eating when you feel much more thirsty than hungry.

Before your workout:
   Water
   Coffee or tea
   Protein shake (made with pesticide-free, fast-assimilating proteins such as whey and milk)
After:
   One liter of water, during and after
   Multivitamin and minerals
   Protein shake (same as pre-workout shake but larger serving)

Extremely Active People

For professional athletes and others who engage in intense, vigorous physical activities during the day and burn thousands of calories, it may be necessary to consume more food during the day to satisfy high-calorie demands and to spare muscle breakdown. In these circumstances, it's okay to have a light carbohydrate meal during the day (such as oatmeal and eggs, rice and eggs, rice soup, or barley soup). However, if your goal is to lose body fat, minimize the amount of carbohydrates during the day and have a light protein meal instead, preferably from a light, fast-assimilating source such as yogurt, kefir, or pesticide-free protein shake.

The Warrior Diet—A Sample Day

Upon awakening:
   1 cup of water
   Amla C: 100 mg
   Multivitamin and minerals (1/3 daily serving)
   Probiotics: 3–6 capsules
   Coffee—black, from freshly ground beans
   Morning shake
   Small glass of grapefruit juice or yogurt or protein shake (15–30g)

Noon:
> Medium-size juice—carrot, beet, and ginger, or a salad with boiled or poached eggs
> Multivitamin and minerals (1/3 daily serving)
> Amla C: 100 mg

Early afternoon:
> A bowl of berries or yogurt

Late afternoon:
> Protein shake
> Coffee—black or espresso with milk foam

Early Evening Workout—during and after:
> 1–1.5 liters of water
> Multivitamin and minerals (1/3 daily serving)
> Calcium and magnesium (500 mg)
> Amla C: 100–200 mg

Recovery meal:
> Protein shake: 30–50 g

Evening: Main Meal (eat as much as you want)
> Mixed green salad (you can add tomatoes, onions, and olive oil)
> Curry fish in spicy tomato broth
> EFA oil, lecithin
> Steamed broccoli, zucchini, and carrots or string beans with garlic

If you are fully satisfied or much more thirsty than hungry, stop eating. If you are still hungry, finish with brown rice topped with EFA or lecithin, or instead finish with 1–3 handfuls of raw almonds, or alternatively, finish with a Warrior Diet dessert like pumpkin cheesecake or green tea with ginger, slightly sweetened with maple syrup.

Late night:
> Protein shake—no sugar added

As you can see, The Warrior Diet can be applied with different food combinations and recipes to accommodate different needs and satisfy different tastes. The food choices can be adjusted according to variables such as food availability, level of physical activity, and health condition.

CHAPTER 7

STUBBORN FAT

STUBBORN FAT IS A MAJOR PROBLEM for many people today. It doesn't matter if they are trying to get rid of it through various diets or exercise routines—the fact is, this fat remains and seems impossible to remove. That's why it's called stubborn fat. Besides the Anti-Estrogenic Diet, I'm not aware of any diet that seriously addresses this problem.

One of the most popular methods today of removing stubborn fat is liposuction, an intrusive and risky procedure. This is a multimillion-dollar business involving sucking out fat tissues through surgery. Not only can it be dangerous, or even fatal, liposuction often doesn't solve the problem. Other methods include crash fad diets and diet pills, often with devastating effects on the hormonal and neural systems, as well as the overall metabolic integrity of the body.

Such extreme measures show how desperate people are. There are natural, noninvasive ways to remove stubborn fat. To understand how to deal with this problem, let me explain what stubborn fat is, why we have it, and how to prevent or lose it.

What Is Stubborn Fat?

Stubborn fat is composed of slow-metabolized, often estrogen-sensitive adipose tissue. To burn fat, a natural hormonal process has to take place. When a fat-burning process is stimulated, the adrenal hormones bind to special receptors in the fat tissues. There are two major groups of receptors in the fat tissues, alpha and beta. The beta adrenoreceptors are the active ones, which respond to the adrenal hormones and burn fat. On the other hand, the alpha receptors are antagonistic to fat-burning.

Stubborn fat tissues often have a lower ratio of beta receptors to alpha receptors. Due to alpha receptors' inhibiting effect on fat breakdown, stubborn fat tissues are generally slow to respond to adrenal hormones.

To make matters worse, stubborn fat is generally an estrogen-sensitive tissue, typically high in estrogen receptors. Estrogen (the female hormone), once it's bound to estrogen receptors, causes enlargement of the adipose tissue and thus induces even more fat gain.

There's much more to it, but I don't want to make this too complicated and overly scientific. So for now, let's just say that stubborn fat presents three major problems:

1. It doesn't have a high enough ratio of beta receptors to alpha receptors, so it doesn't respond to adrenal fat-burning stimulation.
2. It is highly sensitive to estrogen, which promotes the growth of estrogen-sensitive fat tissues and thus accelerates fat gain.

And, on top of all this—

3. Stubborn fat doesn't have a healthy blood circulation. These slowly metabolized fat tissues have fewer blood vessels than a normal fat tissue, and consequently this fat is slower to metabolize and, therefore, more stubborn or difficult to remove.

What Causes Stubborn Fat?

There are many reasons for having stubborn fat. Both men and women suffer from stubborn fat gain as a result of unhealthy diet, exposure to estrogenic chemicals and/or aging. The increase in size of estrogen-sensitive fat tissues has been associated with excess of estrogen in the body. Excess of estrogen often occurs due to the inability of the liver to break down and detoxify estrogenic substances, metabolites, or chemical compounds that mimic estrogen in the body.

Fat gain has also been associated with insulin insensitivity and over-consumption of carbohydrates. Over-consumption of too many carbohydrates—especially sugar and overly processed, refined carbs—places pressure on the pancreas to overproduce insulin in order to lower blood sugar levels.

Hyperinsulinemia causes insulin insensitivity. When this happens, the body converts these extra carbohydrates into triglycerides and fat. Indeed, insulin resistance and diabetes have been associated with excessive belly fat (pear shape), which has been associated with increased levels of circulating estrogen.

Deficiencies in certain nutrients, vitamins, and minerals—such as B vitamins, chromium, magnesium, zinc, and omega-3 essential fatty acid (alpha-linolenic acid)—may also cause insulin insensitivity and compromise fat metabolism.

Stubborn fat can be linked to protein deficiencies as well. Vegetarians and vegans are more likely to suffer from protein deficiencies, and especially the essential amino acid lysine. Lysine, abundant in animal proteins but less so in grains, converts in our bodies to L-carnitine. Carnitine enzymes (carnitine palmitoyle transferase or CPT) mobilize fat for breakdown in the mitochondria (the cell's site for energy production and fat utilization). Carnitine is essential for the fat-burning process. It is found mostly in animal foods, including meat, dairy, eggs, and fish. Without enough carnitine and carnitine-related enzymes in your body, the ability to burn fat may be severely compromised.

Stubborn fat can be an age-related problem for men and women. The older men get, the more testosterone is converted into estrogen. This process, called aromatizing, affects women in a similar way. The older one gets, the more active the aromatase enzyme is. Fat tissues are the sites that produce aromatase enzymes and therefore accelerate the conversion of testosterone into estrogen. There are natural ways to help block this process, involving ingestion of certain foods and herbs. We'll discuss them soon.

Men typically suffer from stubborn fat gain in the belly and chest. Women usually gain stubborn fat around their hips, thighs, and butt. Some women have stubborn-fat tissues around their upper arms or entire legs. Age-related stubborn fat for women may be the result of estrogen dominance in the body, with an increase in estrogen receptors in the tissues. Moreover, age-related insulin insensitivity, chronic stress, liver congestion, low thyroid, vascular permeability, and exhausted adrenals may all make the syndrome even worse for both men and women.

How to Prevent Stubborn Fat

There are several things you can do to avoid stubborn fat:

1. Stay away from crash diets or diets that make you lose fat and gain it again. Second-generation fat would most likely be more stubborn than the first.

2. Avoid consuming foods and herbs that have estrogenic effects on the body, such as soy, clover, and licorice. Also, minimize intake of omega-6 vegetable oils such as canola, corn, safflower, and soy, which have shown the capacity to induce estrogenic effects when not balanced with omega-3 oils.

3. Eat as much organic food as possible, thereby avoiding estrogenic substances that are in our food supply, such as petroleum-based fertilizers, pesticides, herbicides (found in non-organic produce), and hormones, which are found in conventional meats, poultry, and dairy.

4. If the food or water smells like plastic, stay away from it. Certain compounds in plastic called plasticizers, such as bisphenol A, have been found to be highly estrogenic and carcinogenic. Plasticizers can leach into water, milk, or foods that are packaged in plastic.

5. Minimize alcohol consumption. Excessive alcohol may compromise your liver's ability to break down and detoxify estrogenic derivatives. These estrogenic toxins can then penetrate the blood and cause adverse symptoms like bloating, water retention, and stubborn-fat gain. If these toxins remain unchecked, they may cause chronic diseases and even cancer. Alcohol may cause ethanol toxicity in the liver, which is also associated with insulin resistance, hypertension (high blood pressure), and fat gain.

6. Control your insulin. Naturally minimize the amount of carbohydrates you ingest by having whole carbs as the last component of your meal. If needed, supplement your diet with all the vital nutrients for stabilizing your insulin, such as essential fatty acids, vitamins, and minerals. If you're insulin-resistant, switch from carb foods to low-glycemic fat fuel foods such as nuts and seeds.

7. Follow a steady exercise routine. A comprehensive diet and exercise routine is the first defense against stubborn fat. Exercising boosts the metabolic rate, lowers estrogen level, and reduces stress-related symptoms, and thus accelerates the diet's effects. However, avoid overtraining. Chronically overstressing your body may cause the opposite effect and slow down your metabolic rate.

As for plastic, avoiding it altogether would be very impractical and almost impossible today, given how widespread and ubiquitous it is. Therefore I recommend that everyone do their best to check what type of plastic packaging is used before buying and consuming products wrapped or bottled in it. The worst packaging products are made with soft plastic, such as conventional "cloudy" plastic containers for water or milk. And, as noted above, you can use your senses. If anything edible smells like plastic, stay away from it. Moreover, acid-based foods such as lemon juice, vinegar, tomato sauce, and wine should never be packed or stored in plastic containers, since acid is more reactive with plastic material. A few safety measures I use are:

- Cut away a small amount of the outer edge of foods that are wrapped in plastic, such as cheese.
- Store food and beverages in glass or ceramic containers.
- Do not ingest liquids packed in soft, "cloudy" plastic containers.

To sum up how to prevent stubborn fat:
1. Avoid weight fluctuations.
2. Avoid estrogenic foods and herbs such as conventional meat and dairy, inorganic produce, omega-6 vegetable oils—canola, safflower, corn, and soy, all soy protein products, soy isoflavones supplements, clover and licorice supplements.
3. Minimize consumption of non-organic foods.
4. Avoid foods or liquids that smell like plastic.
5. Avoid excessive alcohol consumption.
6. Control your insulin; minimize refined carbohydrates; eat nuts and seeds instead of grains.
7. Follow a steady exercise routine.

The Problem with Plastic

Plastic is a very controversial issue. Its use is widespread in packaging for all types of food and beverages, and many oils. Most of these plastic bottles are made from polyethylene (a type of plastic that's been shown to be acceptably safe packing material for foods and oils). However, some plastics used on the market today for packaging food are quite toxic—in particular, soft plastics which are high in placticizers.

How to Get Rid of Stubborn Fat

If you suffer from stubborn fat, you should consider trying natural supplements, or "stubborn-fat busters," that may help you burn it off, including estrogen inhibitors and liver detoxifiers.

Estrogen Inhibitors

Certain compounds in foods and herbs have shown the capacity to inhibit estrogen and modulate its effects. The most potent estrogen inhibitors are found in cruciferous vegetables (indoles), chamomile flower (containing the flavone apigenine), passion flower (the flavone chrysin), onion and garlic (the flavone quercitin), bee propolis (galangin), citrus fruits (containing the flavonone naringenin), curry (curcumin), red grapes or wine (resveratol), omega-3 oils from fish, flax seeds, or hemp seeds, and milk fat, particularly from grass-fed animals (CLA).

Studies reveal that a combination of estrogen inhibitors has a superior estrogen-inhibiting effect than each of the components alone. When combined properly, estrogen inhibitors counteract estrogen on three levels:

- Lowering or antagonizing the estrogen receptors' activity.
- Inhibiting the aromatase enzyme that produces estrogen (from male androgens).
- Shifting estrogen metabolism to favor the production of beneficial estrogen metabolites instead of harmful estrogen metabolites. Cruciferous indoles (indole-3 carbinol, indole-3 acetate, and diindoly methane or DIM) have demonstrated highly protective anti-

carcinogenic properties by shifting estrogen metabolism to produce beneficial metabolites. The flavones apigenine, chrysin, quercitin, and galangin were found to be potent aromatase inhibitors. So is the citrus flavonone naringenin, although with a lower inhibition potency. Omega-3 oils are most important estrogen modulators, balancing the estrogen-promoting effects of omega-6 vegetable oils. Omega-3 oils antagonize estrogen receptors' positive tumor cells, and so does CLA (conjugated linoleic acid), which is derived from milk fat and found abundantly in aged cheese and butter from grass-fed animals.

Both omega-3 oils and CLA seem to exert anti-estrogenic and anti-cancerous effects in a similar manner. Other estrogen inhibitors, including curcumin from turmeric and resveratol from grapes, were found to work together as potent anti-estrogenic agents and cancer cell destroyers. Overall, when combined with anti-estrogenic foods and applied in sufficient amounts, estrogen inhibitors may help counteract the adverse effects of chemical as well as endogenous estrogen, thereby helping defend the body against estrogen-related fat gain, disorders, and cancer.

It's popular today to take soy isoflavones as a natural preventative aid against estrogen-related cancers, but I believe that a combination of the afore-mentioned estrogen inhibitors is the best alternative. Unlike soy isoflavones, these estrogen inhibitors have no inherent estrogenic effects and therefore are safe and viable. Soy isoflavones were found to be estrogenic and therefore may be part of the problem rather than the solution.

Liver Detoxifiers: Milk Thistle, Dandelion Root, and Amla C

As I've mentioned before, one of the reasons for excessive estrogenic activity in the body is liver congestion. The liver works as a filter organ. Under normal conditions the liver breaks down or neutralizes toxins and estrogen derivatives as well as chemicals, preventing them from reaching the blood. Bad diets and excessive alcohol consumption lower the liver's capacity to break down estrogen. Therefore, toxic estrogen substances reach the bloodstream, thereby inducing adverse estrogenic effects. That's one reason why many heavy drinkers and alcoholics suffer from estrogen-related stubborn fat in the belly and other areas.

As noted, leafy greens and cruciferous vegetables such as broccoli, cauliflower, Brussels sprouts, kale, and cabbage are believed to be great natural aids for the liver's estrogen metabolism. Routinely consuming cruciferous vegetables is a natural, simple way to provide the liver with its first defense against excess estrogen. Those who want to accelerate liver detoxification and rejuvenation should consider supplementing with milk thistle and dandelion root, since these herbs have been shown to help the liver detoxify and recuperate. Dandelion root is a diuretic herb and mildly laxative, so be cautious about the amount you take. Start with a small dosage, see how you feel, and then increase it slightly. Both herbs are available as teas, tinctures, and capsules. As mentioned previously, both amla C and boerhaavia are potent liver detoxifiers as well.

Steroids and the Liver

Those who take steroids, and women who take hormone replacements, place pressure on their liver to break down and detoxify these drugs. An inability to break down steroidal drugs may cause unpleasant symptoms such as bloating, water retention, and weight gain. In these cases, supplementing with natural estrogen inhibitors may help.

Yohimbe Bark, An Alpha Antagonist

Yohimbe bark is an herb derived from a West African tree. Yohimbe is used as an aphrodisiac herb for men who want to boost potency. It may also benefit those who suffer from stubborn fat.

Yohimbe is an alpha-2 adrenergenic antagonist, meaning that yohimbe may block alpha receptors of fat cells. The blocking of alpha receptors makes it possible for a stubborn fat tissue to be more responsive to the adrenal hormones. (The adrenal hormones bind to the beta receptors and activate a fat-burning response.) For both men and women who suffer from stubborn fat, this herb may offer positive effects. However, some people don't react well to yohimbe. Those who suffer from high blood pressure, heart conditions, or thyroid problems should consult their physician before trying it. Due to government regulations, yohimbe isn't easily accessible in stores.

Summary

In summary, the first defense against stubborn fat is to maintain a chemical-free diet, proper nutrition, and a regular exercise routine. It's best to eat anti-estrogenic organic foods, increase intake of omega-3 oil, minimize intake of omega-6 oil, supplement with estrogen-inhibitor herbs, and drink clean water. Try to reduce the purchase, consumption, and storage of foods or liquids packaged in plastic; avoid foods to which you are sensitive or allergic; minimize exposure to industrial estrogenic chemicals; minimize alcohol consumption; and, yes, avoid fluctuating weight through fad or crash diets.

The Warrior Diet can greatly help in preventing and eliminating stubborn fat. As you've already seen, this diet gives you hours of daily detoxification. This, coupled with the fat-burning that happens during the daily Undereating Phase, should keep you lean and healthy. If you follow the overeating rules of the Warrior Diet, you'll know that all the nutritional advice mentioned in this chapter is already part of the Warrior Diet routine, and so you may be able to virtually eliminate the problems that cause stubborn-fat gain. And, if you have stubborn fat and want to get rid of it, ideally you now know what to do.

As an "end note" for this subject, let me reiterate how essential exercise is to accelerate fat-burning and to reduce stress. Maintaining a healthy diet is of utmost importance in order to achieve any positive results. Nonetheless, exercise makes you achieve the results you're hoping for much faster.

CHAPTER 8

THE WARRIOR DIET
VERSUS OTHER DIETS

I RARELY HEAR PEOPLE TALK ABOUT THE STABILITY of specific diets, yet to me, stability is key. Most dietary programs today are missing a critical dimension—time. We are not steel objects; we are living entities in time and space. Time is a crucial factor, and it can't be ignored. Diets need to reflect the fact that human beings, like all living creatures, exist in time and space, and that we are evolving, moving, and always cycling our activities. The easiest way to get people's attention is to make them believe that they live in a simplistic, two-dimensional world. But in life, "one plus one" does not always equal "two." Things manifest in cycles, contradictions, and extremes, balancing each other, existing all together in a dimension called Time. Rotations and changes occur in the differences between seasons, weather, days and nights. So it still puzzles me how can people be brainwashed to believe that their life should be lived within the same parameters every day!

A stable diet is one that, once you're on it, you can live with it regardless of your location, the weather, or the season. To me, a stable diet isn't just a diet. It's a way of life. So even if you change something, or go off your eating regimen for a short while, you'll still be balanced. And that's how human beings should be—balanced—whether they eat a little more carbohydrates or protein on any one day, or even if they fast, they should still be balanced. That's one motto of the Warrior Diet. Our bodies are built to adapt to various situations without losing homeostasis.

If a diet is built on such specifics that you often fail to follow the regimen, it is most likely an "unstable diet." An unstable diet is a bad diet simply because it's almost impossible to stay on it. For instance, The Zone says you should eat 40% carbohydrates, 30% fat, 30% protein, and that if you change the ratio even slightly, you've lost The Zone. As Barry Sears says, "You're as good as your last meal." To me this diet is the very definition of unstable because, according to its creator, any deviation will mess you up. In fact, the truth is quite the opposite. There is substantial evidence that humans have adapted to cycle between different ratios of macronutrients. If we hadn't adapted to these cycles (in ratios of macronutrients), we wouldn't be able to survive climate and seasonal changes.

Most diets are built on a very simple equation and, to me, this is wrong. Many modern diets can't work for very long because it's impossible to follow a specific, straight formula in an un-straight world. It's just not realistic. And anyway, you shouldn't eat the same food or ingest the same number of calories every single day because of changes in your routine. For instance, on some days you may be highly physically active, whereas on others you may not be active at all. You're the same person, but your ratios and needs are changing. Everything in life is evolving. So should your diet.

Light and daylight influence the hormonal system. For some people, there's a peak time of hormone secretion in the afternoon, but for others it's early in the morning. The hormonal system can also be affected if, for instance, you work in the evening as opposed to during the day. Animals and plants are also affected by and react to the cycles of day and night and the seasons. Why do we so often overlook or ignore this?

Since the Industrial Revolution, we've been moving further away from the natural cycle of life, governed by sunrise and sunset. As a result, many people today suffer from symptoms of chronic jet lag as well as related problems, like depression, fatigue, or feelings of deprivation, often leading to chronic cravings for pick-up foods and sweets.

The stability of the Warrior Diet is built on the premise that whether or not you've eaten your main meal, you'll always know where you are in the cycle and what you're supposed to do to keep evolving from one part of the cycle to the next.

I believe that nature is wise, and that we all have deep instincts within us that can provide the wisdom to know when to eat, what to eat, and when to stop eating. Everyone has and needs these primal instincts. The Warrior Diet allows you to make changes, to binge on carbohydrates or fatty foods like nuts, and still be fine. Other diets don't allow this freedom. I believe that feeling free should be a part of your life. By introducing you to the Warrior Diet, I hope to relay how this sense of freedom will enrich your life in many ways.

The Warrior Diet vs. the Frequent-Feeding System

The frequent-feeding system (followed by many people today) is where you eat relatively small, frequent meals throughout the day. Those who advocate frequent feedings say that it puts less pressure on the digestive tract and keeps sugar levels stable. And, especially for physically active individuals, it allegedly enables them to ingest more protein throughout the day to further build muscles.

I understand the philosophy and science behind this, but I also see the down side. With all due respect, the huge disadvantage of the frequent-feeding system is that the body never gets a break to detoxify, to recuperate, and to let the pancreatic system rest. Additionally, when you deposit material so often without giving your body enough time to detoxify, you basically deplete your body's pool of enzymes. This often results in compromised digestion, especially of proteins. The loss of digestive power weakens the immune system, and if this is unchecked, it may lead to waste of lean tissues and disease. A large percentage of those who practice frequent feeding no longer have a healthy feeding cycle. It's no wonder that so many people today suffer from digestive disorders, constipation, weight gain, and related diseases. These problems are so pronounced that the companies who sell drugs to help people become "regular" make a bloody fortune.

The Warrior Diet is built on daily detoxification and enzyme loading. If you practice this diet, you'll eventually reach your own natural cycle and should be able to sustain prime health and increase your resilience to stress and disease. This makes the Warrior Diet radically different from all conventional diets today.

Reviews of Popular Diets

Including How They Differ from the Warrior Diet
I've separated the diet reviews into five major groups:

Group I – The American Diet
- The All-American Diet
- The American Health-Food Diets

Group II – The Low-Fat Diet
- High-Carb/Low-Fat/Low-Protein
- The Pritikin Diet
- Dean Ornish's Diet

Group III – The Protein / Fat / Carb / Ratio Diet
- The Zone: 40-30-30

Group IV – High-Protein, Very Low-Carbohydrate
- Dr. Atkins (New Diet Revolution and Vita-Nutrient Solution)
- Protein Power
- South Beach Diet

Group V – Holistic Diets
- Macrobiotics
- Andrew Weil (Instinctive Healing)
- Harvey Diamond (Fit for Life and Fit for Life: A New Beginning)

To make things clear and simple, I chose to review only those diets that, in my opinion, best characterize their group.

Group I: The All-American (Junk Food) Diet

From Hot Dogs and French Fries to Sodas, Chips, and Cookies

There are no books in this category, other than cookbooks (and fast food or diner menus).

This is a relatively young diet, less than a hundred years old. It cropped up during the twentieth century and is an example of a "scavenger diet." People on this diet don't think about what they eat and blithely consume prepared and overly processed foods. True scavengers don't hunt for food; they eat what's left over by another animal. They pick up and eat dead food. Scavengers have this unique mentality.

The All-American Diet is based on consuming food without thinking. This is a very aggressive diet, high in refined and overly processed foods loaded with chemical preservatives, pesticides, nitrates, and artificial food colors. When I say "aggressive," I refer to taste—meaning there's too much sugar, salt, and grease (unhealthy fat). Sugar overstimulates insulin levels, thereby maintaining the craving for more sugar. Overly processed foods make up the majority of the All-American Diet: hot dogs, hamburgers, fried chicken, cold cuts, cakes, cookies, candies, sodas and other sugar-laden beverages, refined or sugary grains like most muffins, donuts, and cereals, and French fries and other fried foods.

Many of you already know how bad this diet is. A great deal of data show its correlation with obesity, diabetes, heart attacks, and degenerative diseases. It's my contention that even if you try to balance it somewhat by reducing sugar consumption and increasing your intake of olive oil (instead of margarine or other hydrogenated oils), you're still left with too much overly processed food. To add insult to injury, unless you eat organically, much of the food is contaminated with hormones, antibiotics, pesticides, and petroleum-based chemicals and other estrogenic derivatives. You can't win here!

The American "Health Food" Diets

Choosing organic food is definitely a step in the right direction, because it means that there's some awareness of what you eat. You're attempting to avoid the hormones and antibiotics found in most non-organic meat and dairy products, as well as the chemical herbicides, pesticides, and fertilizers used in most of the nation's food supply.

But one of the common mistakes people make when they see a health-food label is going for it without checking the ingredients. A lot of organic foods, including many cereals, contain too much sugar or other sweeteners like fructose, or they have undesirable oils or overly processed fats—all of which are unhealthy for you. Remember, even if your food choices are right, it is *when* you eat that makes *what* you eat matter.

Group II: High-Carbohydrate, Low-Fat, Low-Protein

The Pritikin Diet and Dean Ornish's diet belong in this group, which is still popular today despite massive research showing the insulin impact of high carbohydrate-based diets.

High-carb, low-fat, low-protein diets have proven ineffective in terms of weight loss. Even when calories are reduced, many people who try these diets gain weight. Following high-carb, low-fat, low-protein diets can also lead to major health problems. For example, when there's a chronic imbalance between protein and carbohydrate consumption, it may result in protein deficiencies as well as overspiking of insulin. This can, in turn, lead to insulin insensitivity, hypoglycemia, and even diabetes. Additionally, active people require more protein than those who are sedentary. These diets may not supply enough amino acids for their active muscles.

It's common to find people with "fat phobias" in this territory—people who don't realize that dietary fat plays a critical role in supporting the hormonal, muscular, and neural systems. If one doesn't consume enough healthy fats, particularly essential fatty acids (EFAs), one may suffer from an EFA deficiency. This can lead to metabolic impairments in the brain, inflammation in other parts of the body, excess of estrogen, weight gain, and compromised immunity. Moreover, it may lead to depression, impotency, and eventually full-blown disease.

Group III: The Zone (40/30/30)

I respect many of Barry Sears' theories, and he's taken a great step ahead by explaining to people the mechanism of fat-burning and the difference between insulin and glucagon. However, there's absolutely no reason to conclude from his theory that there is actually a "Zone." In my opinion, if there is something similar to the alleged Zone, it definitely doesn't look like the Zone. I can prove philosophically, not just scientifically, how wrong this assumption of a Zone is. First of all, let's address the amount and proportion of food. There's no proof that all people should consume 40% carbs, 30% protein, and 30% fat daily.

I believe that Sears has made some incorrect assumptions. He believes that this ratio fits everybody—men and women of different ages, athletes, and sedentary people. The truth is that different people have different needs, so you can't say that everybody should follow the same ratio. Moreover, some people suffer from metabolic problems such as gout or hypoglycemia, and their diet absolutely must accommodate their condition. Sears ignores the fact that a diet's protein-to-fat-to-carb ratio depends on one's personal condition. If you're in a phase where you want to lose weight, you should have one ratio; if you want to maintain your weight, you should have another.

To me, the worst thing about the Zone is that it's built—like virtually all diets today—on control and deprivation. The human instinct to reach satiety (satisfaction) from food and to enjoy a sense of freedom cannot be achieved with this diet. Maybe people can fool themselves for a while, but the fact that you have to measure everything, almost like a pharmacist, is very difficult for people to maintain. I think the Zone is a potentially interesting diet, and some people can probably lose weight on it. But in the long run, such a diet would most likely fail due to impracticalities, restrictions, and deprivation. For those who want to build lean tissues while boosting their metabolism and feeling a sense of freedom as well as satisfaction from their meals, I believe the Zone diet is just not good enough.

Group IV: High-Protein, Low- or No-Carbohydrate

- Dr. Atkins' New Diet Revolution
- Vita-Nutrient Solution
- Protein Power
- The Carbohydrate Addict's Diet
- The South Beach Diet

I chose to review Dr. Atkins' New Diet Revolution and Vita-Nutrient Solution for Group IV because I think it represents this group well. Dr. Atkins is a pioneer, since he was the first to introduce the public to some of the science behind fat-burning, as well as the hazards of carbohydrates and overconsumption of sugar. But, unfortunately, his diet suffers from serious downfalls. I believe it's virtually impossible to follow his diet for the long term, mainly because it is impractical and wrong to ask people to deprive themselves of carbs forever. There are other problems too, involving overacidity and imbalance, resulting from not consuming enough raw plant foods, and over-consuming protein and junk fatty foods, such as hot dogs, cold cuts, or bacon, which acidify the body, often load it with chemicals, and deplete its vital enzymes. On top of this, Dr. Atkins overlooks the importance of whole foods and their healing effects on the body. The emphasis on live, raw foods is missing from his diet plan. Human beings were created as an integral part of nature, and consuming whole foods is essential for our health.

In his other book, *Dr. Atkins' Health Revolution* (1990), he suggests a list of vitamins and herbs that you can take to supplement this high-protein, high-fat, low-carbohydrate diet. Nonetheless, he draws the wrong conclusions. Chronically avoiding carbs may compromise the body's natural production of serotonin, a major neurotransmitter that triggers pleasure sensors in the brain, giving a calming effect. Serotonin is the precursor for the hormone melatonin, which promotes sleep and rejuvenation. Dietary carbs also play an important role in sustaining a critical metabolic pathway in the liver (the Pentose Phosphate pathway), responsible for production of DNA, RNA, and some of the most powerful endogenous antioxidant enzymes. Chronic carb restriction may shut down this metabolic pathway, thus leading to accelerated aging and disease.

I contend that there is no substitute for the phytonutrients, minerals, and vitamins we get from whole foods. I also firmly believe that whole carbohydrates should be an essential component of the diet.

Any recommendation to cut out some of what nature provides—fruits, plants, whole grains, and fibers—and instead use synthetic supplements is absolutely wrong. Phytonutrients, minerals, and microorganisms are needed to support all bodily functions. The Atkins Diet misses a lot of potent, living-food forces.

The colors of live food, such as the pigments in plants, are actually nutritious and essential for your health. These phytonutrients are much more potent in their natural state than in synthetic forms. You can't achieve this same potency with processed powder supplements.

Many years ago, when the soil was richer and less contaminated with environmental toxins, food contained much more vitamins, minerals, flavonoids, and other phytonutrients, all of which support our body's hormonal, neural, and muscular systems. Their decline in our food supply is a major problem today. So why follow a diet that makes this problem even more pronounced?

Dr. Atkins almost completely ignores the importance of natural detoxification, which is one of the main roles of living food and food enzymes. I believe, moreover, that following this high-protein, high-fat diet with the absence of daily detoxification will place too much pressure on the liver, and so will eventually increase the overall metabolic stress on the body and thus accelerate aging. Atkins' slogan that "you can eat whatever protein and fat you want," including bacon, salami, cheese, and butter, is a dangerous gimmick. If you choose to go on this gimmicky diet, you may temporarily lose weight but eventually pay the consequences.

In summary, the Atkins Diet overlooks and therefore lacks four major elements:

- The importance of dietary carbs in supporting the body's metabolic integrity.
- The importance of the wholeness of food, derived primarily from plants and grains.
- Daily detoxification
- A sense of freedom (since the diet is built on deprivation)

Group V: Holistic Diets

- Macrobiotic Diets
- Andrew Weil's Instinctive Healing
- Harvey Diamond's Fit for Life and Fit for Life: A New Beginning

Macrobiotics

Macrobiotic diets are based on the ancient Eastern cultural concept of balancing yin and yang. However, we Americans seem to have created a modern mutation of an old Eastern tradition. These diets are based mainly on consumption of cooked food, including cooked fruits and veggies. Grains are the main source of energy.

Yin foods are those that have light, expansive, and often cooling properties, such as fruits, vegetables, sugar, and some herbs and spices. Yang foods have contractive, anabolic, and often warming qualities; they include meat, grains, and beans. Since macrobiotic diets are vegetarian, the yang foods are mainly grains, nuts, seeds, beans, and legumes.

In my opinion, these diets aren't as balanced as they claim to be. They neglect, or nearly avoid, the living-food factor. As a result, people who eat a macrobiotic diet miss the live-food elements, which, as mentioned, are so essential for your health. I also question the wisdom of balancing the yin and yang food with each meal. Some people are more acidic, so they need more yin, alkalizing food, and the opposite holds true, too. Moreover, cooking methods may change the quality of fresh yin-like food to a more yang-like quality. It's confusing. On top of all this, the diet is simply impractical to follow, especially for people on the run. Macrobiotic junkies usually carry precooked food with them in plastic containers. This is inconvenient; furthermore, precooked food may spoil if left for too long without refrigeration.

This diet is built on control and deprivation because your choices are limited, and you can't freely use your own instincts. And as we've said: no freedom, no good!

Andrew Weil's Instinctive Healing

I respect Andrew Weil. He deserves the credit for educating people about the importance of fresh food, the dangers of processing, and making the right choices when it comes to different plants, seeds, and herbs. Dr. Weil puts things in the right perspective when he covers the subjects of healthy oils and natural toxins. He also elaborates wisely about different healthy cooking methods, and the importance of being in tune with nature and seasons when it comes to dieting.

But philosophy is one thing, and a practical diet is another. I suspect that one of Dr. Weil's magic bullets, besides his charisma, is his ability to remove guilt from those who are looking for guidance. Using Weil himself as a living example of his diet philosophy is somewhat confusing. Dr. Weil argues that the lean body image isn't a healthy one. According to him, it's all right to be chunky (like himself), and this point of view suggests to people that it's okay to be overweight. Dr. Weil says that lifting weights (bodybuilding) is bad for you, and that moving yourself from the chair to the kitchen and back is kind of an exercise (well, maybe gardening and walking around the block is mentioned, too). I find this approach to be misleading. People can do better than that. In short, if you want to follow Andrew Weil, you may learn a lot about food and cooking. But you might find yourself looking like, well, Andrew Weil.

Harvey Diamond's *Fit for Life* and *Fit for Life: A New Beginning*

These diets are very popular among people who are looking for a practical way to heal themselves. Harvey Diamond's books are built on three major premises:

1. Food Separation: Carbohydrate and protein meals should be separated. According to Diamond, food separation will guarantee better digestion since carbs and protein need different enzymes under different pH.
2. Detoxification: In his latest book, *Fit for Life: A New Beginning,* Diamond elaborates on the importance of periodic lymphatic system detoxification as the only natural way to prevent disease.
3. Living Food: Diamond explains the vital importance of living food forces as an integral part of the diet.

My main problem with these books was, and I say "was," that in my opinion they appeal to sick or sedentary people. I fully understand and agree with his suggestion of consuming fruits and freshly squeezed fruit and veggie juices, but disagree with Diamond's advice concerning what and how much you're allowed to eat. I, as well as other active people, would literally disappear if I followed Fit for Life. However, after speaking with and meeting Harvey Diamond, I realize that he's much more flexible than I thought before we met. Harvey agreed that his diet doesn't target active people or athletes who need to consume more protein and meat. He admits that in spite of his attack on "flesh foods," he no longer is a vegetarian and does, in fact, enjoy a steak once in a while.

Given the above, I have to say that this is a diet I honestly recommend as one of the most effective means of detoxification, for healing, and for breaking old, unhealthy habits. I personally don't follow food separation since I think that eating carbs alone may cause a rapid rise in insulin, while combining protein, fat, and carbs in one meal prevents high-insulin fluctuations—and has the added benefit of providing more satiety.

Further, some natural whole foods, such as beans and nuts, contain both protein and carbohydrates in an almost equal ratio.

Let me just note that Harvey is also a great writer with a wonderful sense of humor. He cracked me up a few times. No other diet book has ever made me laugh.

As a final note here, let me mention that I didn't find it necessary to review all of today's popular diets. Though they manifest in different variations, virtually all current diets are based on similar dietary restrictions: low fat, low carbs, or low calories. The Warrior Diet is the only diet today that challenges all common dietary concepts and offers a real alternative—guidelines that are not based on superficial restrictions, but rather on true principles of human nutrition.

CHAPTER 9

LESSONS FROM HISTORY

THE MIGHTY ROMAN SOLDIER WAS A LIGHTWEIGHT, 135 pounds on average. Yet in face-to-face combat against Gauls or Celts who weighed about 180 pounds, the Roman warrior came out on top. Julius Caesar was only five feet, six inches tall, and Alexander the Great wasn't physically a big man, but history remembers them both as giant warriors.

One might ask why history and legend remembers these lean people as giants. In my opinion, the answer lies somewhere between the ways these people lived, and how adamantly they followed their convictions.

I've chosen to focus mainly on the ancient Romans and Greeks for two reasons. First, the Greco-Roman culture is considered to be the foundation of modern Western civilization. Western cultural ideals of beauty and body proportions are derived from the Greco-Roman classical period.

Second, I find the Greeks, and especially the Romans, to be great historical examples of people who created large empires and documented their warrior way of life over hundreds of years. There's a lot to learn from ancient warriors, but since this isn't a history book, I have limited myself to major topics relevant to the Warrior Diet. To understand what made these people live as they did, you need to get acquainted with their priorities. What were their aesthetic and moral concepts of beauty and ugliness? What did courage and cowardice mean to them? How did they relate to subjects such as health and sickness? And, especially, what were their attitudes toward pain, pleasure, deprivation, and compensation? I find it all most intriguing. I hope you will, too.

Although I focus mainly on the Romans and Greeks, I do refer to other groups of ancient people. This chapter aims to shed some light on the historical relevance of the Warrior Diet.

At the end of the chapter I offer my conclusions and elaborate on the historical role of nutritional carbohydrates.

The Romans—An Empire of Wanderers

Romans devoured space. They spent most of their lives outdoors. They traveled the length and breadth of Latium, Italy, and the provinces (the regions that were conquered by the Romans, such as Gaul, North Africa, and Palestine) as soldiers, magistrates, or freed men entrusted with their patron's business.

"On the move," these roving Romans had to be constantly alert and able to adapt to different foods, weather conditions, and especially to times of deprivation. It was essential for nomadic people to maintain a tactical nutrition strategy that could sustain them while moving from one place to another. They were, therefore, geared towards eating mostly accessible, seasonal, fresh food. They were also using natural preservation methods for their food supply. As you'll soon see, diet and food supply played quite a large role in their lives. Maintaining a healthy food supply required special strategies, which influenced almost every aspect of their lives, including how they planned war campaigns.

What You See Is What You Get

Physical appearance was crucial to all Romans. They conducted business face to face. Army commanders had to stand before their soldiers and demonstrate physical and rhetorical authority. A positive self-image was an essential factor that could never be taken for granted. Roman awareness of self was derived from the way others looked at them. Their virtues and vices were an open book, manifested in their style of dress, tone of voice, and choice of body movements. They were forever on stage but always played themselves. Because they were judged by their physical appearance, those who neglected it were no longer respected as citizens or men. To look at a man was to know the truth about him.

The famous censor, Cato, wore a close-fitting toga. When giving speeches, he did so with deliberate delivery, few gestures, and careful steps. Thus he would exemplify his political program: austerity and restraint.

Roman people had a very strict, aesthetic concept of physical appearance. They had their own unique style, which they called *cultus*. Cultus involved body washing, hairstyling, beard trimming, and especially, eating adequately. To suspend one's body cultus demonstrated self-neglect. Gluttony was considered a disgrace, and obesity a humiliating weakness. Censors debarred obese cavalrymen from the army. In order to look lean, Romans had to maintain a special diet. This diet had unique rules, which I'll cover later on.

History also tells us that the Spartan warriors paid a great deal of attention to physical appearance. According to Plutarch, Spartans kept their hair long, as they believed that long hair made a strong man look handsome. A shaved head was a sign of defeat and failure. A "skinhead" was a loser. Greeks idealized physical appearance and class. This is apparent when one looks at the way their artists portrayed Olympian athletes, heroes, and gods in paintings and sculpture.

The ancient Greeks had a common saying: "Tell me what you eat, with whom and how, and I will tell you who you are!"

A Soldier's Status

Roman soldiers had to take an oath, called a *Sacramentum,* which released them from the prohibitions and constraints of civilian life. They wore clothing different from civilian men; soldiers didn't wear togas or light-colored garments. They wore dark red tunics that wouldn't show bloodstains.

Being a soldier required a total commitment to obey orders, and kill or die for a cause. The hardship of military life, battle wounds, and the scars of war were all a source of pride. Soldiers enjoyed a high status and great deal of respect.

Great philosophers, historians, and orators often were involved in one way or another with soldiers and warriors. Aristotle (384–322 BC) was a tutor of Alexander the Great. Xenophon (428–354 BC), a leading associate of Socrates, was an Athenian mercenary in the Persian army under Cyrus the Younger. Demosthenes (384–322 BC), the last spokesman of free Athens, was a lifelong rhetorical opponent of Philip of Macedonia and his son, Alexander the Great. He committed suicide with poison.

Philosophy and spirituality went hand in hand with the sword. Warriors surrounded themselves with philosophers and tutors, and spiritual leaders were ready to sacrifice their lives for their ideas.

The Sense of Chivalry

One element of the Warrior Instinct, manifested throughout history, is the way men have carried arms to defend themselves, their honor, and the honor of their loved ones. Males were routinely trained from a young age to acquire fighting skills such as fencing, wrestling, and later, shooting. During the Greco-Roman period, it was the right and privilege of free people to carry arms. Dueling has been popular among free men since biblical times. American statesman Alexander Hamilton and the Russian poet Pushkin are examples of famous people who died in duels while defending their honor. Dueling was an accepted part of life until the twentieth century.

Virtues and Vices

Courage, generosity, devotion, and self-sacrifice were traits adored in the Greco-Roman society. Cowardice, according to the Romans, was to be treated with cruelty. The Romans were driven to be adventurous, to take risks, and were tempted to gamble just to see how far they could venture without tipping over. Being adventurous was regarded as a courageous way of life. Adventure stories of warriors who wandered to remote and dangerous places were part of Roman and Greek mythology. The Warrior Instinct, which drives people to take risks and even put themselves in danger of death, was an inherent part of life.

Self-control was a matter of life and death in the ancient Roman world. Sensual passions and overindulgence were considered serious weaknesses, which threatened to dissolve the body. Ancient Greeks and Romans believed that heroism protected them from death. Let me point out here that the ability to withstand pain, hunger, and fear were thought to be the warrior's main strength. For the Romans, war was a "competition of pain." Those who could withstand the most suffering would win.

Since pain and deprivation were an integral part of warrior life, the warriors would induce both in order to conquer fears and grow tough enough to withstand the hardship of war. Army leaders, such as Pompey and Mucius Scaevola, also physically tortured themselves.

The Greco-Roman Warrior Cycle

Romans cycled between extremities of deprivation and compensation. A typical cycle was based on intense activity during the day, and relaxation during the night. There was also a yearly cycle, based on the seasons:

- Spring through summer was the time for war and work.
- Winter was the time for peace.
- Autumn was the time of transition between war and peace. This was the season for "the Games."

Each cycle had its rules. Following them was not an option. It was a must.

Romans and Greeks were quite class-conscious, and each social class—rich, poor, freed men, or slaves—had its own rules. To keep things simple, I'll cover the most dominant rules and social behaviors.

As you'll see, poor people had a different diet from the elite. You'll also note that hard laborers and soldiers, who were engaged in extreme physical activities, needed to satisfy their high-calorie demands by consuming carbohydrates during the day. However, during peacetime, consumption of carbs during the daily hours was minimized to raw foods such as veggies and fruits.

The Roman Food Police

Food prohibitions were enacted to enforce diet rules, especially during wartime. This meant that certain luxury foods were not allowed for sale on days other than festivals. Caesar sent special supervising brigades to the markets to seize foods in violation of the law. Soldiers broke into houses to check what was being served in people's dining rooms. During wartime, there was a maximum annual sum that citizens could spend on luxuries such as bacon or salty meat.

Daytime Activities

Daytime was dedicated to work and war. A Roman had to struggle throughout the day, dealing with physical stress and anxiety. Being alert was part of the daily routine. Luxuries, pleasures, and ostentation were not allowed.

The only function of food during the day was to restore strength. People ate standing up. In times of necessity, such as during war campaigns, soldiers ate only dry biscuits and water. Given this, Romans in general didn't like dry food; they ate it for nourishment only. When people traveled, they often ate bread and figs, as they didn't have the time or facilities to cook meals.

Poor people—and those unwilling to wait until the evening meal—would gnaw at dry bread, boiled vegetable leftovers, or an onion. The poor were often on the brink of starvation; eating during the day was for them a matter of survival. By comparison, the elite and soldiers ate only one meal, at night. They minimized food consumption during the day to mainly raw, uncooked foods *(crudus)*.

Evening Pleasures

The Roman evening was dedicated to relaxation, pleasure, and socialization, including family gatherings. This time was organized around the evening meal, called the *cena*. Roman citizens went to public baths in the early evening. Taking a bath was a transition ritual between the physical agitation and anxiety of the day, and the evening leisure or *otium*.

It was essential for people to relax at night and avoid all signs of being troubled or worried. They did not talk business. The wealthy had their slaves play music. Those who couldn't relax were thought to be suffering from a stiff or corrupted soul. Given all these relaxation rules, Romans, with their warrior discipline, always retained a certain level of alertness. They sat on Roman chairs, which had no back, and practically allowed them to wear a sword while remaining alert. The evening relaxation prepared them for sleep. Sleep was essential for a Roman who had to awaken at dawn. Insomnia was considered a sign of weakness, remorse, regret, worry, longing or having a bad conscience.

Concept of Food and the Roman Diet

The Roman concept of food was both symbolic and sensual. According to their beliefs, *crudus* (raw food) was considered animal fodder. They felt that if a man ate the same raw food that wild animals ate, he might himself turn into a beast. In spite of the fact that Romans felt this way, they ate *crudus* as part of the daytime austerity.

Romans believed strongly in *humanitas*—human feeling and culture. Food, therefore, was prepared in the evening in ways that would differentiate it from its raw state. Romans preferred soft foods. To them soft foods were the opposite of crude, tough to chew, raw, and therefore "animalistic" foods. During the *cena,* food was cooked, eaten warm, and was of better quality.

The Plebeian Diet

The plebeian (common people) diet was based mainly on grains and legumes. Meat, cheese, fish, seafood, and eggs were available, but only rich people could afford them on a regular basis. Poor and working-class Romans liked to eat cheese, seafood, and bacon if accessible and affordable but were generally forced to compromise, and so consumed a principally vegetarian diet based on grains. As a result, they often suffered from protein deficiencies. To get enough protein, they combined grains with legumes; beans and peas were their main sources of protein. They prepared grains and beans using two methods: grinding it into flour and baking it; and cooking it in water.

Alcohol Rations

I find it interesting to note that army rations of wine and beer in early modern Europe were pretty high. For instance, daily rations of wine for the Spanish navy during the sixteenth century were 1.14 liters per soldier. Daily rations of beer and wine for Russian army soldiers in the eighteenth century were 3.5 liters and 0.25 liters, respectively. A British seaman during the Napoleonic wars enjoyed a daily ration of up to 4.5 liters of beer. Given these rations, one may wonder about the role that alcohol played in historical war campaigns.

Basic Food Preparations

A cooked meal—"gruel"—consisted of grains mixed with legumes, pieces of meat, or fish, all boiled together in water for a long time. Romans preferred boiling to roasting or grilling because boiling adds water to the food and softens it.

Oil was used and consumed only during the evening meal. Fresh olive oil was added to bean purées, gruel, meat, and dry cheese.

Soldiers also liked to fortify their carb meals with protein. Mixing protein, fat, and carbohydrates all together was generally preferred to eating carbs alone.

Wining and Dining in Ancient Rome

Free Romans did not dine with slaves. Slaves and hard laborers ate during the day. Cato fed his slaves barley, fermented fish, olives, and vinegar. During seasons of particularly hard labor, workers ate bread shaped like a dough ball, with cheese and honey in the center. Romans liked to eat with company. Eating alone was considered unwelcome and depressing.

Romans liked to drink wine. Wine was diluted with (sometimes warm and salty) water to reduce its acidity: one part wine to two parts water, or the opposite.

The greatest warriors in history, Alexander the Great and Julius Caesar, drank a lot of wine. Most warriors, in fact, drank wine, and the more they wandered, the more they drank. Roman warriors liked wine and beer.

According to the Greek historian Thucydides (c. 460–400 BC), Spartan soldiers enjoyed a steady supply of both wine and meat. Great mythological heroes like Hercules and the God of Wine, Dionysus, were notorious for their gargantuan drinking habits. Even the Bible regards wine as a source of happiness.

The Evening Meal—*Cena*

The *cena* or evening meal was designed to include three courses. The first course was *gustatio* (taster or appetizer), meant to introduce a variety of tastes and textures. A typical appetizer was a combination of honeyed wine and tasty small tidbits. Roman cooks mixed ground seafood with exotic herbs and oil to create an unrecognizable, mysterious, and tasty appetizer. *Gustatio* might also be something like boiled eggs and olives (egg salad), or bacon, walnuts, and dried figs taken from the cellar.

The second or main course typically included wild boar, turbot (a type of fish), plump chicken—all very well cooked, until the meat fell apart. There was a kind of food hierarchy in regard to evening meals:

- The bottom level consisted of grains, legumes, vegetables, fruits, oil, and wine;
- The middle level was based on cooked, farm-raised animals;
- The top (preferred) level was a meal that included wild game such as boar or hare.

The most popular fish sauce was *garum*—fermented fish mixed with salt and herbs.

Since Romans liked soft food, the most popular evening meals were prepared by mixing vegetables with different ingredients such as grains, lentils, meat, fish, or cheese into one mushy, soft, warm serving. This whole meal included a variety of tastes and textures to satisfy and relax the diner.

Extreme luxury foods for Romans included fatty meats, fish, eel, and especially shellfish. Roman nobles had their own fishponds *(piscinae)* where they cultivated fish and shellfish.

The third course was dessert. Desserts were chiefly based on fresh fruits such as apples, grapes, or figs. Sometimes the Romans consumed their favorite delicacies, such as shrimp, oysters, or snails, as a condiment to finish the meal.

Mixing Carbs and Protein

Those following the Warrior Diet who choose to mix carbs with protein for the main meal can do so as long as the carbs *are not eaten before* the protein. However, those interested in losing body fat should consume carbs as the last component of the meal. In so doing, the quantity of carbs consumed will be minimized naturally without restriction. This method also helps regulate the amount of carbs ingested when cycling between days of high-protein meals and days of high-carb meals.

Carb Content in Ancient Warrior Meals

The ideal ancient warrior meal consisted mainly of animal proteins such as meat, fish, eggs, and cheese. Carbs were a secondary component, meant to add texture and bulk to the cooked food. However, in reality, soldiers were often forced to use carbs as a main source of food because of shortages in animal proteins. Soldiers generally needed more carbs than civilians to satisfy their high calorie and energy expenditures.

Beans: The Main Source of Protein

As mentioned, the typical plebeian diet was based on grains. To avoid protein deficiencies, they mixed grains with legumes. Beans were considered "the poor man's meat." They were also the gladiator's main source of protein, and beans were served to Roman soldiers in times of short supply of meat, cheese, or fish. The bean was a strong symbol. It conjured up images of death, hell, blood, and semen, yet at the same time was considered a good-luck charm.

There were rules for consuming beans. Romans were aware that they caused gas, bloating, and water retention. In time they developed techniques for cooking beans to reduce or eliminate these side effects. Techniques included triple rinsing, then soaking in water overnight, then triple rinsing again, and finally peeling and removing the skins—all before cooking.

Poor people ate beans as part of the main meal. Roman soldiers mixed bean flour with wheat or barley to enrich bread. The wealthy ate beans and other plebeian food to affirm their superiority over the lower classes. They used beans as a condiment. The "elite bean treat" was served at the end of the meal and resembled baked beans mixed with honey. For the Greeks, beans were a symbol of democracy. However, the Greeks preferred oligarchy. They considered democracy to be the rule of the lower classes over the elite. Pitagoras imposed a ban on beans partly because of oligarchy. Like the wealthy Romans, wealthy Greeks ate beans as special dishes only. They ate young, fresh beans, which were soft and tender, as desserts (*tragema*) or in the form of soup or exotic sauces.

Grains

Wheat was the Roman soldiers' main source of grain. For the Greeks and Spartans, it was barley. Roman warriors' rations were about 800–1000 grams of grain daily. During campaigns, a soldier's diet was made up of 80% grain and 20% other foods such as meats, cheese, legumes, and veggies. Thus it appears that an average Roman soldier consumed about 3,000 calories of grains alone per day.

In my opinion, these calorie figures could be misleading. Roman soldiers carried hand mills with them to grind their own flour on a daily basis. Part of this flour was used to bake dry biscuits to be eaten during the day. Reluctant as the Romans normally were to consume dry food, these biscuits were very likely used as a "backup food" and would frequently have been discarded. The Roman warrior preference was high-protein foods. Whole wheat and barley are relatively high in protein and were, therefore, superior to other grains and carbohydrates such as polished rice (which was consumed by many Asians) and roots (consumed by many Africans). Rice and roots are short not only in protein but other vital nutrients, too. Those who lived on such sources of carbohydrates alone suffered from severe protein deficiencies.

Commoners' Diet

The basic diet of both Roman and Greek commoners was vegetarian (but not exclusively). When these people had access to meat, fish, or cheese they preferred it.

- Meat: The most popular meat for Greeks was goat. For Romans it was pork.
- Dairy and milk: Came mostly from sheep and goats. Romans did not use butter.
- Olive oil: Was freshly squeezed, to avoid rancidity. It was used as an alternative to butter and soap.
- Fish: Was domestic, and both fresh and saltwater fish were consumed.
- Poultry: Was eaten occasionally, whenever available.

Pliny the Elder wrote that Romans consumed more meat than the Athenians, particularly pork. Poor people could only occasionally afford to purchase meat, sausages, or blood puddings of dubious content in the sundry cook shops in the city. Choicer food was sometimes available at public festivals, but such events were not frequent enough to have made much difference nutritionally. Common people would eat chickpeas in theaters (the same way people eat popcorn today). Hot "peace pudding" made of chickpeas was sold cheaply on the streets. Poor people could occasionally afford cheap vegetables such as cabbage, leeks, beets, garlic, and onions. They might, at times, have also consumed cheap fish from polluted sections of the Tiber, old smelly fish, small-fry, and low-quality fish sauce. To compensate for a shortage in animal protein consumption, the poor ate legumes, which supplied vitamin A as well as the amino acids that are low in wheat and barley.

Soldiers' Meals

The quickest and easiest way to prepare a soldier's meal was to cook porridge (a mixture of grains, veggies, legumes, and, if accessible, meat or fish boiled in water). It did not require much time to build a fire or to make the porridge. As mentioned, soldiers occasionally fortified bread by adding bean flour to the grains. The historian Herodian reported that Roman soldiers typically made barley cakes and baked them on charcoal. Biscuits were specially prepared breads that were very dry and could be kept for long periods.

Soldiers prepared their own meals. Basic military units were called the *contubernium*. They were made up of eight to ten soldiers who shared a tent and took care of their own daily needs. Soldiers ate at night after toiling and building camps. Nighttime was the best time for cooking and especially baking, which required camping facilities and time. During army campaigns, soldiers had to prepare quick meals. Each meal had to satisfy the warriors' nutritional and caloric needs.

Rules of Eating

There were a few rules or customs that had to be followed during the meal.

1. Introduce all tastes.

Appetizers *(gustatio)* were served at the beginning of the meal to introduce a variety of tastes before the main course. The appetizers were very small, and their function was taste and pleasure only. Roman cooks used leeks, sorrel, salt, pepper, and cumin for *gustatio*.

2. Start with subtle-tasting foods and move to stronger, more aggressive tastes.

Salads were introduced in the beginning of the meal, and not brought out with the wine, which was mainly drunk toward the end of the meal. Falandrian wine (wine that came from Falandria, a Roman region, and was notorious for its strong taste) was not served at the beginning of the meal because it was too strong to drink on an empty stomach. Roman condiments, mostly spicy, with a strong or sweet taste, were served at the end.

3. After the meal—relaxation.

Relaxation after the meal was a must. People would converse. Philosophical, spiritual, and intellectual ideas were discussed. The atmosphere and mood were care-free. Roman people liked humor, especially at night. Music, dancing, and poetry were popular as well.

"High-Sky Foods"

Romans believed that natural energy existed within some raw foods. They believed, for instance, that berries contained sun energy, and therefore these fruits were considered to be "high sky." Sun-strong foods had to be eaten on an empty stomach in order to keep the right energy flow. Too much energy, according to the Romans, was not good, as they felt it would put one out of balance.

Berries and sun-dried fruits were therefore generally consumed on an empty stomach. For example, mulberries picked before the sun was too high in the sky were to be eaten on an empty stomach during the day.

Balancing Overindulgence

Romans treated overindulgence and its presumed consequence, weight gain, in a variety of ways, such as exercising outdoors, collecting wood, digging, running into the Campus Martius, or taking a dip in the freezing Tiber River. These people had an almost obsessive way of creating checks and balances to their physical and mental states.

Elimination

Healthy digestion and elimination were a necessity of warrior life. Being regular was, therefore, already a priority a couple of thousand years ago (at least). Romans used different preparations of mussels, other shellfish, and sorrel cooked in wine from Chios (another Roman region) to make an effective laxative.

Since the plebeian diet was rich in natural fiber—whether cooked or raw—it is reasonable to conclude that the poor didn't use laxatives. Moreover, they couldn't afford them. I assume that the popularity of these laxative food preparations among the elite Romans was a result of their main meal being high in protein and relatively low in fiber. On another note, Alexander the Great is believed to be the first Westerner to have discovered the banana fruit, in India. He originally thought the banana was a type of fig. After his soldiers ate some overripe bananas and suffered from diarrhea, Alexander issued an executive order to avoid them. For the Macedonians, bananas were forbidden because warriors were not supposed to put themselves at risk of suffering from bloating or any other unpleasant digestive symptoms that could slow them down.

Sickness and Medicine

Sick people were suspected of having committed a morally weak action. Romans were extremely superstitious. As advanced as they were in science, politics, and art, they strongly believed in signs, luck, curses, and blessings. Both Romans and Greeks were pagans. Every Roman home had a god or goddess to protect their family. They also strongly believed in "what you see is what you get." In their eyes, morality and physical health went hand in hand.

Traditional Roman healing remedies included:

- Fasting—to heal stomach troubles
- Pomegranate extract—for colic and worms
- Cabbage—According to Cato, cabbage was a universal remedy for almost every illness. Treats such as fried cabbage were used to heal insomnia. The popular "cabbage soup diet" is as old as the Roman Empire.
- Music—For the Romans, music was a most powerful healing aid. The Greeks believed that music could bring the muse of gods to humans. According to Socrates, music was the ultimate art, which brought forth the ideas of harmony, beauty, and health.

Roman Health

Romans were generally in good shape. A Roman soldier, who spent most of his adult life in the army, was able to endure intense physical stress for long periods of time, especially during army campaigns. An infantryman had to carry 40–60 pounds of equipment on his back, march thirty miles, toil, build camps or fight—almost every day. To withstand such physical and mental demands, a Roman warrior obviously had to be in a good state of health.

The majority of health problems that civilian Romans suffered from at that time were related to protein, vitamin, and mineral deficiencies. Ailments such as eye infections, stomach aches, skin disorders, and summer and autumn fever were mostly the result of nutrient deficiencies. The high-grain, low-protein vegetarian diet of the poor often caused protein deficiencies, particularly among children and pregnant women.

Plebeian Roman diets, high in wheat, and low-class Greek or Spartan diets, high in barley, were deficient in the protein lysine, vitamins A, C, and D, and certain minerals such as zinc. The shortage of animal food and the consumption of high-phytate grains (bread or cereal) caused mineral deficiencies, such as iron and calcium. I can list more vitamin and mineral deficiencies, and their symptoms, but since this isn't a history or medical book, I've just outlined some general problems of the time and how people tried to deal with them.

Living Off the Land

Macedonian, Spartan, and Roman warriors lived off the land. Foraging was a fundamental part of warfare, and armies had to rely on local food supplies. A Roman legion of 5,000 soldiers needed to feed almost 10,000 people, including servants, slaves, and allied soldiers. The daily burden of an average Roman army added up to shiploads of wheat and barley, herds of cattle, and wagonloads of wine, vinegar, and olive oil.

Transportation of large amounts of food made it difficult for an army on the move to conduct an efficient war campaign, especially on the mainland. A dependence on transporting the food supply slowed the advance of an army, and sometimes brought it to a halt. Tactical nutrition strategy was a necessity to successfully live off the land. Warriors had to be aware of the seasons when different crops would be available. Choosing the right season could play a major role in whether or not a military campaign was successful. Greek historian Polybius describes the successful gathering of wheat by Hannibal (in July–August near Gerunium during the Carthaginian campaign against the Romans) as a major contributing factor to Hannibal's Victorian campaign.

Training to live off the land began at a young age for Spartan boys. They were taught to look for food outdoors during different seasons, and these hungry boys would steal food if necessary in order to survive. If caught, they were punished. This preparation also triggered their Warrior Instinct, as they became adept at making viable and efficient food choices as well as cycling between the extremities of deprivation and compensation.

For the Roman army, which consisted mostly of heavy infantry, foraging wasn't an easy task. Small groups of soldiers who were sent to the fields to collect wheat crops were often attacked by enemy cavalry units, which were quicker than the Roman infantry.

Supported by light-armed troops, the cavalry was important in the attack and defense of foraging parties. In order to avoid splitting the army into small, vulnerable foraging units, Caesar established an "always-on-the-march" strategy with the aim of getting his supplies more conveniently by moving camps to various places. Foraging and living off the land was practiced during spring and summertime, when crops were ripe. Winter was a bad time for an advancing army that depended on local food supplies; external food supplies were therefore crucial during that season.

The Second and Third Macedonian Wars clearly illustrated the influence of food supply and seasonality on strategy, and vice versa. The Macedonian army moved into the mainland, where during the wintertime they forced the advancing Roman army to retreat as a result of problems with food supply. Winter was a bad time for war campaigns, and it still is today.

In the late Roman Empire (during Hadrian's reign), Roman soldiers cultivated and grew their own crops and vineyards. At that later time, the Roman army was mainly a defensive army. Not being on the move changed these soldier-warriors' routine to a more comfortable, less aggressive phase. That may have been the beginning of the end of the Roman Empire.

Summary

Macedonian, Spartan, and Roman warriors were frequently on the move. Army campaigns on foreign land forced these wandering warriors to adapt to different climates and seasons, and to adjust their diets accordingly. From an early age, they were trained to adapt to different daily, seasonal, and yearly natural cycles. Following the daily cycle, these warriors cooked their own meals at night and ate while camping. Cooking was popular among Romans. Emperors, army leaders, senators, historians, and philosophers created their own recipes.

It's interesting to note that some wealthy people, like Cato or Cicero, were proud of the humble or "modest" meals they ate. It was their way of practicing austerity and sobriety. But in fact, these allegedly modest meals were beyond the reach of the poor.

Common people had to adjust rapidly to changes in conditions due to wars or natural disasters such as famine or drought, since they depleted much of the available food supply. Because of constant dangers, insecurity, and life's hardships, the "nuclear family" predominated in the Greco-Roman world. Family members united to help each other in times of crisis. Evening meals were dedicated to tightening the bonds of family and friends.

Roman men, soldiers, and civilians had to adapt to a warrior way of life. Physical appearance was of crucial importance to these people; being in shape was a must. Therefore they paid attention to their diet, style of dress, and physical activities.

The ancient "Warrior Diet" primarily evolved to effectively nourish these active people, enabling them to stay in shape and be strong enough to endure prolonged physical and mental pressure as well as extreme conditions involving changes in climate, season, and food availability. The Roman diet was based on a combination of all the food groups: vegetables, grains, oil, and legumes with meat, fish, eggs, or dairy. As mentioned, warriors who lived on vegetarian diets, based on grains and legumes only, did so because of shortages in the food supply. They preferred protein sources such as meat, cheese, or fish.

Vegetarian, high-grain diets often caused protein deficiencies, as well as mineral and vitamin malabsorption and deficiencies. Warriors were aware of that, and so they constantly looked for good sources of protein. Digestion and elimination were top priorities for ancient warriors. Fermented foods in the form of raw vinegar, fermented vegetables, fish, or wine supplied these people with the friendly lactic acid-producing bacteria (probiotics) essential for healthy digestive and metabolic systems.

As you've noticed, the diet kept by common people differed from that of the higher classes. Commoners and hard laborers often faced the threat of malnutrition or starvation, and therefore consumed whatever they could afford. Slaves, laborers, and poor people ate during the day. Noble men and soldiers who carried arms followed a diet that was based on a daily cycle—one meal per day, eaten at night. This diet is what I call the "Ancient Warrior Diet." As noted earlier, during war campaigns Roman soldiers ate carbohydrate foods such as dry biscuits or flatbread during the day in order to satisfy their daily calorie needs. Their main meal, however, was eaten at night while camping.

Roman people considered themselves superior to their Greek slaves. Yet Greek slaves were in charge of educating and medically treating their Roman masters. Greek culture, wisdom, and mythology established the basic foundation of the Roman way of life. It's reasonable to conclude that the Roman diet, which consisted of mostly *crudus* (raw food) during the day and warm cooked meals at night, was in fact influenced by ancient Greek, Spartan, Athenian, and Macedonian traditions.

Romans, Spartans, and Macedonians were strong, tough people. Alexander the Great all but took over the world with a group of only sixty thousand men. He conquered the Mediterranean, Middle East, and Egypt. He destroyed a whole Persian army and moved into India, where his army crossed a thousand miles of desert by foot. These Macedonian warriors were so potent that, man for man, they left more offspring in their wake than any other advancing soldiers in history. There are people today living in remote places throughout Asia, India, and Persia (now Iran) who still claim to be descendants of Alexander the Great.

The Spartans frequently demonstrated their courage and awesome might. At the pass of Thermopylae, three hundred Spartan warriors led by King Leonidas stopped a million-man Persian army under King Xerxes.

Roman warriors were notorious for their bravery. Julius Caesar destroyed a Gaul army that outnumbered the Romans two to one. As mentioned, the average Latin warrior was only 135–145 pounds. Yet he successfully fought face-to-face against a 180-pound man from the north, whether a Gaul, Celt, or German.

Looking at Roman and Greek art, you can clearly see that their warriors were lean and muscular. Julius Caesar was in his late fifties when he was assassinated, and at the time of his death he was still lean and in good shape. The "lean 'n' mean" look of the Roman warrior wasn't just an aesthetic concept. For an armed man who spent most of his life outdoors, often under extreme conditions—mobilizing heavy equipment from one place to another, at times marching thirty miles a day and then engaging in face-to-face combat—the strong, lean physique was a must.

Being as light and mighty as one could be was an essential factor for the survival of a warrior. Conversely, being heavy often made soldiers slow or sluggish, unable to react fast enough. For a warrior, that could be fatal. The lean and tough look or—if you wish—the warrior's body proportion was therefore more an issue of function than of fashion. I have to say that being a soldier does not necessarily mean being in good shape. Army leaders like Napoleon, Czar Alexander of Russia, and Norman Schwartzkopf, for that matter, did not look lean or hard. That, of course, is just the physical look. But if you believe in "what you see is what you get," appearance has a lot to do with one's diet. My conclusion is that the ancient warrior diet of cycling between extremities of deprivation and compensation, with physical activities mostly during the day, was a major factor in shaping the characters of ancient warriors, as well as how they looked and the way they fought. Extreme deprivation, agitation, and anxiety during the day, and relaxation and compensation at night, made these warriors tough enough to endure pain and pressure for long periods, and still remain in good shape for life. Their Warrior Instinct kept them constantly alert to changes, and able to adapt quickly to different conditions. It's very likely that a diet similar to this Warrior Diet was followed by other groups of warriors in different parts of the world. The common thread for all warriors was being nomadic. They wandered from one place to another, living off the land—practically fighting their way as they went along.

The Ramadan holy fast of the Muslims (which is based on fasting during the day and eating only at night) mimics, in my opinion, the way that wild Arab warrior tribes lived in the sixth and seventh century in North Africa and the Middle East during Mohammad's time.

Steak Tartar is reminiscent of the way Mongolian warriors would tie meat to the back of their horses and ride until night, by which time the shaken and beaten meat had become soft and tender. Mongols were probably the most ferocious warriors in history. They were meat-eaters—and the tradition of eating meat and milk is still popular among these nomadic people today. Mongolian warriors used to eat at night while camping. Their most nutritional food was mare (horse) milk, which is high in essential fatty acids and close in biological structure to human mother's milk. Mother's milk and colostrum were both popular among Greek and Roman physicians. They prescribed this dairy nectar to treat symptoms such as infections, headaches, or fever.

Conclusions for the Modern "Warrior"

I've tried to relay the story of ancient warriors in a brief, objective, and factual way. But how can anyone be completely objective, or know for sure how people lived centuries ago? It is my considered opinion that the Warrior Diet is an updated ancient diet. I think it would be impractical to follow an ancient diet without taking into account the changes that have occurred over time, and how these changes affect our lives today. Human nature hasn't changed at all, but the world certainly has. Since we know much more today about the science of nutrition and its effects on the human body and mind, I was able to create a diet based on old principles but with appropriate adjustments made for the twenty-first century.

I believe that if Caesar were alive today, he'd follow a diet similar to the Warrior Diet advocated in these pages. In my opinion, a twenty-first-century man or woman who isn't involved in traditional warrior activities can still live like a warrior. As mentioned before, cycling between undereating and overeating, detoxifying on a daily basis, exercising regularly, and gradually shifting from processed foods to whole foods would naturally help unleash the inert Warrior instinct.

Once triggered, this instinct will guide you to perform at your best both physically and mentally. I believe that with time you'll notice how your body naturally transforms itself while adapting to a warrior lifestyle. In other words, you'll become a warrior and look like one. The Warrior Diet is actually a lesson from history. This diet is based on years of research, my own experience, as well as the experience of many others who have gone on the diet—and what I offer below and elsewhere in this book are my personal conclusions.

The Historical Role of Nutritional Carbohydrates and Their Applications Today

Ancient warriors' high consumption of carbohydrates during campaigns may raise questions about the role that carbs should play in diet. Whether this high-carb diet was an ideal warrior diet or not has already been discussed.

However, the role of carbohydrates as a main source of nutrition is still an open issue today—and needs a fresh review. Ever since *Dr. Atkins' New Diet Revolution, The Zone, Protein Power Diet,* and *The Carbohydrate Addict's Diet* hit bookstores and became bestsellers, carbs have become "the bad guys on the block." Millions of people today who desperately wish to lose weight try these low- or no-carb fad diets. And many of these dieters lose weight in the short run but unfortunately gain back more weight than they lost. According to the low-carb diet concept, one will lose weight when carbs aren't available, because the body is forced to burn fat. That's the main trick. However, the issue of carbohydrates as a body fuel isn't so simple. The main argument made by low-carb diet gurus is that carbohydrates are not an essential nutrient food, and therefore one can live very well without them.

Let me offer some facts regarding the role of carbohydrates. Virtually all plant foods and dairy contain naturally occurring carbs. Humans were introduced to these primal pre-agricultural foods long before grains and refined sugars. Thus we are well adapted to whole carbs from primal food sources. Carbohydrate fuel is critical to our survival, providing the following benefits.

Brain Fuel

The brain needs a mixed fuel of carbs, protein, and fat to function properly. Carbs are the main source of energy for the brain. An insufficient supply of carbohydrate fuel to the brain may lead to fatigue, lethargy, and depression. A mixed fuel works by supporting different critical brain functions including energy production, synthesis of hormones and neurotransmitters, as well as the nourishment of brain cells. If dietary carbs are chronically restricted, there may not be enough carb fuel available to the brain, which may lead to energy crushes and excruciating craving for sugar, which may in turn lead to compulsive bingeing.

Stress Blockers

Carbohydrates help balance cortisol (the stress hormone). The insulin hormone is a major cortisol blocker. That's one of the reasons people under stress tend to eat carbohydrate-rich foods. Moreover, without carbs, one may not be able to produce enough serotonin. Serotonin is a protein neurotransmitter in the brain, essential for feeling calm, relaxed, and happy.

Anti-Aging

Serotonin is also the building block of the hormone melatonin. A decline in melatonin levels is associated with sleep disorders and "chronic jet lag." Melatonin is a powerful antioxidant hormone, and it is believed to possess some anti-cancerous and anti-aging properties. The older one gets, the less melatonin is produced. Keeping your melatonin levels high, if nothing else, may help keep you young.

Carbs can help keep you young in more than one way. As noted, carbs play a critical role in nourishing an important metabolic pathway in the liver. Called the pentose phosphate pathway, it is responsible for the synthesis of nucleotides, RNA, DNA, and energy molecules, as well as the most powerful endogenous antioxidant enzymes (glutathione and SOD). Chronic restriction of dietary carbs may shut down this important metabolic pathway, compromising the body's capacity to generate energy, rejuvenate, and resist aging.

Clean Body Fuel

Carbohydrates are the cleanest and most efficient fuel for energy. The body breaks carbs into energy without any toxic byproducts. Conversely, when the body is forced to break protein and fat into energy, there may be toxic byproducts such as ammonia, nitrates, free radicals, or oxidized fatty acids—all of which will tax the overall metabolic system. Carbs are efficient because they metabolize faster than proteins and fats. By rapidly replenishing depleted glycogen reserves in muscle tissues and the liver, carbs are the most viable source of immediate energy. Under extreme conditions they may help spare muscle breakdown.

Metabolic Controllers

A daily supply of complex carbohydrates will keep your thyroid level up. A healthy thyroid controls your body's temperature and keeps your metabolism intact. The thyroid hormone positively affects steroid sex hormone levels. Low thyroid is associated with declining testosterone, loss of libido, and weight gain.

You can see how chronic deprivation of carbohydrates over the long run may have some negative effects on your body and mind. Chronic carb-depletion, for prolonged periods of time, may eventually compromise your mood, your sleep, your energy, your metabolism, and even your ability to stay young and virile. It probably sounds old-fashioned to recommend that people go back to eating carbs, especially today when low-carb diets are so popular, often endorsed by celebrities, fashion models, and diet gurus.

The Warrior Diet is definitely not about carb deprivation. In my opinion, the fact that warriors in the past were in such great shape may have had a lot to do with high carbohydrate consumption. Eating carbs at night proved to be highly effective in nourishing these super-active men with clean fuel. It provided them with important nutrients, such as fibrous brans, germ oils, and certain phytonutrients, that they could not get from any other food source. Most importantly, a supply of carbs at night may have been the major factor that fully completed the compensation effect of the diet. Since warriors lived under "fight or flight" conditions during the day—with all the agitation and anxiety that involved—they needed full compensation at night to calm down and give them a sense of pleasure and relaxation. I firmly believe that this compensation factor is what made these ancient warriors so capable of enduring intense physical and mental stress under extreme conditions for prolonged periods of time.

My conclusions, therefore, are as follows:

1. Without carbs there won't be complete compensation.
2. Only when the cycle of deprivation and compensation is complete can you benefit greatly from the Warrior Diet.
3. Diets based on chronic carb deprivation will eventually leave you feeling constantly deprived and, in the long run, will fail.

Different people have different needs. Competitive athletes and those involved in daily physical activities can have more carbohydrate fuel than weekend warriors. Professional athletes who train twice a day, for example, may need to eat small snacks of carbs during the day, like ancient warriors did, to satisfy their high-calorie needs. People who burn thousands of calories during the day need to replenish their empty glycogen reserves to avoid muscle catabolism. However, since most people are not engaged in prolonged physical activities on a daily basis, the Warrior Diet generally minimizes carbs (to mostly fruits and vegetables) during the day. As noted earlier, you can cycle the diet according to your needs. In Chapter 10, "The Warrior Diet Idea,"

I discuss how to cycle between days of high carbs and days of high fat. Use your instincts to choose the right cycle for you.

All that said, the Warrior Diet isn't necessarily a high-carbohydrate diet. As you've seen with the Overeating Phase, carbohydrates should be consumed during your evening meal—either with your cooked veggies and protein, or preferably after them if your goal is to lose body fat. In the latter case, carbs should be the smallest component of your meal.

In this discussion about nutritional carbohydrates, I refer to complex carbohydrates, preferably from whole foods such as rice, barley, oats, corn, potatoes, and yams. Sugar and other processed simple carbs should be minimized. They may have devastating effects on your body by overstimulating insulin, and may result in insulin insensitivity, food cravings, mood swings, and fat gain.

Primal Fat Fuel and Carbs

It has been suggested that humans and other primates have better adapted throughout evolution to primal fat fuel coming from nuts and seeds. Nonetheless, even these primal high-fat foods provide the body with naturally occurring low-glycemic carbs, which complement the fat content in these foods.

CHAPTER 10

THE WARRIOR DIET IDEA

THE WARRIOR DIET, AS I'VE SAID BEFORE, is not just a diet. It's a way of life. It is, as you know by now, based on triggering the Warrior Instinct through a daily cycle of undereating and overeating. Since this is a controversial diet that challenges conventional "rules," I consider it important to discuss different ideas in relation to diet, nutrition, instincts, and a sense of freedom. I also question some conventional ideas, routines, or habits that, in my opinion, need to be re-evaluated. Some ideas set forth in this chapter go beyond the diet, yet I believe their consideration will greatly benefit those people who make the Warrior Diet a way of life.

Cycling the Warrior Diet

You can cycle the Warrior Diet in different ways: with days of undereating only, and other days where you choose to overeat. You can also alternate between days of high fat and days of high carbohydrates. However, based on Warrior Diet testimonials, if your goal is to lose body fat, high-fat days would most likely be more effective.

There inevitably will be times when you're too busy, stressed, don't feel well, or may be engaged in events that prohibit you from overeating. This is fine; you can undereat for a few days and then resume your Warrior Diet routine. This is part of the leverage you have on this diet. Listen to your instincts. If you crave high carbs, you may need to satisfy energy demands or just calm down. Don't deny yourself any food group.

You can also go off the Warrior Diet, and then come back to it. This way you can practice the right diet for the right moment and always maintain the freedom to make choices. Some people choose to go off the Warrior Diet during holidays or celebrations, to enjoy eating meals both during the day and evening with family or friends. This is okay. You should be able to live with the Warrior Diet without feeling deprived.

Going Off the Warrior Diet

As mentioned, you may choose to go off the Warrior Diet on some days, or for a short while. Let's say you go on a trip, unable to cook, and want to switch to eating small meals throughout the day. This is fine. Every time I've been on trips and gone off the Warrior Diet, my meals are more frequent but smaller, and surprisingly I lose weight. This is probably because my body's metabolism has been accelerated due to adaptation to the practice of overeating. If you choose to go off the Warrior Diet and have small meals throughout the day for a few days, your body will likely burn more than you actually eat. This heightened metabolism will remain for a few days; however, if you go off the Warrior Diet completely and return to a routine of eating a few small meals per day, *I believe your body will readjust to a lower metabolic rate.* It's my contention that once you've practiced the Warrior Diet long enough to have experienced its incredible benefits, you'll eventually come back to it because it's so fulfilling and effective.

How Often Can You Deviate from the Warrior Diet?

You can deviate as often as you want, but my assumption is that you won't want to. Freedom is the most important thing, so do whatever you want. Use your instincts.

Wild cats look their best when they're hungry. So do you.

What Makes You Stay on the Warrior Diet?

The Warrior Diet is so powerful that it can be compared to a gravitational pull; you can't escape it. Because you'll feel great when practicing it! This is partly due to something that happens during undereating, which I call the "brain-boosting factor" or "getting high." This holds especially true for those who like to feel highly energetic, alert, clear-minded, focused, as well as those who want to boost their creative or competitive drive. There's something like a switch that's turned on after you adapt to undereating, and you become almost addicted to this "crispness" of your brain. Who wouldn't enjoy the "high" feeling that the Undereating Phase provides?

During the Undereating Phase, physical hunger can be turned into spiritual hunger. Religious people all over the world have long believed that one can only experience a deep spiritual awareness when fasting. This said, I should mention again the full satisfaction and sense of freedom and calm that you can achieve every day during the Overeating Phase. Every day has a happy end.

Once you experience the Warrior Diet, you should feel the awakening of a deep, deep instinct. Imagine people who've never had sex, and then suddenly they do—and it's great. Would they want to give it up? I truly believe that this diet is so strong that you won't let it go. Once your Warrior Instinct is triggered, no one can take it away from you. It would be like trying to extract raw meat from a tiger's jaws.

Cycling the Autonomic Nervous System (Alertness and Relaxation)

The Warrior Diet is the only diet I'm aware of that achieves the correct balance between the two parts of the autonomic nervous system, the sympathetic and parasympathetic systems. The sympathetic nervous system is responsible for all "fight or flight" activities during the day, and usually works in an acidic environment. It promotes alertness and energy expenditure and is mainly catabolic.

The parasympathetic nervous system, on the other hand, is responsible for digestion and sleep, and usually works in an alkaline environment. It promotes relaxation, recuperation, replenishment of energy reserves, and is mainly anabolic. These two systems are antagonistic to each other when activated simultaneously.

Many people who eat frequent meals during the day and are under stress often suffer from digestive problems, lethargy, or exhaustion. These problems occur because the adrenal "fight or flight" mechanism contradicts the digestive system. However, the Warrior Diet promotes synergy between the sympathetic and parasympathetic nervous systems. During the day, the sympathetic nervous system triggers alertness and the ability to handle stress (the "fight or flight" reactions). By the time you reach the Overeating Phase you've already consumed live foods (fruits, vegetables, and juices made from them) that alkalize the body. Alkalizing your body will reduce the catabolic-acidic effect of the sympathetic nervous system, and prepare you for the parasympathetic nervous system that regulates digestion, relaxation, and sleep. The Warrior Diet is the only diet I'm aware of that works in synergy with both systems without compromising one or the other.

The Instinct to Overeat

Many health practitioners and diet gurus warn us not to overeat and support this advice with reasons like "it places too much pressure on the body" and "it creates an imbalance." Yet people do overeat, and when they do they usually feel guilty. Well, I may be the first one to say that overeating can be good for you—moreover, that doing so is instinctual. And, like any primal instinct, if you try to repress it and shove it inside, it'll come back with vengeance.

The Overeating Syndrome
(Deprivation Leads to Uncontrolled Bingeing)

Overeating is an instinctual way of the body to compensate when it's chronically underfed, malnourished, starving, or emotionally or mentally deprived. The urge to overeat can also be triggered when the body tries to pick up its metabolism, which may have declined as a result of prolonged low-calorie diets. Overeating can work for you if you control it—by inducing it at the right time. This is discussed extensively in Chapter 5.

If you don't let your body overeat when it needs to, this desire or need may haunt you by inducing an excruciating desire to binge. Many people go to the fridge late at night, open it, and start bingeing. When asked why, they often say it's almost like a demonic force that makes them binge, and they can't stop themselves. A fair number of people binge compulsively. I believe that a large percentage of bingers do so because they feel they are deprived. Deprivation is a key factor in uncontrolled bingeing. The real question is whether bingeing is controlled or uncontrolled. When people are out of balance or feel deprived—due to unhealthy diets and eating habits—they often develop chronic food cravings which, in turn, lead to compulsive, uncontrolled bingeing. Bingeing under these circumstances is obviously not a good habit.

Overeating Boosts Metabolism

One of the most important benefits of overeating on the Warrior Diet is the overall metabolic accelerating effect on the body. Mainstream thought regarding dieting is that the most viable influencing factor in weight management is daily caloric intake. Thus, if you want to lose weight, you just have to reduce your calories. This works up to a certain point. But after a while the body's metabolism slows down, so one has to maintain a lower level of calories or continue reducing them to keep the weight off—at that point just an "extra tomato" may cause weight gain. I'm just teasing about the tomato, but you get the point.

Why would your metabolism slow down due to a low-calorie diet? Because when you chronically decrease your calorie intake, the body, through adaptation, will attempt to maintain itself at this new lower level in order to survive. So, if all of a sudden you increase the calories, you may gain weight. That's what happens to bodybuilders and other athletes who try to make weight. In-season, they look lean because of strict calorie reductions. Off-season, they usually gain weight, often quite suddenly.

I believe that the best way to lose body fat without the above side effect is to reduce calories for a few days, then increase them back, in order not to let the body adapt to low-calorie intake. On the Warrior Diet, you go through this process practically every day, cycling between undereating and overeating. Another effective way to sustain a lean body all year round is to shift from carb fuel to fat fuel foods. I've found that those who train their body to gradually shift to mostly fat fuel foods (such as raw nuts) find it easier to sustain a lean body in spite of the overall increase in daily calorie intake (due to the high fat content).

As mentioned above, it is commonly believed that what affects the body's metabolic rate are the calories consumed per day; however, I believe it's the calories per meal. Or, to say it differently, it's the amount of food/intensity of the meal that really counts. This theory also applies to workouts. We already know that you can exercise moderately for three hours without making any progress. Yet a ten-minute intense workout can be effective enough to stimulate muscular development and strength gain. So it's the intensity of a drill that forces your body to adapt, not necessarily the sheer length or the volume.

142 of THE WARRIOR DIET

When you divide your meals into three to six per day, like most typical diets suggest, and each meal is approximately 150 to 300 calories, that's what the body adapts to. The Warrior Diet concept is different. It's built on extremes similar to athletic training. So when you consume, for instance, 1,000 to 1,500 calories in a meal, that's what the body will adapt to. There's an overall thermogenic effect with increased energy expenditure that occurs with such intense meals; the body tries to increase its metabolism in accordance with the high energy intake.

Studies conducted on mice showed that mice fasting for eighteen hours, without being overfed first, suffered from low thyroid and slow metabolism. However, mice that were overfed and then went through an 18-hour fast kept their thyroid hormone at a normal level and their metabolism high.

Based on Warrior Diet testimonials, there is growing evidence that those who undereat and overeat notice a gradual increase in their metabolism.

How Many Calories Should You Consume during the Overeating Phase?

For some people overeating will be 600 calories a meal. For others, like myself, it's 1,500 to 2,500 calories a meal (a main meal means all food intake at night, including late-night snacks). Building up must be done gradually. Don't jump to 3,000 calories per meal too quickly. Once you begin to practice the Warrior Diet, you'll find that your metabolism gradually picks up to the point that when everybody else gains weight during the holidays, with its big meals, you won't since you have been dining this way every day. What people call overeating during the holidays is actually an average meal for a warrior.

Glycogen Stretching

To Boost Metabolism, Improve Performance, Sustain Energy, and Lose Body Fat

Glycogen is a special form of carbohydrate energy storage in our muscles and liver. For sedentary people, glycogen supplies only a couple hundred calories. After these available calories are burned, a physically inactive person may experience some unpleasant symptoms, such as fatigue, dizziness, or virtual paralysis due to accumulation of lactic acid in the muscles. Conversely, a physically trained person will be able to burn about twice or three times as many glycogen-available calories without side effects. Maintaining a proper diet and exercise routine can increase glycogen reserves in the muscle tissues while improving the liver's capacity to convert lactic acid to energy.

Let me explain how can you stretch glycogen reserves. Let's say that you work out like a warrior, on an empty stomach, and then overeat. After a few months you may succeed in increasing glycogen storage in your muscles by extremely depleting and then overcompensating carbs on a daily basis. Your body will most likely adapt to this diet and exercise routine by gradually increasing its glycogen reserves.

Furthermore, depletion of glycogen reserves was found to involve production of certain proteins called AMP kinase, which accelerates fat breakdown while improving insulin sensitivity.

Glycogen holds water in the muscle tissue. That's what gives muscle the "pump." When people are depleted of glycogen, they often look "flat," as if they've lost muscle size. Nonetheless, they haven't lost muscle, they've lost glycogen. Replenishing empty glycogen reserves by proper application of recovery meals and by overeating will give the muscle back its pumped look. The more you deplete and load, the more the adaptation process will occur and the more you'll benefit from "glycogen stretching."

The method of carb depletion and then carb loading is popular among endurance athletes. Those who try this approach can experience a substantial increase in stamina, as well as endurance of prolonged physical drills.

How Much Body Fat Should You Have?

There are a lot of myths out there. I believe that beyond a certain set point of body fat percentage, any excessive fat storage is unnecessary. Fat in any living creature is a storage for toxins. It may also be an active site for producing estrogen. On top of all this, excessive fat has been correlated with insulin insensitivity, hypertension, and diabetes. So, the "bulge" isn't good for you. After a certain minimum amount of fat, any excess may be harmful. Ideally, adult males should have no more than 10% body fat. Women should normally have about 15% body fat. However, people have different genetic predispositions for body fat. Therefore, optimum body fat levels differ slightly from one person to the next.

Some contend that fat tissues are beneficial because they isolate the body and thus keep it warm. I believe this is a fallacy. Other than Eskimos and people who have genetically adapted to live in extreme Arctic weather, there's no correlation between fat and body heat. Body heat depends on one's metabolism—the more efficient the body is in generating energy through the glandular, hormonal, and cellular systems, the more effective it will be in producing heat.

Building Muscles Without Gaining Fat

You can build muscles without gaining fat by proper incorporation of recovery meals after exercise, and by shifting from carb to fat fuel foods at night. Another effective way to build lean muscles is by incorporating a few days of moderate carb loading per week and cycle these moderate-carb days with the previously mentioned high-fat days. If you consume a sufficient amount of protein, the correct vitamin and mineral supplements, and enough carbohydrates (complex carbs) to moderately boost insulin, you may be able to create an anabolic environment without overspiking insulin. There is evidence that the body's ability to utilize protein increases by twofold after undereating. Once you're depleted, you may reach the potential to be at your best capacity to absorb nutrients so that when you do eat you can accelerate the anabolic process of building muscles without gaining fat.

As long as you maintain the Warrior Diet rules of eating and *gradually* increase the amount of calorie intake per meal, you may be able to accelerate muscle gain. Researchers found a positive correlation between calorie intake and protein utilization in the muscle. (Studies on protein were done by the FAO in the U.S. during the 1970s.) Based on my personal experience, the amount of protein intake does affect the capacity to build muscle tissues. Nonetheless, the most influential factors in inducing a natural anabolic process are timing of recovery meals, quality of dietary protein, and the application of fuel foods as well as the overall calorie intake of the evening meals.

Insulin Insensitivity

Many people suffer from insulin insensitivity. As a result, they often convert carbohydrates into triglycerides, which then leads to high cholesterol, water retention, weight gain, and hyperglycemia (also known as pre-diabetes). People develop insulin insensitivity as a result of eating sweets and overly processed carbohydrate foods throughout the day. Other reasons for developing it include overconsumption of bad fats, exposure to estrogenic chemicals, and deficiencies of essential fats, especially omega-3. Insulin insensitivity or resistance can also occur when the liver is overwhelmed by toxins, alcohol, or chemicals. Under such conditions it gradually fails to regulate fat metabolism. This causes accumulation of fat metabolites in the liver, which in turn compromises the liver's capacity to utilize glucose and results in insulin resistance. Consequently, the pancreas becomes overtaxed by the continual oversecretion of insulin and pancreatic enzymes, which desperately work to remove glucose from the blood to avoid raising blood sugar. Eating frequent meals throughout the day doesn't leave the body enough time to recuperate. Meal by meal, the insulin receptors become more insensitive, and so the body secretes even more insulin in order to reduce blood sugar. This leads to high fluctuations of blood sugar, and one may feel hungrier as a result and thus eat even *more* carbohydrates. If this vicious cycle continues unabated, one may eventually gain weight and becomes insulin-resistant or diabetic.

Conversely, after you've gone through the Undereating Phase of the Warrior Diet, your body is at peak insulin sensitivity. By stabilizing your insulin, you can manipulate this hormone to work as an anabolic agent. You'll also be able to effectively metabolize carbs into energy instead of fat. Stabilizing insulin is a key to sustaining prime health.

The Sense of Freedom

I'd like to discuss what a sense of freedom means, what happens when people are deprived of it, and what happens when they have it. I'd like to offer my perspective on how a sense of freedom relates to dieting and also to negative feelings of depression vs. positive feelings of compensation. Freedom is a relative term. Nobody is completely free. Nonetheless, *we experience a sense of freedom when we feel that we have the ability to make choices and satisfy our primal instincts.*

Once you find your own healthy cycle, you'll feel free because you're in control, your body is rejuvenating again and again, and when you eat, you eat what your body craves. You'll enjoy your meals and will stop eating when you want to, not because of guilt, or because others tell you to. This is quite a difference from other diets.

On the Warrior Diet, you'll likely accelerate your metabolism and lose body fat while regaining a great sense of well-being. In earlier chapters you learned how during the Undereating Phase your growth hormone is boosted, and while glucagon levels are elevated, you are granted hours of fat-burning on a daily basis. All these benefits can be even further enhanced if you add exercise (while undereating) to your daily routine. Just think how exhilarating it'll be to realize that by following the right cycle, your body naturally transforms itself and becomes leaner and stronger and healthier!

How a Sense of Freedom Relates to Achieving Your Goals

Instincts create desires. Every time you satisfy a desire that is derived from a deep instinct—such as creative, nurturing, protective, sexual, or aggressive instincts—you feel pleasure and a sense of freedom. People generally fantasize about things when they're deprived of them. A funny example of this is Kurt Vonnegut's book *Breakfast of Champions,* where people go to the movies to watch other people on the screen eating cheesecake. In this futuristic comedy, eating a cheesecake is outlawed. His satire points out how sick we've become.

You may ask, "If I actually fulfill all my fantasies and instincts, does that mean I won't have any others?" Far from it. You'll have greater fantasies—more romantic, more adventurous, more creative, and more spiritual ones. You may take more chances and more risks, such as launch a new business, help the less fortunate, or work in some way to improve your life. In short, you'll become more ambitious and successful in whatever you choose to do because you're not stuck in primitive fantasies like eating a cheesecake. Most importantly, when you satisfy your desires, you regain feelings of pleasure. Without pleasure, you may feel deprived and miserable. Life is too short to not get the best of it.

The Romantic Instinct

A New Definition for Romanticism

What does "romantic" mean? What makes someone a "romantic"? What is a romantic act? Romantic instinct? Romantic aspect? Romantic Period? Since these common words and phrases aren't always clearly defined, I think they need some clarification.

I'm aware that what I am about to say is debatable, so take it any way you want. You may agree with me, and you may not.

It's my strong belief that romanticism is based on an instinct that's related to and comes from the same source as the Warrior Instinct. The romantic instinct is a primal instinct that defines a person's uniqueness, makes him or her question rules, and inspires the person to fight to keep his or her uniqueness or integrity intact.

The core of romanticism is the concept of breaking an established rule in order to build a new one. And a romantic act is the action of doing just that. For example, the story of *Romeo and Juliet* is romantic because of their struggle to build a relationship in spite of their family's rules. *Romeo and Juliet* are romantic heroes. Seeking each other out in spite of their families was a romantic act, and killing themselves made it even more romantic. Sacrificing one's own life because of love goes against the rule—or instinct—to survive. Throughout history, a romantic aura has surrounded those who were ready to sacrifice their lives for a cause they believed in strongly.

A romantic aspect can emerge solely by breaking rules. Criminals, whores, and antiheroes, for instance, who defy and break societal rules have been the subjects of generations of legend and literature (think Balzac and Dostoyevsky). Outlaws like Jesse James, Billy the Kid, Butch Cassidy, and Bonnie and Clyde are considered romantic heroes mainly because they dared to break the rules.

As noted, romanticism is based on an instinct. Children, for example, have an innate and very fresh romantic instinct. When an authority figure such as a parent or teacher tells a young child to do (or not to do) something, they often try to disobey. It's also common for children to joke about their teachers. Kids have a great sense of humor, and humor itself involves breaking rules. I truly believe that it's the romantic instinct deep within our subconscious that makes us enjoy jokes that break taboos, and the child within us that cracks up when we hear or see something funny. Unfortunately, over time children's romantic instincts are crushed, since children seek approval and are inevitably faced with so many parental, religious, political, and societal rules that they often begin feeling guilty when they go against them. Nevertheless, these primal romantic desires and instincts are still engraved deep within each of us. I believe that every romantic story, in literature and in life, somehow involves triggering this instinct.

To "keep order," society creates many taboos that are anti-romantic. This is understandable, since if everyone were wildly romantic, it would be impossible to maintain control. But when this primal instinct is constantly controlled and inhibited, like anything that's chronically inhibited, there are side effects and symptoms, such as feelings of frustration, anger, deprivation, lack of freedom, and aggression. We're living in a world where false romanticism abounds. There isn't enough space here to fully philosophize about this topic, so let me just say that any seemingly romantic idea that appeals to a crowd of people is probably falsely romantic. True romanticism is individualistic and endorses uniqueness. I'm not suggesting that people break rules or laws. However, I am saying that the ability to instinctively question rules and norms is necessary when you want to improve upon something, make a change, or create something new.

How This Relates to the Warrior Diet

As noted, I believe that the Warrior Instinct manifests itself through the romantic instinct. By triggering the Warrior Instinct you'll become more romantic, you'll instinctively identify your uniqueness, and you will be ready to take action as needed to keep it intact.

False vs. True Romanticism

What I call false romanticism is the most common variety. As an example, if you were raised to be civilized, peaceful, and respectful of other people's lives, and then suddenly your country declares war and tells you to break all civilized rules and instead go and fight and kill, you may feel that going to war is patriotic and even romantic. But as you'll soon realize, this is probably false romanticism. Saying that, being a soldier does in fact have a romantic aspect to it, since it implies the readiness to sacrifice one's life for a cause.

However, going to war with all its seemingly "romantic" aspects didn't come from you; it came from political authorities (the establishment), and therefore, in my opinion it's false. Conversely, if you *volunteer* to go and fight and help a cause, then you're doing something that's truly romantic, since you initiated it and are following your personal beliefs while keeping your integrity intact.

Romantic rituals and holidays, like weddings and Valentine's Day, are other examples that I believe have little to do with real romanticism. People mistakenly confuse rituals celebrating mating with the truly romantic act of falling in love. When people fall in love, their romantic instinct kicks in and they may even become "romantic fools," meaning they will do things that are out of the ordinary, like sacrifice time and money just to be with and satisfy a loved one.

Unfortunately, after some time, many married couples no longer act romantically. Their marriages become routine, and the only romantic things left are the so-called "celebrations of love"—holidays like Valentine's Day and wedding anniversaries.

This said, there are people who are constantly romantic, break routines, and continue to fall in love with their mates.

Following stiff routines is the antithesis of romanticism. Breaking routines is like breaking rules. When the romantic instinct is triggered, people are instinctively more adventurous, more creative, and ready to take more risks.

In the matter of love and relationships, I truly believe that once this romantic instinct is unleashed, it'll instinctively guide you to act romantically at all times. When this instinct kicks in, a person is in his or her best shape to attract a mate. Falling in love, with the desire to give to, share with, and protect someone, is based on an instinctual drive that involves a lot of changes. Being with someone and having a family together demands more responsibility and a capacity to handle all the changes necessary to that union. As I've said before, it's the romantic instinct that encourages you to go through all these changes and continue to care for someone else while creating new lives.

You may ask, "Can you be a romantic or do a romantic act without breaking a rule or routine?" My answer to this is No. All romantic acts involve breaking rules or routines, and doing things out of the ordinary. Being romantic extends beyond love, relationships, and the breaking of old habits. It is romantic to break new ground, to "revolutionize," and to create something new. It is romantic to be brave enough to stand up for your rights—or someone else's rights—and be ready to face the consequences. As I've said, true romanticism comes from deep inside you. When you commit a romantic act and go against the rules or routines, you're actually fighting to keep your integrity and uniqueness intact. This, in my opinion, is what makes the romantic instinct a manifestation of the Warrior Instinct.

The Aggressive Instinct

In his controversial book *On Aggression,* anthropologist Desmond Morris tries to prove that aggression is a primal instinct necessary for survival. Aggression doesn't need to be expressed through violence. In a way, violence is a result of suppressed aggression. Once it explodes, it often goes out of control. Aggression has its positive side. It manifests itself through competitive drive, as a potential force needed for self-defense, and for expanding one's territory.

This subject obviously deserves more space, but for now, let me just say that I truly feel aggression is indeed a primal instinct with both bad and good sides, and it should be thought of accordingly. Aggression is essential for survival. Without it, you'll either end up a saint, or just plain dead.

The Myth of Eating Whole Foods Only

Christian Scientists, and some holistic health gurus, believe that you should eat only whole foods. They claim that supplements may cause imbalance and adversely affect the integrity of the body's metabolism. I understand where they're coming from, since whole foods, especially raw foods, should supply virtually all essential nutrients; and synthetic vitamins may indeed cause more damage than benefit. However, we don't live in a pristine world but rather a polluted world. We're constantly exposed to overwhelming amounts of industrial chemicals including xenoestrogens, which are known to cause metabolic disorders, fat gain, and mortal disease in men, women, and children. On the top of all that, due to industrial harvesting methods and soil depletion, the food that we eat today—including organic whole food—is often deficient in critical nutrients even if it isn't covered with pesticide residue. Therefore, I think some supplementation is necessary to make up for the lost nutrients that existed in greater quantities in food in the past. We need to supplement with nutrients that can help protect us from common exposure to chemicals. However, I also believe there's a need for an alternative to commercial synthetic supplements. Ideally, nutritional supplements should be derived from whole food, and they should nourish the body like food.

Chemical and Environmental Toxins, and Other Stressors in Everyday Life

Most diet books start with lots of current statistics on the frightening increase in obesity in the last half of the twentieth century. Many people today are aware of these stats, and so go on this or that diet. One doesn't have to be a rocket scientist to figure out the important role that diet plays in our health, and the link between obesity and heart disease, diabetes, arthritis, and other degenerative diseases, including cancer.

But what many people don't realize is that other factors—some of which are environmental—may contribute to the way people look and feel, and dictate what they suffer from today.

Chemicals such as petroleum-based pesticides, herbicides, and fertilizers, hormones and antibiotics in the meats, poultry, and milk we buy in the grocery store, industrial toxins like bisphenol A and other estrogenic plastic derivatives, as well as oral contraceptives and prescription drugs in our recycled water supply, some of which also contaminate the fish we eat—these are all examples of invisible toxins or "stealth toxins." On a daily basis, we don't realize (and often can't feel) that these chemical toxins exist. There's nothing more dangerous than stealth toxins coupled with ignorance. The inability to see or feel these dangerous compounds makes us extremely vulnerable.

Data show how destructive these (mainly man-made) chemicals are. Food additives, including nitrates or nitrites, pesticides, herbicides, hormones, antibiotics, and plastic derivatives, are all major catalysts for a wide spectrum of modern diseases, ones that barely existed in the past. The National Cancer Institute found an increased risk of leukemia in children whose parents used

pesticides in their garden or home. Food additives and chemical preservatives have been linked to Attention Deficit Disorder (ADD) in children.
Moreover, antibiotic residues found in non-organic meat and dairy are believed
to cause new mutations of antibiotic-resistant bacteria, which limit or inhibit
the ability of antibiotic drugs to halt dangerous infections in people.

Of even more concern are the plastic derivatives, pesticides, and other
estrogen-like chemicals in our food supply. These toxins have been linked to
male sterility and the increase in cancer rates in both sexes. Industrial plasticizers were found to cause chemical castration and cancer in animals and
sterility in humans. The estrogenic hormone BSA, routinely injected in livestock animals, was found to cause abnormalities in reproductive organs as
well as cancer in women and men. Male sterility today is higher than ever.
Other unpleasant estrogenic effects abound, like "stubborn fat" and the "feminization" of men.

According to the American Chemical Society, sperm count in men worldwide is 50% lower than it was fifty years ago. And, if that's not bad enough,
recent reports indicate that men's sperm count has dropped by a staggering 20% in the past twenty years (within only one generation). Are we already
showing the first signs of extinction? Young male alligators in pesticide-
contaminated lakes in Florida were found to have such small penises that
they're unable to function sexually. Countless other species including marine
wildlife are on the brink of extinction. Is our very survival being threatened?
Farmers have been found to have a relatively high incidence of some cancers, including multiple myeloma (cancer of the bones), lymphomas, skin
melanomas, leukemia, and cancer of the lip, stomach, prostate, and brain.
Work-related exposure to chemicals was theorized to be the cause.

Estrogen-related diseases such as breast cancer and prostate cancer are at
all-time highs. According to another report, the incidence of prostate cancer
has doubled in the past fifty years. And, while the incidence of breast cancer
was one in twenty in 1960, it increased to one in nine in 1998. In 1978, Israel
banned three estrogenic pesticides: lindane, DDT, and BHC. By 1986 the
death rate from breast cancer among Israeli women below the age of 44 had
dropped by 30%. Conversely, breast cancer rates among women who live in
other industrialized countries have skyrocketed.

Steroid hormones in our meat and dairy can have devastating effects on everyone, especially children and infants. Premature puberty and child mortality have been linked to the hormones in non-organic meats and milk. These are only some of the consequences of commonly found chemical stealth toxins in the food and water supply.

Among the most dangerous of all stealth factors is radiation. I'm not just referring to nuclear radiation. We live in a world today that is over-radiated and, as a result, we are exposed nonstop to "slow radiation" that, put simply, is slowly killing us. Radioactive minerals penetrate the human food chain and cause different kinds of malignant cancers. These toxic materials aren't cycled like other organic materials. For instance, the life expectancy of iodine 131 is about 160 years. Once this radioactive iodine penetrates the body, it occupies the place of the natural organic iodine mineral, severely damaging the body's metabolic process. Iodine 131 may be the main reason for cancer of the thyroid gland.

Some radioactive isotopes—for example, strontium 90—have a life expectancy of 360 years. Once a radioactive mineral penetrates the body, it binds to the organ that needs this mineral most and creates a chain reaction that causes catastrophic damage. I can go on and on, but let's just say that all of these factors are extremely dangerous to one's health—and not knowing about them leaves us completely defenseless.

As mentioned, those most in danger are infants, children, and the elderly. The immune system of infants and children are not fully developed, and since they have such small bodies, pound for pound, the toxic effect is much greater on them than on adults. The elderly often suffer from age-related, compromised immune systems, so toxins have an accelerated effect on them.

It seems there is nowhere to run. *But*—in fact—there is a lot we can do. We can effectively defend ourselves against these stealth toxins through diet, proper nutritional supplements, and by following eating cycles that promote daily detoxification. Below are several ways to help protect against the effects of environmental toxins.

Protecting Yourself Against Environmental Toxins

The first defense against environmental toxins such as petroleum-based estrogenic chemicals (including pesticides, herbicides, and plasticizers) is to eat mostly anti-estrogenic foods and to supplement with estrogen-inhibitor herbs. As previously discussed, certain foods and herbs have shown substantial protective properties against harmful estrogenic chemicals. Most notable among them are cruciferous vegetables including broccoli, cauliflower, cabbage, and Brussels sprouts. Other anti-estrogenic foods are onion, garlic, citrus fruits, omega-3 EFA oils (derived from fish, flax seeds, hemp seeds), plant sterol-rich foods such as raw nuts and seeds, spices such as turmeric and curry, and herb extracts from passion flower, chamomile, amla berries, and cruciferous vegetables.

It's important to try minimizing exposure to all estrogenic substances. Also minimize consumption of all estrogen-promoting foods, including all conventional produce, meats, poultry, and pork. Minimize intake of omega-6 vegetable oils such as soy, canola, safflower, and corn. Stay away from edible products that smell like plastic. Minimize consumption of processed soy products, as well as estrogenic herbs such as clover and licorice. Refrain from using lotions or sprays or pharmaceutical products with petroleum-based detergents. The ecological problem of estrogenic chemicals is probably the most dangerous factor threatening our lives today. I designed a hormonal balancing diet called *The Anti-Estrogenic Diet* (North Atlantic Books, 2006) to provide solutions to this very problem.

As noted, in addition to estrogenic chemicals we're also constantly exposed to radioactive substances. The first defense against radiation is via "mineral loading." Once cellular mineral saturation occurs, there's less possibility for the radioactive minerals to be absorbed into your body's organs. The best way to ensure mineral loading is by following a daily detoxification routine, which involves ingestion of live fruits and vegetables while undereating during the day. Eating live fruits as well as freshly prepared vegetable juices (as suggested for the Undereating Phase of the Warrior Diet) provide the body with live minerals, antioxidant nutrients, and live enzymes, a lot of which defend the body against radioactive materials and the free radicals created by radiation. Nonetheless, just to be on the safe side, supplementing with minerals and trace minerals is probably the most effective way to achieve mineral loading and prevent often-occurring mineral deficiencies.

There are also certain foods and herbs that have within them special properties to protect the body from environmental radiation; they contain nutrient and mineral complexes that naturally induce chelation. Chelation occurs when a nutrient pulls out, or neutralizes, toxins and radioactive materials that penetrate the body.

Foods, Nutrients, and Herbs with Anti-Radiation Properties

Sea Vegetables—Kelp, arame, kombu, and hijiki are all high in sodium alginate, which is the best chelator for pulling radioactive toxins from the body.

Miso—High in minerals and a strong alkalizer, miso is believed to protect the body against radioactive minerals.

Beet Juice—This is known as a liver and blood detoxifier. Beets are high in naturally occurring iron, which protects the body from plutonium and radioactive iron.

Super-Foods: Bee Pollen, Colostrum, High-Sulfur Vegetables

Bee Pollen—High in minerals, vitamins, and live enzymes. Pound for pound, bee pollen is one of the highest-protein food, higher than meat or dairy. Clinically, bee pollen has been shown to significantly reduce the side effects of chemotherapy. Bee pollen is high in lecithin, which helps protect the nervous system. It's also high in nucleic acids, which protect the cells from radioactive exposure.

Colostrum—The high content of immuno-supportive compounds, minerals, vitamins, and hormonal-supportive nutrients in colostrum make this super-food a great anti-radiation and recuperation supplement.

High-Sulfur Protein-Containing Foods—Broccoli, cabbage, cauliflower, kale, Brussels sprouts, garlic, onions, and eggs are all high in naturally occurring sulfur as well as the antioxidant sulfur-containing amino acid cysteine. Cysteine neutralizes free radicals and protects against x-rays as well as radioactive minerals such as cobalt and sulfur.

Fiber: Vegetable, Grain, Legume, Seed, and Fruit Fibers

Fiber helps chelate radioactive material out of the body, including fibers containing phytates (which are found in grains and legumes) and pectin, a soluble fiber found in fruits, nuts, and seeds. Lignans, which are in flaxseeds, have also been shown to possess great chelation properties. So do proteoglucans found in oats and barley.

High-Chlorophyll Foods: Leafy Green Vegetables, Grass Sprouts, Parsley

Consuming high-chlorophyll foods such as parsley and leafy green vegetables helps to significantly reduce the effects of radiation. The high-enzyme content of grass sprouts (such as in wheat grass or broccoli sprouts) aids in detoxifying and neutralizing free radicals.

Herbs: Siberian Ginseng, Astragalus, Echinacea, Goldenseal

Siberian Ginseng—This adaptogenic herb has been found to rebalance and heal the body from physiological and environmental stresses. Siberian ginseng is believed to be one of the best herbs to combat the dangers associated with environmental radiation, x-ray exposure, and chemotherapy.

Astragalus—This herb boosts the immune system and thus helps to defend the body against radiation.

Echinacea/Goldenseal—Echinacea is an immune booster and blood purifier. Goldenseal, besides being a potent immune booster, is believed to carry some anti-cancerous properties. Combining echinacea with goldenseal, in my opinion, works better than echinacea alone, particularly when you're sick. Pregnant or lactating women should consult their physician before taking these herbs.

The best way to take these herbs is to cycle their supplementation: a few weeks on, a few weeks off.

NOTE

Some of the foods listed, such as fruits, freshly prepared fruit and veggie juices, bee pollen, and colostrum, are best taken during the day on an empty stomach. Doing so will accelerate the detoxification effect and assimilation of their essential nutrients. All the other foods and herbs listed can be ingested at any time of the day, or with your evening meal.

As a general rule, peeling fruits and vegetables reduces the danger of exposure to radioactive fallout toxins.

Prostate Enlargement Problems

Men, who are understandably concerned about prostate cancer, ask whether there is anything they can do to reduce this risk. What follows is my personal opinion and is not meant to suggest or guarantee that it is a cure for those people who already suffer from prostate enlargement-related problems. Nonetheless, based on testimonials of individuals who have noticed substantial alleviation from symptoms and even reversal of their condition, I strongly believe that certain natural therapeutic methods can be highly effective in treating prostate-related disorders.

It is commonly believed that prostate cancer is "accidentally" contracted due to a genetic predisposition. The current consensus in the mainstream medical community is that dehydrotestosterone (DHT), the so-called "bad testosterone," is what causes prostate cancer. DHT is a most active derivative of testosterone that binds to the androgen receptors inside the prostate gland, and therefore is believed to be what makes the cells proliferate and become cancerous. This in theory may seem to be true, but I strongly believe it's not the whole truth.

In fact, I question this theory outright. DHT, the allegedly bad testosterone, appears in highest levels in young adults, who have the lowest rates of prostate problems. And visa versa: the older one gets, the lower testosterone and DHT levels are, and yet the higher the rates of prostate disorders and cancer. Aging is correlated with lower testosterone production. Moreover, aging accelerates the conversion of testosterone into estrogen. So, if the DHT or oversecretion of testosterone causes prostate cancer, why are the majority of men who suffer from it elderly and have already lost quite a bit of their testosterone as well as DHT?

In my opinion, enlargement of the prostate gland and the incidence of prostate cancer are likely caused by a combination of factors, such as increased conversion of androgens to estrogen, exposure to estrogenic chemicals, liver congestion, hormones in foods, and age-related hypertension, as well as blood sugar problems. More and more studies show that prolonged abuse of certain chemicals, exposure to pesticides, excessive alcohol consumption, and an unhealthy diet may all induce overwhelming estrogenic effects on the whole body and in particular the prostate gland.

Prolactin (the hormone that produces milk) is also correlated with prostate enlargement-related diseases. Prolactin can devastate a male body, accelerating the penetration of testosterone to the prostate gland and its conversion into DHT inside the prostate gland. It's this conversion to DHT inside the prostate that makes the cells proliferate and causes enlargement of the prostate. Elevation of prolactin in men can be due to a complex set of factors, including having a low thyroid, aging, and bad diet.

DHT Can Work for You

DHT is not the "bad guy." DHT is the most potent testosterone derivative, which positively affects potency. In fact, DHT cannot penetrate the prostate gland from the blood. Only free testosterone (testosterone that is not bound to GHGB—gonadal hormone-binding globulins) can penetrate the prostate gland. Once inside it can convert to DHT and then, combined with estrogen, possibly cause prostate enlargement or even cancer. It is now known that estrogenic substances can bind to male androgen receptors in the prostate and induce their adverse proliferative effects.

Drugs such as Proscar and Propecia work to reduce blood DHT and allegedly alleviate prostate enlargement symptoms and protect against hair loss, respectively. However, both drugs have side effects, including lowering libido and sexual potency. So, following this line of thinking, the question is: What happens when blood DHT is increased?

Surprisingly, when DHT level increases, testosterone level declines. Therefore, less testosterone penetrates the prostate, less DHT is produced inside the prostate, and as a result, symptoms and damage would most likely be reduced or even cleared.

The Warrior Diet's First Defense Against Prostate-Related Problems

I believe the Warrior Diet can help provide natural defenses against prostate enlargement and prostate cancer. The Undereating Phase lowers the metabolic stress on the body, while enhancing removal of toxins. The high intake of fruits and vegetables or their juices during the day, combined with supplementation of liver detoxifiers and estrogen-inhibitor herbs, will most likely provide the body with sufficient viable antioxidant and anti-estrogenic nutrients to help prevent excess accumulation of estrogenic substances and to counteract their harmful effects.

Conversely, when eating three to six meals per day, there is an inevitable increase in the overall metabolic stress on the body and the liver. This routine gradually exhausts the liver, over time leading to a compromised detoxifying capacity. When the strained liver can't effectively eliminate toxins, then estrogen metabolites and chemicals can infect the blood circulation, causing harmful effects including prostate enlargement and cancer.

Practicing the Undereating Phase on a daily basis is possibly the most important element of the Warrior Diet, and one of the main reasons why it's so effective in enhancing the body's natural defenses.

Avoiding estrogenic foods and chemicals (see list below) further helps the liver to detoxify. Finally, as noted, eating the foods I suggest previously, and taking the right nutritional supplements, enables you to load your body with the nutrients to help protect against the harmful effects of estrogen—while sustaining hormonal balance for maximum metabolic efficiency.

To sum up, if you detoxify daily, eat the right foods, and take the supplements recommended, while minimizing consumption of estrogenic foods and substances, I believe you will stand a far greater chance of keeping yourself healthy and avoiding prostate problems.

Avoid the Following Estrogenic Foods and Substances:

- All meat that is not organic (due to the estrogen hormones inside), including red meat, chicken, turkey, lamb, pork
- All dairy products that are not organic, due to the estrogen and prolactin hormones they contain
- Petroleum-based pesticides, herbicides, and fertilizers, which are found in non-organic produce
- All edible products that are packed in plastic and smell like plastic
- All skin products with petroleum-based detergents (such as surfactants, p-nonylphenol, and synthetic glycerine)
- Soy protein and soy isoflavones products
- Excess of omega-6 vegetable oils (soy, canola, safflower, corn)
- Alcohol

Natural Supplements to Help Alleviate Prostate Enlargement-Related Symptoms and to Protect Against Prostate Cancer

Estrogen-Inhibitor Herbs

There is mounting evidence that estrogen is the main culprit for the current growing rate of men suffering from prostate cancer. As noted, estrogen and its related compounds can bind to androgen (male sex hormone) receptors in the prostate gland and cause cell proliferation and growth. Researchers believe that there is a direct correlation between the global increase in industrial xenoestrogen pollution in the environment, food, and water, and the current epidemic of estrogen-related cancer including prostate cancer.

Herbs known to be estrogen inhibitors may help provide a first defense against estrogen chemicals. When combined together, natural estrogen inhibitors may counteract estrogen and its related chemicals in three ways.

1. Inhibition of the enzyme that converts androgens to estrogen. Natural aromatase inhibitors are flavones derived from passionflower, chamomile, onion, and garlic. Studies reveal that when combined, these flavones inhibit the two different promoters of the aromatase enzyme and thus effectively inhibit estrogen in both healthy and cancerous cells.

2. Antagonizing estrogen receptors' negative and positive (ER- and ER+) cells. To this group belong curcumin (turmeric), resveratol (red grapes, red wine), and apigenine (chamomile). When combined these natural compounds have shown the capacity to antagonize and destroy ER+ tumor cells.

3. Shifting estrogen metabolism to produce beneficial metabolites (2 hydroxy estrogens), rather than the harmful metabolites (16 hydroxy estrogens). To this important group belong indoles (glycosides) in all cruciferous vegetables, including indole 3 carbinol, indole 3 acetate, and diindolymethane (DIM).

In summary, estrogen inhibitors including flavones from passionflower, chamomile, onion and garlic, curcumin, resveratol, and cruciferous indoles may effectively help counteract excess of estrogen in the body. When combined with anti-estrogenic foods and a chemical-free diet, estrogen-inhibitor supplements may be highly effective in preventing and even reversing disorders.

Plant Sterols and Sterolines

Plant sterols support the anti-estrogenic hormones testosterone in men and progesterone in women. The plant sterol beta-sitosterol has shown the capacity to convert in the body to sex steroid hormones. For that matter, plant sterols may help establish a healthier hormonal balance with an anti-aging effect in both sexes. In addition, plant sterols have anti-inflammatory and cholesterol-lowering properties. Best sources of plant sterols are nuts and seeds as well as stabilized rice and wheat germs.

Liver Detoxifiers

The liver is the site that metabolizes and neutralizes estrogen. Liver detoxifiers (as mentioned previously) may help alleviate the metabolic stress on the liver while supporting neutralization and elimination of toxins, including estrogenic substances.

Pygeum Bark and Saw Palmetto

Pygeum bark and saw palmetto berries are natural supplements that have been used traditionally to alleviate symptoms of Benign Prostate Hyperplasia (BPH). Pygeum is an evergreen African tree. The bark of the trunk is the part of the tree used for medicinal purposes. It is often mixed with palm oil or milk.

It's interesting to note that certain substances in pygeum, such as n-docosanol (a triterpene), significantly reduce serum prolactin levels. As noted, prolactin decreases the uptake of testosterone and increases the conversion to dihydrotestosterone (DHT) inside the prostate gland. Clinical trials and numerous studies support the fact that pygeum effectively reduces the symptoms of BPH.

Fertility—Pygeum may improve infertility-related problems in men who suffer from diminished prostatic secretion. Pygeum helps to increase prostatic secretion and improve seminal fluid.

Potency—Pygeum extract can help those who suffer from BPH to improve sexual performance. BPH is often associated with erectile dysfunction and other sexual problems. In this case, pygeum can help men achieve full erections.

Saw Palmetto, A Double-Edged Sword

Saw palmetto is a small West Indian palm tree. It also grows in North America. The American Indians traditionally used saw palmetto berries as a tonic to support the body nutritionally, and they were used by men as a fertility aid. Many herbalists consider it to be an aphrodisiac. This supposition may, however, be false.

Saw palmetto has proven to be an effective supplement to help treat symptoms in those who suffer from BPH. Saw palmetto inhibits the conversion of testosterone to DHT. It also inhibits DHT's activation through cellular binding. However, there is evidence that Saw palmetto also possesses anti-androgenic activity, which means that it may reduce the action of testosterone.

Saw palmetto is still an open issue. While it seems to be an effective natural aid for prostate enlargement-related symptoms, it may, at the same time, reduce sex drive and potency.

Conclusion

Men who suffer from prostate enlargement-related problems should consider taking a combination of standardized estrogen-inhibitor herbs together with anti-estrogenic foods, while minimizing the intake of "conventional" (non-organic) meat, dairy, and produce, as well as avoiding exposure to industrial estrogenic chemicals. Supplementation with pygeum may be beneficial; saw palmetto may lower potency.

If you suffer from prostate enlargement-related problems, you should seek professional medical help. You may also consider incorporating alternative healing methods in your treatment, such as the above herbal remedies, and making adjustments to your diet and lifestyle.

CHAPTER 11

Questions & Answers

I'D LIKE TO ADDRESS SOME frequently asked questions from those who have been practicing the Warrior Diet, and by others who are considering it.

Q: Does exercise influence when and how much you eat?

A: Yes, it does. After exercising, particularly on an empty stomach, your insulin receptors are at peak sensitivity, your growth hormone is at the highest level, and your glycogen reserves are virtually depleted. This is the best time to eat. Your body is now ready to consume large amounts of food without gaining weight.

Q: What if you only exercise two days a week?

A: The Warrior Diet still works.

Q: Can you eat the same amount on the other five days as the two days you exercise? Maybe your body won't want as much.

A: This diet will eventually bring you to a natural rhythm, one in which you'll be able to sense your particular needs at any time. In other words, you should crave and eat exactly what you need and as much as you need on both active and rest days. On the days that you don't exercise, I believe that your hunger will be slightly less, and satiety will come more quickly. However, people who practice a whole day or two of undereating may need to eat more the following day, even if they didn't exercise.

Q: What about individuals who suffer from blood sugar problems and are often told that they need to eat throughout the day in order to maintain steady blood sugar levels?

A: I have to say up front that everyone, especially those who have preexisting conditions or are sick, should use common sense and consult with their physician before going on any diet. I presume that the majority of mainstream physicians will be opposed to the Warrior Diet, even for those who are healthy; regardless, I truly believe this diet will help most people, including those who suffer from hypoglycemia. In fact, we've received testimonials from people who managed to reverse Type II diabetes simply by adjusting the Warrior Diet program and shifting from grains to the lower-glycemic beans, nuts, and seeds as sources of primary fuel. The Warrior Diet aforementioned blood sugar stabilizer herbs may help accelerate the results. (See Chapter 4, the section titled "Supplements for the Undereating Phase.)

Q: What about children? Is this diet good for them?

A: The most important thing for children, in my opinion, is to make sure that they eat the right foods, which include raw vegetables, fruits, good-quality proteins, whole-grain carbohydrates, and good fats. Children need more fat than adults. Essential fatty acids are extremely important for babies and children's brain development and growth.

Children are virtually "pure." Their natural instincts remain sharp if they're not corrupted. The problem, though, is that adults often try to crush their instincts. I believe that children are primarily in tune with the instinct that regulates healthy eating cycles, but unfortunately they are often forced to eat when they don't want to. As a general rule, when children are hungry they should eat, and when they aren't hungry, they shouldn't be forced to eat. Children should not be on the Warrior Diet *per se;* however, having them eat fresh fruits and vegetables and drink freshly prepared juices during the day would be greatly beneficial.

Q: Most children are starving in the morning.

A: Remember, children should not be on the Warrior Diet *per se,* so they should eat breakfast. Nonetheless, they should be trained to enjoy the subtle taste of low-glycemic whole foods.

Q: Why do you think so many kids today only want to eat sweets, sugar-laden beverages, and fast food? And what can be done?

A: Many children develop aggressive tastes from a very early age. As a result, they lose the ability to enjoy the subtle taste of healthy whole foods. When they're given or allowed to eat overly processed foods that contain additives with aggressive tastes, such as sugar, fructose, or other stimulators including salt, fried oils, etc., they begin to crave these unhealthy foods and become addicted to them. This is highly destructive because as noted, children lose their ability to enjoy the subtle tastes that come from nature. Not eating enough natural foods leads to deficiencies of essential nutrients. To make this matter worse, chemicals in foods—such as petroleum-based pesticides, herbicides, nitrates, food colorings, and certain preservatives, as well as toxins such as metal toxins (aluminum-based leavening)—affect children much more than adults. Poor eating habits may lead to serious metabolic problems, retarded growth, and impaired mental development.

When children have unhealthy diets, I often recommend that parents try putting their kids on a moderated Warrior Diet, with a shorter period of undereating, where they're given raw fruits, veggies, and fresh juices— and then feed them the right foods. Healthy instincts should eventually return and they'll gradually develop a subtle taste and enjoy eating healthy foods.

Q: What age is ideal for people to begin the Warrior Diet?
A: I think it's when they reach maturity. Until then, young people should eat more frequent meals. Nonetheless, based on testimonials, teenagers are doing well on the Warrior Diet by simply increasing the amount of protein meals during the day.

Q: At what age does one mature?
A: Sixteen to eighteen.

Q: So this diet is for people who are at least sixteen years old?
A: There is no classified standard as to what age is appropriate to start following the Warrior Diet. Nonetheless, due to the current rates of child obesity as well as teen obesity, it is obvious that mainstream nutritional guidelines are failing to keep children healthy. I believe that a milder version of the Warrior Diet can provide the benefits of daily detoxification as well as complete nourishment for growing children or teenagers. As noted, the diet plan should be adjusted to accommodate their physical needs. For instance, young adults can have fruit or fresh-fruit smoothies or freshly

squeezed vegetable juices until lunchtime, and then have a meal. As mentioned earlier, Spartan boys were trained and fed like warriors, and they grew up to be strong, tough adults. This doesn't mean that I recommend a Spartan way of life. Nonetheless, this is an example that the Warrior Diet indeed works for young adults.

Q: *I've heard that vegetarians are more peaceful and spiritual than meat-eaters. What do you think?*

A: Some vegetarian-diet authors make this claim, and add that we'd live in a better world if people were vegetarian because they are also more compassionate and spiritual than meat-eaters. I strongly believe that this isn't so. Two of the bloodiest killers ever, Adolf Hitler and Joseph Stalin, were vegetarian. However, I can see where vegetarian advocates are coming from, and I respect their concerns about cruelty to animals and the environmental issues.

Q: *How do you think people on the Warrior Diet should deal with social and business events that involve meals?*

A: While on the Warrior Diet, especially during the Undereating Phase, you'll feel alert and focused. This alone is a big advantage for social and business-related events.

Here's my suggestion. For a breakfast meeting, stick to fresh fruit or a fresh fruit smoothie or juice, and coffee or tea. For a lunch meeting, veggie juices, salad, eggs, or sashimi are appropriate. Dinnertime meals should be no problem. Just follow the overeating principles. People will be impressed with the amount of food you can eat during dinner without gaining fat. Explain that you're on the Warrior Diet. Many people today are on diets, so they should understand if you choose not to eat a typical breakfast or lunch. Don't feel a need to apologize. This is a free country.

Q: *Can you have nuts or seeds during the Undereating Phase?*

A: During the adaptation period and days that you feel deprived, yes. Nuts and seeds are very good foods, particularly raw as opposed to roasted or seasoned. However, it's not ideal to eat them during the early hours of the day. Although raw nuts and seeds won't overspike your insulin, they may increase the metabolic stress on your digestive system, and thus may compromise your body's capacity to detoxify.

Q: *What about smoking and alcohol? Are they allowed?*

A: The Warrior Diet is about diet, and it's also about a sense of freedom, not deprivation. When I say that this diet is a way of life, I mean that there are some profound ideas behind it that ideally will improve your life as far as setting priorities, defining goals, and heightening self-esteem, ambition, and creativity. I assume that those who follow the Warrior Diet have enough information to make the right choices when it comes to whether to drink alcohol or smoke, and if they choose to do either (or both), it's up to them. If you smoke or drink, the Warrior Diet will still help you to detoxify and stay in shape. The ability to make choices is what freedom is all about.

Q: *People who drink a lot of alcohol are often overweight.*

A: Alcohol-related problems, including stubborn fat, are discussed in Chapters 6 and 7.

Q: *Do you have anything to say to those people who crave alcohol?*

A: Being on the Warrior Diet may result in less alcohol consumption because the desire to drink excessively diminishes when you reach satiety from what you eat. I believe that excessive drinking has a lot to do with deprivation.

This said, having a glass of wine per day is usually fine for most people. As mentioned before, warriors of great societies in the past used to drink wine habitually.

Q: *Jews and Muslims fast once a year. How does this relate to the Warrior Diet?*

A: People in the past were aware that to cleanse and reach a spiritual state of mind, fasting was the route to take. For Muslims, Ramadan means fasting during the day and eating after sunset. In my opinion, Ramadan is an example of an old, traditional fast that is similar to the Warrior Diet. People who fast during Ramadan say that they feel physically, mentally, and spiritually rejuvenated. Fasting for Jews, such as on Yom Kippur, means spiritual cleansing. Getting away from the materialistic world is a way to cleanse one's body and spirit.

Q: What should I do with all this new energy that I have?

A: If you "suffer" from too much energy, then go and find yourself a life. It's best that I stick to the subject of diet and not become a preacher. I truly believe that once the Warrior Instinct is triggered, people gain more courage to try things they may have been afraid to attempt before. They may become more adventurous, more romantic, more creative, and more competitive. So the question about what to do with all this extra energy is, in my opinion, irrelevant. If you ask a champion athlete "What do you do with your extra energy that comes from all this training?" they'll likely tell you, "Get out o' here."

Q: What about those who find it hard to calm down or sleep at night?

A: If you find it difficult to calm down at night, you may not be consuming enough carbohydrates. Also, sleeping disorders may occur due to hypertension (high blood pressure), hyperglycemia, or stress-related disorders. If this is your case, shift to low-glycemic foods and, if needed, seek professional help.

Enzymes and Live-Food Enzymes

Q: Who needs enzymes?

A: Everybody needs enzymes. Young people have a higher enzyme pool in their bodies than older people. Because of this, enzyme supplementation may be beneficial as one ages.

Q: When is the best time to take enzymes?

A: I always suggest taking enzymes on an empty stomach or just before a meal because this gives them time to reload your system and reach your blood. It's important that enzymes reach the circulation via a proper loading approach. As I've mentioned before, research reveals that enzymes (such as protease enzymes), upon reaching the circulation, can effectively reduce inflammation and may also have the ability to destroy pathogenic bacteria and viruses, so they may have a systemic healing effect on the body.

Q: How many should I take?

A: It depends on the product's manufacturer. Check the label and experiment. One to four capsules before your meal is usually sufficient. Monitor yourself for what works best. You may try to increase the dosage gradually. For some people, high dosage works better.

Q: *What are the best enzymes to take?*
A: The enzymes that have the most healing effects are protease enzymes, which break down protein, thereby aiding in the purification of the blood and working as anti-inflammatory agents. For example, bromelain (derived from pineapple) is a protease enzyme. In addition to breaking down protein, it aids in reducing water retention and inflammation, and thus is generally helpful in the healing process. All protease enzymes, including papain (derived from papayas) and tripzine (pancreatic protease), have a systemic anti-inflammatory effect.

It's preferable to take a combination of protease enzymes rather than just one type, but they will be effective in both cases. Some experts believe that plant enzymes are most effective because they contain the widest variety of live enzymes that support carb, fat, and protein utilization. However, although plant enzymes do contain proteolic enzymes, they're not high in them. Also, plant enzymes work at different pH levels than human enzymes and therefore could be more beneficial systemically for anti-inflammatory purposes than for digestive purposes. The variety of enzymes in plant enzymes is enormous. They are highly accessible in live food and therefore are greatly beneficial nonetheless. Moreover, plant enzymes are more stable in high temperature than animal-based digestive enzymes.

Q: *Are live-food enzymes good enough to enhance digestion?*
A: If you want to ensure maximum digestive potency, especially since people today consume so much processed food, I think it's best to consume live foods and also take digestive enzyme supplements, as well as probiotics. The latter are beneficial bacteria that help correlate the digestion of protein and fiber.

Q: *Are there other enzymes?*
A: Yes, there are antioxidant enzymes. The most important ones are SOD (Super-Oxide Dismutase) and reduced glutathione, both of which the

body produces naturally. These antioxidants are available today in a supplemental form. Nevertheless, the bioavailability of these products is in question. In order to produce enough SOD, your body needs the minerals zinc, manganese, and copper, as well as probiotics. Besides being a super antioxidant and a first defense against gene damage, SOD is also vital for potency and virility. Healthy cells contain SOD, which protects them from nitric oxide (a natural substance that the body produces). Nitric oxide is necessary for regulating blood pressure and sexual arousal. It is also vital for normal brain and heart functions. Nevertheless, without SOD, nitric oxide metabolism can be adversely shifted to produce harmful compounds—nitrites and nitrates. In summary, without nitric oxide you wouldn't be able to survive, and without SOD the nitric oxide mechanism would be severely compromised.

Glutathione enzymes (the other type of endogenous antioxidant enzyme) are vitally important to the body. The body's glutathione pool is an index determining how healthy you are. Your body should produce glutathione naturally from precursors if you eat the right amount of foods containing the amino acids cysteine, glycine, and glutamine.

Unfortunately, cysteine is such a sensitive amino acid that most processing destroys it. Foods such as bean sprouts, cruciferous vegetables, and minimally processed dairy all contain cysteine. Egg yolks are another good natural source of cysteine, as well as whey and colostrum. Maintaining a high pool of cysteine in your body is critically important. That's one reason why it's highly recommended to keep food live and whole.

Glutathione supplements are available, but your body should be able to produce it naturally when you nourish it with the right foods and supplements. Certain sea plants like spirulina and chlorella, as well as raw meat and raw fish, do contain glutathione, but it's usually destroyed by digestive enzymes in the stomach. Therefore the best way to keep glutathione levels high is by ingesting the right natural precursors so your body will be able to produce it. Glycine and glutamine are present in all complete protein foods, including fish, eggs, dairy, and meat.

CHAPTER 12

SEX DRIVE, POTENCY, AND ANIMAL MAGNETISM

THIRTY MILLION MEN IN THE UNITED STATES are impotent. No joke. Richard E. Spark, MD, Associate Clinical Professor of Medicine at Harvard Medical School, says this number is actually an underestimation of how many men suffer from impaired sexual potency. Even more worrisome is the staggering percentage of male infertility. According to the American Chemical Society, sperm count in men worldwide is 50% lower than it was fifty years ago. And as noted in an earlier chapter, recent reports have indicated a staggering 20% decline in men's sperm count in the past twenty years (within only one generation). Needless to say, male performance is a major problem today. The recent boom in sales of Viagra indicates just how popular a potency drug can be in a sex-oriented society when, ironically, such a large number of men can't perform sexually.

Sex, Power, and Instincts

Sex drive and potency were always regarded as indicators of health and power. Since the dawn of humanity, men have competed with each other for the best mate in order to produce the best offspring and carry their genes into future generations. Being unable to perform sexually or to impregnate a woman was considered a humiliating weakness. Like other animals, human alpha males who were leaders of their pack (group) were proud to inseminate more women than the other males. The primal instinct to multiply and expand territory drove males to "conquer" as many females as possible, and the best-looking, most fecund among them.

According to anthropologist Desmond Morris, men used all their senses to select a mate. There is a primal code of health and beauty engraved in a woman's body, which attracts men. This physical code includes visual stimulators such as a woman's curves: her breasts, hips, thighs, and butt. Ancient goddesses of fertility were depicted as all "bust and butt." A well-rounded woman was a visual indication of fertility and motherhood.

Other sensual stimulations that affected attraction, such as smell (body odor and breath) and touch (smooth skin as opposed to dry skin), were also indicators of a woman's health. For example, having bad breath or body odor was thought to be a sign of disease, and therefore these women were considered unappealing as mates and future mothers. Women were aware of this "physical code of attractiveness" and so they would enhance their cleavage, use lotions to soften and moisturize their skin, and apply perfumes and other concoctions made from herbs and flowers to improve their breath and body odor.

Men, suggested Morris, possessed their own "code of attractiveness." Females were attracted to the strongest and most dominant males. A strong male or a leader could protect and provide more for them and their children. The prime "physical" code regarding a man's appeal and level of attractiveness was a powerful, muscular, and healthy look. Other masculine qualities, such as being aggressive enough to fight and wise enough to dominate other males (leadership), were also considered powerful and attractive to women.

Male genitals were regarded as a symbol of power. Ancient weapons of war, such as spears and swords, had symbolic phallic connotations. The term "weapon" remains today a slang expression that refers to a man's penis.

The main point I'm trying to make here is that an inherent, instinctual code has always attracted men and women to each other sexually. And further, this inherent code is based on sensual (aesthetic) attraction.

I believe that this primal, instinctual code is still within us, although the rules of the game have changed. Men no longer need to be physically strong (masculine and hard) in order to be successful in life or with women, and women don't need to be voluptuous to be considered attractive. As a matter of fact, many men today find women who have a lean and firm look to be most attractive, and many women today are attracted to men who look soft and out of shape.

The question is whether these changes in physical codes of attraction, in both men and women today, have had an effect on potency and fertility. I believe it has.

Modern society has created new standards for success. Thousands of years ago, it was necessary for a man and his family's survival that he be physically powerful. Possessing a combination of intelligence, masculinity, and potency was the standard of success. In biblical times and later, kings, rulers, and leaders were often involved in physical fights or duels. Great philosophers in the past have served as spiritual tutors for historical leaders (Aristotle and Alexander the Great). For ancient warriors, the spirit and the sword often went hand in hand. Bravery was an adored virtue, and chivalry was an inherent part of a man's life.

Today, most men no longer need physical power as a means to survive, and being physically brave isn't required to succeed. Money and wealth now seem to be the most predominant parameters for power. Today, if a man has money and accumulated wealth but is not a "physical specimen," a large number of women would overlook this and still be happy to hook up. It seems as though having a "big wallet" has taken the place of having a "big phallus."

I see many men who are out of shape and don't seem to care about their physical appearance. They suffer from ailments such as high blood sugar, high blood pressure, chronic fatigue, and obesity, yet they continue abusing themselves with bad diets and excessive drinking. In spite of this, these men are often successful in modern society because they're smart enough to make loads of money. Or perhaps they just inherited it. It's my contention that the society we live in today no longer emphasizes and thus suppresses the use of some of our most primal instincts to survive or thrive.

On the top of all that, our contemporary world is overwhelmed by estrogenic chemicals, a world that emasculates men and threatens women.

All that said, it's virtually impossible to totally suppress primal instincts. Behind modern male façades, there are primal desires that dictate how we behave. We still adore athletes for their physical performance and masculine, muscular look. And we also greatly admire and respect artists, scientists, and other creative types for their "creative power" and "powerful" minds. I believe it's this primal instinct which lies within us all that still attracts us to both physical and mental power, even though the emphasis formerly placed on physical prowess has diminished.

In my opinion, the confusion about gender identity today, both sexually and aesthetically, is one reason for the rise of what I believe are artificial standards that too often take the place of natural, primal, instinctual standards.

And, as I've noted earlier, when instincts are inhibited, confusion, anxiety, and poor performance result.

Male Performance Factors

Men's ability to perform sexually depends on many health-related factors that work synergistically. The most important ones are:

1. Neuro-Health: the ability to sense psychogenic (such as visual) and physical (such as sensual, touch) stimulation for sexual arousal.
2. Hormonal Balance: necessary to keep optimum testosterone levels in conjunction with other hormones.
3. Vascular Health: allows an uncompromised flow of blood to the right body parts. This includes vasodilators: factors in the form of enzymes and other substances, such as NOS and cyclic GMP (cGMP) which enforce local blood flow to the genitals until a full erection occurs.
4. Mental Health: to feel sexually confident and able to handle stress and anxiety.

All of the above work together to achieve full sexual performance. If any one is not intact, impotency may result.

There's enough data today to show the correlation between impotency and chronic diseases such as diabetes, heart problems, high blood pressure, and high cholesterol. There's also a clear connection between low levels of testosterone—or high estrogen and high prolactin (the female hormone that stimulates milk production)—and male inability to perform sexually. Stress is another major factor in male performance. Psychologists and other therapists make a fortune attempting to heal and console men who have lost their sex drive or ability to perform.

Potency and Diet

Upon looking deeper into what causes male performance problems, I've realized that many, if not most of them, could be avoided by simply following a healthy diet and by practicing different methods of exercise that help manage stress. The connection between diet and potency is well documented and supported with clinical research. It shows a clear correlation between diet, exercise, and hormonal balance. Hormonal deficiency-related diseases affect libido, potency, and fertility.

The Pottenger Cat Study (see below) illustrates the extreme and dramatic effects of deficient diets (diets that lack live food and enzymes) on the degradation of subsequent generations of cats. Even if you're skeptical about the relevance of this study to human beings, it should at least make you wonder whether maintaining a deficient diet can affect human potency—and consequently the ability to create new, healthy generations.

The Pottenger Cat Study

This seminal (no pun intended) study by a scientist named Pottenger was conducted between 1932 and 1942. It was the first clinical report dealing with the process of intergenerational degradation resulting from a deficient diet.

The study used approximately nine hundred cats, divided into two control groups. One control group of cats was fed a whole-food diet including raw meat, raw milk, and cod liver oil. The other control group was put on a deficient diet, including pasteurized milk and cooked meat. The health of the first, second, third, and fourth generation of all cats was studied, with a focus on their immunity, potency, and fertility.

The results were stunning. Those cats on the deficient diets could not produce a fourth generation, and the first generation already showed the initial signs of degradation, such as heart problems, underactive thyroid and bladder, arthritis, inflammation of the nervous system, and various infections. Second and third generations of cats on the deficient diet also suffered from an acceleration of these symptoms and showed a general decrease in the health of the reproductive organs.

Males showed a failure in active spermatogenesis (meaning they had low sperm count and weak sperm). Miscarriages accounted for up to 70% of the attempted births of second-generation deficient cats (i.e., they miscarried their offspring). Skin allergies were frequent and got worse with each subsequent generation. The third-generation cats were so deficient that none survived beyond the sixth month. Needless to say, there was no fourth generation of deficient cats.

In contrast, those cats that were given raw food ("normal cats") were healthy in all generations. Their internal organs were fully developed, and the immune systems of all four generations of these cats were fully intact, with no signs of infections or allergies. They reproduced one homogeneous generation after another, all in good health. It's interesting to note that when a second generation of "deficient cats" was put back on a raw-food diet, some of the deficiency-related symptoms such as allergies diminished, and by the fourth generation some cats had a fully restored immune system.

There also seemed to be a general connection between hypothyroidism (low thyroid) and male sterility. Eighty-three percent of male "deficient" cats in the second generation were sterile. Fifty-three percent of second-generation female "deficient" cats showed under-developed ovaries.

(Let me note here that I oppose studies that involve cruelty and inhumane treatment of animals. Regardless of all "good scientific intentions," many of these studies are unnecessarily done to prove an already existing fact, while killing and torturing innocent animals. I believe there is karma, and that cruelty doesn't come without some adverse consequences.)

According to a Kellogg Report by Joseph Beasley, MD, and Jerry Swift, MA, 44% of thirty million couples surveyed in the United States in 1980 with a woman of childbearing age were unable to have children. In 1965, there were 482,000 couples with a wife younger than thirty who were classified as infertile. By 1976, the number of infertile couples rose to 920,000. Among black couples (ages twenty to twenty-four), the proportion of infertile couples went up from 3% to 15% in the eleven-year span from 1965 to 1976.

Dr. Pottenger theorized that there are similarities between malformations found in animals and those found in humans. My points here are that:

1. *I firmly believe there is indeed a direct connection between diet, health, sexual performance, and fertility for both men and women.*
2. *The lack of whole foods and live nutrients combined with the abundance of synthetic chemicals in the typical American diet makes it a deficient and toxic diet, which causes impotency, sterility, disorders, and cancer in men and women.*

I believe, furthermore, that while direct conclusions cannot be drawn between animal studies and human conditions, the Pottenger Cat Study throws significant light on what may be contributing to the acceleration of immunodeficiency and chronic disease in our culture, such as the current epidemics of hypothyroidism, hypertension, diabetes, depression, and obesity.

The Syndrome of Taking Drugs

As noted, chronic diseases such as heart disease (arteriosclerosis), high blood pressure, high cholesterol, as well as depression, can all cause impotency. Blood pressure medications (such as beta blockers) and some anti-depression drugs can also cause impotency as a side effect. So, here's the catch: in order to solve one problem people take drugs, but drugs can create other problems. Disease-related impotence is often treated with drugs that, ironically, may accelerate the very same problem. When you hear about miracle pills, just remember that in spite of a low statistical rate of side effects, most popular potency pills don't work for everyone. As just stated, men who take blood pressure medications or who suffer from heart problems and take medication often suffer from impotency. Then, when tempted to try a potency drug to restore their virility, side effects as severe as coma or death may occur.

I'm not against the use of drugs *per se*. Taking the right medication can improve or save life. I'd like to strongly suggest here that if you suffer from male performance-related problems, seek professional help. I also recommend that you ask your physician and pharmacist about the side effects of all drugs prescribed to you, so at least you're aware.

Natural Methods to Enhance Potency

As noted, there are many factors involved in male sexual function. There isn't enough space here to discuss the entire scientific complex of hormonal, neurological, and glandular factors that are essential for proper male performance. To put things simply, let me just say that hormonal balance is a key to men's sexual function. If one hormone such as adrenaline is overactive, or if other hormones such as the thyroid or testosterone are underactive, impotency may occur. The hormone responsible for sex drive (in both men and women) is testosterone. This male hormone is also responsible for some critical functions, including:

- Development of male sex organs
- Regulation of healthy sperm production
- Activation and maintenance of sex drive for both men and women
- Maintenance of strong bones
- Building of muscles and burning of fat for both men and women

What Affects Testosterone, Sex Drive, and Libido?

When testosterone levels decline, sex drive and libido diminish. There are many reasons for inadequate testosterone levels. Some of them relate to disease and others to lifestyle stressors, diet, and aging.

I'd like to present here some of the most common variables that affect testosterone production as well as sex drive and libido. As noted, there is a connection between diet and potency, and bad diets are known to negatively affect testosterone level. Also implicated in adversely affecting testosterone production over the short or long run are chronic low-calorie and crash diets, mineral deficiencies of zinc, magnesium, copper, manganese, or iodine, amino acid deficiencies and/or essential fatty acid deficiencies. But the most notable cause of testosterone decline is the common exposure to estrogenic chemicals in the environment, food, and water. As noted, there is substantial evidence for the sterilizing effects of industrial xenoestrogens (such as that found in pesticides, herbicides, and plasticizers) on animals and humans. Estrogenic chemicals in common products, food, and water may be the main culprit for the ever-growing rate of male impotency, prostate enlargement, and cancer.

Crash diets or anorexic habits have been shown to negatively affect thyroid production as well as the overall metabolic integrity of the body. Having a low thyroid may cause elevation of the lactating hormone prolactin. High prolactin levels suppress the production of testosterone as well as growth hormone. High prolactin may cause some devastating symptoms in men, including breast enlargement and feminization of the body. The market is saturated with over-the-counter thyroid-boosting supplements, and prescription thyroid hormones are in widespread use. The thyroid hormones play critical roles in regulating the body's metabolism. Nonetheless, those who take thyroid supplements to boost their thyroid in order to lose weight often don't realize that having an overactive thyroid may be as harmful as having an underactive thyroid. When the thyroid's level is too high, it creates a condition that may promote an increased conversion of testosterone to the female hormone estrogen. This may cause adverse effects including a loss of potency, infertility, and accelerated aging.

Stress is also a major factor that affects testosterone. Excessive physical or mental stress may cause a decrease in testosterone production as well as sex drive.

Aging is another factor that affects testosterone level. Typically, the more one ages, the more testosterone will convert to estrogen, and the lower its circulating levels will be.

Considering all the above, a healthy diet that supplies all essential and hormonal-supportive nutrients, together with stress management techniques and a viable exercise routine, would most likely work as an effective natural means to sustain virility and defend against testosterone decline. I truly believe that the best way to keep your vigor high is to incorporate daily detoxification, and then consume hearty meals with proper fuel foods and hormonal-supportive nutrients that can make you feel satisfied, compensated, and yet highly charged.

Aphrodisiac Supplements (to enhance libido)

The word "aphrodisiac" is attached to many herbs, potions, lotions, and nutritional formulas. Unfortunately, most so-called aphrodisiac supplements don't work. Commercial companies try to cash in on this or that exotic herb, promising great results, but the truth is that it's very unlikely one single herb can help restore healthy performance in those who suffer from impotency. As just discussed, multiple factors are critical for sexual performance. Isolating and targeting one or another usually isn't good enough. Many people who experience diminished libido and impaired performance suffer from a complex set of factors (such as neurological, glandular, hormonal, and mental factors) that together have created imbalance. Often, both physical and psychological issues are involved in impaired sexual performance.

Overtraining vs. Your Sex Drive

Overtraining may rob you of your testosterone. Avoid overstressing your body with long, obsessive, daily physical training routines. It's critical to take at least one to two days off per week. Rest is part of the training cycle and is necessary for recuperation and strength gain.

Symptoms related to overtraining, such as adrenal fatigue, hypothyroidism (low thyroid), a sluggish metabolism, muscle tightening and cramping, exhaustion, depression, and sleep disorders, may also occur or be exacerbated by a deficient diet. Low-calorie diets, low-carb diets, low-protein diets, raw food-deficient diets, as well as diets deficient in essential and hormonal-supportive nutrients—such as vitamins, minerals, essential fatty acids, naturally occurring phytosterols, and estrogen-inhibiting phytonutrients—may not satisfy the body's nutritional requirements for a complete recuperation from prolonged and intense physical stress. Any exercise routine combined with malnutrition may lead to overtraining-related symptoms.

The Warrior Diet—Instinctual Living and Potency

The Warrior Diet isn't a miracle cure for everything. Nonetheless, it encourages instinctual living and thus unleashes the healing power of your inherent survival mechanisms, which can be triggered by actively using your instincts. Primal instincts are based on an innate wisdom that enables the body to react spontaneously and to compensate for both physical and mental stressors. An instinct, once triggered, should activate all the elements that are necessary for its specific action. Conversely, when instincts are suppressed or aren't intact, the body may fail to coordinate the different elements necessary for healthy performance. This is exactly when problems occur. Isolating one relevant element or another as the culprit for impotence is a method which unfortunately has been used by physicians who prefer to prescribe specific drugs to treat specific problems.

I believe that the revival of sexual instincts is the most natural and powerful way to restore and enhance potency. Once unleashed, instinctual actions can help restore performance, regardless of textbook theories, psychological approaches, or medical application protocols. In other words, you'll be able to perform spontaneously simply by letting your body's own wisdom follow through with the right action.

The notion that you can increase your vigor and improve your performance by improving your diet, exercising regularly, and living instinctually may sound over-simplistic and over-romantic, especially today when so many drugs and synthetic supplements have been habitually used to treat numerous metabolic disorders and dysfunctions with promises of a quick fix. Regardless, those who experience the power of raw living know the difference.

Craving Aphrodisiac Foods Instinctively

On a related matter, I believe that we often instinctively crave foods that enhance sexuality. These aphrodisiac foods aren't always mysterious, esoteric, or exotic. Actually, you may consume some very powerful aphrodisiac foods and herbs quite often. Whole dairy, nuts, seeds, seafood, avocado, oats, and berries are all considered to contain some sex-enhancing properties. Herbs and spices such as ginseng, gingko, mukuna, cinnamon, turmeric, and vanilla beans have been used for thousands of years as natural aids or remedies to enhance sexual performance.

Fish and seafood are abundant in zinc, as well as other essential minerals. Maintaining optimum mineral levels is critical for optimum hormonal balance. Zinc is necessary for testosterone production, male virility, and sperm production. Nuts are high in the amino acid arginine, which is essential for the production of nitric oxide (NO)—a neuro-substance necessary for erections. Ginseng and gingko are herbs that stimulate the production of nitric oxide through the enzyme nitric oxide synthase (NOS). Gingko optimizes blood circulation in the brain, and ginseng is believed to be an adaptogenic herb that helps the body handle stress. These qualities make these herbs potent aphrodisiacs.

Almonds have been regarded as an aphrodisiac food since biblical times. The Romans thought of the almond as a symbol of men's genitals. I often recommend that people try "almond and veggie" meals for a couple of days. (For more on almonds, see Chapter 5, "The Overeating Phase.") Almonds are naturally high in zinc, copper, and manganese, as well as phytosterols, which have shown to convert in the body into sex hormones. In its raw state, this nut is a mild alkalizer. I believe almonds are one of the most powerful aphrodisiac foods, especially for men.

Wine has been considered an aphrodisiac for thousands of years. Taste, color, smell, and aroma are all factors that contribute to the sexual nature of this ancient nectar. A glass of wine has a relaxing effect and sheds inhibitions, and from this perspective alone it is an aphrodisiac. Wine is often served as part of a romantic dinner. However, excessive drinking may work in the opposite way. Alcohol has a diminishing effect on blood testosterone and sperm count. Many guys know that when they drink too much, it reduces desire and can make them "talk the talk" instead of "walk the walk."

There are also some so-called "exotic" foods that are thought to be aphrodisiac, such as cherries, passion fruit, fertile eggs, oysters, and of course chocolate. All the above may or may not enhance sexual performance. Nevertheless, the placebo effect is real. If you believe a certain food is aphrodisiac, then for you it most probably is. It's not imperative to know the science behind everything you crave. Use your instincts. Whatever works for you is good, and vice versa.

As a last note for this matter, let me just mention that any food or beverage that stimulates dopamine in your brain could be a natural aid in enhancing sexual desire and performance. Coffee, tea, and hot chocolate (cocoa) are but a few examples of beverages that fall in this category. As mentioned, one notable dopamine booster is the Brazilian herb mucuna. It has been used traditionally to enhance sexual performance. Mucuna has been also used to treat Parkinson's Disease. Food and sex have been bound together for a long time. I guess this is due to the intimate connection between the two most powerful instincts that predominate in life: the instinct to survive and the instinct to multiply. Nourishment and sex give us a great sense of pleasure. Having the wisdom to satisfy both desires—for food and sex—is the art of living well. I truly believe that this wisdom lies within us all.

CHAPTER 13

WOMEN ON THE WARRIOR DIET

IN SPITE OF ALL THE MASCULINE CONNOTATIONS and machismo surrounding the Warrior Diet, I believe it can work equally well for women. I know women who follow my diet with great results.

Women have some specific desires and needs, such as looking healthy and attractive, losing weight, and slowing the aging process, and they are all addressed extensively in this book.

Women also need to feel a sense of freedom, to live instinctually, and especially to enjoy the satisfaction of so-called "wild" pleasures—which, unfortunately, are too often repressed or inhibited.

Artificial aesthetic standards set by Madison Avenue, and society for that matter, tend to dictate that women limit themselves and endure the tyranny of over-restrictive dietary rules just to stay slim. Many books on the market today attempt to capitalize on this with quick-fix fad diets built on restraint— be it calorie-counting, fat or carbohydrate restriction, or the quite popular liquid diets, based on the principle of substituting real food with allegedly "healthy" shakes and smoothies.

As a result, many women today have developed a "fear" of food. Fat phobia, as well as carbohydrate and calorie phobias, affect many women today and are symptoms of an ever-growing despair. Food phobias are obsessive and dangerous, and they can start at an alarmingly young age. More girls today suffer from anorexia and other eating disorders than ever before. Young as well as grown women have fallen victim to popular culture image-makers and so-called "ideals."

Those who try fad diets may lose weight initially, but often gain back even more. Something must be wrong with the way women have been looking at the term "diet." I believe the core of the problem is the fact that, as stated above, many women over-restrict themselves and therefore feel chronically deprived, while continuously acting against their natural instincts and desires.

Adopting artificial body image and lifestyle standards may take away one's freedom of choice—and without this choice, there is no way to reach a sense of freedom or, for that matter, any sense of satiety, especially when the ideal is unattainable. All that is left is a sense of chronic deprivation and unhappiness.

The Warrior Diet takes advantage of the innate power of your instincts. If you practice it, I believe you'll naturally shed obsessive restrictions and yet be able to address your basic needs, such as losing weight, eliminating stubborn fat, maintaining healthy skin, nails, and hair, slowing the aging process, and maybe most importantly, feeling a true sense of freedom and well-being.

Detoxification

People who follow the Warrior Diet will find that daily detoxification during the Undereating Phase is the best natural method for rejuvenating all body tissues. Loading up with live nutrients such as enzymes, minerals, vitamins, and a host of phytonutrients, which naturally come from live veggies and fruits, helps cleanse the body and protect against environmental and internal toxins. There's sufficient evidence to show the direct correlation between live nutrient intake and the overall capacity of the body to sustain a prime state of health with a young and vigorous look.

Overeating

All diets today tell you not to overeat. However, as noted throughout this book, overeating, when done the right way, can work for you. Many women binge at night and feel guilty afterwards, unaware that bingeing isn't bad if you know how and when to do it.

This said, the Warrior Diet definitely does not advocate uncontrolled compulsive bingeing—quite the opposite. When practicing overeating, one should be in full control.

Overeating is a relative matter. For some it means consuming a 500-calorie meal, and for others it means consuming a 1,000-calorie meal. If you follow the Warrior Diet rules of eating, you'll know instinctively what, when, and how much to eat, and when to stop eating. You'll learn how to trust your female instincts. If nothing else, this will give you a great sense of freedom, something that is missing in other diets. Moreover, following the Warrior Diet may help accelerate your body's metabolism and therefore should, in time, allow you to eat even more.

Hormonal Balance

Women often suffer from hormonal imbalance. There's substantial data that show a link between diet, nutrition, and hormonal integrity.

Inadequate diets often cause nutrient deficiencies or chemical toxicity. Daily exposure to estrogenic chemicals in pesticides, plasticizers, solvents, adhesives, petroleum-based lotions, sprays, deodorants and PVC, as well as hormones in meat, poultry and dairy, overwhelms the body's endocrine system. Estrogenic chemicals are known to cause hormonal imbalance, with an excess of estrogen in the body. This condition manifests with symptoms such as weight gain, mood swings, bloating, water retention, headaches, nausea, hot flashes, and a host of female disorders, as well as an increased risk of cancer.

Conversely, following a diet that *detoxifies* your body while *nourishing* it with all essential nutrients and hormonal-supportive nutrients may help alleviate these symptoms as well as reverse their related disorders. On a related matter, women who take hormonal replacements should be aware of the dangers and side effects of this therapy. I'm not against or in favor of hormonal therapy; I believe this decision should be left to you and your physician. Nevertheless, the Warrior Diet can be of great benefit for those who are under such treatment. By practicing daily detoxification, and with the right nutritional supplementation, you may help your liver detoxify and neutralize steroidal derivatives, including estrogenic substances, and thus lower the risk of suffering their related harmful effects.

Stubborn Fat

Like men, women suffer from stubborn fat and its related problems. Most diets don't address this issue. Those who have stubborn fat (usually around the waist, lower butt, thighs, or back of the arms) may find the Warrior Diet—and the suggested nutritional supplements—helpful in fighting and eliminating it. For more on stubborn fat, see Chapter 7.

In conclusion, the Warrior Diet is an instinctual diet that allows *everyone* to feel the power of raw living—to experience a real sense of freedom and at the same time enjoy the pleasure of reaching full satisfaction from meals. And all that while having the gratification of increasing energy levels and a notable improvement in physical appearance! Don't let the references to ancient war-riors dissuade you from trying the Warrior Diet. As stated at the beginning of this book, the term "warrior" refers to an instinct that is deep within all of us—women and men alike—and it can be triggered by following this diet.

Unlike many popular diet books, I have chosen not to fill this book with testimonials of personal success, male or female. Nonetheless, for those who wish to learn how the diet has benefited people from both genders, different ethnic groups, and all ages, we provide plenty of information in our websites, www.warriordiet.com and www.defensenutrition.com.

CHAPTER 14

THE WARRIOR WORKOUT: CONTROLLED-FATIGUE TRAINING

Have you ever asked yourself:

- What is my physical potential?
- Have I tried to reach my limits?
- Do I feel strong in certain areas, but weak in others?
- Am I quick enough?
- Can I jump high a few times without falling apart?
- Can I sprint for more than thirty seconds without collapsing?
- Do I know the difference between being *strong* and being *tough*?
- Do I like what I see in the mirror?

The goal of this training program is to enable you to reach your body's potential and maintain it. What I call *"body potential" is based on function—not fashion.* The exercise emphasis is to activate and strengthen the most essential and functional muscle groups, while increasing the capacity to resist fatigue. In the past, warriors were aware of the importance of a functional body and its effect on balance, speed, explosive moves, strength, and endurance. Sport training in ancient Greece and Rome was based on drills that mimicked warfare or hunting activities. The modern concept of *training to failure* (training until reaching complete muscle exhaustion) was definitely not a warrior way. Failure was simply not allowed.

As mentioned in Chapter 9, "Lessons from History," Romans, Spartans, and Greeks were lean and muscular. Being lean was a must, and building a lean muscular body was a result of strength, speed, and velocity conditioning. To gain strength and speed without adding unnecessary bulk, a special exercise routine is needed.

This exercise program is based on cycling between intense resistance, speed, and high velocity (explosive moves). It includes special supersets aimed at maximizing the natural synergistic effect between different muscle groups. CFT eliminated all aerobic exercise, but its combination of drills confers a profound inherent quality of intense endurance. This training routine is designed for those who are interested in building a lean, functional, and powerful body and have no time to waste.

The first part of this chapter covers the principles of CFT, as well as pre-workout and recovery meals. The second part focuses on specific training concepts and exercises designed to help you follow the CFT's principles.

Lean 'n' Mean for a Lifetime

A few years ago I was watching a TV interview with former Olympic champions. The program showed clips of these athletes during the peak of their careers, and the contrast between how they looked then and now startled me; it was really surprising to see how out of shape most of them had become. For instance, the ex-Olympic champion sprinter Vladimir Borosov, the fastest man in the world during the 1970s, was lean and well defined at his athletic peak. Now a businessman, he looks heavy and sluggish. It got me thinking how competitive athletes in many sports, including football, soccer, boxing, and swimming, who were also "lean 'n' mean" during their competitive careers often look completely out of shape years later.

This "syndrome" is similar among veterans or ex-combat soldiers. While engaged in combat activities, they're in great shape, but when no longer forced to be physically active, they often gain weight and look softer. Why does this happen so frequently? In my opinion, athletes and soldiers who lose their drive to stay in shape tend to do so because their minds and bodies simply became overly exhausted and depleted from years of physical mistraining aimed at scoring rather than living. Exercising, training, and any other physical activity for that matter, whether competitive, combative, or not, should be thought of in a larger context—what works for you over the course of your life. A progressive training routine will only be successful if you can live with it; it should energize you and help trigger your Warrior Instinct, with the drive to continually improve yourself. Without this, sooner or later you'll burn out.

The Warrior Controlled-Fatigue Training Goals

- *Build a functional and tough body*
- *Develop strength, speed, velocity, and endurance*
- *Increase the capacity to resist fatigue*
- *Accelerate fat-burning*
- *Improve body composition*
- *Improve body balance*
- *Sharpen survival instincts*
- *Accelerate alertness and competitive drive*

The Controlled-Fatigue Training Principles

1. *Make strength-training priorities: joints, back, and core.*
2. *Combine strength, speed, and high velocity.*
3. *Train to resist fatigue.*
4. *Do not train to reach complete muscle failure.*
5. *Make your workout short.*

Principle #1: Make strength-training priorities: joints and back.

The first step of a progressive exercise routine is to make priorities. It's necessary to understand the priorities, especially if your goal is to gain strength rather than bulk.

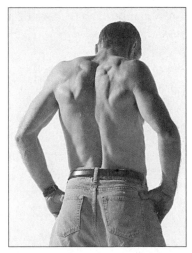

Roman, Spartan, Macedonian, and Greek warriors were lean and light, yet their performance during war campaigns required a great deal of endurance and strength. What made these lean and light people so physically strong? I believe it was due to their joint and back strength, as well as their incredible capacity to endure pain and resist fatigue.

Back Strength (for carrying weapons and loads)

For an ancient warrior, back strength was essential. During the Olympian games, which go back as far as the sixth century BC, Greek athletes competed with full body armor, including helmets, shields, and javelins. Running while fully armed requires back strength. This method of training is still popular among Marines and other combat units today.

Joint Strength (jumping, swinging, stabbing, slashing, pushing, pulling)
Many if not all fighting activities are related to joint and tendon strength. Tendons and ligaments connect the muscles to the bones. Weak tendons compromise muscle elasticity. Joint strength depends on the strength of connective tissues and their related compound muscle groups, which are responsible for all joint movements.

Of top priority for developing a functional, lean body should be strengthening of the shoulders, wrists, elbows, waist, abdominals, buttocks, knees, ankles, and back.

Shoulder strength was necessary for fighting activities including slashing and stabbing. A Macedonian and Roman phalanx infantryman was known to be able to stop a horse attack with his shield. Push (press) and pull activities needed shoulder, elbow, and back strength. Swings required core, back, and knee strength. Running or jumping while carrying a heavy load needed back, knee, buttock, and ankle strength. Fighting with a sword required a strong grip—which meant strong wrists and forearms.

In short, making priorities is essential for warrior training, and thus back, joint, and core strengthening should be priorities for developing a lean and muscular body. Basic training exercises that specialize in back, joint, and core strength are covered later in this chapter.

Strengthen Those Tendons

It doesn't matter how big your muscles are if your tendons are weak; you won't be able to reach your peak level of strength. Moreover, having an overgrown muscle belly (the broadest center part of the muscle) combined with weak tendons may lead to severe injuries, such as torn muscles.

Principle #2: Combine strength, speed, and high-velocity exercise.

During army campaigns, soldiers were under intense physical stress. Ancient warriors had to be constantly alert and ready for a fight. Fighting face to face required the ability to push and pull strongly, as well as mastery of explosive stabbing or slashing movements.

Roman and Macedonian infantrymen used the shield as a pushing board against their enemy. A typical combat strategy was to push an opponent so hard that he'd lose his balance, and at the same time deliver a quick, explosive hit with a sword (slash or stab) that was meant to wound or kill. Intense pulling skills were needed for wrestling when warriors fought holding one another. A strong pull over the opponent's neck could throw him down, or pull him into a dagger. In other words, both power moves and explosive moves were necessary for an ancient warrior engaged in combat activities.

Though Controlled-Fatigue Training (CFT) isn't about fighting *per se*, it may very well prepare one for a fight. The routine's purpose is to mimic the basic activities of a warrior body—forcing it to get stronger, faster, and tougher. The second principle of this workout is to combine strength (intense resistance) with speed (fast repetitive moves) and high velocity (explosive moves). By following this exercise routine, you'll be able to train your body and mind to adapt to these highly intense performance requirements. You'll gain the ability to sustain strength through special weight training "pyramids" that force the body to "come back with vengeance" when extremely fatigued. You'll also be trained to react faster to a sudden stress and be able to sustain highly explosive exercise (such as power punches, kicks, frog jumps, and high jumps).

On top of all that, you'll be trained to maintain speed (rather than just to accelerate speed) via special sprint intervals. Over time, your body will learn to endure super-intense drills that combine strength, speed, and velocity, resulting in substantial increase in your capacity to resist fatigue and stress.

Sustained Strength

To sustain strength, you have to train your body to endure lifting heavy weights for a relatively prolonged period of time (up to a few minutes per set, rather than the typical few seconds per set). I consider a heavy weight to be a load that you can lift for no more than 5-6 repetitions. Heavy weight is also a relative matter. For a beginner, a heavy load could be 20 pounds. For a trained person, it might be 200 pounds. Choose whatever is appropriate for you. Generally, lifting light weights won't lead to anything other than burning calories; however, there are some exceptions to this statement, such as when light weights are combined with heavy weights in specially prolonged supersets ("upside-down pyramids"). These highly intense supersets force one to repetitively go up and down with the weight load, and thereby acquire the ability to "come back," to resist heavy loads again and again, while sustaining performance with no rest in between intervals.

Light weights can also be used to effectively enhance total body conditioning by combining them with speed or velocity exercise such as running, power biking, swinging, or punching. Also, as you'll soon see, CFT uses light weight to maximize the impact of "pre-fatigue" exercises, which are specially designed to prepare the body to swiftly react to sudden stress (rather than the gradual warm-up effect) and increase its ability to reach maximum muscle oxygenation (VO_2 max) in minimum time. I'll explain this further in the second part of this chapter.

Gaining the ability to sustain strength is a matter of adaptation, perseverance, and skill. The goal here is to give your brain a signal that a heavy load—with high tension—must be handled for a few minutes at a time. Once your brain adapts to sustain a certain degree of physical tension for a certain period of time, it's a sign that you've gained some strength and will be able to gradually increase the weight load and the time under tension.

Strength is the ability to resist a force in time and space. The more you can sustain strength, the stronger you get.

The factors that determine strength are:

1. Intensity—The weight load
2. Volume—The time under tension
3. Form—The length of the motion

You must observe these three parameters to maximize your strength gain. The training program presented below provides you with basic exercise routines that activate all three factors: intensity, volume, and form. To gain strength, you need to alternate the weight loads and number of sets per session. Keeping the right form is also a must. Since heavy sets are low reps, the way to build volume is to rotate between heavy and lighter weight loads (medium and light weights) with no rest in between, all of which builds into a giant, intense superset.

This training routine is based on body function, not on body parts. It incorporates different muscle groups, including antagonistic muscles, stabilizing muscles, and upper and lower body compound-muscle groups. It maximizes the synergistic effect of basic body movements such as pushes and pulls, as well as lateral moves. It also enhances the neuromuscular synergy between the hands, the legs, and the core. As stated, don't waste your time with moderate aerobics or moderate exercise—you might as well do something more useful instead, like washing dishes or gardening. If you want to train like a warrior, go intense, but do it wisely. I call this program "Controlled-Fatigue Training" because it enables you to gradually increase the intensity and volume of the exercise and improve your ability to control your fatigue as well as resist intense physical and mental stress.

High Velocity (Explosive Moves)

Explosive moves are not an integral part of a typical strength training (or bodybuilding) routine. Just go to any neighborhood gym and watch how people train. Very few, if any, try explosive moves such as fast clean and presses, speed punches, or power punches. Other exercises such as high jumps, frog jumps, or one-leg jumps are explosive training methods that don't hold muster for an average Joe who's trying to pump his thighs in front of the mirror by doing heavy squats half the way.

In my opinion, explosive strength is essential for the ability to fight or flight (survival). It is also essential for developing a lean and functional body. Ballistic exercises, like cleans or power punching with weight, work the whole body. They require explosive strength, endurance, balance, and skill. By following a training program that incorporates explosive strength exercises (with a gradual increase of weight and volume), you'll be able to tone your body, making it stronger, faster, and tougher. There are quite a few variations for high-velocity training. I'll cover the most basic exercises, which I believe will enable your mind and body to initiate and sustain explosive moves while gaining real functional strength. High-velocity exercises are very demanding. They involve your mind, body, and your instincts. The frequency of this kind of training should be built gradually, starting with one session per week and then adding more according to your progress. If you've already tried it, you know how it feels to do a few repetitive heavy sets of, say, clean presses, or endure a few minutes of heavy bag punching. It takes all you have. But whatever you put in, you're sure to get back. For me, high-velocity training days are fun—I feel like I'm doing something primal and essential to my body and mind. Speed, endurance, and strength are what really counted for a warrior. Size was not an issue. Thousands of years ago, wrestlers and boxers disregarded the body-weight factor when they fought in the Games. That, in my opinion, mimicked real-life war conditions. This training program may not fully teach you the fighting skills needed to face a giant opponent. Nonetheless, it may build the courage to protect yourself if necessary, and most importantly, help you enjoy facing yourself in the mirror.

Principle #3: Train to resist fatigue (train to be tough)

"Controlled fatigue" is a warrior-training concept. Being able to function properly when fatigued was critical to a warrior's life. Romans believed that the winner of a fight was the one who could endure the most pain. As discussed in Chapter 9, "Lessons from History," Roman warriors inflicted pain and torture on themselves in order to prepare for the real thing.

During war, a soldier (particularly an infantryman) had to endure constant and intense physical pain and mental stress. War campaigns have typically forced a soldier to perform combat activities under prolonged fatigue.

Army training is not the same as sport training. The goals of sport training are to make athletes stronger or faster in order to score. Conversely, the goal of military training is to first and foremost make soldiers tougher. Being tough requires the ability to endure stress, whether physical or mental, for a prolonged period of time. Sometimes training to be tough may come at the expense of gaining strength, at least in the short run. However, in the long run, what I call Controlled-Fatigue Training pays back generously. A body that has been trained to resist fatigue learns how to adapt to prolonged periods of intense physical and mental pressure without experiencing failure. It's this intense signal of prolonged stress with the "fatigue factor" that forces the body to switch into a survival mode and thus trigger innate survival mechanisms that sustain alertness and improve energy utilization. When under extreme conditions, the body is forced to make priorities in order to effectively perform and avoid wasting energy. To say it differently, under Controlled-Fatigue Training, there's no "BS." A man really learns about himself when faced with such conditions. And the same holds true for women.

When faced with constant, intense physical strain, your body will instinctively do only the most important functional moves, to effectively sustain performance. Fancy moves are useless when your body's survival instincts kick in.

The more you train under controlled fatigue, the more you'll be able to resist stress. As mentioned, this is a key factor in what makes a person tough. The CFT program incorporates pre-fatigue (pre-exhausting) exercises, followed by intense resistance and explosive exercise. As noted, it incorporates giant supersets built on rotations between heavy and lighter weight loads. All the above can be cycled with different volumes (length of supersets) and levels of intensity (amount of weight lifted). CFT can be done once a week, or three to six days per week.

If your goal is to get tougher, then let the tough get going. If, however, your goal is to gain strength, you should be alternating between Controlled-Fatigue Training and strength-training days. For example, one week of CFT followed by one week of sheer strength conditioning will enable you to strengthen muscle groups while stimulating neuromuscular units that have not been fully activated prior to this routine. Eventually, it all leads to a win-win situation, because you may be able to grind your limits, become tougher, stronger, and most importantly, more in tune with your own body. If you've reached a plateau in your current workout regime, this is one way to break it. Controlled-Fatigue Training, if nothing else, will accelerate your mind-body connection in an instinctual way, enabling you to react, initiate, and perform at any time.

CFT isn't necessarily a long workout routine. It puts your body under a continuous intense tension, which lasts for up to a few minutes at a time. Compared to a typical 10-rep set that takes about 30 seconds, a giant superset (a "workout unit") under Controlled-Fatigue Training could take 3 to 10 minutes, and maybe even more. Nonetheless, a relatively long time under intense pressure doesn't make the workout session long. Quite the opposite. As you'll see in Principle #5, the workout should be short, and literally, you should be able to finish your training within 15 to 30 minutes.

As a last note, I'd like to briefly cover the effect of this routine on lactic-acid efficiency. Under Controlled-Fatigue Training, the body becomes more and more efficient in metabolizing lactic acid and converting it into energy. The burn that you feel when intensely working out is a result of accumulating lactic acid in your muscle tissues. Lactic acid is a byproduct of glucose metabolism. Under prolonged intense exercise, accumulation of this substance in the muscle may suppress its ability to contract. This is the bad news.

The good news is that lactic acid can convert into pyruvate, which in turn converts to energy, and may also help accelerate the body's metabolic rate. Moreover, researchers believe that by lowering the pH in the working muscle tissues, lactic acid may play an important role in boosting anabolic hormones required for recuperation and muscular development. A physically trained body should be more efficient in metabolizing lactic acid into energy, and therefore be able to handle longer periods of intense exercise and to recuperate faster compared to an untrained body. CFT is one of the best and most efficient methods to boost the body's metabolism and burn fat. For those interested in accelerating the Warrior Diet's effects, this is the way to go.

Principle #4: Do not train to reach failure

As stated, training to reach failure (or total collapse) is not a warrior way. For a warrior, failure was not allowed. Ancient warriors, especially Spartans and Romans, considered failure worse than death. A Roman soldier was virtually ready at any time to fight until the end. Surrendering was a disgrace.

I believe the concept of not reaching failure has much more to do with the mental state than the physical state. When you train your body to avoid failure, you'll learn by trial and error how to keep performing and improving, without losing control. Conversely, if you chronically train to reach failure, your mind will surrender every time you feel that your body has reached its limit. Subconsciously, your mind will "pre-fail" before your body, because that's the way it was trained. When you're used to failure, it stops your body from crossing barriers. In other words, if you train to reach failure, you will fail. Training not to reach failure does not necessarily mean that you won't fail. It does mean training in a way that encourages you to avoid failure—by stopping one step before reaching this dead end. While training, you may continually encounter a point where your body can no longer perform. This is a way to study your current limits, so next time you'll know when to stop. Stopping one step before failure gives your brain the signal that you're still in full control. Over time you'll learn how to "trick" your body to recharge itself and in no time (a few seconds) be able to grind a "sticking point" that you haven't been able to cross previously. CFT trains your body to sustain performance, rather than gradually decline until reaching failure.

Failure brings its own psychosomatic effects. Muscle failure during training is often a result of a defense mechanism. Your brain gives your muscles an order to fail, out of fear of injury. The reason why ancient warriors tortured themselves was mainly to conquer the fear of pain. Conquering the fear of pain or injury could be the main reason why a 130-pound Olympian weightlifter could successfully press 300-pound weights. Nonetheless, training to failure remains popular among strength athletes and bodybuilders today. This issue is controversial, especially for those who are mainly interested in gaining sheer strength and muscle size.

Those who believe in reaching failure argue that only by pushing to the limit—meaning reaching failure—will one be able to gain muscle size. According to this line of thinking, it's the last two failed reps that count. Training to reach failure needs spotting, by a trainer or a training partner. Based on this theory, without spotting, it's almost impossible to exercise the effect of the last two failed reps. I'm not trying to dismiss this method of training, because it might work well as far as gaining muscle size. However, I do question it as far as strength is concerned.

My points are simple:

1. When you depend on a spotter to lift you up every time that you reach failure, then you fail to reach your own limits.
2. By chronically reaching failure, you exhaust yourself, and therefore rob yourself of the mental capacity to grind limits as well as the mental aggression to go on and sustain performance.

A good workout session should charge your energy, not deplete it. Knowing that you will not reach failure is a state of mind. This state of mind should be yours before, during, and especially after your workout. You should at all times feel you can "kick ass."

Principle #5: Make your workout short

Make your workout short and intense. Long aerobics or resistance workouts may compromise your strength and hormonal levels. There's evidence that after 45 minutes of intense resistance training, there is a notable decline in blood testosterone. You should finish your workout while your hormones are at a peak level. Manipulating your hormones is one of the Warrior Diet goals, and it should be the same goal for the Warrior Workout.

The timeframe for a constructive intense-training session is between 15 and 45 minutes. CFT is designed to be no longer than this very timeframe per session.

Short, intense training sessions are more practical, and for busy people this is a great advantage. To be successful, a progressive workout program should be easy to follow—one you can live with on a daily basis. If you know why you're training and how to do it, you're almost there. Knowing that it'll only take 15–45 minutes—and then you can go back to resuming your daily activities—is encouraging. Short sessions make it easier to monitor and stay focused. When you finish each workout you should be able to say, as Julius Caesar once declared: *"Veni, vidi, vici"*—"I came, I saw, I conquered."

"Pre-Fatigue" Exercise

Pre-fatigue exercise is an essential part of the Warrior Workout. The goals of pre-fatigue exercise are:

- *Pre-fatigue the body for the core workout*
- *Improve endurance and speed*
- *Improve the body's ability to swiftly react and initiate perform-ance*
- *Accelerate fat-burning*

Pre-fatigue exercise can be cycled between short sessions of specially designed intense exercise such as sprint intervals and power-biking intervals. Generally, they should last 3-10 minutes, but sometimes pre-fatigue exercise could be turned into "killer" fat-burning drills lasting up to 20 minutes. Doing pre-fatigue exercise on an empty stomach will accelerate the Warrior Diet effects of boosting growth hormone, depleting glycogen reserves, and accelerating fat-burning. Certain advanced pre-fatigue exercise can facilitate a short but nonetheless complete workout. Pre-fatigue exercises are covered in the second part of this chapter. Note that aerobics is not an integral part of CFT. Nonetheless, by virtue of its combined pre-fatigue and intense "non-stop" core exercise, CFT increases total body endurance and the capacity to sustain intense performance for a prolonged period of time.

Pre-Workout and Recovery Meals

To take full advantage of the workout, one must know how to apply recovery meals. Pre-workout meals are optional, whereas post-workout recovery meals are critical. The logic behind recovery meals is to minimize the catabolic and stress effects of the workout, replenish energy reserves in the muscles, and accelerate the anabolic effects after the workout.

Always make sure that you drink plenty of water before, during, and immediately after your workout.

Pre-workout meals are best for endurance athletes and individuals engaged in prolonged, intense drills.

Pre-Workout Meal Principle:
To supply the body with nutrients that help initiate performance and sustain it without boosting insulin.

Pre-Workout Goals:
- *Initiate performance*
- *Boost neurotransmitters (alertness)*
- *Keep hormones at a peak level*
- *Keep insulin low*

Pre-workout meals should be designed similarly to post-exercise recovery meals, with only two differences: They should be very low glycemic; and their servings should be half the size of recovery meals. Pre-workout and recovery meals should be composed of light, fresh, fast-assimilating proteins such as yogurt, kefir, whey, or milk protein, together with slow-releasing carbs. Individuals engaged in prolonged drills can have a bowl of oatmeal about an hour before training.

Pre-Workout Meal Alternatives

Those who skip a pre-workout meal can have coffee or tea instead. Good, fresh coffee is a wonderful natural stimulator before a workout. Caffeine, which is a strong alkaloid, may boost your metabolism up to 20%, and therefore may help accelerate the fat-burning effects. Caffeine boosts dopamine (a major brain neurotransmitter, giving you a feeling of alertness and well-being). In general, a shot or two of good espresso will do it; or a cup of, say, English Breakfast tea.

Caffeine works best when ingested on an empty stomach, with no carbs. In my opinion, adding one teaspoon of unrefined sugar won't change much for active people, but to be on the safe side, skip the carbs if you can. Sugar may overspike your insulin and as a result may cause a hypoglycemic reaction during the workout; consequently, you may feel dizzy, drained, or exhausted. You can add milk, preferably milk foam, to the coffee or tea. Too much milk will slow the absorption of the caffeine and may cause an upset stomach during the workout. Those sensitive to coffee can substitute with caffeinated teas such as green tea or guarana. Guarana tea is a natural source of pure caffeine without the acidity. It's a mild pickup. I find guarana to be too alkaline, so I mix it with ginger. Guarana with ginger tastes better to me. Guarana is sold in many health-food stores.

Post-Exercise Recovery Meals

Post-workout recovery meals are more important than pre-workout meals. After an intense workout, the body is at a peak metabolic state to absorb amino acids and other nutrients to the muscle tissue. The insulin hormone reaches peak sensitivity, which further enhances the body's capacity to replenish energy reserves and effectively utilize carbs without gaining fat. This is the best time to eat.

Recovery Meal Principle:
- *Provide the body with fast-assimilating proteins and slow-releasing carbs after exercise*

Recovery Meal Goals:
- *Finalize the anabolic effect of the workout*
- *Replenish nutrients to depleted muscles*
- *Boost immunity*

Recovery meals should be composed of fast-assimilating proteins, good fat, and slow-releasing carbs: serving size 25–30 grams of protein and 10–25 g of carbs. The best fast-assimilating proteins are whey and milk proteins. One of the best foods for recovery and a great source of hormonal-supportive nutrients is stabilized rice germ and bran soluble fiber. It is a natural, most viable source of plant sterols, tocotrients (natural vitamin E), as well as anti-inflammatory and antioxidant nutrients including ferulic acid and naturally occurring vitamins. I highly recommend taking a mineral supplement before and particularly right after the workout to avoid mineral deficiency-related symptoms, including muscle cramps and soreness.

Exercising on an Empty Stomach—The Fat-Burning Factor
If enduring prolonged drills is not your main goal, then the pre-workout meal isn't necessary. Training on an empty stomach will accelerate the undereating effects of the diet. As discussed in previous chapters, when you exercise on virtually empty, your body's main source of energy will come from burning fat. People who suffer from stubborn fat should take advantage of the "exercise on empty" factor. It may help accelerate fat-burning in areas that diet alone won't accomplish as rapidly. For those interested in having lean definition, this is the best way to go.

Timing of Recovery Meals

The best time to have a recovery meal is right after the workout. If you train in the late afternoon or early evening, have your recovery meal after exercise and then, about an hour later—or whenever you start feeling hungry—go for your evening meal. If you work out in the morning or during the day, it's usually best to have a recovery meal right after the workout and then continue with a second and even a third recovery meal every hour or so after the initial recovery meal. Then resume the Undereating Phase until evening. This should sustain you for the rest of the day, without compromising the goals of the Undereating Phase. However, people who feel the need for whole protein foods during the day can have eggs or light dairy such as yogurt, kefir, or fresh cheese (rather than aged cheese or processed cheese).

The Evolution of Fight or Flight

The survival of humans and other species has primarily depended on their ability to initiate and sustain fight or flight activities. Fight or flight activities are most likely the origin of all exercise. Thus, the inherent fight or flight program has been correlated with biological mechanisms that increase the body's ability to generate energy and get stronger, faster, and tougher to better survive.

The Exercise Program

Controlled-Fatigue Training applies survival principles to its exercise manuals. The program incorporates exercise that mimics fight or flight activities, combining strength, speed, velocity, and endurance. The exercises are divided into three major groups: pre-fatigue exercise, the core exercise, and post-fatigue exercise.

Pre-Fatigue Exercise

The pre-fatigue exercise incorporates short, high-velocity speed and endurance drills that train the body to swiftly react to sudden stress. Pre-fatigue exercise increases muscle oxygenation (VO2 max) and total body capacity to initiate and sustain performance, without the typical symptoms of shock, fatigue, and loss of mechanical control.

The Core Exercise

The core exercise consists of special supersets, called workout units, that incorporate strength, speed, and explosive elements, all in one complex set. By rotating between weight load and volume levels, individuals are trained to be able to "come back with a vengeance" repeatedly, even when extremely fatigued. The core exercise promotes cross-interactions between different neuro-motor units, with an increased neuromuscular efficiency to sustain strength, speed, and explosive performance. For a competitive athlete, that can make the difference between winning and losing.

Post-Fatigue Exercise

Post-fatigue exercises train the body and mind to never give up and to sustain power, even when the mission seems to be done. Post-fatigue can be either explosive exercise or sheer strength exercise. It is this ability to sustain total body power after "being dragged around" that can make the difference between submission and victory. Post-fatigue exercise trains individuals to immensely stretch their capacity to sustain alertness, swiftly resume performance, and regain control when unexpectedly forced to do that.

CFT vs. Other Training Methods

- Unlike most training programs, CFT trains the body to resist fatigue and sustain power in a way that mimics primal fight or flight activities.
- Unlike other training methods today that typically separate resistance and endurance, CFT combines both with a substantial emphasis on exercise intensity.
- While the common goal of strength conditioning programs is to gain strength, CFT's goal is to sustain strength.
- Unlike mainstream fitness programs, CFT does not incorporate aerobics.
- Different from training methods that typically separate between resistance and other sport-specific exercises, CFT combines resistance with speed and explosive exercise.

- While other exercise programs typically work on isolation of body parts (arms, chest, legs, shoulders, etc.), CFT works the whole body, with a superior emphasis on the core.
- While other exercise programs generally fail to provide clear functional principles, CFT is based on survival principles, with a profound functional appeal and clearly defined priorities as to what comes first and what is secondary.
- While other exercise programs promise a "straight line" progress (i.e., gradual increase in weight load, etc.), CFT gradually increases strength, speed, and velocity together with the capacity to resist fatigue. By virtue of methodically rotating between levels of exercise complexity, work load, and volume, CFT features repetitive cycles of training sessions, providing steady progress in a spiral-like manner.

Intensity:
- Intensity levels of exercise complexity and work load in a work-load unit.

Volume:
- Volume, length, and number of workout units per workout.

The CFT's Ten Commandments

1. Base your training on workout units that incorporate strength, speed, and velocity exercise in one complex set.
2. Incorporate pre-fatigue and post-fatigue exercise with the workout units.
3. Rotate between sessions with pre-fatigue exercise, sessions with pre-fatigue and post-fatigue exercise, and sessions of sheer resistance.
4. Incorporate special abdominal and back supersets in the end of the workout sessions.
5. Exercise within a fixed time frame.
6. Increase intensity (increase work load or complexity) while reducing volume (less workout units/time).
7. Increase volume while decreasing intensity (more units with less weight load or complexity).
8. Increase intensity with a fixed volume.

9. Increase volume with a fixed intensity.
10. Rotate among 6, 7, 8, and 9.

CFT Nutritional Tips

- Cycle between high-fat and high-carb days (or detox) to train your body to maximize fuel utilization.
- Have a recovery meal of 15–30 grams of protein and 10–25 g of carbs after your workout (ideally within the first hour post-exercise).
- Have a light protein meal with minimum carbs every couple of hours after the initial post-exercise recovery meal (15–30 g protein/5–10 g carbs).
- If you work out in the early evening, your evening main meal could be a great recovery meal.

As mentioned, CFT deserves much more space than this chapter. The following chart provides some basic information as to the progress involved from basic to advanced levels.

CFT: Basic to Advanced Levels

- *CFT Level I—Resistance to fatigue:* Introducing pre-fatigue and post-fatigue exercise together with basic workout units, with an emphasis on increased capacity to resist fatigue (total body endurance).
- *CFT Level II—Sustained strength:* Decreasing pre-fatigue and post-fatigue exercise, while increasing complexity and work load, with an emphasis on sustained strength.
- *CFT Level III—Sustained velocity:* Combining pre-fatigue exercise with workout units that incorporate high-velocity exercise such as heavy bag punching and post-fatigue resistance exercise, with an emphasis on sustained speed, sustained velocity, and repetitive capacity to "come back with a vengeance" when extremely fatigued.
- *CFT Level IV—The Master Level:* Maximizing the workout unit's complexity by combining basic and advanced units (Levels I–III), with an emphasis on maximizing total sustained power.

Applications

CFT can be carried out with or without weights. The exercises induce maximum impact in minimum time and space. CFT can utilize any available weight (dumbbells, barbells, kettlebells, shots, etc.). CFT uses simple accessories such as towels, ropes, and even stones, thus being highly effective without a standard gym space and equipment.

Breathing Properly

Proper breathing is critical for performance and overall health. Breathing deeply alkalizes your system and thereby reduces the acid-stress factor on your body. Deep inhalations (from the diaphragm) followed by deep exhalations supply your tissues with vital oxygen while eliminating carbon dioxide. Conversely, shallow or improper breathing causes an oxygen deficiency and retention of carbon dioxide, which accelerates the build-up of carbonic acid in the blood. Poor oxygenation of the cells and an overly acidic system lead to muscle fatigue and stiffness, and stress-related exhaustion.

The Exercise Manuals

As noted, the main goal of Controlled-Fatigue Training is to increase the body's capacity to sustain power and resist fatigue. Note that CFT incorporates new training concepts in its exercise manuals. Since there isn't enough space in this book for a complete training program, I had to minimize the number of exercises to a mere few that may help individuals jump-start the program while they try the Warrior Diet. (Interested readers can learn more in our newsletter, from our workshops, and in forthcoming e-books and DVDs.) The following exercises are divided into three groups: pre-fatigue, post-fatigue, and core. The exercise manuals should be followed as instructed, but the levels of intensity and the number of reps can be adjusted according to the individual's level of fitness.

Pre-Fatigue Exercise

The purpose of pre-fatigue exercise is to increase the body's ability to initiate and sustain performance. Following is one of a few versions of pre-fatigue exercise that I believe is simple, effective, and viable, even for beginners.

Warrior's (Fight or Flight) Sprint Intervals

This 5-minute exercise incorporates special running intervals of 30 seconds each. Unlike typical jogging routines, CFT incorporates defense or military press hand positions while running. The first interval incorporates a defense position in which the fists are raised slightly above the forehead; hands bent in a 90-degree angle in front of the body. The second interval incorporates an overhead stretched-hand position. Note that the exercise can be done on a treadmill or outdoors.

Treadmill: Choose two levels of speed, max level and maintenance.
- Go up to max speed. Start with the first interval. Run for about 30 seconds while your hands are in a defense position, your fists in front of your forehead (step 1).
- Follow by raising your hands overhead to a stretched position (high above your head); keep running for 30 seconds (step 2).

Step 1   Step 2

- Lower the speed to maintenance level. Follow with 30 seconds of defense position (step 1), followed by another 30 seconds of overhead-hands position (step 2).
- You may feel the burn in your shoulders and back; nevertheless, try to repeat this cycle once more. Go up to max speed level; 30 seconds defense position, followed by 30 seconds overhead hands; and then lower the speed to maintenance and resume 2-minute intervals (i.e., 30-second defense followed by 30-second overhead hands, repeated twice).

Notes
- One can increase intervals to 1 minute rather than 30 seconds (thereby doing 5 intervals/5 minutes rather than 10).
- Advanced trainees can use very light weights while running.
- If the drill gets too tough, lower the speed or do 3 minutes instead of 5 minutes.

Outdoors: Intervals should be paced similar to treadmill intervals. If you exercise outdoors, try to fix distance per interval. For instance, if the distance is 100 yards, do each interval for a 100-yard distance (with different hand positions and different levels of speed).

Pre-Fatigue Exercise, Version II
Warrior's Walking Intervals

Compared to the previous exercise, Warrior's Walking Intervals have a lower impact on the knees, yet they are highly effective in improving upper to lower body synergy and lateral coordination. They also increase the capacity to initiate and sustain total body strength and explosive performance. Like the previous pre-fatigue exercise, Warrior's Walking Intervals can be done either on a treadmill or outdoors.

- Pick up a pair of light or medium-weight dumbbells.
- Step on a treadmill and put the dumbbells on the front board or on the sides. Set the machine to a walking speed level (3.0–3.6, step 1).
- Pick up the dumbbells, push the speed button, lift the dumbbells to shoulder level, and begin walking (step 2).

Step 1   Step 2   Step 3   Step 4

- While walking, start overhead lateral presses, rotating between right hand and left hand presses. Most importantly, adjust the rhythm of the legs' movement to the rhythm of the hands' movement. Work left leg–right hand, followed by right leg–left hand. (I.e., while your left leg moves forward, press your right hand overhead and vice versa. While your right leg moves forward, press your left hand overhead.) Continue overhead lateral presses while walking for 30 seconds (step 3).
- Move to the next intervals in the following way: while walking, press both dumbbells to an overhead "freeze" (stretched hands) position. Continue walking while holding both weights in an overhead freeze position for 30 seconds (step 4).
- Repeat the above intervals 2–4 times.
- You may feel extreme burn in the shoulders and back, but try to sustain the drill for at least 3 minutes.
- If you feel that it's getting too tough, put down the weights and resume the intervals without weights.
- You can also rotate between intervals with weights and intervals without weights.
- Beginners should start with very light weights and gradually increase the weight load.
- The heavier the weight load gets, the shorter the exercise should be. Nonetheless, try to sustain a 3-minute pre-fatigue drill at the minimum.

Pre-Fatigue Exercise, Version III
Incline Bike Power Intervals

The purpose of this exercise is to maximize total body capacity to initiate and sustain push and pull activities. Like other pre-fatigue exercises, Incline Bike Power Intervals induce an extreme physical demand on the body. The exercise incorporates power biking (push) intervals with power walking (pull) intervals. During the intervals, the body is forced to perform power pedaling (max power level) followed by power walking intervals (pedaling in a way that resembles walking, where the butt rises slightly above the seat, forcing the body to continue pedaling while under a "high" mechanical disadvantage due to an extreme shift of the gravitational center backward). Each interval lasts 30 seconds. In between there is a maintenance interval involving overhead lateral presses with light dumbbells.

- Choose a pair of lightweight dumbbells and put them on top of the bike handle (leaning on the front board) or put them on the floor next to the bike in an accessible place.
- Pick up the weights, raise them to shoulder level, and press them overhead, laterally (one hand at a time), while pedaling for 30 seconds (step 1, p. 211).
- Put the weights down and prepare to begin the power pedaling interval (step 2).
- Go up to max power level and try to sustain pushing the pedals for 30 seconds.
- Lower the speed to a maintenance level. Pick up the weights and resume maintenance interval (do overhead lateral presses while pedaling for 30 seconds, step 1).
- Move to power walking. Hold the bike's handle and pull your body forward, while raising your butt slightly above the seat. (Your upper body should be bent forward while your arms are pulling the handle toward you, thus keeping your body forward, step 3.)
- Try to sustain this position, pulling and pedaling for 30 seconds. If you can't sustain 30 seconds, try a few seconds at a time, until reaching a total 30-second interval. Note that due to an extreme shift in the gravitational center backward, you'll be forced to continuously resist

| Step 1 | Step 2 | Step 3 |

the body's tendency to fall backward by pulling and pushing (from the arms, gluts and knees, respectively).
- Pick up the weights and resume maintenance (overhead lateral presses while pedaling for 30 seconds, step 1).
- Repeat the aforementioned intervals (power pedaling–maintenance–power walking) for an additional 3 minutes until completing a 5-minute drill (steps 1, 2, and 3).

Notes
- Once in a while, try to grind up to 10 minutes of drilling.
- Do not waste your time attempting to do the above exercise on a vertical stationary bike.

Post-Fatigue Exercise

CFT incorporates various post-fatigue exercises. I present here only the high-velocity explosive exercises, which tend to be the missing element in most strength conditioning programs. In fact, many trainers today fail to even define what velocity is. The so-called "ballistic exercise" isn't as ballistic as they claim it to be, often using momentum (passive swings) instead of a real explosive force. Velocity is the epitome of all exercise. The ability to take flight effectively or to deliver explosive fighting moves was critically important for human survival. Velocity can be defined as the combination of strength and speed. Indeed, it is this ratio of strength to speed that dictates the nature of velocity. For instance, when a lion chases an antelope, the big cat incorporates *strength velocity*, whereas the antelope incorporates *speed velocity*.

CFT trains individuals to incorporate both. Just to keep things clear, all post-fatigue exercise should be incorporated at the end of every workout unit or right after the core exercise.

Post-Fatigue Exercise, Version I
Towel Swiping

Towel Swiping is a high-velocity exercise with a profound impact on the shoulders, back, and core. I believe it puts the body in a highly explosive fight or flight-like mode. Towel swiping can be done in various strength and speed velocity levels. Beach towels are best. We call them "bitch towels." Towel swiping is highly effective in increasing neuromuscular capacity to combine strength and speed and be able to sustain it.

- Hold the towel at the two corners, stretching the width part (not the length, step 1).
- Stand with your knees slightly bent, your back arched, and the torso slightly bent forward at the waist (step 1).
- Bring your arms (slightly curved) just above your forehead (step 1).
- Swipe the towel down (below waist) and up (above forehead) in swift and decisive moves (step 2). Hear the snapping sound of the towel with every swipe. Try to incorporate speed velocity (faster reps within a shorter range of motion, step 3) together with strength velocity (stronger and slower reps within a larger range of motion, step 4).
- Try to sustain swiping for 1 to 3 minutes. Use this exercise as a post-fatigue part of workout units or at the end of the core exercise.

Step 1   Step 2   Step 3   Step 4

Notes

- Towel swiping can be done with a partner. Try to mutually adjust speed and strength to the same rhythm. Try to push each other to sustain performance.
- You can hold two towels instead of one. The rebound of the towel on your face is "part of the game."
- You can try to incorporate towel swiping standing in shallow water (pool, sea, or river). Every time that you slow down the speed or strength velocity beyond a certain level, the towel will touch the water, get wet, and thus become substantially heavier. Water swiping is a tough drill that trains the body to sustain optimum speed and velocity or otherwise be forced to swipe a heavier load with increased level of difficulty.
- You can try to gradually increase the exercise's duration from 3 minutes up to 5 minutes and once in a while, up to 10 minutes.
- Towels are accessible exercise tools. If nothing else, towel swiping can constitute the whole core of the workout unit, without the need for any gym equipment or a typical gym space. In this case, you can incorporate a core of towel swiping together with pre- or post-fatigue exercise such as Warrior Sprint Intervals or Frog Jumps, respectively.
- When you exercise towel swiping as the core of the workout, do it for 5 to 10 minutes. Occasionally, try to go beyond 10 minutes and grind your limits.

Post-Fatigue Exercise, Version II
Frog Jumps

Frog Jumps are high-velocity exercises that train the body to sustain low explosive and rapid jumps. The exercise forces the body to strengthen joints and tendons with an emphasis on knees and ankle mobility. It also improves dynamic form control with a complete (360°) peripheral orientation. Frog jumps have been incorporated in traditional military training routines, increasing soldiers' ability to sustain performance while "staying low." Frog jumps can be combined with towel swiping, thus facilitating a total-body explosive workout.

| Step 1 | Step 2 | Step 3 |

- Go down to a low squat position (step 1).
- Stand on the balls of your feet, hands slightly curved at the sides of your body (step 1).
- Do 5 rapid low jumps to the right followed by 5 jumps to the left, followed by 5 jumps forward, followed by 5 jumps backward (to starting position, step 2).
- Repeat the same with only 4 reps (jumps) to each direction.
- Repeat the same—do 3 reps.
- Repeat the same—do 2 reps.
- Repeat the same—do 1 rep.
- Finish with 3 to 5 high jumps. Explode as high as possible above the ground, land on the balls of your feet softly and quietly (like a cat) for a split second only, and resume jumping (step 3).
- Frog jumps can be incorporated as a post-fatigue exercise with or instead of other high-velocity post-fatigue exercises.
- Frog jumps can be done with light weights. Start with very light weights, and be careful with the landing.

The Core Exercise

The main purpose of the core exercise is to increase the body's capacity to sustain strength. It also trains the body to effectively perform when forced to endure combined strength, speed, and explosive elements.

The core exercise is based on special supersets called workout units. Each workout unit is composed of a complex set of exercises that apply a "zig-zag" training principle. This training principle forces the body to go down and up with the weight load, in a repetitive manner, and thus acquire the ability to come back again and again and be able to intensely perform while resisting fatigue. The skill to "come back" is missing in most strength conditioning programs, which generally attempt to slow down the typical decline in strength. Thus they gradually give up to the inevitable failure. Instead, CFT trains the body to bounce back, even when feeling fatigued, and to regain the capacity to sustain peak strength.

Among the top priorities for human survival, the ability to sustain strength is far superior to the ability to gain strength. Being able to endure a prolonged, intense strength drill is by far more beneficial to the overall conditioning of the human body than the ability to perform a short burst of resistance exercise and then "fall apart." The typical short resistance sets train the body to gain strength but fail to train for sustaining the acquired strength. Sooner or later, strength athletes reach training plateaus, upon which they fail to score or gain. For a martial artist or a boxer, the ability to sustain strength is a key element in their quest to become tougher and to be able to knock out an opponent in late rounds. By virtue of applying exercises that train the body to sustain strength (a unit's complex set can last up to 15 minutes), CFT helps improve neuromuscular efficiency as well as muscle capacity to utilize carbohydrate and fat fuel for energy. These neuromuscular and fueling benefits can help boost the overall capacity to generate energy, burn fat, and build a tough and powerful body. CFT incorporates a few versions of core exercise. I feature here some core exercises that I believe represent this group well.

Since CFT may initially appear too extreme to some people, let me elaborate a bit more about some of its training concepts.

The single most important feature of Controlled-Fatigue Training is the incorporation of survival principles in its training concepts. In this respect, CFT appeals to all human beings. All of us—men, women, and children alike—share the same survival mechanisms. These inherent biological mechanisms must be triggered in order to induce their beneficial effects on the body. CFT applies training concepts that trigger these primal mechanisms. While putting the body in a survival mode, CFT forces individuals to actively survive, regardless of their age, gender, occupation, or lifestyle. The same training concepts that benefit a young individual can benefit an older individual. As noted, the exercise manuals should be customized to one's level of fitness (via adjustments in weight load, volume, and complexity of the workout). We've discussed previously how exercising in a way that mimics fight or flight activities is inherently beneficial to our survival. Following the presentations of pre-fatigue and post-fatigue exercise, I'd like to present here some concepts of the core exercise.

Upside-Down Pyramid

Like some of the exercises we have already encountered, this training concept is based on repetitive rotations between weight loads. It is called "upside-down pyramids" because you go down and up with the weight loads in a way that somewhat resembles an upside-down pyramid.

When combined, upside-down pyramids induce a "zig-zag" effect that forces repetitive climbs to the top (heavy) points of the pyramids. Thus, individuals are trained to repetitively "come back" to lifting heavy, and still continue exercising.

A combination of 1–5 pyramids constitutes a workout unit, and a combination of 1–5 workout units constitutes the core exercise.

- Put in front of you three pairs of dumbbells: heavy, medium, and light. Adjust the weights according to the heavy weight—one that you can lift about 5–6 reps (step 1).
- Start with the heavy weights. Clean both weights to shoulder level and press them overhead. Do 5–3 reps (steps 2 and 3).
- Slowly lower the weight to the ground while keeping your back arched at all times (step 4).

| Step 1 | Step 2 | Step 3 | Step 4 |

| Step 5 | Step 6 | Step 7 | Step 8 |

- Pick up the medium weights; clean and press them overhead. Do 5–3 reps (steps 2 and 3).
- Move to lightweight lateral raises: Do 5–3 side laterals (steps 5 and 6), followed by 5–3 back laterals (steps 7 and 8), followed by 5–3 front overhead raises (steps 9-11).
- Go up-back to medium weight (5–3 reps, all steps).
- Go up-back to heavy weight (3–1 reps, all steps).
- Go down to medium weight (3–1 reps, all steps).
- Finish with lightweight lateral raises (5–3 reps) (step 5 to 8).

| Step 9 | Step 10 | Step 11 |

Notes

- You can try to incorporate a more intense Upside-Down Pyramid by turning all presses into cleans and presses (clean and press both heavy and medium weights for 5 to 3 reps, rather than cleaning and then pressing for 5 to 3 reps).

- To form a simple workout unit, incorporate post-fatigue exercise such as Towel Swiping or Frog Jumping at the end of each Upside-Down Pyramid.
- To form a complex workout unit, combine 2–5 Upside-Down Pyramids, followed by post-fatigue exercise.
- The core exercise can be composed of 1–5 workout units, regardless of their level of complexity.
- Do not delay your exercise continuity. Do not fall into the trap of desperately attempting to jerk or swing another rep. Instead, put the weight down and move forward to the next weight, while lowering your reps. Your ability to continue coming back and sustaining strength is more important than your ability to jerk another rep.

Laterals

Another important concept of CFT is the methodical incorporation of lateral moves in its exercise manuals. Most humans' functional moves are lateral. We write, walk, sprint, and punch laterally. Our brain operates laterally (with a full orientation to the left and right), even when we do bilateral moves (using both our arms and legs at the same time). Human survival dictates a hierarchy of functional moves. And as noted, the top priority of human moves are those involved in fight or flight activities. All through evolution, the survival of the fittest depended primarily on the ability to run away rapidly (flight) or to deliver powerful punches, pulls, hits, and kicks (fight). Since fight or flight activities are primarily lateral (sprint, punch), it is probable that the human body is preprogrammed to better adapt and improve when exercised laterally. In fact, it is now known that exercising one ligament at a time enhances neuromuscular activity in the other (lateral) ligament. This lateral compensation mechanism may have evolved primarily due to the necessity to survive in extreme conditions when being forced to perform on one arm or one leg at a time.

When we exercise laterally, rotating between left and right ligaments (such as during running or boxing), we naturally swing the core of the body in the opposite direction of the moving ligament. This repetitive swing shifts the gravitational center again and again, from the sides of the body back to the core, thus preventing us from falling sideways. For instance, a left hook requires a swing to the right (shift of the hips toward the right side) and vice versa. This lateral swing in the opposite direction of the moving arm helps counter the accelerated-velocity impact of the punch outwards and thus keeps the body from losing its balance.

Lateral Upside-Down Pyramid

This exercise is similar to the previous upside-down pyramid (UDP), only here the lifting is lateral and may require slightly lighter weights.

- Put in front of you three pairs of dumbbells: heavy, medium, and light weights. Adjust weights according to the heavy weight—one that you can lift about 6–7 reps (step 1).
- Start with the heavy weight. Clean the weights to your shoulders (step 2).

| Step 1 | Step 2 | Step 3 | Step 4 |

| Step 5 | Step 6 | Step 7 | Step 8 |

- Do 5–3 alternating left and right one-arm military presses. Slightly swing your hips according to the rhythm of your lift. Your hip bone should be alternately positioned under the lifted weight (steps 3 and 4).
- Do the same with the medium weights (5–3 reps).
- Move to the light weights (step 5). Do lateral raises: side laterals (5–3 reps, steps 5 and 6) followed by back laterals (5–3 reps, steps 7 and 8). Finish with front raises (5–3 reps). Raise your hands above your head, rather than just to shoulder level (steps 9-11, p. 217).
- Go up to medium weights (5–3 reps, all steps).
- Go up to heavy weights (3–1 reps, all steps).
- Go down to medium weights (3–1 reps, all steps).
- Finish with lightweight lateral raises (5–3 reps, steps 5 and 6).

Notes
- In all lightweight lateral raises, keep your hands tight, "frozen" in a hook-like position.
- At the end of each lateral UDP, try to incorporate 1–3 minutes of post-fatigue velocity exercise such as towel swiping. This will create a simple workout unit.
- You can combine 2–5 lateral UDPs to form a complex workout unit. However, it is recommended that you start with 2 lateral UDPs and gradually increase the number until reaching 5 lateral UDPs per complex unit.
- Incorporate post-fatigue velocity exercise right after each complex unit.
- The core exercise can be composed of 1 to 5 workout units.

Heavy Units for Max Strength
One of CFT's main goals is to gain strength and increase the capacity to sustain it. One way of doing that is by applying a training cycle that gradually increases the weight load. Following the CFT principles, any initial increase in max weight load requires an initial decrease in volume (duration of exercise). There are two ways to lower the exercise volume:

- Shorten the length of the basic upside-down pyramid unit.

- Reduce the number of workout units per session (for instance, 1–3 instead of 3–5).

Let's go into a bit more detail.

- Shorten the basic upside-down pyramid:
  A heavy UDP unit can be shortened by omitting the medium weight. Thus, the shortened heavy UDP is based on only two levels of weight (heavy and light). Yet it is still possible to maintain or increase the overall complexity. Combining short and heavy UDPs will form a highly intense complex unit. Based on a zigzag principle, such a workout unit forces rapid "comebacks" to max weight, thus increasing weight load without decreasing complexity. Due to the high level of intensity, it's recommended that you gradually incorporate 1–3 heavy UDPs/unit (1–3 "comebacks" to heavy weight). Start with one heavy UDP and build it up gradually until reaching a maximum complexity of 3 UDPs/per unit.
- Reduce the number of workout units per session:
  When increasing the weight load and intensity of the unit, one can lower the overall number of units per session and thus lower the overall volume of the workout. The higher the increase in the weight load and complexity of the unit, the lower the number of units per session should be.

  For instance, an initial increase of 20–25% in max weight (heavy weight) should lower the number of minimum units per session from 3 to 1. And the same holds true with the number of maximum units per session: they should be lowered from 5 to 3.

Notes
- If needed, drop the reps from 5 to 1, but do not delay your exercise continuity. As noted elsewhere in these pages, do not fall into the trap of desperately attempting to jerk or swing another rep. Instead, put the weight down and move forward to the next weight while lowering your reps. Your ability to continue to "come back" and sustain strength is more important than your ability to jerk another rep.
- Use common sense. If max weight increase is 5%, you may be able to maintain volume. If the increase is 15%, you should lower the

number of units per session. If max weight increases by 20–25%, you should shorten both the basic UDP and the number of units per session.

Supportive Manual Exercise (Abs, Back, Shoulders)

CFT incorporates various post-fatigue exercises, some of which are mandatory whereas others are optional. Since the core and back are top priorities, I present here a few exercise manuals that target the abdominal muscles and the back. These exercises can all be incorporated into the end of the workout.

As noted, CFT can be incorporated with sheer resistance training. But because resistance exercise has been featured in virtually all strength conditioning and bodybuilding programs, I chose to present here only exercise manuals that are uniquely part of the CFT routine.

Abdominals

Abdominal muscles (abs) are divided into three main groups:

1. *Rectus Abdominus* (the "six-pack")
2. *Serratus Anterior* (sides of the upper abs)
3. *External Obliques* (sides of the lower abs)

However, you should note that all abdominal muscles are bound together by connective tissues into one large muscle.

Abdominal training is a controversial issue. There are differing opinions about abdominal muscle development. Trainers who use specific ab-training methods often try to prove that theirs are superior to other ab routines. People who want to define their midsection spend a great deal of time on ab-training methods such as sit-ups, crunches, reverse crunches, hanging leg raises, Roman chair sit-ups, ab-flexor machines, rollers, and more.

The problem with many of these methods is not the efficiency of the exercises, but the fact that they're built on isolating one ab part or another. Isolating one part of a large muscle group may cause imbalance and weakness in other parts of the same muscle. That's why it's so important to understand that abs are, in fact, one large muscle group working as a unit. They have primary functions, essential for body movements and posture. Let me put it simply: the prime function of the abdominals is to stabilize the midsection of your body, and thus protect your organs and support your spine. Abs should always be toned and ready for action. Sluggish, soft abs will cause vulnerability and dysfunction.

As a stabilizer of your midsection, the ab muscles are responsible for all waist movements such as swings, twists, bends, and crunches. The stabilizing function of abs manifests

clearly when you're engaged in explosive moves such as punching or kicking. Notice that without the reflexive tightening of your abs, you can't deliver a powerful punch or an explosive kick. Abdominal muscles respond instinctively to explosive or powerful frontal arm and leg movements. By contracting, and thus stabilizing, your midsection as a solid column or base for all explosive moves, ab muscles protect your spine from the rebound forces of your arm and leg movements. To perform with maximum strength, you need to tighten your midsection. A soft or weak waist may force you to compromise on your ability to lift weights, kick, or punch. Moreover, without abdominal support at all, you wouldn't be able to stand or walk.

We tend to take ab function for granted. A trained gymnast will tell you that there's no way to successfully stand on your hands without tightening your midsection. If your abs and lower back are loose, your body will collapse. This fact is not just true for standing on your hands. Without abdominal support, as stated above, you wouldn't be able to sing, "I'm still standing." Martial artists and boxers are particularly aware of this.

A trained warrior is ready at any time to absorb a hit on his midsection. A warrior's abs instinctively contract to protect the spine and inner organs, while absorbing the punch or kick. Habitual reflexive toning of the ab muscles enables a warrior to instinctively swing, punch, or kick whenever necessary.

The Warrior Posture

A trained warrior often adopts a unique posture, which I call the "Warrior Posture." People engaged in intense physical activities, including martial artists, gymnasts, some professional competitive athletes—or even hard laborers, for that matter—often develop a posture where their abs are slightly flexed, and their back is ever so slightly bent forward. This isn't a fashion model's or a dandy's posture; it looks quite different.

Some fashion models, as well as many guys who want to look tall, often push their chest out, pumping air into their lungs, and try to walk as tall as they can. This stiff walk, without a bounce, makes them look pumped and vulnerable. When I see people walk this way (usually men), it often reminds me of a strolling penguin.

What I call a "Warrior Posture" has nothing to do with posing in front of a mirror. It is, in fact, the result of a natural adaptation of the body to tough, physical strain. I'm not trying to persuade people to walk like warriors. I'm just trying to point out what a Warrior Posture is and how it's naturally designed to enhance agility. If you find yourself instinctively walking like a warrior, I'd say it's a clear sign that you've been around the block a few times. Okay, enough of all this bravado. Let's go to the exercises.

There are many variations of abdominal training. I cover here only a basic approach—but nonetheless enough to get you started. Let me note here that "basic" doesn't mean easy. The Warrior Abs Routine activates all abdominal muscles in one giant superset and is, in fact, quite intense.

It works on the serratus anterior muscles, the external obliques, the upper and lower rectus abdominis, and the connective tissues between the serratus, the obliques, and the rectus abdominus.

This giant superset incorporates a rotation between two kinds of exercise: hanging leg raises and crunches. It takes about 2–3 minutes (and everything you have) to finish a set. All you need is one set per day, preferably at the end of each workout day. As noted, the main function of the abs is to stabilize the midsection while protecting the spine and inner organs. Therefore, it's important to incorporate isometric exercises together with isotonic exercises.

- *Isometric*—static exercises that contract the muscles without shortening them.
- *Isotonic*—dynamic exercises that involve movement, and shortening (thickening) of the muscles.

Most people are weak in the side layers of the abs (the serratus and the external obliques). In addition to the aesthetic factor (these muscles give you fine definition, and a compact look), the serratus and the obliques are necessary for all swings, punches, kicks, and leg raises.

Having tight, strong sides will give you a flat and strong midsection. I believe that the best way to work the sides of your midsection is by combining special isometric (freezing) exercises with isotonic exercises (movement). Static intense pressure on the abs will trigger a reflex of maximum contraction, thus forcing them to function the way they're meant to—as stabilizers and protectors of your midsection.

Ab Superset: First Exercise—Hanging Leg Raise

Stand under a chin-up bar. Grab the bar with both hands, palms down, at about shoulder width. Hang. Your feet should be flexed, pointing forward (step 1). Slowly raise your feet toward your hands. Your toes should touch the bar (step 2). Advanced exercisers should try to keep their legs almost

| Step 1 | Step 2 | Step 3 | Step 4 |

Step 5

straight. Beginners can bend their legs to ease the tension.

Slowly lower your legs to eye level. Keep your legs at that level for 10 seconds while rotating them with small movements: 2–3 to the right side and 2–3 to the left side (step 3). Slowly lower your legs to about a 45-degree angle with your torso and then lift them up again to eye level (steps 4 to 3).

Try to keep them at about eye level for another 5–10 seconds. If it's too hard, bend your knees. Slowly bring your legs down to 45 degrees. Bend your knees and then bring them up to your chest, keep them there for 3 seconds (step 5), and then bring them down (step 1). Repeat 5–10 times. When done, bring them up to your chest again. Keep your knees as high and as close to your chest as you can, and keep them in that position for another 5–10 seconds (step 5). When you're done, you'll feel your lower abs and sides burning.

If you haven't collapsed by now, bring your legs down slowly. Now, grab a bench. You're going to do the crunches as part of this exercise; no resting in between.

Second Exercise: Crunches

Sit on a bench. Lie down on your back and raise your legs slightly above the bench for a count of 10–60 seconds (step 1). Bring your legs to where your thighs form a 90-degree angle with your body; and while your knees are bent (also in a 90-degree angle), your shins are parallel to your body and the bench.

Step 1   Step 2   Step 3

Your hands should be behind your head, and your elbows should point to the side (step 2). Slowly lift your torso as high as you can. Don't bounce or use any momentum. Use your abs only. When you reach the top, stay for 5–7 seconds, and on each second count, squeeze the crunch as if trying to reach with your chin farther and farther forward. Your chin should be raised slightly and your elbows pointing to the sides at all times (step 3). Go slowly down to starting position without losing muscle contraction (step 2). Always keep your abs contracted. Repeat 10–30 times.

When done, stretch your legs to a position slightly raised above the bench for a count of 5–10 (step 1); follow with crunches again (steps 2 and 3). If you can, repeat this drill and move back to the first exercise (Hanging Leg Raises).

Second (Final) Set—Hanging Leg Raises

After finishing crunches, you'll most likely be in pain. Nevertheless, try to go on and do one more set of leg raises. Hang on the chin-up bar with your feet flexed, pointing forward. With whatever is left within you, bring your feet to eye level. If you can't do it with straight legs, do it with your knees bent. Hold the position for a few seconds, and then slowly bring the legs down. Repeat 5–7 times, or do as many reps as you can. When you feel the sharp pain in your rib cage, and your lower and upper abs, you can stop drilling. Hang for a second, stretch your abs, arch your back ever so slightly, then stretch your abs again—and you're all done.

Note: The only way that you can reach maximum performance with your midsection is to incorporate lower-back stretching with ab exercises. The lower back and abs balance each other. A weakness in either may create imbalance, bad posture, injuries, and may compromise your strength.

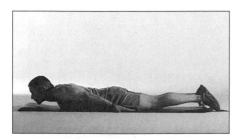

Step 1

Step 2

Back

Lower Back Stretch: 1–3 Sets

Lie down flat on your abdominals. Your arms should be straight and at your sides, with your hands palms down to the floor. Your head should be facing forward (see step 1, previous page). With the palms of your hands pushing downward, lift your lower body up. Your legs should be practically straight. Push your lower body up, without jerking, as high as you can. When you reach maximum contraction, hold for 10 full seconds (see step 2, previous page). Relax and repeat again.

Pull-Ups

Pull-Ups constitute an important exercise that works the lats, back, and biceps. It enhances the capacity to pull and thus helps balance push and pull activities. Pull-ups should be incorporated as a post-fatigue exercise at the end of each workout unit or the end of the core exercise.

Stand under an overhead bar. Most gyms have a special rack for pull-ups, where the overhead bar is marked for wide grip and narrow grip. Grab the bar in a wide grip (step 1). Your arms should be about 45 degrees from your body. Pull yourself up until your upper chest almost touches the bar (step 2). Try to keep your back arched all the way up. Stay on the top for a second, and then lower your body back to hanging position (step 1). Do as many reps as you can.

Step 1

Step 2

When you pull yourself up, keep your chest forward while pushing your body away from the overhead bar. This way you use more of your lats than your biceps.

When you're done, take a 5-second rest, and then pull yourself up and stay on top for 10–15 seconds. Count the seconds, and on each count try to bounce up. Then, on a count of five, slowly lower your body. When done, immediately start shoulder laterals. Don't rest between sets.

Note: Keeping the right form is more important than how many reps you perform.

Shoulders

Shoulder Lateral Raises

Shoulder Lateral Raises are part of the workout units. The following exercise manuals are presented here for the purpose of clarity and the maintenance of a proper form.

Shoulder Side Lateral Raises

Hold the dumbbells by your sides (step 1).

Bend your elbows slightly. Raise both arms to just a bit higher than shoulder height (step 2). While you lift, rotate your hands so that your thumb is facing downward. When you reach peak contraction, try to hold it for a second. It's going to be hard, but make the attempt nonetheless. Then slowly lower your arms back to starting position (step 3). Don't jerk at all. When you're done, start Bent-Over Laterals.

Step 1   Step 2   Step 3

Back Lateral Raises (Bent-Over Laterals)

This is the same as Side Lateral Raises, only here you bend forward and put more pressure on your rear deltoids. Raise or push the weight upward. Your hands should be slightly bent. When you feel the burn, you can bend your elbows more and keep pushing the weight up through your rear delts. Do 5–10 reps.

Note: Shoulder back laterals look like a bird taking flight. Think of your arms as wings.

Bow and Arrow—Shoulder Stretch

This stretch routine mimics how ancient warriors used the bow and arrow. It works on the rear deltoids, back, trapezoids, triceps, elbows, and tendons. It can be incorporated at the end of each workout unit or after the core exercise.

Get yourself a training bungee cord or, if that's unavailable, you can use a towel. Fold the bungee cord. Hold the handles attached to the cord with one hand, and the edge of the folded cord with the other hand. Bring the cord up to shoulder level. Stretch the hand holding the cord to the side of your body at shoulder height, as if you are holding a bow. The stretched hand should be at a 90-degree angle from your body. The other hand should hold the handles with the elbow bent, as if you are holding an arrow. Slowly pull the "bow-

string" with the bent hand through your shoulder and elbow in the opposite direction of the stretched hand, as if you're about to shoot an arrow. At all times, keep the other hand in a stretched and locked position. When you reach peak contraction, stay for 10 seconds. On each second count, slightly pull through your elbow and the shoulder of the pulling hand. Return the pulling hand to starting position. Repeat 5–10 times.

When you're done, reverse your hand position. Repeat 5–10 times. At all times, your eyes should stare at the outstretched far hand, as if you're aiming an imaginary arrow at a target.

As mentioned, this is part of a basic routine that activates all deltoid muscle groups and tendons. Those interested in more information on advanced Warrior's CFT Workouts should visit our website: www.warriordiet.com.

Lat Pull-Down

Lat Pull-Downs can be incorporated at the end of each workout unit, as well as the end of the core exercise.

Sit on the attached pull-down seat of the weight equipment. Hold the bar with a wide grip. Arch your back. Keep your chin high. Pull the bar down to the front of your chest. Pause for a couple of seconds. Squeeze backward (not downward, as most people mistakenly do) as hard as you can. You'll feel your traps and the lower part of your upper back. Return slowly to starting position. Do 5–7 heavy reps. Then lower the weight. Bend backward until your back is about 45 degrees to the floor. Keep your back arched at all times. Slowly pull the bar to your front (chest). Pause 5–7 seconds, count the seconds, and with each count squeeze the bar toward your chest. Then slowly return the bar to starting position. Do 5 reps. When you're done, go to the incline chest rack. Don't rest between sets.

Seated Pulley Rows

This exercise can be supersetted together with Lat Pull-Downs after each workout unit, as well as after the core exercise. Do 10 reps, including cheat reps.

Sit on the pulley rack bench. Bend your knees. Hold the handle or bar attached to the pulley's cable. Arch your back and sit at a 90-degree angle. Pull the bar or handle to your upper abs, just below the chest. Pause for a second. Squeeze and then slowly return to arm stretch (starting position). On the fifth rep, pause at peak contraction for 5 to 7 seconds. Squeeze the bar to your body on each second count. Then slowly return to arm-stretch position, and bend forward fully stretched.

Now you can do a few cheat reps. Pull the bar to your body, bouncing slightly with your back. Don't bend backward further than 90 degrees at any time. Bring the bar slowly back to stretch position. Do 5 cheat reps—for a total of 10 reps. The first 5 slow reps work your middle and lower back. The last 5 cheat reps work the lower part of your mid-back and the sides of your lower back. When you're done, go to the flat bench rack. Don't rest between sets.

Keep the bar close to the body as you lift and try to maintain a constant arch in your back. Slowly push through your back, butt, knees, and heels, until you are standing straight. When you reach the top, keep your abs and lower back tight. Squeeze your traps, shoulder blades, and buttocks at the top

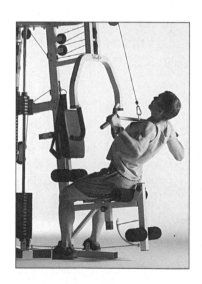

position. Take a deep breath and slowly bend your knees, push your butt backward, and keep staring upward while your back is arched and tight. Put the bar on the floor. Do 5–7 reps. I like to use a regular grip (hands palm down). This grip will accelerate forearm and wrist strength.

Clean and Press—3–5 sets, 5 reps

The Clean and Press is one exercise that works practically all of your body. It's the best exercise for overall muscle synergy, agility, and functional strength. It works your quads, hamstrings, knees, back, traps, shoulders, triceps, biceps, and wrists. If I had to choose only one exercise that would be an effective full-body strength conditioning drill, it would be the Clean and Press.

Clean and press exercises could be incorporated in the core exercise together with pull-ups, followed by high-velocity post-fatigue towel swiping as well as speed or power punching.

Stand behind the barbell with your feet under the center of the barbell, shoulder-width apart. Bend down and grab the bar with an overhand grip, slightly wider than shoulder width (step 1). Keep your back arched and tight, with your eyes staring upward. Take a deep breath. In one explosive motion lift the bar to your shoulders (steps 1–3).

A clean motion in "slow-mo" should look like this: first the bar moves from just above your ankles to knee level. Then, while your butt lowers and moves a bit backward, your upper body moves upward, with your arms bending and moving the barbell toward your shoulders. Your knees bounce a little, yet stay slightly bent. At that point, pause for a second, take another deep

| Step 1 | Step 2 | Step 3 | Step 4 |

breath, and press the weight overhead (steps 3 and 4). When you reach the top overhead position, hold for a second. Keep your lower back and abs tight. Stand still. Do not bounce. Then slowly lower the bar back to your front shoulders, and from here bring it slowly down to your knees, and then return the weight to starting position (step 1). When you bend down, always keep your back arched to avoid injury. Repeat 5 times. The weight should be heavy enough that you would fail at about 6 or 7 reps. This way you may be able to perform 3–5 repetitive sets of about 5 reps as the core exercise.

Those who want to accelerate the intensity of this exercise should consider using the following tips.

Partial-Press Reps

Once you're done with the last rep you can go on and do Partial-Press Reps. Hold the bar on your front shoulders, and then with a count of 5–7 seconds, lift the weight slightly up and down on each second count. Partial reps should be performed on the last two sets.

Clean and Jerk

Once you feel the burn, you can still go on and grind more forced reps of Clean and Jerk. Once you clean the barbell to your shoulders, slightly jerk through your bent knees and back. The jerk motion will help you to lift the weight overhead. At the top overhead position, hold for a second and then slowly bring the bar back to your shoulders. Bend your knees slightly and then repeat again 2 or 3 times. Clean and Press, followed by Clean and Jerk, will take everything you have. This is one exercise in which you go all out. As noted, it works on strength, endurance, and balance. Incorporating Controlled-Fatigue Training with clean and press exercises will help you burn fat and accelerate strength gain simultaneously.

Summary

Controlled-Fatigue Training was designed for individuals interested in maximizing their true physical potential. The purpose of this workout routine goes beyond losing fat or gaining muscles—it provides the basis for developing a functional body. Following this exercise routine, you may notice how your body's proportions are changing in a way that complements your functionality.

You may realize that having a heavy body isn't always a parameter for strength. A human body, first and foremost, is destined to be functional. From this aspect, being as light and mighty as one can be is an advantage. Being heavy is okay as long as one is able to effectively run, sprint, and jump. If any of these natural functions are compromised, then something must be wrong. CFT trains your body to resist fatigue under pressure, while gaining the capacity to sustain strength, speed, and explosive performance. It also takes advantage of the inherent synergy between different body movements and muscle groups.

Following this routine is a progressive method. As long as you follow the CFT principles, you can choose various exercises and combine them according to your personal needs. Trust your instincts. Be creative. More information about CFT beginner and advanced training is available at www.warriordiet.com.

Workout and Diet

It takes some time to adjust to exercising on an empty stomach. I've already discussed the advantages of such a strategy as far as fat-burning efficiency and hormonal manipulation. Nonetheless, there is also a connection between your last big meal (the night before) and your performance. Those who practice carb depletion (high-protein, low-carbs or extreme detox) may need to reduce the pre-fatigue component as well as the volume of Controlled-Fatigue Training on days following a low-carb diet. Those who practice carb-loading (high-carb meals) will likely find it easier to perform controlled-fatigue training. Those on high-fat days may initially compromise on their endurance, but over time they will most likely overcompensate and be able to supercharge their energy levels to endure prolonged intense drills without "hitting the wall." I recommend cycling between days of low carbs and days of high carbs (or high fat), and to cycle accordingly training days without pre-fatigue exercise and training days with pre-fatigue exercise. Another option is to cycle between sheer resistance days and days of CFT. I want to mention again how important it is that you use your instincts in planning each workout day. Only you know what's best for you.

Women Who Follow the Warrior Workout

Women are generally smaller than men; they have different needs, and as a result, different priorities. Some women may ask themselves, "What do all these workout principles, based on macho-like moves such as slashing, stabbing, swinging, or punching, have to do with me?" The answer is that all the exercises outlined here are essential to create a truly functional body. You may choose to skip these aggressive moves, but why give up the chance to build a truly functional body?

The exercise routine outlined in this chapter mimics the impact of fight or flight activities without actually doing them. I assume that some women, especially those engaged in martial arts, will have no problem with CFT's masculine connotations—or, for that matter, the concept of this book.

My suggestion for women who want to follow the CFT program is to make sure that the weights used can be handled all throughout the supersets (which constitute the core exercise of this routine).

Women generally like to work specifically on their legs and buttocks more often than men. I guess this is due to feminine self-awareness, and a desire to keep them in good shape. CFT pre-fatigue, core, and post-fatigue exercises constantly incorporate leg exercise, forcing improvement in the legs' functionality and muscularity. I highly suggest that women start pre-fatigue exercise with no weight. If you use nothing, make sure that your hands are positioned in the correct form. You'll be surprised how demanding this is.

If you'd like to accelerate the tension on your knees and butt, you can try to incorporate slow repetitive squats as post-fatigue exercise. When you squat, go slowly down for a count of 5 seconds, then pause for a couple of seconds on the bottom, then slowly rise up for another count of 5 seconds. To maximize even further the tension on your knees and butt, try to freeze and pause for 10–15 seconds in a low squat position. Keep your back arched at all times.

You can build strong, lean, and functional legs without using weights. Nonetheless, over time, when you feel stronger you can try to work your legs also with special resistance exercise.

As mentioned before, my best advice for you is to be creative and use your instincts to design a program that feels right for you.

CHAPTER 15

WARRIOR MEALS AND RECIPES

I'D LIKE TO THANK NATASHA, MY WIFE, for creating some of the Warrior Diet recipes and for improving others. I'm having the most fun of my life every night with my family while enjoying these homemade meals. The Warrior Meals are based on recipes and preparation methods that I have been using for years and have continually improved upon with the help of family and friends, as well as feedback from Warrior Diet followers.

For years I've cooked my own meals as part of my daily routine. I've found that when cooking, you treat yourself and those around you to something that satisfies a most basic primal need—nourishment.

Cooking is one way of being in control. In my opinion, it's a humane means of showing respect for yourself and your surroundings. Many of these meals closely mimic old warrior traditions of cooking. The purpose of the recipes included here is to help you prepare basic warrior meals. I believe they'll appeal to most people, but since everyone obviously has different tastes, I encourage you to be creative and feel free to tweak them.

All that said, let me note here that there is no mandatory obligation for cooking in order to practice the Warrior Diet. But I highly recommend trying it. When you cook your own meals, you become more in tune with yourself and with the food you're eating—and this will enhance your sense of pleasure and satisfaction.

The recipes here are unique to the Warrior Diet. Most aren't available anywhere (that I know of). I haven't explained how to boil eggs, make salads, cook rice, or steam vegetables since I believe this is common knowledge. Serving sizes and calories per meal are also not included, since they depend on individual needs.

Almost all of the following recipes were featured in the first edition of this book. However, my food choices have changed since that time. One of the changes is that I no longer eat meat. This is partly because (as noted previously) I strongly believe that humans aren't well adapted to eating meat, but mostly because of humane reasons. In any case, I chose to keep the recipes containing meat, since in general this section of the book has proven useful to people learning about the Warrior Diet.

Meats

Animal and marine food, including beef, chicken, and fish, should be cooked in a way that mimics the ancient warrior tradition of cooking in broth—with different herbs and spices to enhance flavor and aroma. I highly recommended rotating among beef, veal, chicken, and fish. Also, through trial and error, you'll learn what works best for you.

As noted in "The Overeating Phase" and "Lessons from History" chapters, cooking meats in liquids is healthier than frying, grilling, or even baking. Moreover, when cooking in liquids, the meat becomes soft and tender, while absorbing all the flavors of the herbs, spices, and veggies in the broth. When these meals are fully cooked, you can try shredding the meat with a fork and then add some essential oil and lecithin on top.

This way, you'll enjoy a soft, mushy, delicious protein meal, which ideally will provide a great deal of pleasure as well as nourishment—the old-fashioned way.

While reading this chapter, you may realize that some traditional ethnic dishes, such as bouillabaisse, paella, gumbo, and stews, closely resemble traditional warrior meals.

I recommend that you add essential fatty acids (oils) and lecithin on top of meals just before eating. It enriches the nutritional composition of the food and, in my opinion, enhances flavor. Some people, however, may find their taste too strong. Although these additions are optional, they are nonetheless essential to have in your diet, especially the EFA.

Curry Chicken in Spicy Tomato Broth

1½ pounds boneless, skinless chicken breast, cut into medium-sized chunks
1 can stewed tomatoes, chopped (or crushed tomatoes)
1 can fat-free chicken broth
3 cloves garlic
½ small onion
1 bay leaf
1 tablespoon curry powder

1 tablespoon turmeric powder
1 tablespoon dried parsley
¾ teaspoon dried basil
¾ teaspoon dried oregano
¾ teaspoon dried cumin
¼ teaspoon ground coriander
Salt and pepper to taste
Garnish with ½ cup coarsely chopped cilantro

Clean and wash chicken with filtered water.

In a large Pyrex bowl (with oven-safe cover) mix all ingredients, excluding the cilantro.

Marinate chicken in the bowl (with cover on) overnight in the refrigerator. Marinating overnight is optional.

Preheat oven to 375° F. Cook for one hour in a Pyrex bowl with an oven-safe cover.

Serve garnished with chopped cilantro.

This meal goes very well with steamed carrots, zucchini, and broccoli. Starches that best complement this meal are mashed butternut squash, pumpkin, sweet potatoes, mashed potatoes, sweet yellow corn, and rice.

Fish and Eggplant in Curry Tomato Sauce

This meal is recommended for people interested in rapid weight loss.

1½ pounds white fish fillet (sole, flounder, turbot)
1 can diced or crushed tomatoes (14.5 ounces)
2 medium or large eggplants, peeled and cut into medium-sized chunks
1 tablespoon olive oil
3 cloves garlic
½ small onion (optional)
1 tablespoon curry powder
1 tablespoon caraway seeds (optional)
¾ teaspoon oregano
¾ teaspoon thyme
Salt and cayenne pepper to taste (optional)
½ cup chopped fresh cilantro or parsley for garnish

Prepare the sauce in a large Pyrex bowl (with cover). Mix all ingredients excluding the cilantro, parsley, and eggplant.

Clean and wash the fish fillet with filtered or spring water. Place the eggplant chunks in a steamer and cook until they are soft (about 15 minutes). Marinate the fish in the Pyrex bowl with the sauce.

Preheat oven to 375º F and cook the fish in the sauce for one hour. When done, remove from oven, add the steamed eggplant, and mash it all together with a fork. Garnish with chopped fresh cilantro or parsley.

This meal also mimics an old tradition of warrior cooking. You'll be surprised how large this dish looks; however, it's very light and delicious. Fish meals go very well with steamed carrots, broccoli, cauliflower, rice, millet, and corn.

Beef and Carrots in Chicken–Tomato Broth

1½ pounds trimmed natural lean beef (top round), cut into medium-sized chunks
1 large peeled carrot, cut into small medallions
1 can crushed tomatoes or tomato sauce
1 can fat-free chicken broth
3 cloves garlic
½ onion
1 teaspoon dried basil
¾ teaspoon dried oregano
1 tablespoon caraway seeds (optional)
Coarsely chopped parsley or cilantro as garnish

Clean and wash the meat with filtered or spring water. If you want the meat to be more tender, beat it with the bottom of one of your cooking pans. No joke! It'll make it softer and able to absorb more flavor from the broth.

In a large Pyrex bowl, mix all ingredients, excluding the parsley (or cilantro). Marinate the meat overnight in the refrigerator (optional).

Preheat oven to 375º F and cook for 1½ hours. Garnish with chopped parsley or cilantro. This meal goes very well with steamed broccoli, cauliflower, and zucchini, and for starches try mashed potatoes, mashed butternut squash, and sweet potatoes.

Eggs

Most egg meals take almost no time to prepare and cook, yet they're delicious and very nourishing. On days of being too busy, or just in the mood for a light protein meal, eggs can be a most viable choice, as well as a great alternative to meat or fish. Moreover, on egg days you can try indulging every once in a while in dairy foods as well. I believe eggs and cheese complement each other nicely. Egg meals can be well incorporated with either carb fuel (grains) or fat fuel (nuts and seeds).

Egg Omelet with Tomato Sauce (high-protein meal)

    16 egg whites with 3-4 yolks (for 2 servings)
    ¼ cup tomato sauce or crushed tomatoes
    ¼ small onion, diced (optional)
    1 tablespoon olive oil
    Salt and cayenne pepper to taste
    Garnish with chopped parsley or cilantro

Preheat olive oil in a large, deep skillet. Add diced onions and sear until browned. Slowly add tomato sauce, and mix with onions. When sauce is boiling, add the eggs. Scramble and mix the eggs while cooking.

When mixture thickens, remove from the stove, put in a large bowl, and cover. Garnish with the chopped parsley or cilantro.

Those people who like mushrooms can steam shiitake or portabella mushrooms, or sauté them in olive oil, and put them on top of the omelet. Or you can cook them with the omelet.

Egg omelets go very well with steamed zucchini, butternut squash, steamed pumpkin, sweet peas, and black bean soup, which you can also put on top of the omelet.

Egg Omelet with Black Beans (high-protein meal)

This is the same preparation as the egg-white omelet with tomato sauce, only here you use black bean soup instead of tomato sauce. You can use a half can of organic black bean soup, which is available in most health-food stores and supermarkets.

Egg Omelet with Lentil and Bean Chili (high-protein meal)

This is the same preparation as the other omelets, only here you use a half can of organic chili, which is available in most health-food stores and supermarkets

Oatmeal and Eggs (high-carbohydrate meal)

I used to eat this meal years ago, when I was a student. This was one of my so-called "poor man meals," since my budget at that time was very limited. Regardless, I always enjoyed it, and still do.

2-3 cups oatmeal (rolled oats or steel-cut oats)
6-12 egg whites with 2-4 yolks
¼ teaspoon turmeric (optional)
¼ teaspoon cumin (optional)
Salt and pepper to taste
½ cup coarsely chopped cilantro for garnish

If you choose steel-cut oats, soak them overnight in purified, steam-distilled, or spring water (to cut down on cooking time).

Fill a large pot with 4–5 cups water and bring to a boil. Add oatmeal and spices. Rolled oats need half the time that steel-cut oats need. Check the preparation instructions on the box.

Reduce heat and let it cook until almost done. Make sure you stir it to avoid clumping. When you notice that very little water is left, add the eggs and slowly mix it all together while still cooking. Once the eggs are thickening, turn the stove off, cover the pot, and let it simmer for a couple of minutes. Garnish with cilantro and serve.

This meal goes very well with buttermilk or kefir, which will supply additional protein to this high-carbohydrate meal, as well as beneficial bacteria. They can be used as a cool sauce you put on top. Oatmeal and eggs also go well with steamed broccoli and cauliflower.

If you'd like to make this dish spicy, you can add curry or cumin. It can also be garnished with scallions or chopped onions. Use your imagination. With trial and error, you'll find what's best for you.

Rice 'n' Eggs (high-carbohydrate meal)

This was my second favorite meal during my student days. Once you taste it, you'll realize that a poor man's meal isn't necessarily poor. It is, in fact, rich in flavor and nutrients.

2 cups uncooked brown rice or, if accessible, sweet brown rice. If you prefer, use white rice instead (sushi rice is best).
1 clove chopped garlic
½ teaspoon curry
½ teaspoon cumin
½ teaspoon basil
6-12 egg whites and 2-4 yolks
Chopped cilantro, onions, or scallions as garnish

Rinse the rice with purified water. In a large pot, add 4 cups of water with the garlic and spices. Bring to a boil. Stir in the rice, reduce heat, cover, and simmer until water is almost absorbed. Add the eggs and mix it with the rice while it's still cooking. When the eggs start to thicken with the mixture, remove from the stove, cover, and let sit for a few minutes. Garnish with cilantro, onions, or scallions and serve. This meal goes very well with cucumber and dill salad. It also goes well with black bean soup that can be used as a sauce on top of the meal. Those who like to experiment can try grated Parmesan cheese on top, or goat cheese as a side dish.

Angel Hair Rice Pasta with Eggs (high-carbohydrate meal)

1 package of angel hair rice pasta
½ to 1 can tomato sauce
2 cloves crushed garlic
¾ teaspoon dried basil
¾ teaspoon dried oregano
6-12 egg whites and 2-4 yolks
Salt and pepper to taste
Parsley or cilantro as garnish

Cook pasta until done. Drain and place the pasta in a large bowl. Mix tomato sauce, garlic, and spices in a large pot and cook on medium-high heat. Add pasta. When hot, add the eggs and mix it all together. When eggs start to thicken, remove from the stove and serve, garnished with cilantro.

You can opt to prepare pasta and eggs without the tomato. In this case, use olive oil as a base to simmer the pasta and eggs in a large, deep pan or pot. Pasta and eggs, done without tomatoes, can be served with buttermilk or kefir as a cool sauce on top of this hot meal. It also goes very well with steamed carrots, zucchini, or broccoli.

If you'd like to increase the amount of protein in this meal, you can add low-fat, organic cottage cheese on the side, or goat cheese on top.

Baked and Grilled Meals

Once in a while, especially when friends are coming over, my wife prepares grilled meats or fish. These meals are more than delicious. They're awesome. Grilling isn't the preferred way to cook on a daily basis. However, when you marinate meat or fish before grilling, you reduce the risk of burning or caramelizing the protein. Further, adding herbs like basil, oregano, and thyme, in addition to improving taste, mimics an old tradition of curing meats while enhancing flavors. Most herbs contain healing properties. For instance, thyme and oregano are believed to have antibacterial and antiviral properties; turmeric is a powerful antioxidant and anti-cancerous agent; and as discussed earlier, parsley is a powerful detoxifier.

Grilled Chicken

    2 packages of boneless, skinless chicken thighs
    Juice of two lemons
    3 large cloves garlic
    1 small onion
    1 tablespoon Dijon mustard
    1 tablespoon fresh thyme (leaves only, not the stem)
    1 tablespoon fresh oregano
    1 tablespoon fresh parsley
    2 tablespoons fresh basil
    3 tablespoons olive oil
    Salt and pepper to taste

Combine garlic, onion, mustard, thyme, oregano, parsley, basil, and olive oil in a food processor. Pulse until all ingredients are finely chopped. Season with salt and pepper to taste. Set aside in the fridge for approximately 45 minutes to an hour.

To prepare the chicken for outdoor grilling:

Wash and clean chicken thoroughly. In a bowl combine lemon juice and the mustard mixture with the chicken. Mix well. Let it sit in the fridge for 30 minutes, or until ready to grill. If you don't want to grill, the broiler works fine, too.

Grill for approximately 15 minutes on each side on a low to medium flame (check sooner if you're broiling). Just make sure the chicken juices run clear.

Baked Red Snapper

    1 medium whole red snapper
    2 large onions, sliced
    3 ripe tomatoes sliced
    5 lemons
    4 cloves garlic, finely chopped
    3 tablespoons olive oil
    Salt and pepper to taste

Make sure the fish is properly cleaned of all scales. Preheat oven to 375º F.

Place ⅓ of the onion and tomato slices on the bottom of a baking pan. Sprinkle a portion of the garlic on the onion and tomatoes. Squeeze the juice of one lemon.

Before placing fish on the onion and tomatoes, rub fish with salt and pepper. Stuff ⅓ of the onion, tomato, and garlic inside the belly of the snapper. Place the remaining onion, tomato, and garlic on top of the snapper. Take one lemon; cut into slices and spread over the top of fish. Squeeze the remaining lemon on top. Drizzle olive oil over the fish.

Cover with aluminum foil. Cook 40–50 minutes (depending on the size of the fish). To test for doneness, poke fish with a fork—the meat should be flaky.

Soups

Soups are great appetizers. In addition to introducing different tastes, smells, textures, and aromas, they can be highly nutritious and nourishing. Having a soup at the beginning of a meal may help balance cravings and enhance the overall feeling of satisfaction.

Soups can also be the basis for a whole meal. As noted, by combining meat, fish, or eggs with beans, and occasionally with carbs such as potatoes, rice, or barley in the broth, you can create a whole, delicious, nutritious meal in the traditional way.

Potato–Onion Tomato Soup

    2 pounds potatoes, peeled and cut into chunks
    1 35-ounce can plum tomatoes with juice, coarsely chopped (total of 4 cups)
    1 quart chicken stock
    ½ teaspoon coarse sea salt
    ¼ teaspoon freshly ground black pepper
    3 tablespoons extra virgin olive oil
    4 medium onions, thinly sliced

In a four- to six-quart non-aluminum saucepan, combine the potatoes, tomatoes, and chicken stock. Season with salt and pepper. Bring to a boil, then reduce heat and simmer gently, partly covered. Stir occasionally, for one and a half hours, or until tender.

Meanwhile, in a skillet, warm olive oil over medium heat and sauté the onions until translucent.

To finish soup, break up potatoes, mashing slightly with a wooden spoon. Add onions to tomato-potato mixture, and simmer together for 5 minutes, stirring occasionally. Add chicken stock as necessary to slightly thin out the soup. Garnish and serve with fresh basil.

Miso Soup

Miso is made from unpasteurized fermented soybeans. Miso soup is high in minerals and is a great alkalizer. Miso, unlike processed soy foods, is also believed to be highly nutritious, with anti-radiation protective properties. It's rich in enzymes and lactic acid-producing bacteria—which is highly beneficial for digestion and elimination.

1 tablespoon miso paste (from organic unpasteurized fermented soy)
½ small onion
½ ounce dried wakame or nori seaweed (optional)
2 cups purified or spring water

In a medium pot, combine all ingredients. Bring everything except the miso paste to a boil for 5 minutes, then add the paste. Serve warm.

Desserts

The Warrior Desserts can be great alternatives to sugar-loaded commercial or homemade treats that are high in saturated fat, There aren't many desserts listed here. However, in my opinion, you'll be better off enjoying the taste of a few healthy delicious desserts that will nourish and provide you with a great sense of pleasure than trying a variety of popular desserts and sweets which usually leave you sluggish, bloated, and heavier, not to mention the obvious guilt.

Pumpkin Cheesecake

1 teaspoon ground cinnamon
½ teaspoon ground ginger
Pinch of ground nutmeg
Pinch of salt (optional)
½ teaspoon vanilla extract
2 whole eggs
4 egg whites
¼ to ½ cup maple syrup (adjust sweetness according to taste)
1 15-ounce can organic pumpkin

15 ounces nonfat ricotta cheese (or farmer cheese)
4 ounces fat-free cream cheese

You can substitute organic low-fat cottage cheese for the listed cheeses. However, this will change the texture of the cake slightly.

Combine cinnamon, ginger, nutmeg, and salt (optional) in a small bowl. Set aside.

Lightly beat vanilla, eggs, and maple syrup in a small bowl. Set aside.

In a food processor, combine pumpkin and cheese until smooth. Alternate adding egg mixture and spice mixture to the pumpkin and cheese mixture. (If you don't have a food processor, a blender will work, but mix eggs first, then gradually add pumpkin mixture.) Mix well, approximately 3 minutes.

Bake in a preheated 425° F oven for 15 minutes. Reduce temperature to 350° F. Bake for 40–50 minutes or until a knife inserted near the center comes out clean. Cool on a baking rack for about 2 hours. Serve room temperature or chilled. Do not freeze; freezing causes the filling to separate.

Pumpkin cheesecake tastes so good that, unfortunately, it disappears too quickly. It's like an open invitation for a binge.

The sweetness can be adjusted according to your taste. It goes very well with organic yogurt or low-fat sour cream. As you can see, this dessert is high in protein, low in fat, and relatively low in carbs. It's also highly nutritious, supplying you with abundant carotenes and soft fiber.

Crepe Blintzes

1 egg
8 ounces low-fat cottage cheese (small curds)
1 teaspoon vanilla extract
Pure maple syrup to taste
1 package prepared crepes
Cooking spray (butter-flavored)

Preheat oven to 350° F.

Combine cottage cheese, egg, vanilla, and maple syrup in a small bowl. Take individual crepe, place on a flat surface, and spoon one and a half tablespoons of cottage cheese onto the center. Fold all four sides together to secure cottage cheese mixture. Place each crepe on a nonstick cookie sheet, folded side down. Repeat until cottage cheese mixture is finished. Spray each crepe with butter-flavored spray.

Bake in oven 5–8 minutes, until slightly brown. Serve warm with Live Berries.

Live Berries Dessert

    1 cup blackberries
    1 cup sliced strawberries
    1 cup raspberries
    1 cinnamon stick
    Pure maple syrup to taste (enough to cover berries)

Combine all ingredients in a small bowl and place in fridge 3–4 hours to chill (may remain in fridge overnight). Serve over warm crepe blintzes. Live Berries can also be served over yogurt.

This is a meal with total appeal: a feast that screams calories but really is a bounty of low-fat, low-cal goodness. Enjoy!

Milk Gelatin Dessert

I began making this treat years ago. Surprisingly, it has turned out to be one of my favorites. Milk Gelatin is a good complement to the fruits and veggies you consume during the day while you go through the Undereating Phase. It's most useful to eat this on an empty stomach.

    1-2 tablespoons organic nonfat milk powder
    1-2 teaspoons brown rice syrup (adjust sweetness according to taste)
    1 packet unflavored (if available, kosher vegetarian) gelatin
    1-2 cups filtered or spring water (*Check instructions on the gelatin box regarding amount of water to add, but feel free to alter depending on level of density desired.*)
    3 tablespoons cool or cold water
    2 tablespoons hot water
    Vanilla extract to taste (approx. 1/8 teaspoon)
    Approximately 3-10 crushed organic almonds (optional)
    1-2 tablespoons minced, organic, unsulfured, unsweetened coconut (optional)

In a small bowl, mix the milk powder, brown rice syrup, and 1 tablespoon of cool water until it turns into a thick paste. Set aside.

To prepare gelatin:

Mix gelatin in another small bowl with 2 tablespoons of cool or cold water. When it turns into a gummy paste, add 2 more tablespoons of hot water and mix. Combine gelatin mixture with milk paste and then place it in a blender with 2 cups of water. Blend for one minute. Pour mixture into several cups or one large bowl. Refrigerate for a couple of hours until it turns into gelatin form.

You can opt to add more milk powder to make the mixture thicker or more dense. You can also blend a few crushed almonds with the mixture if you want to add texture. And you can do the same with minced coconut, or else sprinkle it on top once you've poured the completed mixture into a bowl or cups. When it's ready, Milk Gelatin becomes a three-layered treat with a light, white foam on top. It's quite unique. I hope you'll like it.

Papaya Gelatin Dessert

This dessert is good for digestion and detoxification. It can also be consumed as a delicious light treat during the Undereating Phase. Gelatin is a natural source of silicon and proteoglycans, which support your skin, hair, nails, and connective tissues. It's also a great detoxifying agent. Papaya contains digestive enzymes. When eaten on an empty stomach, Papaya Gelatin Dessert soothes your hunger while helping to eliminate toxins, fat, and cholesterol from your intestines.

1 packet unflavored (if available, kosher vegetarian) gelatin, which is equivalent to 1 level tablespoon

1 cup papaya puree (no sugar added). This is sold in glass juice bottles in some health food stores and supermarkets. Or you can puree a fresh papaya yourself. Peel, remove seeds, and cut papaya. Place papaya slices in a blender with a little water and blend until pureed.

½ cup hot water (filtered or spring water)

3 tablespoons cool or cold water

2 tablespoons hot water

1 teaspoon maple syrup (optional)

1 tablespoon minced organic unsulfured, unsweetened coconut (optional)

Heat water on stove. Meanwhile, mix gelatin with 2 tablespoons of cool or cold water in a small bowl. When it turns into a gummy paste, add 2 tablespoons of hot water and mix again. Pour this mixture plus 1 cup of papaya puree (per packet of gelatin puree) and the half cup of hot water into a blender. Blend for 30 seconds or so. Pour mixture into glass cups or a large bowl. Refrigerate for a couple of hours until it turns into "Jell-O" form. Enjoy!

You can also blend 1 tablespoon of minced coconut to the mixture if you want to add texture, or sprinkle it on top once you've poured the completed mixture into a bowl or cups.

Warm Raspberries and Yogurt

This is a wonderful dessert that combines and polarizes sweet and sour, warm and cold tastes. It's delicious and can also be used as a nourishing treat during the Undereating Phase.

1 cup fresh or frozen raspberries
1 teaspoon honey or maple syrup
1 cup organic, nonfat plain yogurt

In a small pot, add raspberries and honey (or maple syrup). Turn on the stove to a medium heat and stir. When the mixture turns fluid and begins to boil, reduce the heat and simmer for a few minutes.

Take off heat and set aside for a minute. Put yogurt in a small bowl. Slowly pour the warm berries on top of the yogurt. Enjoy!

Note: You can substitute blueberries or blackberries for the raspberries. Adjust the sweetness according to your taste.

REFERENCES

Airola, P. *Every Woman's Book.* Sherwood, OR: Health Plus Publishers, 1979.

Diamond, J. *Guns, Germs, and Steel: The Fates of Human Societies.* New York and London: Norton, 1999.

Dupont, F. *Daily Life in Ancient Rome.* Malden, MA, and Oxford, UK: Blackwell, 1993.

Erasmus, U. *Fats That Heal, Fats That Kill.* Burnaby, BC, Canada: Alive Books, 1986, 1993.

Erdkamp, P. *Hunger and the Sword.* Amsterdam: Gieben, 1998.

Garnsey, P. *Cities, Peasants, and Food in Classical Antiquity.* Cambridge, UK: Cambridge University Press.

Giacosa, I.G. *A Taste of Ancient Rome.* Chicago and London: University of Chicago Press, 1992.

Hamilton, E. *Mythology.* Massada Ltd. Israel, 1982 [[There is probably a Penguin version of this published in the US—I read it in college]]

Jensen, B. *Foods That Heal.* New York: Avery, 1988, 1993.

Karch, B. *Herbal Medicine.* Hauppauge, NY: Advanced Research Press, 1999.

Murray, M.T. *Encyclopedia of Nutritional Supplements.* Roseville, CA: Prima Health, 1996.

Murray, M.T. *The Healing Power of Herbs.* Roseville, CA: Prima Health, 1992, 1995.

Plutarch. *Greeks.* Jerusalem: Bialik Institute, 1986.

Solomon, J. *Ancient Roman Feasts and Recipes Adapted For Modern Cooking.* Miami: Seemann Publications, 1977.

Spark, R. *Sexual Health for Men.* New York: Perseus Books, 2000.

Additional Research References:

Andriamampandry, M.D., et al., Centre d'Ecologie et Physiologie Energetiques, Strasbourg, France. "Food deprivation modifies fatty acid partitioning and betaoxidation capacity in rat liver." *J Nutr* 126(8): 2020–27 (Aug 1996).

Anson, R.M., Guo, Z., de Cabo, R., Iyun, T., Rios, M., Hagepanos, A., Ingram, D.K., Lane, M.A., and Mattson, M.P. "Intermittent fasting dissociates beneficial effects of dietary restriction on glucose metabolism and neuronal resistance to injury from calorie intake." Laboratory of Neurosciences, Gerontology Research Center, National Institute on Aging, 2003.

Beck, B., Stricker-Krongrad, A., Burlet, A., Nicolas, J.P., and Burlet, C. "Specific hypothalamic neuropeptide Y variation with diet parameters in rats with food choice." *Neuroreport* 3(7): 571–74 (July 1992).

Benthem, L., van der Leest, J., Steffens, A.B., Zijlstra, W.G., Department of Medical Physiology, University of Groningen, The Netherlands. "Metabolic and hormonal responses to adrenoceptor antagonists in 48-hour-starved exercising rats." *Metabolism* 44(10): 1332–39 (Oct 1995).

Bereket, A., Wilson, T.A., Kolasa, A.J., Fan, J., and Lang, C.H., Department of Pediatrics, State University of New York, Stony Brook. "Regulation of the insulin-like growth factor system by acute acidosis." *Endocrinology* 137(6): 2238–45 (June 1996).

Bergstrom, J., Hermansen, L., Hultman, E., and Saltin, B. "Diet, muscle glycogen and physical performance." *Acta Physiol Scand* 71: 140–50 (1967).

Bogardus, C., LaGrange, B.M., Horton, E.S., and Sims, E.A. "Comparison of carbohydrate-containing and carbohydrate-restricted hypocaloric diets in the treatment of obesity" and "Endurance and metabolic fuel homeostasis during strenuous exercise." *J Clin Invest* 68(2): 399–404 (August 1981).

Bravo, L. "Polyphenols: chemistry, dietary sources, metabolism, and nutritional significance." *Nutr Rev* 56: 317–33 (1998).

Brun, S., et al., Departamento de Bioquimica y Biologia Molecular, Universitat de Barcelona, Spain. "Uncoupling protein-3 gene expression in skeletal muscle during development is regulated by nutritional factors that alter circulating non-esterified fatty acids." *FEBS Lett* 453(1-2): 205–209 (June 18, 1999).

Cai, X.J., et al. "Hypothalamic orexin expression: modulation by blood glucose and feeding." Diabetes 48(11): 2132-37 (Nov 1999).

Campbell, D.R., and Kurzer, M.S. "Flavonoid inhibition of aromatase enzyme activity in human preadipocytes." *J Steroid Biochem Mol Biol* 46: 381–88 (1993).

Carreau, S., Lambard, S., Delalande, C., Denis-Galeraud, I., Bilinska, B., and Bourguiba, S. "Aromatase expression and role of estrogens in male gonad: a review." *Reprod Biol Endocrinol* 1: 35 (2003).

Cassidy, A. "Physiological effects of phyto-oestrogens in relation to cancer and other human health risks." *Proc Nutr Soc* 55: 399–417 (1996).

Chorazy, P.A., Himelhoch, S., Hopwood, N.J., Greger, N.G., and Postellon. D.C. "Persistent hypothyroidism in an infant receiving a soy formula: case report and review of the literature." *Pediatrics* 96: 148–50 (1995).

Clark, M.G., et al. "Hypertension in obesity may reflect a homeostatic thermo-genic response." *Life Sci* 48(10): 939–47 (1991).

Coleman, E. "Carbohydrates: the master fuel." In: *Sports Nutrition for the '90s*, eds. J.R. Berning and S.N. Stenn. Aspen Publishers, 1991.

Conlee, R.E. "Muscle glycogen and exercise endurance: a twenty-year perspective." *Exercise and Sports Science Reviews* 15: 1–28 (1987).

Constantinou, A., Kiguchi, K., and Huberman, E. "Induction of differentiation and strand breakage in human HL-60 and K-562 leukemia cells by genistein." *Cancer Res* 50: 2618–24 (1990).

Costill, D.L., Sherman, W.M., Fink, W.W.J., Witten, M.W., and Miller, J.M. "The role of dietary carbohydrates in muscle glycogen resynthesis after strenuous running." *Am J Clin Nutr* 34: 1831–36 (1981).

Cotroneo, M.S., and Lamartiniere, C.A. "Pharmacologic, but not dietary, genistein supports endometriosis in a rat model." *J Toxicol Sci* 61: 68–75 (2001).

Covasa, M., and Ritter, R.C. "Rats maintained on high-fat diets exhibit reduced satiety in response to CCK and bombesin." *Peptides* 19(8): 1407–15 (1998).

Dauchy, R.T., Dauchy, E.M., Sauer, L.A., Blask, D.F., Davidson, L.K., Krause, J.A., and Lynch, D.T. "Differential inhibition of fatty acid transport in tissue-iso-lated steroid receptor negative human breast cancer xenografts perfused in situ with isomers of conjugated linoleic acid." *Cancer Lett* 209 (1): 7–15 (2004).

Deferrari, G., Garibotto, G., Robaudo, C., Saffioti, S., Russo, R., and Sofia, A., Department of Internal Medicine, University of Genoa, Italy. "Protein and amino acid metabolism in splanchnic organs in metabolic acidosis." *Miner Electrolyte Metab* 1997; 23(3&-6): 229–33.

Divi, R.L., Chang, H.C., and Doerge, D.R. "Anti-thyroid isoflavones from soybean isolation, characterization, and mechanisms of action." *Biochem Pharmacol* 54: 1087–96 (1997).

Dulloo, A.G., Jacquet, J., and Girardier, L., University of Geneva, Switzerland. "Autoregulation of body composition during weight recovery in human: the Minnesota Experiment revisited." *Int J Obes Relat Metab Disord* 20(5): 393–405 (May 1996).

Evans, S.J., Lo, H.C., Ney, D.M., and Welbourne, T.C., Department of Nutritional Sciences, University of Wisconsin. "Acid-base homeostasis parallels anabolism in surgically stressed rats treated with GH and IGF-I." *Am J Physiol* 270(6 Pt 1): E968–74 (June 1996).

Forslund, A.H., et al., Department of Medical Sciences and Nutrition, Uppsala University, Uppsala, Sweden. "Effect of protein intake and physical activity on 24-h pattern and rate of macronutrient utilization." *Am J Physiol* 276(5 Pt 1): E964–76 (May 1999).

Gaullier, J.M., Halse, J., Hoye, K., Kristiansen, K., Fagertun, H., Vik, H., and Gudmundsen, O. "Conjugated linoleic acid supplementation for 1 y reduces body fat mass in healthy overweight humans." *Am J Clin Nutr* 79(6): 1118–25 (2004).

Hagan, M.M., Havel, P.J., Seely, R.J., Woods, S.C., Ekhator, N.N., et al., Department of Psychiatry, University of Cincinnati College of Medicine. "Cerebrospinal fluid and plasma leptin measurements: covariability with dopamine and cortisol in fasting humans." *J Clin Endocrinol Metab* 84(10): 3579–85 (Oct 1999).

Heinz, Rupp, PhD. "Hypercaloric nutrition, sympathetic activity and hypertension." Editorial to the Symposium "The Excess Catecholamine Syndrome. From Cause To Therapy."

Hocman, G. "Prevention of cancer: restriction of nutritional energy intake (joules)." *Comp Biochem Physiol A* 91(2): 209–20 (1988).

Holness, M.J., and Sugden, M.C., Department of Biochemistry, London Hospital Medical College, UK. "Pyruvate dehydrogenase activities and rates of lipogenesis during the fed-to-starved transition in liver and brown adipose tissue of the rat." *Biochem J* 268(1): 77–81 (May 15, 1990).

Ibrahim, A.R., and Abul-Haij, Y.J. "Aromatase inhibition by flavonoids." *J Steroid Biochem Mol Biol* 37: 257–60 (1990).

Isidori, A.M., et al. "Leptin and androgens in male obesity: evidence for leptin contribution to reduced androgen levels." *J Clin Endocrinol Metab* 84(10): 3673–80 (Oct 1999).

Jassim, S.A., and Naji, M.A. "Novel antiviral agents: a medicinal plant perspective." *J Appl Microbiol* 95: 412–27 (2003).

Jones, B.S., Yeaman, S.J., Sugden, M.C., and Holness, M.J., Department of Biochemistry and Genetics, Medical School, University of New Castle-upon-

Tyne, UK. "Hepatic pyruvate dehydrogenase kinase activities during the starved-to-fed transition." *Biochim Biophys Acta* 1134(2): 164–68 (March 16, 1992).

Ju, Y.H., Allred, C.D., Allred, K.F., Karko, K.L., Doerge, D.R., and Helferich, W.G. "Physiological concentrations of dietary genistein dose-dependently stimulate growth of estrogen-dependent human breast cancer (MCF-7) tumors implanted in athymic nude mice." *J Nutr* 131: 2957–62 (2001).

Jungestrom, M.B., Thompson, L.U., and Dabrosin, C. "Flaxseed and its lignans inhibit estradiol-induced growth, angiogenesis, and secretion of vascular endothelial growth factor in human breast cancer xenografts in vivo." *Clin Cancer Res* 13: 1061–67 (2007).

Kao, Y.C., Zhou, C., Sherman, M., Laughton, C.A., and Chen, S. "Molecular basis of the inhibition of human aromatase (estrogen synthetase) by flavone and isoflavone phytoestrogens: A site-directed mutagenesis study." *Environ Health Perspect* 10685–92 (1998).

Kersten, S., et al., Institute de Biologie Animale, Universite de Lausanne, Switzerland. Department de Physiologie, Faculte de Medecine, Universite de Geneve, Laboratory of Metabolism, National Cancer Institute. "Peroxisome proliferator-activated receptor alpha mediates the adaptive response to fasting." *J Clin Invest* 103(11): 1489–98 (June 1999).

Kuppusamy, U.R., and Das, N.P. "Effects of flavonoids on cyclic AMP phosphodiesterase and lipid mobilization in rat adipocytes." *Biochem Pharmacol* 44: 1307–15 (1992).

Lambert, E.V., et al. "Enhanced endurance in trained cyclists during moderate intensity exercise following 2 weeks adaptation to a high-fat diet." *Eur J Apply Phyiol* 69: 387–93 (1994).

Levin, B.E., and Sullivan, A.C. "Regulation of thermogenesis in obesity." *Int J Obes* 8 Suppl 1:159–80 (1984).

Ludwig, D.S., et al. "High glycemic index foods, overeating, and obesity." *Pediatrics* 103(3): E26 (March 1999).

Marti, A., Berraondo, B., and Martinez, J.A. "Leptin: physiological actions." *J Physiol Biochem* 55(1): 43–49 (March 1999).

Mattson, M. "The need for controlled studies of the effects of meal frequency on health." *Lancet* 365: 1978–80 (2005).

Metabolism 32(8): 769–76 (Aug 1983).

Middleton, E., Jr. "Effect of plant flavonoids on immune and inflammatory cell function." *Adv Exp Med Biol* 439: 175–82 (1998).

Minassian, C., Montana, S., and Mithieux, G. "Regulatory role of glucose-6 phosphatase in the repletion of liver glycogen during refeeding in fasted rats." *Biochim Biophys Acta* 1452(2): 172–78 (Nov 11, 1999).

Moore, N.P. "The oestrogenic potential of the phthalate esters." *Reprod Toxicol* 14:183–92 (2000).

Moral, R., Russo, J., Balogh, G.A., Mailo, D.A., Russo, I.H., and Lamartiniere, C. "Compounds in plastic packaging acts as environmental estrogens altering breast genes." *96th Annual Meeting of the American Association for Cancer Research* (2005).

Munro, I.C., Harwood, M., Hlywka, J.J., Stephen, A.M., Doull, J., Flamm, W.G., and Adlercreutz, H. "Soy isoflavones: a safety review." *Nutr Rev* 61 (1): 1–33 (2003).

Newby, F.D., Wilson, L.K., Thacker, S.V., and DiGirolamo. M., Department of Medicine, Emory University School of Medicine. "Adipocyte lactate production remains elevated during refeeding after fasting." *Am J Physiol* 259(6 Pt 1): E865-71 (Dec 1990).

Nutrition Department, University of California, Davis. "Effective nutritional ergogenic aids." *Int J Sport Nutr* 9(2): 229–39 (June 1999).

O'Dea, K., et al. "Noradrenaline turnover during under- and over-eating in normal weight subjects." *Metabolism* 31(9): 896–99 (Sept 1982).

Ogihara, H., et al., Gunma University School of Medicine, Maebashi, Japan. "Peptide transporter in the rat small intestine: ultrastructural localization and the effect of starvation and administration of amino acids." *Histochem J* 31(3): 169–74 (March 1999).

Oh, Y.S., Lee, H.S., Cho, H.J., Lee, S.G., Jung, K.C., and Park, J.H. "Conjugated linoleic acid inhibits DNA synthesis and induces apoptosis in TSU-Pr1 human bladder cancer cells." *Anticancer Res* 23 (6C): 4765–72 (2003).

Pelissero, C., Lenczowski, M.J., Chinzi, D., Davail-Cuisset, B., Sumpter, J.P., and Fostier, A. "Effects of flavonoids on aromatase activity, an in vitro study." *J Steroid Biochem Mol Bio* 57: 215–23 (1996).

Phinney, S. "Exercise during and after very low-calorie dieting." *Am J Clin Nutr* 56: 190S–94S (1992).

Phinney, S.D., et al. "Effects of aerobic exercise on energy expenditure and nitrogen balance during very low-calorie dieting." *Metabolism* 37: 758–65 (1988).

Phinney, S.D., Bistrian, B.R., Evans, W.J., Gervino, E., and Blackburn, G.L. "The human metabolic response to chronic ketosis without caloric restriction: preservation of submaximal exercise capability with reduced oxidation." *Metabolism* 32: 769–76 (1983).

Plata-Salaman, C.R. "Regulation of hunger and satiety in man." *Dig Dis* 9(5): 253–68 (1991).

Radomski, M.W., Cross, M., and Buguet, A., Defense and Civil Institute of Environmental Medicine, North York, ON, Canada. "Exercise-induced hyperthermia and hormonal responses to exercise." *Can J Physiol Pharmacol* 76(5): 547–52 (May 1998).

Recchia, A.G., Vivacqua, A., Gabriele, S., Carpino, A., Fasanella, G., Rago, V., Bonofiglio, D., and Maggiolini, M. "Xenoestrogens and the induction of proliferative effects in breast cancer cells via direct activation of oestrogen receptor alpha." *Food Additives & Contaminants* 21: 134–44 (2004).

Reuters. "Mice That Overexpress Human UCP-3 Eat More Yet Weigh Less Than Wild-Type Mice." July 27, 2000.

Samec, S., Seydoux, J., and Dulloo, A.G. "Inter-organ signaling between adipose tissue metabolism and skeletal muscle uncoupling protein homologs: is there a role for circulating free fatty acids?" *Diabetes* 47(11): 1693–98 (November 1998).

Sandberg, P.R. "Carbohydrate loading and deploying forces." Bravo Company, 2nd Battalion, 3rd Special Forces Group (Airborne), Fort Bragg, NC 28307. *Mil Med* 164(9): 636–42 (Sept 1999).

Sanderson, J.T., Hordijk, J., Denison, M.S., Springsteel, M.F., Nantz, M.H., and van den Ber, M. "Induction and inhibition of aromatase (CYP10) activity by natural and synthetic flavonoid compounds in H295R human adrenocortical carcinoma cells." *Toxicol Sci* 82: 70–79 (2004).

Schreihofer, D.A, Parfitt, D.B., and Cameron, J.L., Department of Behavioral Neuroscience, University of Pittsburgh, Pennsylvania. "Suppression of luteinizing hormone secretion during short-term fasting in male rhesus monkeys: the role of metabolic versus stress signals." *Endocrinology* 132(5): 1881–89 (May 1993).

Selvais, P.L., et al. "Cyclic feeding behavior and changes in hypothalamic galanin and neuropeptide Y gene expression induced by zinc deficiency in the rat." *J Neuroendocrinol* 9(1): 55–62 (January 1997).

Shafie, S., and Brooks, S. "Effect of prolactin on growth and the estrogen receptor level of breast cancer cells (MCF-7)." *Cancer Res* 37: 792–99 (1977).

Sherman, W.M., Coastal, D.J., Fink, W.J., and Miller, J.M. "Effect of exercise-diet manipulation on muscle glycogen supercompensation and its subsequent utilization during performance." *Int J Sports Med* 2: 114–18 (1981).

Sherman, W. "Carbohydrates, muscle glycogen, and muscle glycogen supercompensation." In: *Ergogenic Aids in Sports*, ed. M. Williams. Human Kinetics Publishers, 1983.

Singleton, D.W., Feng, Y., Chen, Y., Busch, S.J., Lee, A.V., Puga, A., and Khan, S.A. "Bisphenol-A and estradiol exert novel gene regulation in human MCF-7 derived breast cancer cells." *Mol Cell Endocrinol* 221: 47–55 (2004).

Singleton, D.W., Feng, Y., Yang, J., Puga, A., Lee, A.V., and Khan, S.A. "Gene expression profiling reveals novel regulation by bisphenol-A in estrogen receptor-alpha-positive human cells." *Environ Res Online*, November 2005.

Sivitz, W.I., Fink, B.D., and Donohue, P.A., Department of Internal Medicine, University of Iowa, and the Iowa City Veterans Affairs Medical Center. "Fasting and leptin modulate adipose and muscle uncoupling protein: divergent effects between messenger ribonucleic acid and protein expression." *Endocrinology* 140(4): 1511-19 (April 1999).

Sohoni, P., and Sumpter, J.P. "Several environmental oestrogens are also anti-androgens." *J Endocrinol* 158: 327–39 (1998).

Sower, S.A., Reed, K.L., and Babbitt, K.J. "Limb malformations and abnormal sex hormone concentrations in frogs." *Environ Health Perspec* 108: 1085–90 (2000).

Strack, A.M., Akana, S.F., Horsley, C.J., and Dallman, M.F., Department of Physiology, University of California, San Francisco. "A hypercaloric load induces thermogenesis but inhibits stress responses in the SNS and HPA system." *Am J Physiol* 272 (Pt 2 of 3): R840–48 (March 1997).

Svanberg, Elizabeth, et al., University Hospital, University of Goteborg, Sweden, College of Medicine, Pennsylvania State University. "Postprandial stimulation of muscle protein synthesis is mediated through translation initiation and is independent of changes in insulin." *APStracts* 19 (Feb 1997).

Thain, R.I. "Bovine infertility possibly caused by subterranean clover: a preliminary report." *Aust Vet J* 41: 277–81 (1965).

Van Wyk, J.J., Arnold, M.B., Wynn, J., and Pepper, F. "The effects of a soybean product on thyroid function in humans." *Pediatrics* 24: 752–60 (1959).

Wang, J., and Leibowitz, K.L. "Central insulin inhibits hypothalamic galanin and neuropeptide Y gene expression and peptide release in intact rats." *Brain Res* 777(1-2): 231–36 (Nov 28, 1997).

Wantanabe, M., and Nakajin, S. "Forskolin up-regulates aromatase (CYP19) activity and gene transcripts in the human adrenocortical carcinoma cell line H295R. *J Endocrinol* 180: 125–33 (2004).

Welbourne, T.C., Milford, L., and Carter, P., Department of Molecular and Cellular Physiology, Louisiana State University Medical Center. "The role of growth hormone in substrate utilization." *Baillieres Clin Endocrinol Metab* 11(4): 699–707 (Dec 1997).

Willingham, E., Rhen, T., Sakata, J.T., and Crews, D. "Embryonic treatment with xenobiotics disrupts steroid hormone profiles in hatchling red-eared slider turtles (Trachemys scripta elegans)." *Environ Health Perspect* 108: 329–32 (2000).

Wozniak, A.L., Nataliya, N.B., and Watson, C.S. "Xenoestrogens at picomolar to nanomolar concentrations trigger membrane estrogen receptor-a-mediated Ca^+ fluxes and prolactin release in GH3/B6 pituitary tumor cells." *Environ Health Perspect* 113(4): 431–39 (2005).

Zand, R.S., Jenkins, D.J., and Diamandis, E.P. "Steroid hormone activity of flavonoids and related compounds." *Breast Cancer Res Treat* 62: 35–49 (2000).

Zhai, S., Dai, R., Friedman, F.K., and Vestal, R.E. "Comparative inhibition of human cytochromes P450 1A1 and 1A2 by flavonoids." *Drug Metab Disposition* 26(10): 989–92 (1998).

Zhou, X., Sun, C., Jiang, L., and Wang, H. "Effect of conjugated linoleic acid on PPAR gamma gene expression and serum leptin in obese rat." *Wei Sheng Yan Jiu* 33(3): 307–309 (2004).

INDEX

ABOUT THE AUTHOR

Ori Hofmekler is a modern Renaissance man whose life has been driven by two passions: art and health. His formative experience as a young man with the Israeli Special Forces prompted a life interest in diet and fitness regimes that would help improve human survival. After the army, Hofmekler attended the Bezalel Academy of Art and the Hebrew University, Jerusalem, where he studied art, philosophy, and biology and received a degree in Human Sciences.

A world-renowned painter best known for his controversial political satire, Hofmekler's work has been featured in magazines and newspapers worldwide, including *Time, Newsweek, L'Express, Die Zeit, Der Spiegel, The New York Times, People, Rolling Stone, Esquire, The New Republic,* and *Playboy,* as well as *Penthouse,* where he was a monthly columnist for seventeen years and health editor from 1998 to 2000.

Hofmekler has published two books of political art, *Hofmekler's People* and *Hofmekler's Gallery.* As founder, editor-in-chief, and publisher of *Mind & Muscle Power,* a national health and fitness magazine, he introduced his Warrior Diet to the public in a monthly column to immediate acclaim from readers and professionals in the health and fitness fields.

With numerous readers worldwide, *The Warrior Diet* has been translated into Italian and French, and featured in health and lifestyle magazines as well as the prestigious medical journal *The Lancet.* Hofmekler's dietary and training methods have been endorsed by nutritional and medical experts, scientists, champion athletes, martial artists, and military and law enforcement instructors, as well as by authors of best-selling books.

The Warrior Diet, LLC, and Defense Nutrition, LLC, currently provide nutritional and training workshops for their followers, as well as certification seminars for health experts, medical clinicians, coaches, trainers, and military and law enforcement instructors.

Hofmekler resides with his wife and children in Tarzana, California. To contact the author, log into www.warriordiet.com.